The Proceedings of the Twenty-eighth Annual
Child Language Research Forum

The Proceedings of the Twenty-eighth Annual

CHILD LANGUAGE RESEARCH FORUM

edited by
Eve V. Clark

28

Published for the
Stanford Linguistics Association
by the
Center for the Study of Language and Information

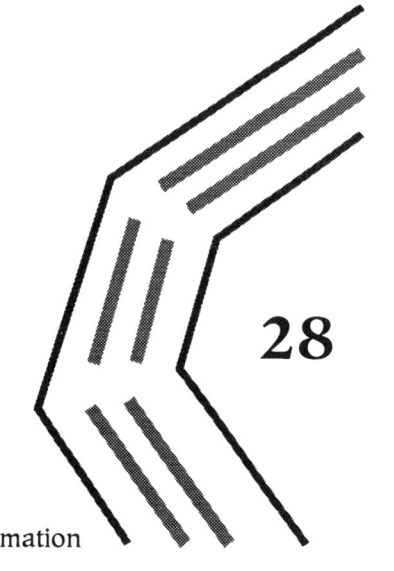

Copyright © 1997
Center for the Study of Language and Information
Leland Stanford Junior University
Printed in the United States

   ISBN (cloth): 1–57586–063-5
   ISBN (paper): 1–57586–062-7
   ISSN: 1042–1080

∞The acid-free paper used in this book meets the minimum requirements of the American National Standard for Information Sciences—Permanence of Paper for Printed Library Materials, ANSI Z39.48-1984.

Contents

Foreword ix

A Study of Chinese Children's Comprehension of Universal Quantifiers   1
XIANGDONG JIA, PATRICIA J. BROOKS, AND MARTIN D.S. BRAINE

Workshop

Perspectives on an Emerging Language   15
JUDY A. KEGL & JOHN MCWHORTER

Papers

Isolating the CVC Root in Tzeltal Mayan: A Study of Children's First Verbs   41
PENELOPE BROWN

Functors in Early On-Line Sentence Comprehension   53
ALLYSON CARTER & LOU ANN GERKEN

Pragmatic Comprehension: Development of Mandarin-Speaking Children's Strategies for Interpretation of Given and New Information   63
SHU-HUI EILEEN CHEN

Reference and Representation: What Polynomy Tells Us About Children's Conceptual Studies   73
GEDEON DEÁK & MICHAEL MARATSOS

From Adam('s) and Eve('s) to Mine and Yours in German Singletons and Siblings   85
WERNER DEUTSCH, ANGELA WARNER, RENATE BURCHARDT, KAREN JAHN, & NINA SCHULZ

Is the Simultaneous Acquisition of Two Languages in Early Childhood Equal to Acquiring Each of the Two Languages Individually?   95
SUSANNE DÖPKE

Codas, Word-minimality, and Empty-headed Syllables   113
HEATHER GOAD

Pronominal reference in 3-year-olds narratives   123
NORMA JEAN GOMME & CAROLYN E. JOHNSON

The Acquisition of Controlled PRO: A Crosslinguistic Perspective   133
HELEN GOODLUCK, ARHONTO TERZI, & GEMA CHOCANO DÍAZ

Evidence in Phonological Acquisition: Implications for the Initial Ranking of Faithfulness Constraints   143
MARK HALE & CHARLES REISS

The Role of Input in the Acquisition of Past Verb Forms in English and Dutch: Evidence from a Bilingual Child   153
ANNICK DE HOUWER

The Role of Prosody in the Acquisition of Grammatical Morphemes   163
RICHARD F.-S. HUNG

Scope and Distributivity in Child Mandarin   173
THOMAS LEE

Vertical Path in Tzotzil (Mayan) Early Acquisition: Linguistic vs Cognitive Determinants   183
LOURDES DE LEÓN

Are English-speaking One-year-olds Verb Learners Too?   199
LETICIA NAIGLES

Gender-based Differences in the Language of Japanese Preschool Children: A Look at Metalinguistic Awareness   213
KEI NAKAMURA

Rhythm in Newborns' Language Processing   223
THIERRY NAZZI

Overextension of Intransitive Verbs in the Acquisition of Japanese   233
MASAMI NOMURA & YASUHIRO SHIRAI

Pronominalizations in the Narratives of Turkish-speaking Children   243
F. HÜLYA ÖZCAN

The Acquisition of Past Tense Inflection in Icelandic and Norwegian Children   259
HRAFNHILDUR RAGNARSDÓTTIR, HANNE GRAM SIMONSEN, & KIM PLUNKETT

The Linguistic Encoding of Spatial Relations in Scandinavian Child Language Development   271
HRAFNHILDUR RAGNARSDÓTTIR & SVEN STRÖMQVIST

Using the Semantics Associated with Syntactic Frames for Interpretation without the Aid of Context   283
NITYA SETHURAMAN, ADELE E. GOLDBERG, & JUDITH C. GOODMAN

The Verbalisation of Motion Events in Arrernte   295
DAVID P. WILKINS

Foreword

The 28th annual meeting of the Child Language Research Forum was held on April 12–14, 1996, in Cordura Hall at the Center for the Study of Language and Information (CSLI), Stanford. (This will also be the venue for the next meeting.) This 28th meeting was ably run by the coordinating committee whose members included Jennifer Arnold, Martina Faller, Dawn Hannah, Tracy King, Andrea Kortenhoven, Meredyth Krych, Peggy Li, Yukiko Morimoto, Maria-Eugenia Niño, Rachel Nordlinger, Eunjin Oh, Christine Poulin, Jennifer Rothblatt, Lauren Shapiro, Helen Shwe, Ida Toivonen, and Qing Zhang. Special thanks go to Christine Poulin and Ida Toivonen for organizing the book display; to Rachel Nordlinger, Maria-Eugenia Niño, and Martina Faller for producing the program handbook; and to Jennifer Arnold and Lori van Houten for overseeing the refreshments. The organizing committee is particularly grateful to Judy A. Kegl (Rutgers University) and John McWhorter (UC Berkeley) for organizing the very stimulating Friday evening Workshop on "Perspectives on an emerging language: Creolization and critical periods." The general focus at this meeting was on crosslinguistic comparisons, and we thank all the presenters for bringing together, between them, data from some 19 languages. Lastly, I would like to thank the administrative staff in the Linguistics Department for all their help: we depend on them critically in planning and organizing the annual Child Language Research Forum: Michelle Collette Murray, Gina Wein, and, especially, Kyle Wohlmut. Without them, the meeting could not take place.

The present volume is the fifth since the Center for the Study of Language and Information took over publication of the annual Proceedings of the Child Language Research Forum. In two of the previous volumes, we outlined the history of this meeting – in the Proceedings of the 25th annual meeting, published in 1993 – and listed all the papers published in the earlier working-paper series from previous meetings – in the Proceedings of the 26th annual meeting, published in 1995. (The Proceedings prior to 1992 were published in a working paper series, and are still available through the ERIC Clearinghouse for Languages and Linguistics, at the Center for Applied Linguistics in Washington, D. C.) Many studies first presented at the Child Language Research Forum have since been published in fuller form in linguistics and psychology journals concerned with language and the acquisition of language.

The next meeting of the Child Language Research Forum will take place on April 25-27, 1997. Further details are available from the Coordinators of CLRF-97, Department of Linguistics, Stanford University, Stanford, CA 94305-2150, and will be posted on the psyling and childes email lists.

Eve V. Clark
Editor
For the CLRF-96 Organizing Committee

August 1996

A Study of Chinese Children's Comprehension of Universal Quantifiers[1]

XIANGDONG JIA,* PATRICIA J. BROOKS,† & MARTIN D.S. BRAINE*
*New York University & †Emory University

Introduction

Many languages have universal quantifiers with functions similar to the English quantifiers *all* and *each* (Ioup, 1975). Universal quantifiers play an essential role in deductive reasoning because of the rich set of inferences to which they give rise. A study of children's developing understanding of universal quantifiers serves as a good way to explore children's cognitive development at the interface of reasoning and language. Early studies (see Inhelder and Piaget 1958; 1964) indicate that young children have a limited understanding of universal quantifiers. Recent work of Philip and his colleagues (see Philip 1992; Philip & Takahashi 1991) suggests that preschoolers are biased to interpret quantified sentences symmetrically, i.e., their representations of universally quantified sentences are undifferentiated in the sense that the quantifier is not restricted to a particular noun phrase.

Brooks and Braine (1996) examined children's understanding of English universal quantifiers and looked for evidence of emerging awareness of lexical and syntactic distinctions that influence quantifier interpretation. Their hypothesis was that children gradually discover the semantics of quantification by acquiring correspondences between linguistic cues and salient semantic categories or representations. They examined cue-category mappings for three semantic representations coinciding with relationships frequently associated with English sentences containing universal quantifiers. Borrowing from Vendler (1967), the first representation was collective: a group of people or animals interacting with one object, or a group of objects located in one container (e.g., *All of the flowers are in a vase* with the interpretation that all of the flowers are in the same vase). Another representation was distributive: people or animals individually interacting with an object, or objects paired off with unique containers (e.g., *Each girl is riding a bicycle* meaning that girls and bicycles are associated

---

[1] This paper originally appeared in incomplete form in the *Proceedings of the Twenty-Seventh Annual Child Language Research Forum*.

in one-to-one correspondence). A third representation was exhaustive: all of the people or animals interacting with all of the objects, or all of the objects arranged among all of the containers (e.g., *The boys are washing the dogs* with the interpretation that all of the boys are washing dogs and all of the dogs are being washed). Brooks and Braine (1996) examined the accessibility of collective, distributive, and exhaustive representations using a picture selection task in which children chose from sets of two or three pictures the one that best fit a sentence read aloud. Their work provides evidence that young children attend to a variety of lexical and syntactic cues to quantifier interpretation.

In this study, we adopted the Brooks and Braine task to investigate Chinese children's acquisition of universal quantifiers. Children's grasp of the Mandarin quantifier system is of particular interest because Mandarin has a drastically different grammar from that of English. We start with an introduction to Mandarin grammar focusing on features related to our study.

Universal Quantifiers and Related Grammar in Mandarin

While English has four universal quantifiers, *all, each, every,* and *any,* Mandarin has a more complicated quantifier system. To begin with, the word *dou1* is of special importance (numerals 1-4 indicate tones). Although *dou1* is identified as a quantifier equivalent to *all* by Li and Thompson (1981), it is described as a scope adverb by most Chinese linguists (see Xu, 1993). It occurs before a verb and modifies the plural noun preceding it, indicating that the meaning of the predicate is applied to everything within the scope of *dou1* (the example below is from Li & Thompson 1981:336).

(1) Zhe4-xie1   hai2-zi   wo3   ***dou1***   xi3-huan1.
  this-PL   child   I   all   like
  I like all these children.

Dou1 may collocate with other universal quantifiers, e.g., *suo3-you3, yi1-qie4, yi1-gai4, yi1-lui4, quan2, quan2-ti3,* and *quan2-bu3,* to emphasize the quality of the scope. When *dou1* follows the noun modified by a universal quantifier, the noun phrase is emphasized as a single unit (we refer to this semantic relation as collective). Although all of the above quantifiers are translated as *all,* they differ in whether they modify animate or inanimate objects, whether they are used in formal or less formal language, and whether they go before or after the modified noun. *Suo3-you3* is the most frequently cited Mandarin equivalent of *all.* It occurs before a noun, which may be either countable or mass, animate or inanimate.

(2) ***Suo3-you3***   de   hua1   ***dou1***   zai4   yi1-ge2   hua1-ping2   li3.
  all   NOM   flower   all   in   one-CL   vase   in
  All of the flowers are in one vase.

Da4-jia1, which literally means "big-family", is usually translated as *everybody* and is regarded as a mixture of an universal quantifier and a noun. It is a very colloquial term which emphasizes a collective interpretation.

(3) **Da4-jia1** zai4 ban1 yi1-ge4 xiang1-zi.
everybody DUR carry one-CL box
All of the men are carrying one box.

In sum, there are many Mandarin universal quantifiers which emphasize a collective semantic relation. In this study, we present sentences containing *suo3-you3, dou1,* and *da4-jia1* because they appropriately modify concrete objects that are easily depicted.

Another kind of universal quantifier is exemplified by *mei3* and *ge4*. These quantifiers modify count nouns, and emphasize that the objects referred to are to be taken one by one (we refer to this semantic relation as distributive). *Mei3* is the most common translation of *each*. It occurs before the word it modifies and combines with a classifier, e.g., *ge4, zhi1* (CL=classifier).

(4) **Mei3** yi1-zhi1 hua1 dou1 cha1 zai4 yi1-ge4 hua1-ping2 li3.
each one-CL flower all put in one-CL vase in
Each flower is in one vase.

Ge4 usually combines with *ge4* (classifier) or *zhong3* (type) to modify a noun that follows it, e.g. *ge4-ge shang1-dian4* (each store), *ge4-zhong3 xian1-hua1* (each kind of fresh flower). Another way to refer to a distributive relationship is to collocate *yi1-CL* with *yi1-CL* in a sentence.

(5) **Yi1-ge4** ren2 zai4 ban1 **yi1-ge4** xiang1-zi.
one-CL person DUR carry one-CL box
One man is carrying one box.

This sentence literally means there is one man carrying one box. Because Mandarin does not mark the singular/plural distinction on the noun, it turns out to be a very colloquial way of describing one-to-one correspondence. In this study, *mei3* and *yi1-CL...yi1-CL* were presented because they appropriately modify concrete entities easily depicted in pictures.

Plurality of Nouns. Mandarin does not mark a singular/plural distinction on nouns. To express plurality, one typically uses a separate word, e.g., *yi1-xie1* (some), *xu3-duo1* (many). For pronouns, plurality is marked with the suffix *men* (e.g., *ta1,* she, he; *ta1-men2,* they).

Classifiers. One of the most striking features of the Mandarin noun phrase is the classifier. A classifier must occur with a number, e.g., *yi1* (one), demonstrative, e.g., *na4* (that), or quantifier, e.g., *mei3* (each), before the noun. Mandarin has several dozen classifiers.

(6) yi1-**ge4** ren2 yi1-**zhi1** hua1 yi1-**tou2** niou2
one-CL person one-CL flower one-CL cow

Articles. The Mandarin definite article has both a singular and a plural form: *zhe4-ge* is singular, and *zhe4-xie1* is plural (e.g., *zhe4-ge ping2-guo3*, the apple; *zhe4-xie1 ping2-guo3*, the apples). Mandarin does not allow indefinite topic noun phrases. Although sentences can omit articles, nouns that are unmarked for definiteness are interpreted as definite or generic when topic. Although the indefinite article *a* is usually translated as *yil-ge4*, *yil-ge4* is definite when modifying a topic NP.

Our Study

A picture-selection task was used to investigate whether Chinese children and adults show similar preferences in assigning collective, distributive, and exhaustive interpretations to sentences containing universal quantifiers. One goal was to see whether children distinguish *suo3-you3* (all) and *mei3* (each). A second goal was to examine whether young children understand other colloquial ways of talking about collective and distributive events.

Subjects. Subjects were 40 three- and four-year-olds, 40 five- and six-year-olds, 40 seven-and eight-year-olds, 40 nine- and ten-year-olds, and 40 adults from public schools and one university in Beijing, China.

Materials. The stimuli consisted of two sets of nine triads of pictures depicting collective, distributive, and exhaustive events.

One set of triads depicted various objects positioned among containers (see Figure 1) and are referred to as locative pictures. A collective picture showed three objects in a single container along with two additional empty containers (Figure 1a). A distributive picture showed three objects individually placed in three separate containers with two additional empty containers (Figure 1b). An exhaustive picture showed five objects arranged in three containers with no additional objects or containers (Figure 1c). The empty containers were included in the collective and distributive pictures to distinguish them from the exhaustive picture in which all the containers and entities were used up. Children who do not restrict the quantifier to the appropariate noun phrase were expected to reject the non-exhaustive collective and distributive pictures because of the presence of the left-over containers.

The second set of pictures depicted people engaged in various activities such as men carrying boxes, women washing dogs, or boys feeding monkeys (see Figure 2) and are referred to as actional pictures. A collective picture showed three actors engaged with a single object along with two additional objects not directly involved in the activity (Figure 2a). A distributive representation depicted three actors individually engaged with three distinct objects and included two additional objects not directly involved in the activity (Figure 2b). An exhaustive picture showed three actors engaged in an activity involving five objects; all objects depicted were directly involved in the activity (Figure 2c).

Nine additional triads of pictures were used as filler items to ensure that children understood the task. Filler items depicted boys and girls interacting with a variety of objects (e.g., a boy smelling a pie, a girl cutting a flower). Filler sentences were constructed to refer unambiguously to one of the

Figure 1.

1a: Example of a collective picture for the locative sentences.

1b: Example of a distributive picture for the locative sentences.

1c: Example of an exhaustive picture for the locative sentences.

Figure 2

2a: Example of a collective picture for the actional sentences.

2b: Example of a distributive picture for the actional sentences.

2c: Example of an exhaustive picture for the actional sentences.

pictures of a triad; these sentences did not contain universal quantifiers.

Sentences. Sentences were selected to be natural Mandarin ways of expressing universal quantification. For the locative picture sets (see Figure 1), four sentence types were presented using unique sets of pictures (e.g., flowers in vases, alligators in bathtubs, etc). Sentence 1 with *suo3-you3* and *dou1* was targeted for the collective picture. Sentence 2 with *mei3* and *dou1* was targeted for the distributive picture. Sentence 3 is sentence 2 leaving out *dou1*. It is a less natural sentence, but was included to see the effect of *dou1* on sentence interpretation. Sentence 4 with *yi1-CL...yi1-CL* structure is a very colloquial way of describing a distributive relationship. The four sentence types are illustrated for the context of flowers in vases.

1. ***Suo3-you3*** *de   hua1 **dou1** cha1 zai4 yi1-ge4 hua1-ping2 li3.*
   all   NOM flower all   put in   one-CL   vase   in
   All the flowers are in one vase.

2. ***Mei3*** *yi1-zhi1 hua1 **dou1** cha1 zai4 yi1-ge4 hua1-ping2 li3.*
   each one-CL flower all   put in   one-CL vase   in
   Each flower is in one vase.

3. ***Mei3*** *yi1-zhi1 hua1 cha1 zai4 yi1-ge4 hua1-ping2 li3.*
   each one-CL flower put in   one-CL vase   in
   Each flower is in one vase.

4. ***Yi1-zhi1*** *hua1 cha1 zai4 **yi1-ge4** hua1-ping2 li3.*
   one-CL flower put in   one-CL   vase   in
   One flower is in one vase.

For the actional picture sets (see Figure 2), five sentence types were presented with unique sets of pictures. Sentence 5 with *suo3-you3* and *dou1* was targeted for the collective picture. Sentence 6 with *da4-jia1* emphasizes a collective interpretation. Sentence 7 with *mei3* and *dou1* was targeted for the distributive picture. Sentence 8 omits *dou1* and was used to examine the function of *dou1*. *Ta1-men2* was added at the beginning of the sentence and *mei3 yi1-ge4 ren2* was contracted to *mei3-ren2* to make the sentence more natural. Sentence 9 has *yi1-CL...yi1-CL* structure, with *ta1-men2* added to make it more colloquial.

5. ***Suo3-you3*** *de   ren2 dou zai4 ban1 yi1-ge4 xiang1-zi.*
   all   NOM person all DUR carry one-CL   box
   All the men are carrying one box.

6. ***Da4-jia1*** *zai4 ban1 yi1-ge4 xiang1-zi.*
   everyone DUR carry one-CL   box
   All the men are carrying one box.

7. ***Mei3*** *yi1-ge4   ren2 **dou1** zai4 ban1 yi1-ge4 xiang1-zi.*
   each one-CL person all DUR carry one-CL   box
   Each man is carrying one box.

8. *Ta1-men2* **mei3-ren2** *zai4 ban1 yi1-ge4 xiang1-zi.*
      they   each-person DUR carry one-CL   box
   Each man is carrying one box.

9. *Ta1-men2* **yi1-ren2** *zai4 ban1* **yi1-ge4** *xiang1-zi.*
      they   one-person DUR carry one-CL   box
   One man is carrying one box.

Procedure. Participants were tested individually in 15 minute sessions. The experimenter presented three pictures at a time and asked participants to point to the picture that went best with a sentence heard aloud. Half of the participants at each age heard sentences 1 to 4 containing locative predicates and chose among the locative pictures; the remaining subjects heard sentences 5 to 9 containing actional verbs and chose among the actional pictures. Before reading the sentence the experimenter instructed participants to look carefully at the three pictures. Participants were instructed to select only one picture--whichever picture depicted exactly what the experimenter said. The first three sentences were filler items to ensure that participants understood the task. Presentation of experimental items was interspersed with filler items so that no more than three experimental items occurred consecutively. Order of presentation of sentence types was randomize so that identical sentence types were not presented consecutively. No corrective feedback was given; participants were given periodic encouragement.

Results. Mean percentages of collective, distributive, and exhaustive pictures selected for each sentence are presented in Table 1. Adults selected almost exclusively collective pictures for sentences with *suo3-you3...dou1*. Children as young as three to four years were less unanimous, but also preferred a collective interpretation of *suo3-you3...dou1*. For the sentence with *da4-jia1*, all groups selected mostly collective interpretations. *Da4-jia1* is a very colloquial expression which children seem to grasp at a young age. Adults selected mostly distributive pictures for sentences containing *mei3...dou1*. The youngest children found these sentences to be very ambiguous and split their responses between collective and distributive choices. We suspect that these sentences were ambiguous because *dou1* is a collective cue and *mei3* is a distributive cue; ambiguity results when two conflicting cues appear together in a sentence. Leaving out *dou1* made the sentences with *mei3* less ambiguous for all groups who showed a clear preference for the distributive interpretation. Children and adults also selected mostly distributive pictures for sentences with *yi1-CL...yi1-CL* structure, another very colloquial expression. It should be noted that all groups of children increased their choices for the targeted pictures when more colloquial expressions were adopted (sentences 4, 6, and 9) and when conflicting cues were eliminated (sentences 3 and 8). Chinese children never associated any of the sentences with exhaustive pictures at an above chance level. Taken together, the results show that young Chinese children have considerable mastery of the complicated Mandarin quantifier system.

Table 1. Percentages of picture selections for each sentence.

	PICTURE SELECTED		
	Collective	Distributive	Exhaustive

Suo3-you3 de hua1 dou1 cha1 zai4 yi1-ge4 hua1-ping2 li3.
(All the flowers are in one vase.)

3 and 4-year-olds	55	32	12
5 and 6-year-olds	73	10	17
7 and 8-year-olds	88	5	7
9 and 10-year-olds	100	0	0
Adults	100	0	0

Suo3-you3 de ren2 dou1 zai4 ban1 yi1-ge4 xiang1-zi.
(All of the men are carrying one box.)

3 and 4-year-olds	55	23	22
5 and 6-year-olds	68	23	9
7 and 8-year-olds	98	2	0
9 and 10-year-olds	100	0	0
Adults	95	5	0

Da4-jia1 zai4 ban1 yi1-ge4 xiang1-zi.
(All of the men are carrying one box.)

3 and 4-year-olds	60	10	30
5 and 6-year-olds	95	5	0
7 and 8-year-olds	100	0	0
9 and 10-year-olds	100	0	0
Adults	100	0	0

Mei3 yi1-zhi1 hua1 dou1 cha1 zai4 yi1-ge4 hua1-ping2 li3.
(Each flower is in one vase.)

3 and 4-year-olds	30	30	40
5 and 6-year-olds	53	33	14
7 and 8-year-olds	47	48	5
9 and 10-year-olds	35	60	5
Adults	25	75	0

Mei3 yi1-ge4 ren2 dou1 zai4 ban1 yi1-ge4 xiang1-zi.
(Each man is carrying one box.)

3 and 4-year-olds	38	33	29
5 and 6-year-olds	50	40	10
7 and 8-year-olds	48	50	2
9 and 10-year-olds	7	93	0
Adults	10	90	0

Mei3 yi1-zhi1 hua1 cha1 zai4 yi1-ge4 hua1-ping2 li3.
(Each flower is in one vase.)

3 and 4-year-olds	20	60	20
5 and 6-year-olds	25	65	10
7 and 8-year-olds	30	65	5
9 and 10-year-olds	15	85	0
Adults	5	90	5

Table 1. Continued.

	PICTURE SELECTED		
	Collective	Distributive	Exhaustive

Ta1-men2 mei3-ren2 zai4 ban1 yi1-ge4 xiang1-zi.
(Each man is carrying one box.)

3 and 4-year-olds	30	40	30
5 and 6-year-olds	15	85	0
7 and 8-year-olds	10	90	0
9 and 10-year-olds	0	100	0
Adults	0	100	0

Yi1-zhi1 hua1 cha1 zai4 yi1-ge4 hua1-ping2 li3.
(One flower is in one vase.)

3 and 4-year-olds	5	75	20
5 and 6-year-olds	0	95	5
7 and 8-year-olds	5	95	0
9 and 10-year-olds	0	100	0
Adults	0	100	0

Ta1-men2 yi1-ren2 zai4 ban1 yi1-ge4 xiang1-zi.
(One man is carrying one box.)

3 and 4-year-olds	15	55	30
5 and 6-year-olds	5	95	0
7 and 8-year-olds	5	95	0
9 and 10-year-olds	5	95	0
Adults	0	100	0

General Discussion

In our work, we have examined Chinese children's understanding of two Mandarin universal quantifiers, *suo3-you3* and *mei3*, which are translational equivalents of the English quantifiers *all* and *each*. In some of the sentences presented *suo3-you3* and *mei3* were used in combination with the scope adverb *dou1*. Sentences containing *suo3-you3...dou1* were consistently assigned collective interpretations from age five to six years on. The scope adverb *dou1* was shown to have contributed to sentence interpretation. It is a collective cue which forms a functional unit with *suo3-you3*. Sentences containing *mei3...dou1* were often assigned either collective or distributive pictures by the youngest subjects. When *dou1* was dropped, children as young as five years associated *mei3* with a distributive interpretation. *Dou1*, a collective cue, appears to compete with the distributive cue *mei3* when present in the same sentence. We also examined children's understanding of other very colloquial Chinese sentences which quantify events. This provided us with an opportunity to examine how children understand references to collective and distributive representations before they have acquired some universal quantifiers. Children as young as three to four years associated the quantifier-noun *da4-jia1* with a collective meaning and the colloquial *yi1-CL...yi1-CL* structure with a distributive interpretation.

The results are consistent with a framework we are developing to explain how children acquire an understanding of universal quantification (see Brooks & Braine 1996). Children may start with a representational system that distinguishes among mental representations such as the collective and distributive ones. Children learn to associate a core universal meaning, i.e., that a property applies to the whole or all of a set, with salient universal quantifiers and other appropriate colloquial expressions. Children gradually learn to differentiate among quantifiers by identifying them with collective and distributive representations. Children discover cues in their language that correspond to particular semantic relations. Some cues are fairly unambiguous and occur frequently in daily language, children acquire these cues first and associate them correctly with corresponding mental representations. Since many different sorts of cues for collective or distributive meaning may exist in a language, children must learn which cues are consistent with each other and how to handle conflicting cues by weighting one cue over another. Children gradually develop flexible comprehension strategies for combining the various cues to quantifier scope.

References

Brooks, P. J., and M. D. S. Braine. 1996. What do children know about the universal quantifiers 'all' and 'each'? *Cognition, 60,* 235-268.

Inhelder, B., and J. Piaget. 1958. *The growth of logical thinking from childhood to adolescence.* New York: Basic Books.

Inhelder, B., and J. Piaget. 1964. *The early growth of logic in the child.* London: Routledge and Kegan Paul.

Ioup, G. 1975. Some universals for quantifier scope. *Syntax and Semantics, 4,* 37-58.

Li, C. N., and S. A. Thompson. 1981. *Mandarian Chinese: a functional reference grammar.* Berkeley, CA: University of California Press.

Philip, W. 1992. Event quantification and the symmetrical interpretation of universal quantifiers in child language. In K. von Fintel and H. Rullman (Eds.), *University of Massachusetts Occasional Papers in Linguistics: Semantics Issues.* Linguistics Department, UMASS, Amherst, MA: Graduate Linguistics Students Association.

Philip, W., and M. Takahashi. 1991. Quantifier spreading in the acquisition of "every". In T. Maxfield and B. Plunkett, eds., *Papers in the Acquisition of WH: Proceedings of the UMass Roundtable, May 1990.* Linguistics Department, UMASS, Amherst, MA: Graduate Linguistics Students Association.

Vendler, Z. 1967. *Linguistics in philosophy.* Ithaca: Cornell University Press.

Xu, S.L. 1993. Semantics of "dou" as a scope indicator. *Language Teaching and Research,* Vol.4, 75-86.

WORKSHOP

Perspectives on an Emerging Language

JUDY A. KEGL & JOHN MCWHORTER
Rutgers University & University of California, Berkeley

1. Introduction

If we choose to subscribe to the hypothesis that language is a capacity of the human brain that exists independent of any specific body of knowledge in our environment that must be learned, how can we amass evidence for its validity?[*] We as language acquirers are exposed to the language of our parents, peers, casual acquaintances, and overheard snippets of conversation on a continual basis. The input, whether a prerequisite to language emergence or not, is already language.

The argument has been made that because language input in general is noisy, inconsistent, and incomplete, the language competence a given acquirer exhibits is dependent upon something more than extrinsic language input. A filtering device or set of innate language expectations supposedly serves to clue us in to those features and exemplars in the input that are relevant to making the linguistic generalizations or determining the finite set of linguistic choices that lead to acquisition of a human language. This mechanism accounts for the acquisition of language not only in marked

---

[*] Kegl's work has been partially funded by National Science Foundation Grant #SBR-9513762 to Rutgers University. We are grateful to the Nicaraguan Sign Language Project archive for access to the data and fieldnotes on Nicaraguan Sign Language, to the members of that project, past and present, who have teamed their resources to collect those data and make them available.

contexts (creoles, first language learning of a dominant-culture language by the children of immigrants, etc.) but also in the canonical situation where young learners acquire their native language in the context of a community of native speakers of that language. All these cases share in common a Phoenix-like scenario where language emerges from the remnants of language.

Here we begin by discussing two lines of research that have been driven by a desire to uncover the human bioprogram for language. The first is the study of creolization and the second is a series of studies of first language acquisition under conditions of non-optimal input, where learners surpass their models in terms of language competence. In both cases, we argue that the remnants of language that contribute to the language acquisition process preclude us from conclusively crediting the spontaneous creation of grammars to the brains of the children acquiring them. We conclude with a discussion of one study where language did not beget language—the case of Nicaraguan Sign Language, which emerged as a consequence of the social interaction of large numbers of home signers with no access to any remnants of a signed language in their input. We argue that while the prior studies set the research paradigm for the study of spontaneous language emergence, it is the Nicaraguan case that instantiates the idealized scenario.

2. The Creolist's Perspective

To be sure, the claim to have espied the spontaneous creation of grammars by children has previously come from the creolist field. Specifically, Bickerton (1981, 1984, 1988) has identified Hawaiian Creole English as a manifestation of a "bioprogram," an array of innate parameter settings underlying the human language competence, obscured in regular languages by historical accretion. With the Hawaiian data as a demonstration case, Bickerton has analogized the bioprogram scenario to Caribbean plantation contexts, the resultant claim being that not only Hawaiian Creole English, but also other creoles like Jamaican patois and Haitian Creole, are Universal Grammar on virtually unmediated display. Bickerton's hypothesis has been immensely stimulating to creolistics and beyond, framing creoles as potential sources of insight into Universal Grammar, so often elusive to the generative syntactician or semanticist. For this reason, the bioprogram is represented as virtual canon in many textbooks and other sources on linguistics, such as Steven Pinker's *The Language Instinct* (Pinker, 1994) and articles in magazines such as *Discover* (Berreby, 1992).

The irony here is that few working creolists subscribe to Bickerton's hypothesis to any great degree. This lack of acceptance stems from criticisms of Bickerton's interpretations of sociohistorical and comparative evidence, as yet largely unanswered.

2.1 The Sociohistory of Hawaiian Creole English

A principal stumbling block is Bickerton's reconstruction of the history of Hawaiian Creole English. In the mid-1970s, Bickerton interviewed elderly

Hawaiians who had immigrated early in the century from, mainly, Japan and the Philippines to work sugar plantations. These informants spoke a relatively structureless, highly substrate-influenced pidgin English. Subsequent generations, born in Hawaii, spoke a fluent, elaborated and structured creole, contrasting strikingly with the rudimentary jargon controlled by the immigrants. Bickerton interpreted the disjunction between the immigrants' pidgin and the native-born's creole as evidence that the creole speakers had spontaneously created their language from the fragmentary input received from their parents. This spontaneous creation would theoretically have been via the direct expression of Universal Grammar settings. Bickerton hypothesizes that in learning regular languages, children must "unlearn" these settings. The Hawaiian situation was presumably a rare one in which children had no choice but to express these settings directly, the pidgin data being too inconsistent to build a grammar upon, and immigrants' native languages being too varied to serve any use in the new communities.

Bickerton situates this scenario around the turn of the century, at which point Chinese, Portuguese, Japanese, and Filipino immigrants had all settled in Hawaii and began reproducing, while at the same time the United States had annexed Hawaii (in 1898), imposing English as the main medium of government and instruction. Before the turn of the century, Bickerton hypothesizes that the main *lingua franca* in Hawaii was a pidginized Hawaiian, rather than a pidginized English. Thus Bickerton proposes this basic timeline:

Pidgin Hawaiian   Pidgin English ----> Creole English
_____
                              1898
                       Annexation by USA

This timeline is extremely problematic, however, in view of rich evidence that a pidginized English was well in place in Hawaii long before the turn of the century, well before the American hegemony that Bickerton considers the spark for children's purported creation of the creole. Hawaiian men were serving long terms on English whaling ships from the middle of the nineteenth century, which would have served as an initial context in which an English-based pidgin would have emerged among Hawaiians. An English-Hawaiian jargon, *hapa haole*, is in fact attested from this time, and Portuguese plantation foremen are documented to have spoken a restructured variety of English (McWhorter 1996:62). More to the point, however, in 1887 a newspaper editorial notes that (Goodman 1985:111-2).

> The colloquial English of Hawaii *nei* is even now sufficiently *sui generis* to be noticeable to strangers. It is not a dialect, but a new language with English as its basic element, wrought upon by the subtle forces of other languages, not so much in the matter of a changed vocabulary as a changed diction.

This description is strikingly reminiscent of laypeople's descriptions of pidgins and creoles. It is crucial because it indicates that a relatively stabilized pidginized or creolized English was in place in Hawaii long before the turn of the century, especially given that we can assume that its public mention in 1887 implies that it had taken shape long before even this date. We see further evidence in reminiscences collected in the 1930s by pioneer creolist John Reinecke from people who immigrated to Hawaii in the late 1800s. These reminiscences depict a sociolinguistically variegated situation in Hawaii of this time, but pidginized English is one of the common threads, exemplified in this comment (thanks to Julian Roberts for access to this document):

> When I returned to the Islands in the year 1885 the English language, mostly in a crude form, was generally used in Honolulu by the Hawaiians in their intercourse with whites, aided by the addition of many expressive Hawaiian words common up to the present time such as Pau, Kupu, Wikiwiki, etc.

Documentary tokens such as these, then, make it difficult to accept that restructured English only became a general presence in Hawaii at the turn of the century. To be sure, the existence of a pidginized *Hawaiian* as well in the 1800s is uncontestable (Bickerton & Wilson 1987, Roberts 1995), and appears even to have been dominant. This, however, hardly disallows the concomitant existence of a pidginized English. Many societies have harbored more than one pidgin at a time, such as Lingala and Kituba in Zaire or Tok Pisin and Hiri Motu in Papua New Guinea. The evidence suggests a revision of Bickerton's timeline:

Pidgin Hawaiian   ----> (Extinction)
Pidgin English   ----> Creole English
_____
                         1898
                    Annexation by USA

The implications of this timeline for Bickerton's hypothesis are dire: if pidgin English was spoken in Hawaii as far back as the mid-1800s, how likely is it that the elderly people Bickerton interviewed in the 1970s were the creators of the variety they were speaking? It is difficult to avoid the conclusion that these people were simply second-language speakers of a contact English that already existed when they arrived.

2.2 Problems with Child Invention

The extension of the bioprogram scenario to other creoles is based upon similarities Bickerton noted between Hawaiian Creole English and various Caribbean creoles. Bickerton hypothesizes that Caribbean plantations, like the Hawaiian, were settings where adults spoke native languages of little use to subsequent generations, and English too rudimentary to be viably transmitted. Thus the bioprogram hypothesis predicts that there would be correspondences between Hawaiian Creole and Caribbean creoles unattributable to any particular European or substrate language, and only explainable as innate universals. However, regardless of the tenability of Bickerton's interpretation of Hawaii, there are severe problems with his identification of creole grammar with creation by children.

For example, the prime demonstration of the bioprogram has been the trio of preverbal tense-mood-aspect markers visible in most creoles. In both Hawaiian Creole English and a great many Caribbean creoles, one finds that the complex European and substrate verb-marking systems have been reduced to a focus upon three distinctions, anterior, progressive, and irrealis:

	Sranan Creole E.	Haitian Creole F.	Hawaiian Creole E.
I am going	Mi **e** go	M'**ap** ale	Ai **stei** go
I went/had gone	Mi **ben** go	M **te** ale	Ai **wen** go
I will go	Mi **sa** go	M **va** ale	Ai **go** go

The status of these distinctions as universal is hardly unpromising, as none of the West African languages spoken by Caribbean creole originators display this particular array of distinctions, and there is even cross-linguistic evidence that these distinctions are the foundation of regular language syntaxes (Givon 1979). What is questionable, however, is whether or not these distinctions are diagnostic of child invention, as Bickerton claims. A comprehensive perspective on pidgin-creole data suggests not.

Despite emphasis in the literature on plantation creoles, the fact is that as often as not, contact languages are expanded and stabilized by adults rather than children. Crucially, many adult-created pidgins and creoles display the same array of anterior-progressive-irrealis as do the plantation creoles. For example, Tok Pisin was created by adult men on British ships and plantations (Keesing 1988); by the time children were acquiring it natively, it has long since acquired expanded structure. Nubi Arabic was created by adult male soldiers in a context in which children were a distinctly marginal presence (Owens 1990). Yet these languages pattern like Sranan and Haitian:

	Tok Pisin Creole E.	Nubi Creole Arabic
I am going	Mi **stap** go	Ána **gi**-rúwa
I went / had gone	Mi **bin** go	Ána **kán** rúwa
I will go	Mi **bai** go	Ána **bi**-rúwa

Another serious problem for Bickerton's analysis is that these TMA markers are among the very few cross-creole correspondences that lend themselves to analysis as "universal" in any sense at all. A great many structures that Bickerton designates innate are in fact much more likely to have been transfers from the languages spoken by the slaves first brought to the Caribbean. Bickerton's claim has been that any such similarities between creole and African structures are mere accidents. While it is hardly impossible that such accidents could have occurred -- especially given the "unmarked" nature of many of the structures in question -- comparative analysis makes it relatively unequivocal that many of the Caribbean-African correspondences are indeed transfers, not spontaneous creations.

An example is serial verb constructions, grammatically central both in deep Caribbean creoles like Saramaccan Creole English, and in West African languages spoken on the coast of present-day Côte D'Ivoire through Nigeria (particularly the Akan dialects, the Gbe dialects, Yoruba and Igbo):

SARAMACCAN	GBE (EWE)
INSTRUMENTAL:	
A téi góni súti dí píngo.	àyí kè àtó tsɔ̀ wónù.
he take gun shoot the pig	Ayi take ladle pour soup
He shot the pig with a gun.	Ayi poured soup with a ladle.
BENEFACTIVE:	
Kófi bái soní dá dí mujéɛ.	é-flè sɔ́ ná-m.
Kofi buy thing give the woman	he-bought horse gave-me
Kofi bought something for the woman.	He bought something for the horse.
DIRECTIONAL:	
A wáka gó a dí opoláni.	wó-tsɔ-nɛ yi keta.
he walk go LOC the airplane	one-take-him go Keta
He walked to the airplane.	One carries him to Keta.
COMPARATIVE:	
A bígi pása dí míi.	sɔ́ lolo wú tédzi.
he be-big pass the child	horse big pass donkey
He is bigger than the child.	The horse is bigger than the donkey.
COMPLETIVE:	
Kófi nján dí ganía kabá.	mí-awɔ-e vɔ égbê.
Kofi eat the chicken finish	we-do-it finish today
Kofi finished eating the chicken.	We will finish it today.

(McWhorter 1996:34-5)

Bickerton claims (1981:118–32, 1984:179, 1988:303–4) that serialization is an innate strategy for encoding certain grammatical relations in the absence of prepositions, case markers, etc., and that its presence in West African languages was irrelevant to its emergence in Caribbean creoles.

This is difficult to support, however, in view of the simple distributional facts:

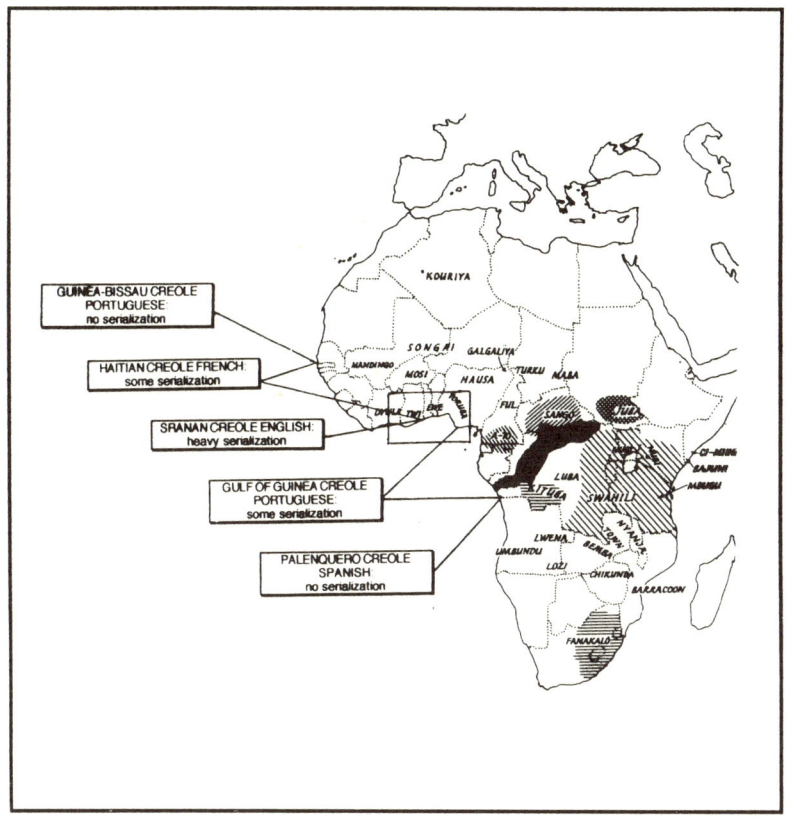

Figure 1.

Evidence suggests that most of the slaves originating Sranan came from the serializing area in the square in the figure (McWhorter in press). Sranan is a heavily serializing creole. On the other hand, Cape Verdean Portuguese does not have serial verbs; neither do the West Atlantic and Mande languages spoken in the region slaves were brought to Cape Verde from. Similarly, the slaves who originated the Palenquero Creole Spanish spoken in Colombia were brought from present-day Angola, where non-serializing Bantu languages are spoken; Palenquero has no serial verbs. Could this distribution be accidental? It seems unlikely when, for example, Negerhollands Creole Dutch, heavily serializing (Sabino 1992), was seeded by slaves mostly from Ghana (Stolz & Stein 1986).

However, the case seems particularly clear from the calibrated cases. Haitian slaves were brought partly from the serializing region, but as many were also brought from non-serializing regions farther west (Singler 1993). Haitian indeed serializes, but only about half as richly as does Sranan (Muysken 1994). Is this an accident? Unlikely when we note that the Gulf of Guinea Portuguese creoles serialize to a similarly moderate extent (Ferraz 1979, Post 1992), and its creators were brought partly from the serializing region, but just as many from Bantu-speaking regions. (See McWhorter 1996 for fuller discussion.)

A similar case could be made for other features, such as predicate clefting and postnominal positional markers. The result is that there is little in Caribbean creole structure that is plausibly treated as a child invention.

2.3 Children and Caribbean Plantation Demographics

A final problem with Bickerton's analysis concerns plantation demographics. The bioprogram scenario depends upon the emergence of a first generation of local-born children quickly enough that the pidgin spoken by the African-born slaves has not yet had time to stabilize into a full language, as Tok Pisin did. However, all evidence indicates that on early Caribbean plantations, children were a relatively marginal presence. Planters preferred men as slaves when most Caribbean plantations were founded in the mid 1600s, with new imports seen as a more cost-effective strategy for increase than reproduction and child care. Thus local-born children were few on most plantations until the 1700s, by which time the creoles are documented to have already taken shape (Singler 1992).

Bickerton has countered that even if children were a minority presence, they would still have transformed pidgin input into a creole, and would thus have served as linguistic models for the community as a whole (1991:38). It remains to be explained why a few children's speech habits would be imitated by a community of adults? Bickerton has also claimed that at some point, such children would come to outnumber African-born slaves, and that finally, creolized speech would be the community norm. But this runs up against the fact that, by this late date, the adults' pidgin could have stabilized into a language suitable for child acquisition, eliminating the impetus for children to express the bioprogram.

2.4 Where the creole program falls short of addressing the bioprogram issue

The above observations lead one to the conclusion that if there is a such thing as a bioprogram, then creoles and language learning from non-native models happen not to be the place to look for them. For one thing, the linguistic input on the plantations was, if anything, richer than the ordinary one rather than poorer.

For example, while the textbook conception of the plantation depicts hundreds of slaves receiving superstrate input from a few whites, the current consensus in creole studies is that disproportion of black to white was a gradual development on Caribbean plantations. Most plantation societies concentrated upon small-scale agriculture at their founding, most plantations having only a few slaves, with white indentured servants as numerous as these. Only with the transformation to sugar cultivation, a highly labor-intensive activity, were massive black labor forces imported, generally several decades after the founding of a colony if not even later. What this means is that the superstrate model was only gradually withdrawn from the slave forces. On early plantations (termed *sociétés d'habitation* by Chaudenson 1979), it is likely that blacks acquired a second-language, but hardly pidginized, register of the dominant European language. Thus the emergence of the creole can be thought to have occurred later, more via gradual transformation of lexifier input than via immediate extreme deprivation of such. This leaves little room for Bickerton's conception of superstrate input as only a fragmented jargon.

A concomitant problem in the plantation context is substrate input to children. Evidence as to how vigorously, and how long, African languages survived in daily use on plantations appears to be essentially lost forever. However, it hardly seems implausible that African-born parents would have spoken to their children in their native language, rather than in a language they controlled only partially and had learned under adverse circumstances. The survival of African languages, in relatively viable form at least, for at least one generation would have been even more likely in cases where a single language was spoken by a significant number, such as Twi in Jamaica. Thus it is likely that the first generation of children were often bilingual in the local pidgin/creole and an African language. If so, then the question arises as to why they would resort to the bioprogram in developing the pidgin, rather than transferring African structures into the pidgin. The West African-Caribbean correspondences such as serial verb constructions indicate that at some point in the developmental process, be it by adults or children, native languages had a significant impact upon plantation creoles.

In summary, a closer look at the historical context in which spoken language creoles have arisen reveals that we cannot look to creoles as the source of evidence for the spontaneous creation of grammars via the brains of children. We need to look elsewhere for conclusive evidence of a human bioprogram for language. This is not to say that creole studies provide no evidence in this regard. Creoles acquired by children, afford us the same evidence for the bioprogram that canonical language acquisition by a child of a single language from native-speaking parents provides.

3. The problem with language remnants in the input

Creoles hold a fascination in the sense that they take multiple existing languages and restructure them into a new linguistic form or variant. Like all creative processes, creolization takes pre-existing structures and materials and organizes them in a new way. As long as language remnants are available, the full extent of the contribution of the human brain to the language acquisition process will be difficult to determine. Even if we could determine that a child was only exposed to pidgin forms and never to exemplars of substrate or superstrate languages, the possibility will always remain that covertly encoded in the fragments of language material to which a young acquirer is exposed is sufficient linguistic evidence to condition language acquisition without the need to recruit previously missing or default linguistic structure from the bioprogram.

Another line of research seeking to uncover the human bioprogram for language looks for cases where there is a mismatch between the richness of the linguistic input and the output of language acquisition such that learners surpass their models. Note that if we take native acquisition of a language as a benchmark, creoles do not provide us with this case. The models in the context of pidginization controlled full-blown native languages, whether or not they used them exclusively. Children acquiring a creole did not surpass the language capacities of their parents. Their parents were already native speakers of various languages that participated in the creole mix.

3.1 Recreolization to a language specific target

To push the bioprogram hypothesis further, we need to identify a case where the generation providing input to young language acquirers did not have native mastery of any language and yet, their children surpassed them in developing native mastery of a language. A number of researchers have discussed a specific scenario that instantiates this case—the native-like acquisition of ASL by the children of first generation, late-learners of ASL.

Only six percent of the U.S. deaf population learn American Sign Language (ASL) from deaf native-signing parents. A majority have hearing parents and their earliest communication is "home sign," a gestural system having little internal morphology, with grammatical relations indicated by isolated words in a fairly rigid word order (Goldin-Meadow 1979)[1]. Newport (1982) looked at the 90% or more of the deaf population who are deaf children of hearing parents, terming them "first generation deaf." (By virtue of lack of auditory access to spoken English, these same deaf individuals, unless late-deafened, tend to also be late-learners or only partially in control of the grammar of English.) The earliest communication of first generation deaf signers involves home sign and they often go on later in life to acquire predominantly the frozen lexicon of ASL. First generation signers frequently intermarry and it is their children who pose an interesting linguistic puzzle.

The children of first generation signers are exposed to inconsistent and non-optimal models of ASL. Their parents communicate using frozen signs and a syntactic and morphological system that is highly inconsistent not only among various of these first generation signers, but across the individual utterances of a single first generation signer as well. Outside of the family situation, second generation signers will be exposed to a highly variable language community of whom only 6% at best will have native competency in ASL. Yet, second generation deaf signers, the children of these first generation deaf signers, produce forms with complex word-internal morphology, indicating that they have performed complex internal morphological analysis on input from first generation signers that clearly do

---

[1] This is an early citation to a massive series of studies that offer a carefully detailed analysis of home sign.

not make use of this productive morphology. It has been reported that these second generation signers exhibit native fluency in ASL and are indistinguishable from children of native signing parents.

Noting that pidgins tend to have isolating morphology while creoles universally include morphology internal to the word, Newport (1982:480-484) argued that the elaboration in morphology seen in second generation signers can be viewed as a "recreolization" of the pidgin input of their first generation deaf parents. She used the term "recreolization"[2] because the recurrent influx of deaf children born to hearing parents repeatedly recreates the conditions leading to creolization of pidgin input by their offspring. Newport (1982:481) characterized recreolization by second generation signers as follows:

> "complex internal morphological analysis is performed by second-generation deaf on an input that does not itself contain this morphology...The frozen lexicon of ASL, which is the predominant linguistic input for most second generation signers, includes the handshapes, movements, and so on of complex verbs of motion and location as phonological entities inconsistently associated with particular components of meaning. The second generation learner, then, regularizes these associations, ending up with productive form-meaning components that were not characteristic of the language of his or her parents."

This perspective, as stated, loses sight of the fact that children actually seem to learn language from slightly older peers rather than their parents (Baron 1975) and that most of these second generation deaf children have additional sources of input from the Deaf community at large, including at least some native-signing peers in schools for the deaf. Still, since 90-94% of the deaf population are deaf children of hearing parents, the source of input as a whole is heterogeneous, even though it also may include native signers.

Later, more controlled studies by Singleton and Newport (1987) and Singleton (1989) documented a deaf child (Simon) acquiring American Sign Language in a family environment where no native-signing models of the language were available; and where, until school age, the parents, Deaf late-learners of ASL themselves, were the sole language input to the child. Until school age, Simon did not have significant contact with other members of the Deaf community. Even after entry into school, Singleton (1989) argued that Simon was the best signer in his class, in which the primary mode of communication was a form of manually-coded English and not ASL. Like other late learners, Simon's parents had a vocabulary of frozen signs and used many of the grammatical constructions in ASL unsystematically. By

---

[2]The term *recreolization* actually goes back to a paper on sign languages as creoles by Fischer (1978:329) where she noted the large proportion of non-native speakers in the communication environment of deaf children (including, but not limited to their parents) and pointed out that "most deaf children are forced to re-creolize ASL in every generation."

the age of seven, Simon's ASL had already surpassed the input he was receiving from his parents, particularly with respect to verbs of motion and location. Simon did not invent new forms. He took morphemes that were used sporadically in his parents' signing, and used them more consistently and systematically in his own signing.

Simon's situation offers a more controlled case of exclusively non-native signing input to a first language learner, but conditions being as they are in the United States, complete isolation from signed language input other than from his parents was impossible to maintain.[3] Manually-coded English still involves frozen lexical items from ASL, and these frozen signs also contain within them the remnants of the complex morphology and syntax of ASL (Kegl and Schley 1986), preserved in such a way that the analytical mind of this young first language learner could undoubtedly tease out systematic aspects of their linguistic organization. ASL signs are particularly rich in this regard since verbs tend to be sentential and most nouns result from a process of nominalizing them (Shepard-Kegl 1985). By learning and transmitting these signs as frozen forms, Simon's parent's were actually preserving the consistency and integrity of these language remnants in a form ready for Simon's analysis. Although frozen and therefore non-productive for his parents, the signs that they did use as late-learners of ASL provided Simon with sufficient regularity to allow him to "remorphologize" and decode the syntactic regularities of the grammar of ASL. The input to Simon's language acquisition therefore indirectly involved morphologically rich data input from a full-fledged language, ASL.

Kegl (1986) made the point that if second generation signers are indeed indistinguishable from native signers, then this would mean that they are not just recreolizing a non-optimal input or pidgin form; they would be simultaneously de-creolizing to a language specific target--namely, ASL. A simpler account would be that, like children of native signers, second generation signers are simply learning ASL on the basis of noisy, partial, inconsistent input.

It is important to consider what factors condition the outcome where second generation signers surpass their models in terms of exhibiting native-like competence in ASL. First generation signers (children of hearing parents) are typically not exposed to formal signed input until their school years, possibly beyond. First generation signers do have early access to some degree of home sign, but home sign comes from gesture rather than from a pre-existing language and does not come packed full of remnants of a morphologically and syntactically complex signed language. Home sign may not constitute a form of input rich enough to support the first language

---

[3] By the way, although the focus in these and the home sign studies of Goldin-Meadow and her colleagues focus upon signing development, all of these children upon entering school are being intensively trained in English, spoken and written, with varying levels of success.

acquisition process. Furthermore, delay in exposure to formal signed language input has consequences for language acquisition down the line.

3.2 Where the recreolization program falls short of addressing the bioprogram issue

The early studies of recreolization by second generation signers is confounded by the fact that their language models are not strictly limited to their parents and by the fact that the language pool to which they are exposed has the potential to contain 6-10% native signers. By school age, which typically comes earlier for deaf children, these children are being taught English, albeit formally and not in any rich natural context. In many cases, they are also being exposed to manually coded forms of English that contain frozen forms of morphologically complex signs drawn from ASL. While Simon's case solved some of the input problems by his experiencing more limited contact with the Deaf community and no access to native ASL signers, there was one factor that still confounds the case. Simon and other recreolizers are being exposed to remnants of ASL, however frozen and inconsistently used they may be.

These cases can be taken to demonstrate that children bring to the language acquisition process certain innate expectations of how languages work. These expectations lead them in their quest to mine the full morphological and syntactic richness hidden in the frozen forms to which they are exposed and to ignore irrelevant and inconsistent data, settling in on a viable grammar. But, what these studies cannot tell us is exactly what structural expectations or tendencies the bioprogram can contribute de novo in the course of the acquisition process. The fact that recreolizers can recreolize to a language specific target, ASL, attests to the fact that the linguistic input is rich enough in linguistic cues to support ASL acquisition despite its non-productive and inconsistent use by first generation signers. It is not clear what sole reliance on the bioprogram in the absence of a language blueprint encoded in the input would yield in terms of structural choices and linguistic innovations. To address this question, we need a situation where the input to first language acquisition does not consist of remnants of pre-existing languages.

4. The Value of the Nicaraguan Sign Language Data

The above observations lead one to the conclusion that if there is a such thing as a bioprogram, then creoles and language learning from non-native, but signed language using, models happen not to be the place to look for it. In this final part of the paper, we will discuss some findings accumulated over the past 10 years in Nicaragua, where a language seems to have emerged from non-language roots, namely from the idiosyncratic gesture systems used by isolated Deaf individuals in interacting with their hearing family members. These idiosyncratic gestures systems are what were referred to above as home signs, but in the Nicaraguan case these home sign systems initially existed in an environment devoid of any formal signed language(s) that could have provided fragments of pre-existing signed language grammars to these home signers.

4.1 The Initial Setting

In 1980, one year after the triumph of the revolution, a commitment on the part of the newly installed Sandinista government to improving health care and providing a minimum fourth grade education to all Nicaraguans led to the establishment of public schools throughout Nicaragua. This educational commitment extended to individuals with disabilities, and as a consequence, schools for special education sprang up all over the country. The largest schools were established in Managua and along the Pacific Coast, with limited resources diffusing inland and, to only a limited extent, to the Atlantic Coast as well.[4] We will focus upon Managua, the capital, where Kegl has been doing field work since 1986.

While we query every family and service provider that we contact in our research concerning the existence of any signed languages or families with deaf children prior to the 1980s, our best information on the prior situation in Nicaragua comes from Laura Polich, an audiologist who went to Nicaragua first in 1987, then later in 1994 and again in 1995 and did an extensive amount of interviewing to compile background on audiological services in Nicaragua. During her 1994 visit, she also conducted a series of interviews to determine a bit of the history of deaf education in Nicaragua. A summary of her findings from the 1994 interviews appears in Polich (1994), but she has also shared her extensive field notes with the Nicaraguan Sign Language Project archive. Her work confirms our findings that prior to the 1980s, socialization of deaf individuals with each other or the community at large was limited by stigmatization.

> ...because of the stigma that such children represented for their parents, or as a means of protecting them from public ridicule, until recently, it was common for deaf children to be hidden from public view. (Polich 1994:1)

A further consequence of this stigmatization, persisting to this day, is the fact that there is to date not a single case of a deaf child of deaf parents that has been identified in the country. This is not to say that genetic deafness does not exist, rather it appears to have simply been suppressed. We have found pockets of Usher's Syndrome (San Marcos and possibly Corn Island; deafness at birth plus gradual development of tunnel vision around puberty),

---

[4] The Atlantic Coast was more heavily populated with counter-revolutionary supporters, cut off from the Pacific coast by an impassable rain forest and mountain range, and prone to the dangers of easy attack by air or boat. Cultural distinctions existed as well since the inhabitants of the Pacific Coast were primarily mestizo and Spanish speaking; while the inhabitants of the Atlantic Coast are of African descent (former British slaves and creole English speakers) as well as a variety of indigenous groups with their own languages and cultures (Miskitu, Rama, Sumu/Mayanna, etc.). In addition, limited monetary funds dwindled the farther one got from the governmental center in Managua.

several families with more than one deaf child whose etiology of deafness was not illness related, and a few families with deaf individuals at different generations (aunt and uncle plus nephew; grandmother, uncle, niece; etc.). We suspect that genetic deafness is in the population, but because of the lack of socialization prior to the 1980s, marriage of deaf people, even to hearing spouses, was not happening.

In an interview with Polich (1995:1), Silvia Ayon, whose child was diagnosed with a hearing impairment in 1961, reported that the first "school" for children with disabilities, a private institution focusing on children with mental retardation, but willing to accept deaf pupils, began in 1946. She described it a follows:[5]

> Literacy was never a goal, and activities focused upon providing a pleasant atmosphere for the children, all of whom came from wealthy families, to spend their days. The pattern of educating mentally-retarded, blind, and deaf children at the same school is followed to this day in Nicaragua, although classrooms are now grouped according to disability.

Polich also notes that another private school (of similar organization), founded around 1960 with help from the local Lion's and Rotary Clubs, was seriously damaged in the 1972 earthquake, and rebuilt in 1977, re-opening with 82 pupils, a handful of whom were deaf. Closing with the intensifying of the revolution, this school reopened in 1980 as the Melania Morales School, the largest special education school in the country with 488 students in 1994, 40% of whom were deaf. Because of the continuity in students from 1977 through the reopening of the Melania Morales School in 1980, we include in what we term the first generation of deaf students those students who entered the school in 1977, even though they report not sharing classes and using no signed language of any sort with each other at that time.[6]

According to Polich, "[s]peech and language therapy for deaf individuals using oral methods was not available until 1963, when Ayon who had gone

---

[5] We have found that grouping by disability is not yet a practice on the Atlantic coast, with the exception of the school (Escuelita de Bluefields) jointly founded in 1995 by our organization, the Nicaraguan National Deaf Association and a parents' advocacy group in Bluefields, Los Pipitos.

[6] A small group of men (3-4) who attended a special education school (entering after age 10) in the 60s and still socialize with each other was identified in the summer of 1995. Richard Senghas, Juan Carlos Druetta and members of the Deaf Association interviewed and collected a language sample on them. Juan Druetta reports their signing to be distinct from the signing we see currently and pidgin-like in nature--more akin to the contact signing observed to emerge between home signers. While not likely to have been an input to the signed language that has emerged given the discontinuity between these men and the children who entered the schools in the 80s, we see this group as important in terms of tracking any potential adult-centered stabilization of a signed pidgin over time in the absence of child acquirers.

to Mexico for two years of training established a private practice as a speech and language therapist. The only individual with formal audiology training to date (also trained in Mexico) is Dr. Acuña de Izaba, who established her practice in 1967. Furthermore, even with the opening of the Melania Morales School in 1980, the facilities to allow speech training in the school were highly inadequate:

> Noel Lam Herrera, who is in charge of the hearing-impaired program at the Ministry of Education, recalls that after about five years the totally oral approach was increasingly unsatisfactory. "The students just weren't making progress. We had even a special, less-demanding curriculum, and they weren't even attaining that."..."Realistically," Lam explained, "we couldn't have a totally oral program even if we wanted to. What are the bases of a good oral program? Good auditory perception and speech training, excellent individual amplification, and highly trained teachers. We don't have even one of those: there is one group auditory trainer and it is ancient—it is out of order more than it is working. Not even 10% of our students have individual hearing aids, and most of them only have one, and often it is poorly fit. And finally, we have no special education training course. [Polich 1994:4]

In general, the students categorized as "deaf" in Nicaragua typically function as profoundly deaf. Some who are moderate to severe generally have their hearing loss exacerbated by chronic infection. In general, to be "deaf" is to not speak.

> "I was really puzzled my first few days of teaching...I asked my fellow teachers: 'What's wrong--these kids don't talk!' 'Of course not,' they told me 'they're deaf.' But at that time I didn't know that deafness and not talking went together!" [interview with Iliana Ruiz, presently the audiometric technician for the Ministry of Education, who was a teacher of the deaf in the early 1980s, Polich 1994:4]

Even now, we successfully track down isolated deaf individuals in remote areas only by asking for whether there are any "mudos" (mutes), never by asking for individuals who cannot hear. The above discussion establishes the fact that the system selects for individuals unable to process any sound in the speech range and that transmission of spoken Spanish to deaf students via the schools in the early 1980's was not happening. Deaf children in Nicaragua were clearly barred from acquisition of Spanish by the simple fact of being unable to hear it -- any input they received via oral instruction can have had highly marginal impact at best upon the distinct and elaborated sign language they have developed. Thus, the input to the first generation of deaf students in the schools was neither a full-fledged spoken or signed language. In 1992, to their credit, the Ministry of Education turned to advocating signed language in the curriculum. Yet, well before then, a full-fledged indigenous signed language had spontaneously emerged and was fortunately available to meet the needs of this new curriculum.

The Nicaraguan context, eliminates all of the insurmountable problems with seeking spontaneous language creation on plantations where, after all, the linguistic input was, if anything, richer than the ordinary one rather than poorer. To borrow terms from creolistics, in Nicaragua, language emerged without a full-fledged language as "superstrate" and without full-fledged signed languages in the "substrate." The only possible "substrate" among these deaf children would have been the individual and idiosyncratic home signs each had developed. Not only were these not "languages" at all in the true sense, but more importantly they were not a system consistent across a community -- transfer of these systems would result in only the broadest, if any, uniformities. Thus there, unlike the plantation, is a context where children were incontestably forced to build a full language from no language input. There were no language fragments available for first language acquirers to mine for frozen clues to morphology and syntax. In this case, we argue, they were indeed forced to rely heavily on the elusive human bioprogram for language. If there indeed exists a bioprogram, we could ask for no better a demonstration.

4.2 The Spontaneous Emergence of Nicaraguan Sign Language

The beauty of the Nicaraguan case is that not only can we establish that it meets the criteria for emergence of a language in the absence of language input, but we have actually been able to observe the process as it unfolds— empirical creolistics! From the observer's perspective, we would now like to overview the process by which Nicaraguan Sign Language emerged, commenting upon ways in which it fits with or diverges from previous speculations about language emergence. Detailed discussion of the grammatical features that characterize the various stages in the development of Nicaraguan Sign Language would require far more space than is available here; therefore we will add only new information and refer the reader to relevant articles where other details can be found as we go along.

The process begins with home sign[7], the sole means of communication available to prelinguistic deaf children and their families. The home sign of isolates is far more impoverished than one might imagine. It is easy to assume that homesign is akin to what the average person would do communicating through gesture alone, but what we have observed in Nicaragua indicates that this is not the case. The Nicaraguan data reveals that much of how we gesture is tempered by the language knowledge we have. Deaf homesigners do not have that knowledge base.

Since 1995, Kegl and Morford have been collecting a home sign battery on isolates, acquired whenever possible upon first contact, consisting of two narratives elicited via non-verbal cartoons (the Koumal Stories (Animovanéhu Filmu 1969, 1973), a narrative elicited via a non-verbal picturebook (*Frog, Where Are you?* (Mayer 1969)), a supplemented form of a picture naming inventory compiled by Dr. Karen Emmorey, a background

---

[7] For a lucid and straightforward review of the basic literature on home sign see Morford (1996).

questionnaire, and a informal family interview (including some parallel testing of family members)—all videotaped. We are currently analyzing data from 45 homesigners (for preliminary findings see Kegl and Morford 1995, to appear and Morford and Kegl 1996). Upon initial contact, the most prolific homesigners tested generally use gesture to label events that are retrievable based on shared knowledge. Eliciting names for objects typically yields a single gesture indicating how the object moves or is used. If the object is in the immediate environment or a known location, it will be indicated with a pointing gesture. Home signs tend to be action oriented rather than expressing names for things. Notions like colors, emotions, and tense, tend not to be encoded. Single gestures spread to cover a range of concepts like "breasts" for woman, mother, sister, etc "beard" for man, father, brother, etc. and "eat" for all edible items. Home signs are slightly more discrete and conventional than mimetic gesture but tend not to use multiple discrete signs in a relational way that resembles syntactic organization. Family members can generally list and identify most of the small gestural repertoire the homesigner commands. Because home signs draw heavily on the gesture system in general use among hearing people, isolated home signs are generally transparent to other Nicaraguans in the same cultural sphere but without exposure to deaf homesigners, even those gestures that to non-Nicaraguans seem opaque.

We discovered that older Nicaraguan homesigners, while possibly developing increased conventionality in their home sign systems, do not end up spontaneously generating a language. A single home signer left until adulthood in the canonical home sign environment—the home and immediate hearing community—remains "native language-less" and appears unable to acquire a language to the point of native-like competency.[8] In fact, those well past the critical period for language acquisition (ages 15 and above) are oftentimes unable to acquire even the most rudimentary language components beyond naming. The critical period for acquiring a full-language exemplar is an issue we hope to determine longitudinally in a project on the Atlantic Coast of Nicaragua where Nicaraguan Sign Language is being explicitly taught to individuals (ages 3-37) who prior to December 1994 were home signers.

---

[8] By "native language-less" we mean failing to have achieved native-level competence in some human language. Ability to communicate via some alternative mode such as, drawing pictures, mime-like gesture, laundry-list like stringing together of gestural labels that elicit an interpretation, or even partial mastery of a pidgin-like system of signing do not on our definition constitute having fully acquired a language. It is important to note that individuals without a language can exhibit a continuum of communicative competencies ranging from high communicative skills (strong ability to convey information in an alternate way) to low communicative skills (virtual inability to convey information).

Home sign alone is insufficient to support spontaneous generation of a signed language. In Nicaragua, an intermediate stage of development mediated between home sign and the emergence of a full-fledged signed language. When hundreds of deaf students came together in the schools in the early 80s, their individual home sign systems were brought into contact on a large scale. The cross-fertilization, conventionalization, expanded use and critical mass of interlocutors yielded a form of intercommunication (a "pidgin" between home sign systems) that crossed a line between non-language (home sign) and a form of communication that was sufficient to support first language acquisition. The result of the subsequent first language acquisition process using this intermediate form as input was a first language in every sense of the word. It was both the first language of these individual acquirers and the first language of the community as a whole.

Kegl and Morford (1995, to appear) and Morford and Kegl (1996) track particular grammatical forms in Nicaraguan Sign Language back to their homologues in the pidgin as well as to their pre-cursors in home sign in an attempt to characterize the process of grammaticization that occurred and to identify those components of the process that are gradual (gesture to home sign to pidgin) and those that are abrupt (pidgin to full-fledged signed language). Senghas focused upon the statistical occurrence of grammatical features identified in earlier work by Kegl and Iwata (1989), Kegl and Senghas (1991) and subsequent studies and correlated them with age at entry into the Deaf community to build an argument "that the [y]oung children who entered into the signing environment since the early 80s have abruptly changed the language" (Senghas 1995:157). By looking not only at age of entry, but also year of entry, Senghas was also able to capture quantitatively the observation that with each successive class entering the schools, the make up of the language pool to which they were exposed changed in content and proportion. First there were only home signers, then pidgin signers were added to the mix, and finally full-fledged signed language users as well. Over time the proportions of these groups shifted toward more and more full-fledged language users, and with each successive generation the language input to first language acquirers became richer and richer.

We now know that what has occurred over the last 15 years in Nicaragua is spontaneous emergence of language. We also know that abrupt spontaneous emergence will not occur in the absence of the right kind of input, which itself need not be a fully formed language. But, is the human bioprogram for language currently on view in Nicaragua? The answer is that for a brief evolutionary instant, it was. Luckily, we were able to document some of that instant as it was happening. One thing we have learned is that that period of language emergence is <u>extremely</u> rapid, even more rapid than has been assumed. Home sign changes once it leaves the home, i.e. once a critical mass of deaf homesigners come into contact. In contrast to the pidginization that occurs in a plantation context where full-language input yields to a process of leveling and regularization to accommodate the conflicting grammatical cues being contributed by an overly rich set of linguistic choices offered by the input, the pidginization of home sign systems allows bits and pieces of language pre-cursors, contributed by non-language using contributors, to accumulate in the language pool.

The same mechanism that allows a first language learner to creolize pidgin input, reconstituting a new language from pidginized multiple language input, kicks in in the Nicaraguan case as well. While older home signers may expand their variable repertoires to some degree as a consequence of exposure to additional options in their communication environment; young home signers, we argue, recruit the bioprogram for language to <u>force</u> the pidginized home sign input to conform to their innate expectations of what a language is. When the bioprogram forces the decision, we see its direct expression, albeit tempered by the non-language gestural input it had to work with. In contrast, where creolizers sift through language fragments to settle on a language that satisfies their innate expectations, the bioprogram serves as an adjudicator rather than an innovator, yielding the types of statistical correlations between grammatical options in the input languages and degree of expression in the creole, as seen in Figure 1.

While the serial verb distribution in spoken language creoles argues in favor of systematic substrate influence, Bickerton's original claim that serial verb constructions are favored by the bioprogam may also be justified. In the emergence of Nicaraguan Sign Language, we observed that home sign encodes actions and events, leaving participant roles unspecified. Early grammaticization in the signing of home signers post contact favors the expression of single verbs or verbs plus a single argument. Lexical conceptual structures involving multiple participant roles are generally expressed by a series of verb plus single argument clauses. The transition to the fully grammaticized form of Nicaraguan Sign Language is associated with increased grammatical fine-tuning of a range of serial verb constructions in addition to the emergence of multiple argument taking verbs (see Kegl, Senghas, and Coppola in press). Interestingly, the Atlantic Coast homesigners being formally exposed to the fully articulated form of Nicaraguan Sign Language, while producing some serial verbs, are skipping the strictly one-verb-one-argument stage and jumping straight to the expression of multiple argument verbs; although they favor all arguments in preverbal position.

The recreolization by second generation signers to a specific ASL target that we discussed earlier further attests to the fact that when specific language cues are retrievable from the input, young acquirers will use them. They may initially overregularize, but they will eventually reflect the tendencies toward grammatical options reflected by full-fledged language fragments in the input. What the bioprogram does seem to contribute is a kind of "species recognition," the ability to identify relevant human language input in the context of a morass of potential candidates and a statistical tendency to reflect its relative contribution in the output of the acquisition process. It is this same process that accounts for the effects of contact with other languages on the development of an evolving language.

Since the early 1990s,[9] the development of Nicaraguan Sign Language has been turning a new page in its development, incorporation of the products of contact with other signed languages into Nicaraguan Sign Language. With the emergence of a pidgin between homesigners came the parallel emergence of a Deaf community. Since the mid-80s the elaboration of the social organization of the Deaf community has dovetailed the development of the language. With the emergence and stabilization of a full-fledged language came the ability of the Deaf community to interact on an international scale with signers of other languages. As a result, we see language contact effects of ASL, Swedish Sign Language and a variety of Central and South American signed languages having an impact on the lexicon and bits of the grammar of Nicaraguan Sign Language. In the course of a population study we are conducting, we have the ability to track the course of these influences both temporally and geographically as they spread from the Association in Managua outward. While there are up and down fluctuations in terms of the degree on impact external signed languages are having, the lexical diffusion of foreign borrowings has occurred very rapidly. In addition, fluency in a full-fledged signed language (Nicaraguan Sign Language), the present existence of interpreters (also a phenomenon of the 90s), and support (since 1992) from the Ministry of Education for the use of Nicaraguan Signed Language in the school curriculum has also led to increased access to Spanish for Deaf Nicaraguans. This has increased language contact between Spanish and Nicaraguan Sign Language, leading to the introduction of increased initialization (use of a fingerspelled letter corresponding to the beginning of a Spanish word in the articulation of signs), introduction of some lexical items (particularly function words) that were not previously a part of Nicaraguan Sign Language (although their use is currently marginal), and the use of Spanish glosses in the documentation and dissemination of signed vocabulary in the standardization program. In less than 10 years into its history, we have already seen the kinds of influences on the newly emerged language that could, had we not collected earlier data, have forever obscured its roots.

In reviewing the Nicaraguan case, we have observed the extreme rapidity and transiency of that period in which a language emerges and have come to

---

[9] Two factors played a role in this shift: 1) the increased travel to and from Nicaragua by Deaf people as a consequence of the waning of the counter-revolutionary war after the 1990 elections and 2) the shift in control of the Deaf Association, centered primarily in Managua, to Deaf individuals with a goal of standardizing and disseminating Nicaraguan Sign Language throughout Nicaragua.

appreciate the serendipity that led researchers to be in the right place at the right time. These observations also lead us to appreciate the necessarily speculative nature of creole research and the immensity of the task involved in retrospectively searching for evidence of that glimmer of a second of linguistic history in which a given language may have emerged.

References

Andersen, R. (1983). A language acquisition interpretation of pidginization and creolization. In R. Andersen, (ed), *Pidginization and creolization as language acquisition.* Rowley, Mass.: Newbury House.

Baron, N. 1975. Trade jargons and pidgins: A functionalist approach. Paper presented at *the International Conference on Pidgins and Creoles.* Honolulu.

Berreby, D. 1992. Kids, creoles and the coconuts. *Discover* 13:44-9.

Bickerton, Derek. 1981. *Roots of language.* Ann Arbor, MI: Karoma.

_____. 1984. The Language Bioprogram Hypothesis. *The Behavioral and Brain Sciences* 7:173-88.

_____. 1988. Creole languages and the Bioprogram. In F. Newmeyer, (ed.), *Linguistics: The Cambridge Survey, Vol. II: Linguistic theory: Extensions and implications.* Cambridge: Cambridge University Press, pp. 268-82.

_____. 1991. On the supposed "gradualness" of creole development. *Journal of Pidgin and Creole Languages* 6:25-58.

_____ and William Wilson. 1987. Pidgin Hawaiian. *Pidgin and creole languages*, ed. by Glenn G. Gilbert, 61-76. Honolulu: University of Hawaii Press.

Chaudenson, R. 1979. *Les créoles français.* Évreux: Nathan.

Ferraz, Luis Ivens. 1979. *The creole of São Tomé.* Johannesburg: Witwatersrand University Press.

Fischer, S. 1978. Sign language and creoles. In P. Siple, (ed.), *Understanding language through sign language research.* New York: Academic Press, pp. 309-333.

Givón, Talmy. 1979. Tense-aspect-modality: The creole prototype and beyond. In Hopper, P. J., (ed.), *Tense-aspect: Between semantics and pragmatics.* Amsterdam: John Benjamins, pp. 115-63.

Goldin-Meadow, S. (1979). Structure in a manual communication system developed without a conventional language model: Language without a helping hand. In H. Whitaker & H. A. Whitaker (eds), *Studies in Neurolinguistics, Vol. 4.* New York: Academic Press, pp. 125-209.

Goodman, Morris F.. 1985. Review of Bickerton (1981). *International Journal of American Linguistics* 51:109-37.

Kegl, J. 1986. The Role of Sub-Lexical Structure in Recreolization. Presented at *the 18th Annual Stanford Child Language Research Forum*, Stanford University. April 6.

Kegl, J. and J. Morford. (to appear) Gestural Precursors to Linguistic Constructs. In McNeill, D. and A. Kendon, (eds.), *Gesture: An Emerging Field of Study.* Cambridge: Cambridge University Press. (Invited presentation at conference on Gestures Compared Cross-Linguistically. Organizers David McNeill and Adam Kendon. Albuquerque, NM, July 8.)

Kegl, J. and S. Schley. 1986. "When Is a Classifier No Longer a Classifier?" In N. Nikiforidou, M. Van Clay, M. Niepokuj and D. Feder, eds., *Proceedings of the Twelfth Annual Meeting of the Berkeley Linguistic Society*, Berkeley, Calif.: Berkeley Linguistics Society, pp. 425-441.

Kegl, J., A. Senghas, and M. Coppola. In press. Creation through contact: Sign Language Emergence and Sign Language Change in Nicaragua.. In M. DeGraff, ed., *Comparative Grammatical Change: The Intersection of Language Acquisition, Creole Genesis, and Diachronic Syntax*. Cambridge, MA: MIT Press.

McWhorter, John H. 1996. *Towards a new model of creole genesis*. NY: Peter Lang.

_____. In press. It happened at Cormantin: Tracing the birthplace of the Atlantic English-based creoles. *Journal of Pidgin and Creole Languages*.

Morford, J. 1996. Insights into language from the study of gesture: A review of research on the gestural communication of non-signing deaf people? *Language and Communication*, vol. 16, no. 2., pp. 165-178.

Morford, J. and J. Kegl. 1996. Grammaticization in a newly emerging signed language in Nicaragua. Poster presented at *TISLR V, Fifth International Conference on Theoretical Issues in Sign Language Research*. Montreal, Sept 19-22.

Muysken, Pieter. 1994. Column: Saramaccan and Haitian: A comparison. *Journal of Pidgin and Creole Languages* 9:305-14.

Owens, Jonathan. 1990. East African Nubi: Bioprogram vs. inheritance. *Diachronica* 7:217–50.

Pinker, S. 1994. *The Language Instinct*. New York: William Morrow and Company, Inc.

Post, Marike. 1992. The serial verb constructions in Fa d'Ambu. *Actas do Coloquio sobre Crioulos de Base Lexical Portguesa*, ed. by E. D'Andrade and Alain Kihm, 153–71. Lisbon: Colibri.

Roberts, Julian. 1995a. Pidgin Hawaiian: A sociohistorical study. *Journal of Pidgin and Creole Languages* 10:1–56.

Sabino, Robin. 1992. A point of detail: Serial verbs in Negerhollands. Paper presented at *the Society for Pidgin and Creole Linguistics conference*, Philadelphia.

Senghas, A. 1995. *Children's Contribution to the Birth of Nicaraguan Sign Language*. Dissertation, distributed by MIT Working Papers in Linguistics, Cambridge, MA.

Shepard-Kegl, J. 1985. *Locative Relations in American Sign Language Word Formation, Syntax, and Discourse*. Dissertation, distributed by MIT Working Papers in Linguistics, Cambridge, MA.

Singler, John. 1992. Nativization and pidgin/creole genesis: A reply to Bickerton. *Journal of Pidgin and Creole Languages* 7:319-33.

Singleton, J. (1989). *Restructuring of language from impoverished input.* Unpublished doctoral dissertation, University of Illinois at Urbana-Champaign.

Singleton, J. and E. Newport. (1987). When learners surpass their models: The acquisition of American Sign Language from impoverished input. Poster presented at *the Biennial Meeting of the Society for Research in Child Development*, Baltimore, MD.

Stolz, Thomas and Peter Stein. 1986. Social history and genesis of Negerhollands. Amsterdam Creole Studies 9:103–22.

PAPERS

Isolating the CVC Root in Tzeltal Mayan: A Study of Children's First Verbs

PENELOPE BROWN

Max Planck Institute for Psycholinguistics, Nijmege, The Netherlands

1. Introduction

The verbs of Mayan languages have an important structural property: they are based on canonically CVC roots, which underived belong to a certain form class (Transitive, Intransitive, Positional) and take affixes characteristic of their form class. There is a very productive derivational morphology that can shift a word's form class from transitive to intransitive, from verb to noun or adjective, and so on. The basic building blocks of the language are these CVC roots; these are the core semantic packages which stay constant across many different derived forms. These are the forms which are entered in dictionaries, which a child learning the language must somehow enter in her mental lexicon.

However, in natural speech these CVC roots do not often occur in isolation; they are accompanied by the prefixes and suffixes appropriate to their form class (which depend in turn on whether and how the roots have been derived). Furthermore the rhythmic structure of the language tends to mask the identity of roots; Tzeltal Mayan[1] seems to be *syllable-timed* (a bit like French, with neither intervocalic intervals nor vowel amplitude varying very much - in contrast to a *stress-timed* language like English). In Tzeltal stress is word-final, clause-final, and there is special prosodic emphasis on the utterance-final syllable. There is massive resyllabification, so this utterance-final syllable often consists of the final consonant of the root plus a suffix or particle; this, not the root, receives the prosodic prominence. Now Pye (1983) has shown that, in K'iche' Mayan acquisition, prosodic salience overrides semantic salience, so that children's first verbs in K'iche' are often composed of only the final (stressed) syllable constituted by the final consonant of the CVC root and a "meaningless" termination suffix.

---

[1] This paper is based on fieldwork in the Tzeltal Mayan community of Tenejapa, Chiapas, Mexico. The longitudinal data base consists of several hundred hours of taped recorded and/or videotaped natural interaction of children ranging in age from 1;6 to 5;0 and their caregivers, in five extended family households, collected monthly (audio) and every six weeks (video) over two and a half years.

Intonation thus plays a crucial role in early K'iche' morphological development, promoting the very early production of these suffixes. In Tzeltal, however, we do *not* find children doing this, despite what appears to be a comparable prosodic structure of the languages. The first words of Tzeltal children starting around the age of 1;6 are predominantly bare roots; children strip off all prefixes and suffixes which are obligatory in adult speech. They gradually produce them, starting with the suffixes (which tend to receive the main stress), but the development is not linear from the end of the verb to the beginning as Pye reports for K'iche' - certain person prefixes and one aspectual prefix (obligatory, and always produced, in adult speech) which are verb-internal (neither first nor last in the verb) are systematically omitted in some contexts for one to two years after the child starts to talk.

How can we explain the Tzeltal child's initial faultless isolation of the root despite the complex input, and how can we explain the differences from K'iche'? An account in terms of intonation or stress cannot explain the Tzeltal children's ability to isolate the root (neither the prefixes nor the roots are always syllables; the roots are often not stressed). In this paper I will look first at the child's segmentation problem in detail, then at what children actually produce as their first verbs, and try to tease apart the factors which help them in what seems a daunting task.

2. The Child's Segmentation Problem

2.1. Structure of the Tzeltal Verb

Tzeltal has ergative/absolutive person cross-referencing on the verb. The minimally required morphology for a transitive verb is:[2]

(1) ASPECT + ERG. PREFIX + ROOT + ABS. SUFFIX
 ya s-**nutz**-on [syllabifies as: yas nu tzon]
 ICP 3ERG-push-1ABS
 'He is chasing me.'

For a ditransitive verb it is the same, with the addition of a **'benefactive'** suffix:

(2) ASPECT + ERG. PREFIX + ROOT + BENEFACTIVE + ABS.
 ya j-**pas**-bet [syllabifies as: yaj pas bet]
 ICP 1ERG-do-2BEN
 'I'll do it for you.'

For intransitive verbs, aspect particles and an absolutive suffix flank the root:

---

[2] Verb roots are in boldface in the Tzeltal examples. A practical orthography is used, with symbols corresponding roughly to their English equivalents except that j=h, x=sh, and ' indicates a glottal stop or glottalization of the preceding consonant.

(3) ASPECT + <u>ROOT</u> + ABS. SUFFIX
 ya x-'**och**-at   [syllabifies as yax 'o chat]
 ICP ASP-come-2ABS
 'You enter.'

For transitive and intransitive verbs, there is often resyllabification such that the syllable consists of the final consonant of the root plus the suffix. There is also a large set of optional particles that can occur between the aspect and person markers, so that the latter syllabicize with the root. The root, therefore, rarely constitutes a syllable by itself.

The difficulty of identifying of the root is exacerbated because there are two sets of ergative person-markers (which cross-reference both *agent* of transitive verbs and *possessor* of nouns). One set is for consonant-initial roots (including most verb roots) and another for vowel-initial roots, so that a child has to distinguish between, for example, *k-il* meaning 'I see' and *kil* meaning 'drag it', or between *y-al* 'she says' and *yal* 'fall'. The two sets are given in Table 1.

Table 1: Ergative prefixes in Tzeltal

	Before a root beginning with a consonant:	Before a root beginning with a vowel:
1st	j-	k-
2nd	a'-	a'w-
3rd	s-	y-
	Examples:	
1st	j-pas 'I make (it)'	k-uch' 'I drink (it)'
2nd	a'-pas 'you make (it)'	a'w-uch' 'you drink (it)'
3rd	s-pas 'he/she/it makes (it)'	y-uch' 'he/she/it drinks (it)'

So Tzeltal verbs present segmentation problems at the front (non-syllabic prefixes, non-canonical VC roots), and problems at the end (resyllabification), which should cause difficulties for the child in identifying the root.

2.2 Null Affixes.

Against these problems we may set some helpful structural and distributional facts. There are some linguistic contexts where prefixes or suffixes "aren't there" so the beginning or ending of the root is bared. <u>Positive imperatives</u> have no prefix, only a suffix (*-a* for transitives, *-be* for ditransitives, *-an* for intransitives):

(4) Transitive: **pas**-a 'Do it!'

(5) Ditransitive: **k'an**-be 'Ask him for it!'

(6) Intransitive: **'och**-an 'Enter!'

However, this does not help with some verbs which never occur imperatively (eg. *-tak'* 'be able to do it') but which children still use at the one-word stage. And many directives (including all negative and volitive ones) use another form which does have a prefix:

(7) ma x-a'-**pik.** 'Don't touch it!'

(8) x-a'w-**ak'** xan tal ya'tik.
     'Give (the fire) some more (wood) in a little while.'

There are also null places in the <u>intransitive verb paradigms</u>: some forms of completive aspect, and third person singular person-marking are null:

(9) 0-**tal**-on ta lum. 'I came to town.'

(10) ya x-**tal**-0 ta lum j'alux. 'Alux is coming to town.'

(11) 0 **tal**-0 ta lum j'alux. 'Alux came to town.'

Intransitives with perfective aspect have no prefix, just a suffix:

(12) '**och**-em 'He/she has entered.'

The <u>transitive paradigms</u> also have null places: 3rd singular absolutive (marking transitive objects) is a null suffix:

(13) ya s-**maj**-0 swix 'He is hitting his elder-sister.'

and passive and adjectival forms of the verb have no prefix:

(14) **maj**-ot yijtz'in. '(She was) hit (by) her younger-brother.'

(15) **tz'us**-ul, **tz'us**-bil 'closed, having been closed.'

Hearing verbs in these linguistic contexts must help children distinguish the stable root from the contextually varying and sometimes non-present (null) affixes, although, as we will see in a moment, these contexts are not overwhelmingly frequent in the input to 2-year-olds. Most input verbs in the sample I looked at have linguistic material before and after the verb root.

But let's look first at the structure of children's early verbs.

3. Children's Performance

Here I present the first 35 verbs produced in my samples by two Tzeltal children.

3.1 Mikel

The first child, a boy named Mikel, was recorded from the age of 1;0, his first intelligible utterances were at 1;6 when he was not yet walking freely. His first verbs appeared at 1;8, and from age 2;0 new verb types exceed new noun types in his data. His first 35 verbs are listed in Table 2. Note that all of this child's first verbs are CV(C) except for one -VC (-*ak*', 'to give'), and all are correctly analyzed. All are bare roots, no affixes are produced yet. This child's first verb productions support the view expressed by Demuth (1996), that children have accurate phonological representations of words (and in this case roots) very early - in her view, by the end of their first year, certainly by the time they begin to use verbs.

3.2 X'anton

Recording of a second child, a girl X'anton, started before she was 1 1/2. Her first words appeared at around 1;6, but her first verbs in my data not until 2;1. At this point she was at a more advanced stage than Mikel, with many 2- and 3-morpheme utterances. Her first 35 verbal utterances are listed in Table 3 (with a blank _ indicating where obligatory grammatical morphemes are missing). In these utterances, aspect marking is missing except on three verbs: *ya _xi'* (probably rote-learned), *ya _we' ch'o* (repeated from the preceding utterance) and *a pach* (with *a* as syllable-holder for the aspect particle *ya*). Ergative person-marking is missing except in the two vowel-initial roots (*k-a'y* and *k-ak'be*); there is no evidence yet that these are productive, but they are used correctly. This set seems among all the children to be the first ergative person-markers learned. Absolutive suffixes are sometimes present, if not always correct: *_ti'at wakan* '(It) bit your foot', and *_we'on* 'I('ll) eat'. The missing grammatical morphemes are missing even in contexts immediately preceded by a parental correct model - the child's repeats *edit out* these grammatical morphemes:

(16) Mo; ma ba ya j**tek**' uta i. 'I won't tread on it, say.'
    Ch; ju'uk, _**tek**'. 'No, tread.'

A relevant point to mention here is that Tzeltal offers a discourse model of natural 'elicited repetition': it is conversationally appropriate to repeat an interlocutor's words as backchannel, and children do this from very early on, demonstrating their ability to extract the appropriate part to repeat from a long stream of speech:

(17) Mo; ya me s**we**' ch'o waj teme ya 'wixlane.
        'Mice will eat the tortillas if you play with them.'
    Ch; aj ya _**we**' ch'o.
        'Ah, mice eat.'

3.3 Resistent grammatical morphemes

In Tzeltal verb development is *not* strictly linear (back to front) - unlike in K'iche'. There are systematic "holes" in the verb which persist for up to two years after the child begins to talk. Taking a long-term look at the verb productions of a third child, a girl called Slus, we can see that certain

Table 2: First 35 verb types of Mikel

[age 1;8-2;0. mlu 1.0. Criterion: not a repeat of previous utterance, and meaning clear in the context]

Age	Utterance	Target (if different)	Gloss
1;8	ba		'go'
	la'		'come!'
1;9	ak	ak'	'give'
	tzak ~ tak		'take'
1;10	po	poj	'take away'
	ay		'exist'
	muk		'cover'
	tak	ma s-tak'	'(I) can('t)'
	wa ~ way	way	'sleep'
	ajx	ajch'	'get wet'
	we wa	ya j-we' waj	'(I) eat tortilla'
1;11	pas ~ pax	pas	'do'
	laj		'finish'
	tek'		'step on'
	chux		'pee'
	tap' ~ ta'p	tz'ap	'insert'
	kan	k'an	'want'
	'och		'enter'
	ka	kay	'open (door)'
	ti'		'eat meat, bite'
	pach		'set down upright (bowl)'
2;0	nu	nuj	'invert'
	k'ux ~ kus	k'ux	'hurt'
	xi'		'fear'
	pet		'carry'
	ch'ay ~ tz'ay	ch'ay	'fall/drop'
	pok	pok'	'wash'
	lap		'put on (clothes)'
	'ok'		'cry'
	lok'		'exit'
	mal		'spill'
	chu'	tuy	'cut (wood)'
	tup	tup'	'turn off (light, recorder)'
	ja' ni	ja' ini	'this is it'
	pa'y	ba'ay	'where is it?'

Table 3: First 36 verb tokens of X'anton [age 2;1-2;2 (mlu 1.13-1.47)]

Utterance	Target (where different)	Gloss
_lo' matz'	ya j-lo' matz'	'(I) eat corngruel'
_chi'	ya j-chik'	'(I) burn (wood)'
xi		'he/she said'
_ta	ma j-ta	'(I can't) reach'
ba'	bajt	'he/she went'
bajt-ix _ paxyal	bajt-ix ta paxyal	'he's gone (for a) walk'
_tij son	ya s-tij son	'(he) play(s) radio'
k-ak'-be	ya k-ak'-be	'I'll give (it to) them'
laj mamal		'old one died' [chicken]
we'_	we'-ix	'(it has) eaten (corn)'
_k'op-oj son	ya x-k'op-oj son	'the radio is talking'
tal-ix		'it has come'
li' ay i		'here it is'
tal we' i		'came (to) eat'
poch'-em s-jol		'its head is peeled' [chicken]
_k'ux	ya s-k'ux	'(he) eat(s) (beans)'
ay _chu'	ay x-chu'	'it has a breast' [balloon]
och ini		'entered here'
och ja'		'water entered'
_juch' painil	ya j-juch' painil	'(I) grind corn'
juch' bojnuk'	ya j-juch'-be bojnuk'	'(I'll) grind (corn for) cutneck' [a chicken]
laj		'(it's) finished'
_kuch	ya s-kuch	'(he) carry(s)'
_t'ux	ya j-tz'us	'(I) shut it'
_k'ej	ya j-k'ej	'(I) put it away'
ya _xi'	ya j-xi'	'(I'm) afraid of it'
lok' bel		'It went out'
k-a'y chux	ya x-ba k-a'y chuxnel	'I'm (going for a) pee'
til-ix		'it's burning'
ya _we' ch'o	ya s-we' ch'o	'a mouse will eat it'
_ti'-at w-akan	la s-ti'-bet a'w-akan	'(it) bit your foot'
ba-em il wakax	baem ta il wakax	'he's gone (to) see the bull'
puk' tat	ya s-puk'-ben jtat	'father will mix it (corn-gruel)'
puk' ja'at	ya '-puk'-ben	'you mix it'
_'ok ek	ya x-'ok' ek	'it's crying too'
_a pach	ya j-pach	'(I) carry (bowl) (upright)'

grammatical morphemes continue to be systematically omitted even after her fourth birthday. At 2;0 Slus was more advanced than X'anton at 2;1; she could already produce consonant clusters. But at 2;0 her repeats of others' utterances systematically omit the ergative prefixes: for example *ya s-tij-ben k-akan* 'he's biting my foot' is repeated as _*ti'be* _*akan*, showing a *selective* omission of the ergative prefix. There are persistent gaps in her verb productions, for example the third person singular ergative prefix for consonant-initial roots is an omission characteristic of her utterances for another two years; their production gradually increases but does not reach 90% criterion even by age 4;3. The most persistent omission is the neutral aspect marker *x-* which is obligatory with intransitive incompletives. Some examples from Slus's speech across the years (where _ marks the missing *x'-*) follow:

At age 2;6:

(18) ma _**'och.** 'It doesn't go in.'

(19) ya _**a'tej**onix. 'I'm already working.'

At 3;6:

(20) ya _**ba**on ta na, ya _**tal**on xan tatil.
 'I'm going home, I'll come back again, boy.'

At 3;8:

(21) ma me ya _**tajin** _tukeli mali. 'Xmal herself can't play (with us).'

At 4;3:

(22) ya _**a'tej**. 'He's working.'

The aspectual marker *x-* is resistent even in the salient 'repeat' slot:

(23) Fa; ya x**ben** 'It's going (tape recorder).'
 Ch; ya _**ben**, ya _**ben** 'It's going.'
 Fa; ya x**ben** 'It's going.'

It is resistent even though it would make a good CVC syllable with the *ya*.

Ergative prefixes appear much earlier for vowel-initial roots, in some children by 2;0, and in all cases well before the consonant-initial set of prefixes are produced to criterion. In all the children's data is there is only very rare evidence of misanalysis of VC roots as CVC (incorportating an ergative prefix). Double marking in third person (using *both* the *s-* for C-initial and the *y-* for V-initial roots) does occur occasionally on nouns, but never on verbs (for example, s-y-**awil** 'its place', s-y-**axib** 'its shade'). There are, however, very few such errors. Basically children do not misanalyze these vowel-initial roots.

3.4 Summary

Children when they start to talk are isolating the CVC and VC verb roots correctly. They are recognizing and repeating the verb appropriately having extracted it from mid-stream of the input utterance. They are adding suffixes respecting the integrity of the root despite resyllabification. So Tzeltal children in this respect are not behaving like their K'iche' counterparts. What could be the explanation for this?

One possibility is that these differences are attributable to different input. Pye says K'iche' mothers simplify (leave off prefixes) in talking to children, whereas the Tzeltal caregivers never do. But is there a lot of speech in linguistic contexts with a bare root (bare at front or at back)?

4. Input

Tzeltal adults in my data never omit aspectual particles, or cross-referencing prefixes or suffixes.[3] In a sample of speech to X'anton[4] comprising 748 input utterances (intonationally complete chunks of speech), 2/3 are clausal and 1/3 are not. The total number of verbs[5] is 556. Of the 495 clausal utterances in the sample, 34% are directives, 52% are declaratives, and 15% are questions. Only 1/2 of directives are root-initial; the others (volative and negative) have prefixes like the declaratives and questions. So only 17% of input utterances are of the speech act type that can have root-initial verbs in them. But other linguistic contexts have root-initial or root-final verbs. Table 4 shows the position of the verb root in the input utterance across all clauses; we find only 11% of verb roots in the sample in a position to carry stress.

Table 4: Position of verb root in input utterance

	Tokens	Types	Percent
Root alone + stress	12		2%
Root final + stress	51		9%
Root final but - stress	21		4%
Root initial, - stress	151		27%
Root medial, - stress	321		58%
TOTAL	556		100%

---

[3] In rapid speech the aspect prefix *ya* may elide to *a*, but it remains syllabic; and *ya + a'w-* (incompletive + 2nd ergative) may elide to *ya 'w-*.
[4] The sample comprised two session of about 1.5 hours total, audiotaped by X'anton's father when I wasn't there, including the speech of her mother, father, or brother (age 5) addressed to her. She was 2;1 - 2;2, her mlu was 1.15 - 1.30.
[5] Counted as 'verbs' for this purpose were all predicates taking aspect, plus positional and existence predicates.

This apears to go against one of the arguments (Aslin et al, 1996) proferred for the early identification of words - that new words tend to be introduced in utterance-final position: loud, lengthened, and high-pitched. This is definitely not the case for Tzeltal verbs, yet children correctly segment them.

5. Explanations for Tzeltal Children's Performance

On semantic grounds we would predict roots to appear first, along the lines first argued by Roger Brown (1973). Verb roots are semantically weightier than affixes - their meanings express basic semantic roles not modulations. This however was not what Pye found in his K'iche' data.

5.1. Phonological and Prosodic Cues

Peters (in press) suggests that the more reliably in a language stress or pitch accent predicts word, phrase, or clause boundaries, the easier it will be for children to add morphemes along the boundaries. On these grounds, Tzeltal children should have difficulty adding morphemes at word boundaries. There are, however, some other helpful cues to root boundaries in Tzeltal:
i. The predictability of root shape (CVC) and the absence of consonant clusters in morphemes (but not in syllables) are good cues to the root.
ii. As in other syllable-timed languages there is a very limited number of syllable-types: (C)CV, (C)CVC and (C)CVhC, and only a limited number of word-shapes built on them.
iii. Beyond this, phonotactic patterns don't provide many cues: any C can occur root-initially or root-finally or utterance-initially or finally, but there are relatively minimal morphophonemic alternations at morpheme boundaries: roots keep their shape across linguistic contexts.[6]
iv. However, in general the perceptual salience of Tzeltal roots in speech is relatively low: they are susceptible to heavy stress and high pitch only in utterance-final position. But in utterances, any particle or word that can be utterance-final can receive the intonational/stress prominence. And these in the input are verb roots only 11% of the time. Thus there must be other factors than phonology/prosody helping the child to segment the roots.

5.2. Distributional Cues

For verbs which appear frequently in CDS in contexts where the root is bare at the front or back, that is, in intranstive completive, transitive or

---

[6] There is one class of exceptions: An infix -j- is inserted in positional roots when they are derived into transitive or intransitive verbs, or numeral classifiers. The frequency in child-directed speech of these non-canonical root forms is not known; the lack of such insertions is an acknowledged feature of Tzeltal child speech. Nor do we have information about the frequency of an analogous disruption in verb roots in K'iche'. This might turn out to be an important difference between the two languages. Other cues may exist - for example vowel lengthening at the ends of words, as in French, but an acoustic analysis of Tzeltal CDS has yet to be done.

intransitive third person, or in the imperative form, children are provided with direct evidence of the beginning or end of the root. Another frequent source of distributional cues is the discourse context: the Tzeltal convention of repeating part of the preceding utterance as backchannel support highlights the constant root, in contrast to the changing affixes. This may play a role in teaching noun and verb morphology, being perhaps especially helpful for the V-initial root prefixes which are acoustically salient:

(24) [Slus is almost 2;6]:
   slus; k-ich' ja' ini 'I get this one.'
   me't; ya 'w-ich' ini 'You get this one.'

5.5 Differences from K'iche'

At the one-syllable per word production limit, according to Pye (1983), K'iche' children choose perceptual salience over semantic salience and produce the stressed final syllable of their verb; Tzeltal children choose semantic salience and produce the root. What could cause these differences between Tzeltal and K'iche' children's performance? Three factors may make the difference:

i. K'iche' morphological order is different; Tzeltal has no "terminations" linked to verb type, aspect, and location in clause, and K'iche' is relatively prefix-heavy, while Tzeltal is suffix-heavy.

ii. K'iche' verb structure is more variable than Tzeltal: the termination depends on aspect and on presence or absence of a movement particle, and the root itself can change in derived stems. So children may rely more on prosody.

iii. In K'iche' stress on the verb shifts reliably with linguistic context: in clause-final position, the termination is stressed; in clause-medial position, the verb stem receives the primary stress. In Tzeltal stress is less predictably associated with the root, so prosody is a less reliable cue to the root.

6. Conclusions

Prosody plays a smaller role in children's initial segmentation strategies in Tzeltal than in K'iche', illustrating the point that dramatic differences in segmenting strategies are possible between even closely related languages. This underlines the importance of cross-linguistic studies of production in closely related languages where prosodic and distributional phenomena may vary, affecting the relative weighting of each.

Many factors provide the child with cues to what the roots are in Tzeltal speech; no single one is determinative. The child must combine the statistical and distributional evidence across many contexts to achieve correct segmentation. Tzeltal children have accomplished this feat for the verbs they use when they start to speak. This observation fits with the consensus reported in Morgan and Demuth (1996), that children have word-level segmentation more or less intact by the time they begin to produce structured utterances. To achieve this they have to "at minimum be able to attend to, discriminate, represent, and integrate metrical, phonotactic and distributional properties of input speech, all under the guidance of certain preprogrammed constraints" on what can be a word. (Morgan and Demuth 1996:10). The Tzeltal data suggests that this conclusion applies to the identification of roots as well as words, and in addition there is another factor playing a potentially significant role in the Tzeltal case. The discourse convention of repeating an interlocutor's informationally salient word or words as the response to his utterance provides Tzeltal children with immediate feedback on appropriate verb morphology, analogous to the "variation sets" described by Küntay and Slobin (in press) for Turkish input. It has the effect of making the verb stand out, as a constant Figure against a shifting Ground of affixes. Tzeltal CDS is overall much less accommodating to the child than Turkish seems to be, but an analogous effect is achieved by this stylistic trait of Tzeltal speech in general, not just speech to children. Children show sensitivity to this convention by the time they are 2;0.

References:

Aslin, Richard N., Julide Z. Woodward, Nicholas P. LaMendola, and Thomas G. Bever. et all 1996. Models of Word Segmentation in Fluent Maternal Speech to Infants. In James L. Morgan and Katherine Demuth, eds., *From Signal to Syntax: Bootstrapping from Speech to Grammar in Early Acquisition*, 117-34. Hillsdale, N.J.: Erlbaum.

Brown, Roger 1973. *A First Language: The Early Stages*. Cambridge, MA: Harvard University Press.

Demuth, Katherine. 1996. The Prosodic Structure of Early Words. In James L. Morgan and Katherine Demuth, eds., *From Signal to Syntax: Bootstrapping from Speech to Grammar in Early Acquisition*, 171-84. Hillsdale, N.J.: Erlbaum.

Küntay, A. and Slobin, D.I. Listening to a Turkish Mother: Some Puzzles for Acquisition. To appear in D.I. Slobin, et al, eds. 1996. *Social Interaction, Social Context, and Language: Essays in Honor of Susan Ervin-Tripp*. Hillsdale, N.J.: Erlbaum.

Morgan, James L., and Katherine Demuth. 1996. Signal to Syntax: An Overview. In James L. Morgan and Katherine Demuth, eds., *From Signal to Syntax: Bootstrapping from Speech to Grammar in Early Acquisition*, 1-22. Hillsdale, N.J.: Erlbaum.

Peters, Ann. in press. Language Typology, Prosody, and the Acquisition of Grammatical Morphemes. To appear in D. I. Slobin, ed. *The Crosslinguistic Study of Language Acquisition*, volume 4. Hillsdale, N.J.: Erlbaum.

Pye, Clifton. 1983. Mayan Telegraphese: Intonation Determinants of Inflectional Development in Quiche' Mayan. *Language* 59(3):583-604.

Pye, Clifton. 1995. The Acquisition of K'iche' Mayan. In D. I. Slobin (ed) *The Cross-cultural Study of Language Acquisition*, volume 3, 221-308. Hillsdale, N.J.: Erlbaum.

Functors in Early On-Line Sentence Comprehension

ALLYSON CARTER & LOUANN GERKEN
University of Arizona

1. Introduction

This paper discusses recent work with young children, examining how they begin to break apart the speech stream and whether function morphemes are useful as an aid in parsing. How do children begin to recognize lexical and syntactic categories in the speech stream? One possible starting point is functors, such as articles and auxiliaries. These closed class parts of speech have certain fundamental properties that children may begin to focus on. Many functors exhibit canonical phonological properties. For example, English functors often contain reduced vowels (such as [ə] in the words *the*, *was*, and *a*) and fricative consonants (such as [ð] in *the* and [z] in *was* and *is*). They also appear in particular positions with respect to co-occurring lexical categories (Clark & Clark, 1977; Maratsos, 1982, Maratsos & Chalkley, 1980). For instance, English articles occur only at the left edge of a noun phrase (as in "the big dog"), and auxiliaries occur only at the left edge of a verb phrase (as in "was barking").

However, there has been a debate over the representation of functors in early language. On the one hand, it has been argued that because telegraphic speakers do not produce functors, they are not aware of them (Bowerman, 1973; Brown, 1973). On the other hand, there are proposals that even though young children fail to produce functors, they are sensitive to their presence (Gerken & McIntosh, 1993; Katz, Baker, & McNamara, 1974; Shipley, Smith, & Gleitman, 1969).

Gerken and McIntosh (1993) examined this issue to determine whether young children are sensitive to linguistic contexts in which particular functors occur. They used a picture selection task with two-year-olds, in which they presented children with three types of declarative sentences, as in (1), below. The first sentence contains a grammatical functor, the second contains a functor appearing in an ungrammatical position, and the third contains a nonsense word that is different from the function morphemes in that it contains only stop consonants, which are rare in functors.

(1) a. Find *the* dog for me.

 c. Find *was* dog for me.

 d. Find *gub* dog for me.

In the task, children heard tape-recorded sentences like those in (1) that were produced by the DECtalk text-to-speech system (in order to equate stress and intonation across the sentences). Following each sentence, they were shown a page containing four pictures: a target (e.g., dog) and three unrelated distractors (e.g., shoe, baby, fork). The results clearly showed that the children chose the correct picture when they heard a grammatical sentence with the functor *the* more than when they heard a sentence with either an ungrammatical morpheme (*was*) or a nonsense word (*gub*). This finding suggests that children who do not produce functors nevertheless are aware of functors in comprehension and that they are sensitive to the co-occurrence of specific functors with specific lexical categories.

There are two ways to interpret these initial results. The first interpretation, and the hypothesis we propose in this paper, is that children use functors in on-line comprehension to aid in parsing and word recognition. On this view, children's sentence processing is disrupted by ungrammatical functors, and their ability to derive meaning is impeded. The second interpretation of the grammaticality effect is that two-year-old children are capable of discriminating between grammatical and ungrammatical functors, but these functors are not necessarily used during sentence comprehension. The grammaticality effect occurs because children understand sentences with nonsense and ungrammatical functors while they are listening, but become confused after the fact, due to the sentence's unusual form.

2. Experiment 1

In order to compare these two hypotheses, we used the same technique as Gerken and McIntosh (1993) and modified the picture stimuli to include related distractors. We included pictures representing words that were phonologically related to the target words by a shared first phoneme. For example, a picture of a door might be the phonological distractor when the target word is *dog*. We also included distractor pictures representing words that were semantically related to the targets. For example, a picture of a cat might be the semantic distractor for the target word *dog*. Along with these two types of related distractors, there was an unrelated distractor (e.g. a picture of a ball). The question addressed was whether, when children make errors, they choose randomly among the pictures on the page, or whether incorrect picture choices reveal something about children's sentence representations. In particular, we wanted to see whether, in certain contexts, children choose phonological and/or semantic distractors more frequently than unrelated distractors.

2.1 Methods

Subjects were 15 children (7 males and 8 females) ranging in age from 24 to 26 months, with a mean age of 25 months. MLUs (Mean Length of Utterance, Brown 1973) ranged from 1.11 to 3.12, with a mean of 2.02. The children were presented with 21 sentences, seven containing each type of functor (*the*, *was*, *gub*). Stimuli were tape recorded from a DECtalk text-to-speech synthesizer to control for differences in stress and naturalness. The experimenter set a toy robot next to a portable speaker and asked the child if she wanted to play with the robot. The robot "read" through a children's alphabet picture book, naming all of the pictures in order to familiarize children with the synthetic speech. After this, the child was presented with a new book created for this study, with a blank page covering each picture page. The child heard the robot "say" a sentence, after which the experimenter lifted the blank page and encouraged the child to point at what she thought she had heard. Most children understood the task and responded by pointing to a picture on the page. If the child succeeded in selecting a picture, the experimenter played each subsequent test sentence with the page covered.

2.2 Predictions

The hypothesis that children use function morphemes in on-line sentence comprehension makes three predictions. First, as in the study by Gerken and McIntosh (1993), children should demonstrate more correct picture choices when presented with sentences containing grammatical functors (*the*) than ungrammatical functors (*was*) or nonsense words (*gub*).

The second two predictions of the on-line hypothesis concern children's incorrect picture selections. In the grammatical condition, children should pick both phonological and semantic distractors more than unrelated distractors. This is because children should reach a phonological and semantic representation of the word they hear. When they are unable to retain this word in memory until the picture is revealed, they choose a distracting picture that has some relationship to the target. In the ungrammatical condition, children should pick phonological distractors, but not semantic distractors, more than unrelated distractors. This is because the presence of an ungrammatical functor decreases their ability to reach a full semantic representation of the sentence. In the nonsense condition, it was more difficult to make a prediction, because the nonsense word may act like a novel content word due to its different phonetic properties from function words. Interpreting the nonsense word as a novel content word (with which two-year-olds are being constantly bombarded) would allow children to extract at least a partial meaning of the sentence. Therefore, they should choose both phonological and semantic distractors more than unrelated distractors (as in the grammatical condition).

The hypothesis that functors do not show their effect on-line, but instead after comprehension, predicts that, although children may show a grammaticality effect for correct picture selections, their patten of incorrect picture choices should be the same for each condition. In particular, children should pick both the phonological and semantic distractors more than the unrelated distractors in all three conditions. This is because children reach a phonological and semantic representation of all three sentence types, and when they make errors, they choose distractors related to the target based on these representations. Note that unlike the on-line model, an ungrammatical functor should not have a different effect on sentence comprehension from a grammatical functor or nonsense word.

2.3 Results and Discussion

An Analysis of Variance (ANOVA) performed on children's correct picture selections showed a significant main effect of sentence type: $F(2,28) = 3.99$, $p < .05$, such that grammatical sentences elicited more correct selections (69%) than sentences with either ungrammatical functors (56%) or nonsense words (55%). These results replicated the findings of Gerken and McIntosh (1993).

A two-way ANOVA (Distractor Type X Sentence Type) was performed on incorrect responses in order to determine if children selected the phonological distractor or semantic distractor more frequently than the unrelated distractor (see Figure 1). There was a significant effect of Distractor Type ($F(2,28) = 11.44$, $p < .001$), such that children chose the phonological distractor significantly more than the unrelated distractor in each of the three sentence conditions. These results suggest that when making errors, children do not choose randomly, but instead, choose based on the phonological properties of the target. No significant difference was found between the semantic and unrelated distractors in the grammatical condition, as had been predicted. There was no main effect of Sentence Type and no interaction.

Figure 1.
Percent Incorrect Picture Choices

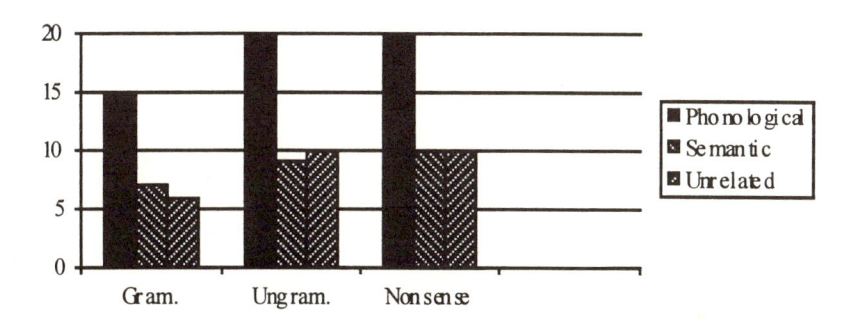

In summary, for correct picture selection, children did better in the grammatical functor condition than in the ungrammatical or nonsense conditions. When making errors, they chose the phonological distractors more than the unrelated distractors. Therefore, children seem to show evidence of phonological processing, in that they choose a picture that is phonologically related to the target. They chose the semantic distractor no more frequently than the unrelated distractor.

The lack of a semantic effect was not predicted by either the on-line or post-comprehension hypotheses. There are several possible explanations for this null result. First, it could be that semantic priming does not occur in children. Second, it could be that the wrong semantic associates were tested for these two-year-olds. The third and most likely explanation is that the phonological distractor may be more salient than the semantic distractor. To tease apart these hypotheses and determine whether or not the related distractor technique taps children's semantic processing, we performed a second experiment.

3. Experiment 2

In this experiment we removed the phonological distractor from the picture sets to determine whether there is a semantic effect when no phonological distractor is present. The predictions of the on-line hypothesis were the same as for the first experiment. In the grammatical functor condition, children should choose the semantic distractor more than the unrelated distractors. In the ungrammatical condition, children should choose the semantic distractor equally frequently as with the unrelated distractors. In the nonsense condition, if children treat the nonsense word like a novel content word, they should choose the semantic distractor more than the unrelated distractors (as in the grammatical condition). The predictions for the post-comprehension hypothesis, on the other hand, were that children should choose the semantically related distractor more than the unrelated distractors in all three conditions.

3.1 Methods

Subjects were 15 children (5 males and 10 females) ranging in age from 24 to 28 months, with a mean age of 25 months. MLUs ranged from 1.00 to 2.77 with a mean of 1.88. The materials and procedures were identical to Experiment 1, with the exception that without the presence of a phonological distractor, the possible responses contained a target (e.g. dog), a semantic distractor (e.g. cat), and two unrelated distractors (e.g. ball and shoe).

3.2 Results and Discussion

A two-way (Distractor Type X Sentence Type) ANOVA performed on children's incorrect picture selections yielded a main effect of Distractor Type: $F(1,14) = 10.12, p < .01$. There was also a significant effect of Sentence Type $F(2,28) = 3.42, p < .05$. An examination of Figure 2 reveals that, as predicted by the on-line hypothesis, children chose semantic distractors more frequently than unrelated distractors in the grammatical and nonsense conditions, but not in the ungrammatical condition. Therefore, it seems that children were less likely to reach a semantic representation in ungrammatical sentences. Note that children actually chose fewer distractors overall in the ungrammatical condition, which was the basis of the main effect of Sentence Type. We interpret this effect to mean that children's lack of a semantic representation for ungrammatical sentences caused them to be less tempted by semantic distractors in this condition than in the grammatical and nonsense conditions.

Figure 2.
Percent Incorrect Picture Choices

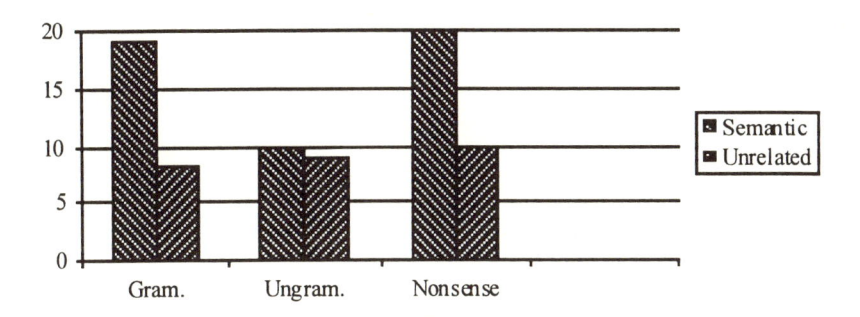

[Bar chart showing percent incorrect picture choices across three conditions (Gram., Ungram., Nonsense) with Semantic and Unrelated bars. Gram.: Semantic ~19, Unrelated ~8. Ungram.: Semantic ~10, Unrelated ~9. Nonsense: Semantic ~20, Unrelated ~10.]

It is interesting to note the results with the nonsense condition. Although the nonsense word elicited more errors than the grammatical functor, it showed the same pattern (semantic > unrelated). This suggests that the presence of an ungrammatical functor, and not just the presence of an uninterpretable word, hinders comprehension.

To summarize the two experiments, a significant phonological effect was found in all three sentence conditions (grammatical, ungrammatical, and nonsense) in Experiment 1. A significant semantic effect was also found in the grammatical and nonsense conditions, but not in the ungrammatical condition (in the absence of the stronger phonological effect) in Experiment 2.

4. Conclusion

These results provide evidence for the on-line hypothesis of children's sentence comprehension. The fact that children in Experiment 2 chose the semantic distractor in the grammatical and nonsense conditions, but not in the ungrammatical condition, suggests that an ungrammatical function morpheme makes it more difficult for them to achieve a semantic representation.

The current study may explain differences between findings of Gerken and McIntosh (1993) and Swingley, Fernald, McRoberts and Pinto (1995). The latter study used a preferential looking task, in which the children were presented on video monitors with two pictures, the target and an unrelated distractor. Sentences contained either a grammatical functor (*the*) or a nonsense word (*gef*).

The researchers found no difference in children's ability to discriminate the grammatical functor from the nonsense word.

The lack of a grammaticality effect in the study by Swingley et al., contrasted with the presence of this effect in research by Gerken and McIntosh and the present studies, may be explained by two differences in the method and materials used. First, the picture selection task used by Gerken and McIntosh and the present studies, which presents four pictures, requires a greater memory capacity than the task used by Swingley et al., which presents two pictures. Furthermore, children in the research by Gerken and McIntosh and in the current studies don't see the pictures until after they have heard the sentences; this is not the case in the task used by Swingely et al.

The second difference concerns a contrast in how the subjects in Experiment 2 reported here responded to sentences with ungrammatical functors versus nonsense words. Recall that children in that experiment appeared to reach a semantic representation of the target in the nonsense word condition, but not in the ungrammatical morpheme condition. The nonsense word condition in the study by Swingley et al. (1995) was more similar to the nonsense word condition than the ungrammatical functor condition in the current studies. Therefore, it is not surprising that the subjects in the Swingley, et.al. study, given the reduced memory demands of the task, were able to reach a semantic representation of the target word even when a nonsense word preceded it.

A final point to note concerns our finding that children's errors in sentence comprehension are not random. Rather, they can be used to reveal aspects of children's word and sentence representations. We hope to use the task to continue to explore how children access and organize their lexicons. For example, one question to ask is whether there is a certain part of a syllable that children use more than another to access words, such as the onset, rime, or first CV? To do this, children could be presented with phonologically distracting pictures that resemble the target by the onset, rime, or other syllable component. One could then look at the nature of children's picture selection mistakes to see if there is a difference in which distractors are chosen or not. We are hopeful that this technique, perhaps coupled with a reaction time component, can give us a better understanding of children's on-line sentence processing.

References

Bowerman, Melissa. 1973. *Early Syntactic Development: A Cross-Linguistic Study with Special Reference to Finnish.* Cambridge, England: Cambridge University Press.

Brown, Roger. 1973. *A First Language.* Cambridge, Mass.: Harvard University Press.

Clark, Herbert and Eve Clark. 1977. *Psychology of Language: An Introduction to Psycholinguistics.* New York: Harcourt Brace Jovanovich.

Gerken, LouAnn and Bonnie McIntosh. 1993. Interplay of Function Morphemes and Prosody in Early Language. *Developmental Psychology* 29:3.448-457.

Katz, Nancy, Erica Baker, and John Macnamara. 1974. What's In a Name? A Study of How Children Learn Common and Proper Names. *Child Development* 45.469-473.

Maratsos, Michael. 1982. The Child's Construction of Grammatical Categories, in E. Wanner and L. Gleitman, eds., *Language Acquisition: The State of the Art.* Cambridge, England: Cambridge University Press. 240-266.

Maratsos, Michael, and Marianne Chalkley. 1980. The Internal Language of Children's Syntax, in K. Nelson, ed., *Children's Language.* New York: Gardner Press. Vol. 2, 102-137.

Shipley, Elizabeth, Carlota Smith and Lila Gleitman. 1969. A Study in the Acquisition of Language: Free Responses to Commands. *Language* 45.322-343.

Swingley, Daniel, Anne Fernald, Gerald McRoberts, and John Pinto. 1995. Prosody, Functors, and Word Recognition in Young Children. *Proceedings of the 20th Annual Boston University Conference on Language Development*, Boston, Mass.

Pragmatic Comprehension: Development of Mandarin-Speaking Children's Strategies for Interpretation of Given and New Information

SHU-HUI EILEEN CHEN
University of Hawaii at Manoa

1. Introduction

Ever since the 1970s, there has been seen one strand of interest among researchers of language acquisition, focusing on the cognitive, functional, and processing dimensions (Ervin-Tripp & Mitchell-Kernan 1977; Slobin 1985; Peters & Boggs 1986; Bates & MacWhinney 1989). From this functionalist perspective, child language development is viewed as a process involving the acquisition of the abilities to map linguistic forms (syntactic, semantic, prosodic and morphological) onto the meanings and functions of sentences (Bates & MacWhinney 1989). One of the most important communicative functions that language serves is to effectively impart whether a particular piece of information is Given, i.e., assumed to be known to the hearer, or New, i.e., assumed to be unknown to the hearer (Clark & Haviland 1974). As their language develops, children are also developing their processing strategies to utilize linguistic forms to interpret such Given and New distinctions.

Natural languages and communication channels utilize several means for encoding information as Given or New. In Mandarin Chinese, word order and stress are two of the commonly used linguistic devices for this pragmatic function. Preverbal position tends to be used to encode Given information, while postverbal position is obligatory for marking New information. NPs denoting Given information (such as a nominal preceded by a demonstrative and a classifier, or a bare nominal) can occur either in preverbal or postverbal position, but NPs denoting New information (such as a nominal preceded by a numeral or a bare nominal) can only occur in postverbal position (Sun & Givón 1985; Hickmann & Liang 1990). In Chinese, local markings of Newness, such as numerals, are optional, but global ones (postverbal position) are obligatory (Hickmann & Liang 1990).

Stress is an available prosodic device that tends to be used to denote New information in Mandarin Chinese. Acoustic studies in Mandarin Chinese show that the stressed element has "heavy prosodic weight", characterized by a raising of pitch on the high tones and a lowering of pitch on the low tones, and/or by a lengthening of the syllable duration within the sentence (Shen 1990; Firbas 1992). According to the Competition model, stress may compete with word order to convey the pragmatic function for encoding information as Given or New (Bates & MacWhinney 1989).

There have been some studies investigating how English-speaking adults and children employ linguistic marking for Given and New in comprehension (Hornby 1973, 1974; Carpenter & Just 1977; MacWhinney & Bates 1978; MacWhinney & Price 1980; Paul 1985). English and Chinese are *quantitatively* different in that, for example, postverbal position is an obligatory means of marking New information in Mandarin Chinese (Hickmann et al. in press), while it is not obligatory in English (Bates & MacWhinney 1989). Hence, the findings that have been reported in studies of English-speaking children can not be generalized to Mandarin-speaking children. The present study attempts to investigate how Mandarin-speaking children and adults use surface cues of word order and competing stress (stress placed on preverbal element) to interpret Given and New information, both in isolated (hereafter IC) and contextualized (hereafter CC) sentences.

2. The study

The present study investigated the following questions: (1) Can Mandarin-speaking children aged 5, 7, 9, 11, and 13 utilize word order in IC and CC? (2) Can stress override word order when they are in competition? (3) Will developmental patterns of strategies vary as a function of context?

Two experiments were conducted to address these questions: Verification/Correction and Picture-choice, modeled after Hornby (1974) and Paul (1985) respectively. In the former, test sentences were presented in isolation, while in the latter, test sentences were presented in a contextualized condition. In both conditions, stress was manipulated on the target sentence in two ways: normal stress on the postverbal element versus emphatic stress on the preverbal element.

In IC, subjects first heard a yes-no question e.g., *Wugui zhui mao ma?*

'Does the turtle chase the cat?' and were then presented a pair of pictures depicting, e.g., the turtle chasing the rabbit and the monkey chasing the cat, each of which contradicted either the Given or the New information in the stimulus question. They were told in advance that although there was something wrong with the pictures, they should choose one, and then correctly describe the selected picture. In CC, each of a pair of pictures was first labeled with a title and an accurate contextualizing sentence e.g., *Zai taiyang de gushi li, shouxian yi-zhi wugui zhui yi-zhi tuzi.* 'In the sun story, first a turtle chases a rabbit.' and *Zai yueliang de gushi li, shouxian yi-zhi houzi zhui yi-zhi mao.* 'In the moon story, a monkey chases a cat.' Subjects were then presented a stimulus sentence e.g., *Ranhou, houzi zhui tuzi.* 'Then, (the) monkey chases (the) rabbit.' Their task was to choose that one of the two pictures that the stimulus went with. Subjects' choice and description of pictures in IC, and choice of context sentence in CC were considered to be measures of their comprehension of the Given and New distinctions implied in a particular stimulus. It was hypothesized that: (1) **in IC, subjects would assume Given information to be true, and would focus their attention on New information; (2) in CC, subjects would choose the picture that contained the Given information in the stimulus sentence.**

Two predictions were tested in the present study:
1. Younger children will rely more on stress than older children and adults for interpreting Given and New information.
2. The use of any linguistic cue to interpret Given and New information will vary as a function of context.

The study reported on here is one part of a larger study in which syntactic structures such as passives, clefts, and pseudoclefts were also manipulated (cf. Chen 1996).

2.1 Experiment I: Verification/Correction experiment

Subjects

Subjects participating in the present study were 15 5-year-olds, 15 7-year-olds, 15 9-year-olds, 15 11-year-olds, 15 13-year-olds and 15 adults, with eight males and seven females in each age group. Children were selected from Yü-Te Kindergarten, An-Ting Primary School, Hsilo and Tung-Nan Junior Middle School in Taiwan. The adult subjects were undergraduates from the Yünlin Institute of Technology in Taiwan.

Materials

All sentences reported on here were in the active voice. Stress was manipulated in two ways: normal stress on the postverbal element associated with New information, and emphatic stress on the element associated with Given information. Each stimulus sentence was in interrogative, presented before the corresponding pair of pictures was shown, either of which contradicted either the Given or New information in the stimulus question. The sentences were constructed around two commonly-used semantic types: semantically-reversible (both agent and object are animate) and semantically-irreversible (only agent is animate). The nouns (bare nominals) and verbs used are:

NOUNS

wugui 'turtle'	tuzi 'rabbit'	houzi 'monkey'	mao 'cat'
yelang 'wolf'	xiaoya 'duckling'	laoying 'hawk'	chabei 'cup'
nanhai 'boy'	xiaoniao 'bird'	nühai 'girl'	chezi 'car'
hudie ' 'butterfly'	gongji 'cock'	yizi 'chair'	hezi 'box'
xiaoji 'chicken'	emama 'goose'	xiaoxia 'shrimp'	nanren 'man'
chuanghu 'window'	xiaogou 'dog'	haibau 'seal'	huapin 'vase'
xingxing 'gorilla'	nüren 'woman'	daxiang 'elephant'	
bingxiang 'fridge'	ügang 'fish bowl'		

VERBS

| zhui 'chase' | zhuazhu 'catch' | yaozhu 'bite' | dapo 'break' |
| fangzou 'release' | caihuai 'trample' | nongdau 'topple' | xiuli 'fix' |

There were a total of 16 nonveridical randomly-arranged test sentences presented with no context given. Eight corresponding pairs of pictures were used for verification.

Procedure

Subjects were visited at predetermined times in the library of their school. Interpretation tests for Given and New information were conducted in a single session. As part of a larger study, this part took about 3 minutes per subject. Subjects were asked to verify each stimulus question against each pair of pictures.

Coding and analysis

Subjects' scores consisted of the number of times that the element conveying New information in each nonveridical sentence was corrected. In Mandarin Chinese, the postverbal element in an active sentence under normal stress, and the emphatically-stressed part of the sentence are considered to encode New information. Subjects scored a point when the New information were corrected. Table 1 lists scoring rules for the Verification/Correction Task.

Table 1. Scoring rules for the Verification/Correction task

condition		subjects' response	score
stress type	stress placement		
normal	New	patient corrected	1
emphatic	Given	agent corrected	1

Answers which involved correction to the Given information or unanswered questions were scored as zero. After all responses were checked as correct or incorrect, the number of correct choices was recorded.

2.2 Experiment II: Picture-choice experiment

Subjects

The subjects consisted of the same groups of subjects who participated in the previous experiment. They were tested a few weeks after they finished the decontextualized task.

Materials

The same eight pairs of pictures used in IC were used again, each labeled with a different title. The stimulus sentences, however, were different although the construction method was similar. Let's call each pair of pictures the X picture and the Y picture. In the contextualized picture-pointing task, the stimulus sentence contained an agent depicted in the Y picture and a patient depicted in the X picture (example below). There were a total of 16 randomly-arranged target active sentences presented with such context sentences, with 8 each in semantically-reversible and semantically-irreversible conditions. Stress was manipulated in two ways: normal stress on the element associated with New information vs. emphatic stress on the element associated with Given information. Each audio-recorded stimulus sentence was preceded by the two context sentences describing each picture (examples shown above in section 2). Their task was to choose that one of the two pictures that the stimulus went with. Verbs for both context sentences matched; agents and objects differed. The stimulus sentence always replaced either the agent or the object of the context sentence to be chosen with that of the context sentence not to be chosen.

Procedure

Subjects were visited in the library of their school. This part of the Given and New interpretation test in the contextualized condition lasted for about 10 minutes.

On each trial, the two context pictures were presented simultaneously side by side. Subjects were told that each context sentence was the first part of a different story. They were told to repeat each context sentence after they heard it in order to aid memory. The experimenter pointed to each context picture while its sentence was being played. Subjects were then instructed to choose the context story that went with the stimulus sentence.

Coding and analysis

The preverbal element in the sentence with normal stress and the unstressed part in the sentence employing emphatic stress are considered to encode the Given information. Subjects' scores consisted of the number of times that the context sentence containing the Given information of the stimulus was chosen. Answers which involved the choice of the context sentence containing the New information or unanswered questions were scored as zero. Table 2 lists the set of scoring rules for the Picture-choice Experiment.

Table 2. Scoring rules for the Picture-choice task

condition		subjects' response	score
stress type	stress placement		
normal	New	choice of the context sentence containing the agent	1
emphatic	Given	choice of the context sentence containing the patient	1

3. Results and discussion

3.1 Results and discussion of Verification/Correction experiment

ANOVAs were run to evaluate the effects of age, stress and interactions of the two. Probabilities up to 0.05 were considered to be significant. The main effect of age did not reach significance in IC, while the main effect of stress did ($F (1,84) = 16.923, p \leq 0.0001$). The interaction of age and stress also reached significance ($F = (5, 84) = 6.237, p \leq 0.0001$).

Word order effect

When New information receives normal stress, word order is probably the only surface cue that subjects can rely on to distinguish Given from New information in active NVN sentences. In Mandarin Chinese, preverbal position tends to be used to encode Given information, while postverbal placement is obligatory for New information. Figure 1 shows the scores in IC and CC when New information receives normal stress. It can be seen that in IC, the percentage of children's correct responses was well below 50%, suggesting that Mandarin-speaking children were unable to use postverbal position effectively to identify Given and New information in IC.

Two explanations for children's poor use of word order are offered. First, the poor performance might be related to their frequent exposure to narratives. Although in Mandarin Chinese, postverbal position is generally obligatory for marking New information, preverbal position can be used to introduce New referents at the beginning of a narrative. According to the Competition model, any cue that consistently signals a particular meaning or function is <u>reliable</u>. If children are very frequently exposed to narratives, the weight of the postverbal cue for indicating New information would be relatively weaker, particularly in IC. However, a text analysis of materials children are often exposed will be needed to confirm the speculation. Secondly, animacy is a potential factor that influences children's processing strategies. While children's performance in semantically-reversible constructions (both agent and patient are animate) was below average, their performance in semantically-irreversible constructions (animate agent and inanimate inanimate patient) was even worse because animate subjects were the attentional focus and got corrected. Adults, however, relied more on word order than on animacy in semantically-irreversible constructions. This suggests the existence of a developmental shift from reliance on animacy to reliance on word order after age 13.

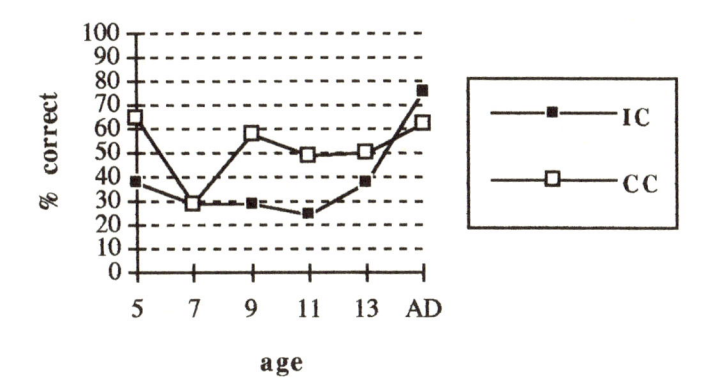

Figure 1: Use of word order (normal stress on New)

Competition between stress and word order

When stress competes with word order, i.e., when emphatic stress was placed on Given, children relied more on stress than word order, but not adults (see Figure 3 where n=normal stress on New, eg=emphatic stress on Given). The difference in performance between the condition when normal stress was placed on New and when emphatic stress was placed on Given was significant for each age group ($p < 0.05$).

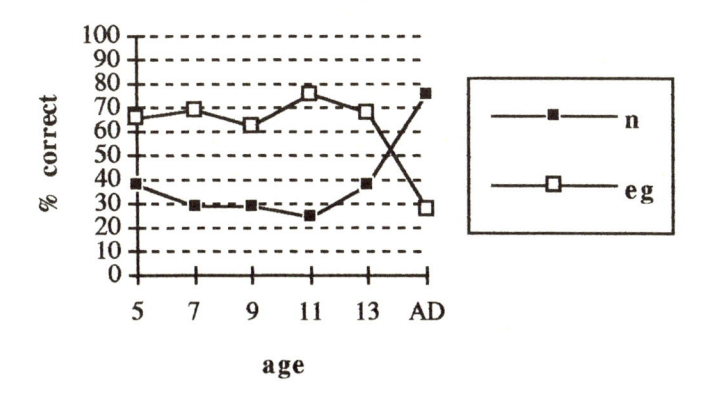

Figure 3: Competition between stress and word order (Isolated)

3.2 Results and discussion of Picture-choice experiment

AVOVAs were run on the data to evaluate the main effects of age, stress, and interactional factors. (no significant sex difference was found, $p > 0.05$). Probabilities up to 0.05 were considered significant. The main effects of age and stress did not reach significance in CC, while the interaction of age and stress did ($F = (5, 84) = 22.246, p \leq 0.0439$).

Word order effect

Children can use word order cues more effectively in CC than in IC. A U-shaped developmental curve, a pattern of acquisition in which performance initially appears adult-like, then deteriorates, and then improves again, is found between 5- and 9-year-olds. The difference between 5- and 7-year-olds ($F (1,28) = 8.775, p \leq 0.0062$) and between 7- and 9-year-olds is significant ($F (1,28) = 6.551, p \leq 0.0162$). This may be due to overgeneralization of processing strategies from clefts to actives. (In cleft sentences, the early occurring clefted element identifies New information.) At age 7, children had better control of cleft structure; this can be seen from their production data, in that they often used cleft sentences to describe their chosen pictures in sentence-picture verification tasks, even when the stimulus sentence was active. We speculate that, because acquisition of clefted structure was more advanced, 7-year-olds overgeneralized this strategy to active sentences by identifying the first element instead of the second as New.

Competition between stress and word order

When stress competes with word order, i.e., when emphatic stress was placed on Given, in CC, only 7-, 11-, and 13-year- seem to rely more on stress to interpret New information, while 5-, and 9-year-olds, and adults seem to rely more on word order (see Figure 4). Univariate ANOVA and contrast tests show that the overriding effect of stress was not significant, nor was the overriding effect of word order.

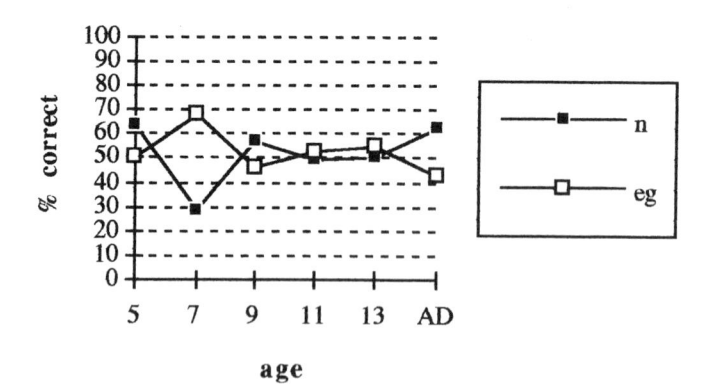

Figure 4: Competition between stress and word order (contextualized)

Context as a variable

By comparing the curves in Figures 1 and 5, it can be seen that the development of processing strategies for Given and New interpretation varied as a function of context. When comparing similarities or differences of processing strategies within the same language or crosslinguistically, we should consider context as one potential variable producing variations.

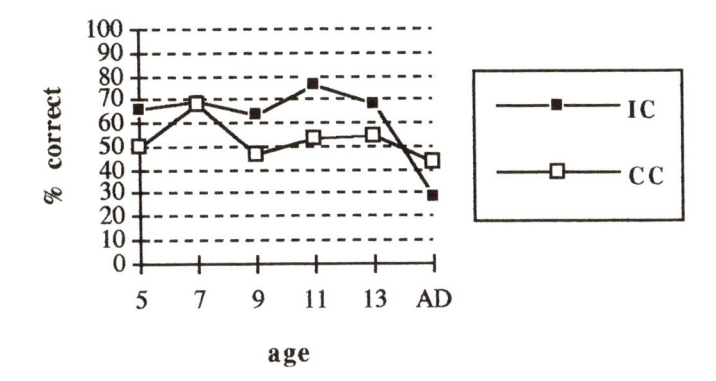

Figure 5: Patterns of interpretation strategies (emphatic stress on Given)

4. Conclusion

The main findings of this study can be summarized as follows:

(1) Mandarin-speaking children develop strategies for interpretation of Given and New information after age 5. In IC, children of all age groups do not demonstrate an ability to effectively utilize postverbal position in actives. A developmental shift is seen from reliance on animacy to reliance on word order after 13. Animacy is a potential factor that may influence children's processing strategies. In CC, 5- and 9-year-olds seem to utilize postverbal position effectively, but not the other age groups of children. A U-shaped developmental curve is found between 5 and 9 years. Seven-year-olds might overgeneralize strategies from clefts to actives.

(2) When emphatic stress is imposed on the preverbal element in IC, children, but not adults, rely significantly more on emphatic stress than on word order to interpret Given and New information. This implies that a developmental shift is made from a stress strategy to a word order strategy after 13. In CC, when emphatic stress in imposed on the preverbal element, children do not repond uniformly. Emphatic stress overrides word order for 7-, 11- and 13-year-olds, but not for other age groups.

(3) There are variations in developmental patterns as a function of context, as shown by the differing developmental curves in IC and CC.When we compare studies from different researchers and/or from different languages to investigate the development of children's processing strategies in sentence interpretation, the variable of context should not be ignored.

(4) Children perform better in marked syntactic structures, particularly passives and pseudoclefts, than actives (see Chen 1996).

5. References

Bates, E. and B. MacWhinney. 1989. Functionalism and the Competition model, in B. MacWhinney and E. Bates, ed., *The Crosslinguistic Study of Sentence Processing*. New York: Cambridge University Press.

Carpenter, P. A. and M. A. Just. 1977. Integrating Process in Comprehension, in D. Laberge and S. J. Samuels, ed., *Basic Processes in Reading: Perception and Comprehension*. Hillsdale, New Jersey: Lawrence Erlbaum Associates, Publishers.

Clark, H. H. and S. E. Haviland. 1977. Comprehension and the Given/New Contract, in R. O. Freedle, ed., *Discourse Production and Comprehension*. Norwood, N.J.: Ablex Publishing.

Ervin-Tripp, S. and C. Mitchell-Kernan. 1977. *Child Discourse*. New York: Academic Press.

Firbas, J. 1992. *Functional Sentence Perspective in Written and Spoken Communication*. Cambridge: University Press.

Hickmann, M. and J. Liang. 1990. Clause-structure Variation in Chinese Narrative Discourse: A Developmental Analysis. *Linguistics* 28:1167-1200.

Hornby, P. A. 1973. Intonation and Syntactic Structure in the Development of Presupposition. Paper presented at the Biennial Meeting of Society for Research in Child Development, Philadelphia.

Hornby, P. A. 1974. Surface Structure and Presupposition. *Journal of Verbal Learning and Verbal Behavior* 13.538-550.

MacWhinney, B. and E. Bates. 1978. Sentence Devices for Conveying Givenness and Newness: A Cross-cultural Developmental Study. *Journal of Verbal Learning and Verbal Behavior* 17.539-558.

Paul, R. 1985. The Emergence of Pragmatic Comprehension: A Study of Children's Understanding of Sentence-structure Cues to Given/New Information. *Journal of Child Language* 12.161-179.

Peters, A. M. and S. T. Boggs. 1986. Interaction Routines as Cultural Influences upon Language Acquisition, in B. B. Schieffelin and E. Ochs, ed., *Language Socialization across Cultures*. Cambridge, MA: Cambridge University Press.

Shen, X.-N. 1990. *The Prosody of Mandarin Chinese*. Berkeley and Los Angeles: University of California Press.

Slobin, D. I. 1985. Crosslinguistic Evidence for the Language-making Capacity, in Dan I. Slobin, ed., *The Crosslinguistic Study of Language Acquisition, Vol. II: Theoretical Issues*. Hillsdale, New Jersey: Lawrence Erlbaum Associates, Publishers.

Sun, C.-F. and T. Givón. 1985. On the so-called Word Order in Mandarin Chinese: A Quantified Text Study and its Implications. *Language* 61.2.329-351.

Reference and Representation: What Polynomy Tells Us About Children's Conceptual Studies

GEDEON DEÁK & MICHAEL MARATSOS*

Vanderbilt University & University of Minnesota

Introduction. It is no understatement that the great majority of research in cognitive science is concerned with representation: investigating which information from the environment is induced and represented, the form and format in which it is represented, and the processes by which representations are structured and coordinated. In principle, one of the simplest ways to access representation is through reference. Referential acts are overt behaviors that specify correspondences between the world and abstract mental entities, or concepts, in the form of intentional communication.

Cognitive psychologists have, with some exceptions (see Brown, 1958; Ogden & Richards, 1923; Olson, 1970; and studies of overextension, e.g., Clark, 1973; Fremgen & Fay, 1980; Rescorla, 1980), seldom specified *how* reference supports inferences about representation, in spite of the fact that much research assumes reference-representation mapping (e.g., studies in which children name items, or pick out examples of [X]). Specifying this relationship is crucial, however, because overt verbal reports (e.g., reference)

---

* This work was supported by a University of Minnesota graduate school grant. Thanks to Loulee Yen for helpful comments. Address correspondences to G. Deák at the Dept. of Psychology and Human Development, Box 512 GPC, Vanderbilt University, Nashville, TN 37203, or deakgo@ctrvax.vanderbilt.edu.

are inaccurate reflections of underlying cognitive organization (e.g., Nisbett & Wilson, 1977; Reber, 1993). We elaborate on the shortcomings of reference as a window on representation, then suggest several procedures that can avoid these shortcomings, illustrated by ongoing research.

<u>Limitations of using reference to access representation</u>. Many referential acts provide only minimal information about underlying representations. The most extreme examples are primitive referential acts such as pointing. Though such acts may be referential, they do not necessarily rest on conceptual representations. For example, one can imagine a scenario in which an infant has learned to point toward an event that exceeds an "interestingness" threshold, if caretaker's attention is elsewhere. This allows reference without an articulated representation (although no doubt *something* is represented, if only the contingencies of the interactions between distal events and infant's and adult's attentive states).

Similarly, we assume that joint attention (e.g., Butterworth & Jarrett, 1991; Tomasello & Farrar, 1986) results in shared representation of an entity or event. Butterworth (see Butterworth, 1991, for review) has shown that during the second year babies more accurately focus on the target attended to by an adult. But what *is the* target? It is virtually impossible to verify that two people are attending to the same thing, even following an explicit deictic gesture (pointing). For example, a parent may look at the target's internal contours while the child looks at external contours. With regard to children's referential acts, this raises a troublesome issue: can we ever infer with certainty the object of a child's reference? This is of course a version of Quine's (1960) problem of induction, which points out the inherent ambiguities of reference.

Another version of the Quinean dilemma is ethnographers' practice of translating foreign languages by eliciting the names of various objects from an informant. As Frake (1963) notes, in this method foreign terms are mapped onto the anthropologist's culture-bound ontological boundaries and distinctions.

Yet another example is standardized instruments such as the Peabody Picture Vocabulary Test (Dunn & Dunn, 1981), which presents subjects with plates of four line drawings. Subjects are told a word and asked to point to the corresponding picture. A correct choice is taken to reflect understanding of meaning--a discrete, well-formed item in the child's lexicon. In fact, the child's representation of the meaning of "umbrella," for example, need suffice only to distinguish a drawing of an umbrella from that of, say, a stroller, a magazine, and a fork. This requires a fairly minimal semantic entry. A similar problem occurs in word learning studies. For example, in "fast mapping" children are purported to learn a new word after minimal exposure. Using semantic contrast (e.g., "Bring me the chartreuse one...not the blue one, the chartreuse one.") children occasionally learn something about the new word (Carey & Bartlett, 1978; Heibeck &

Markman, 1987). However, children may not learn anything more precise than that chartreuse is a color, which hardly constitutes an unqualified understanding of "chartreuse."

All these examples point to a basic problem: referential acts sometimes do not reflect mental representations, and even when they do, such acts can be impoverished, ambiguous indices of representations.

The matter is in the method: Referential measures of representation. This is a serious problems, but it does not eliminate reference as a tool for assessing representation. For one thing, all methods used to study conceptual representations (e.g., priming and reaction time, similarity judgments, typicality ratings) are inferential. The ambiguities of reaction time data, for example, are no less serious. Second, as Malt (1991) points out, there are some advantages to studying people's extensions (as opposed to intensions): in such studies the words are not chosen by the experimenter, and subjects are not required to access (or invent) knowledge about word meanings (e.g., definitions, feature lists).

In research on young children's thought and language, which has not adopted many adult measures, referential acts may be our primary means for assessing conceptual representations. Concerns over the accuracy of verbal reports of underlying cognitive content and process (Nisbett and Wilson, 1977) are less serious with children who, relative to adults, are generally less concerned with producing consistent, logical reports. They are also less serious in spontaneous conversation, wherein many unplanned behaviors (e.g., gestures, pauses, hedges, etc.) seem to reflect underlying cognitive activity. In the pragmatic context of an ongoing conversation, reference may reveal speakers' knowledge about the objects of conversation, and their representations of the terms used to refer to those objects. This is critical in the study of child language, because young children can seldom sensibly justify their verbal responses. If researchers are interested in how young children represent relationships among words, and the features or aspects denoted by particular words (see Clark, in review), an alternative to verbal elaboration is desirable.

We contend that reference is not *inherently* problematic. It may in fact be the best way to elicit information about semantic representations from preschoolers. The problems noted above are attributable to specific methodological limitations, and in some cases can be avoided by carefully-designed procedures. The specific procedures we will discuss rely on a general pragmatic principle: Discourse focuses on a given aspect of the topic of discussion (e.g., an object) until a *frame shift* (i.e., switching to discus a different aspect) is indicated. In some cases this is done by verbal constructions such as "a kind of." In other cases it is done by introducing new information (e.g., by demonstration).

The following section describes research that uses this principle to elicit names from preschoolers, in a sequence that reflects underlying representations. First, semantic contrast (Au & Markman, 1987) was used to establish a level of inclusion (e.g., superordinate) of a name. Second, new information was introduced by demonstrating a previously-unnoticed aspect of an object (e.g., function). In addition, we describe a third technique which, if carefully designed, can reveal additional information about underlying representations. This is the established method of having subjects choose from a set of systematically-varied exemplars to test the extension of a word. These procedures are illustrated below.

Polynomy in preschoolers. The theoretical questions motivating this research have implications for both reference and representation. First, representation: A striking and poorly-understood feature of human cognition is the ability to hold multifaceted representations of an entity. With regard to categorization abilities, we can represent an entity as belonging to a large number of categories, each defined by different criteria, and each with different contrast classes. So, for example, a particular dog is a member of categories like Spaniel, dog, canine, carnivore, mammal, animal, living thing, pet, companion and beast; as well as "furry things." The ability to refer to some hypothetical entity, "Fido," by various category labels is extremely useful. For example I may refer to Fido as a "beast" after he chews my shoe; on another occasion (e.g., a discussion of different breeds) I may call him a Spaniel (see Clark, in review).

In natural language this representational flexibility is reflected in *polynomy*, the capacity to refer to an entity by several words. Polynomy facilitates communication through selection of a word that names a specific category of interest, out of several alternatives. So just as multiple, flexible representation is a crucial cognitive ability, polynomy is a crucial linguistic ability. We further assume that the cognitive (representational) ability is a prerequisite for the linguistic ability (i.e., polynomy).

Given all this, it is striking that for decades there have arisen proposals that young children are systematically limited in their ability to construct or maintain multifaceted representations, and limited in their ability to apply or accept multiple words for a single entity. Two such proposals are relevant here. The first echoes Piaget's assertion that preschoolers have difficulty holding in mind more than one variable or aspect of a situation. This is Flavell's *dual encoding* hypothesis (Flavell, Green, & Flavell, 1986): preschoolers, and particularly 3-year-olds, have trouble simultaneously representing two aspects of an object, as seen in the appearance-reality task. For example, they frequently respond that a sponge which looks like a rock both *looks like* and *is* a rock, or that it both *is* and *looks like* a sponge. One interpretation is that preschoolers have trouble coordinating the various categories corresponding to different aspects of the object. And this is reflected in a failure of polynomy, because children apply the same name to both aspects of the object.

The second idea is Markman's *Mutual Exclusivity* hypothesis. Mutual exclusivity (ME) is a proposed bias in preschoolers' construal of novel word meanings. It is designed to deal with Quine's indeterminacy problem, the fact that logically, an unknown word has an infinite number of possible meanings. The ME hypothesis stipulates that children tend to assume that one object only has one name, until they receive clear evidence (of unspecified nature) to the contrary (see Markman & Wachtel, 1988:122-125; Merriman & Bowman, 1989:2-3). This clearly implies that polynomy is laboriously achieved by preschoolers from 3 to 4 years.

Both Markman and Flavell have speculated that ME and dual encoding difficulties are related. Markman (1992) has suggested that ME stems from general difficulty in maintaining multiple aspects, or category memberships, of an entity. Our question, then, was whether preschoolers understand that an entity simultaneously belongs to several categories, as reflected by labeling. In other words, are preschoolers spontaneously polynomous?

An empirical illustration: Evidence of early articulated conceptual networks. The method and results summarized below are reported in detail in Deák and Maratsos (in review). Sixteen 3-year-olds and 16 4-year-olds participated in the first experiment, and 22 3- to 5-year-olds participated in the second experiment. The two experiments differed in subject recruitment, experimenters, setting, and other factors.

In both experiments, children completed several tasks. In the *labeling task*, which is the focus of our discussion, children were shown eight "representational" objects in which appearance and function were dissociated (e.g., a dinosaur-shaped crayon; a car-shaped book). Children named each object; the experimenter then elicited additional names via two procedures (see above): (1) semantic contrast (to establish frame) and (2) demonstration (to introduce new information). We illustrate these procedures with a typical example.

If a child called the dinosaur crayon "dinosaur," the experimenter asked, "What kind of thing is a dinosaur--a plant?" Typically children objected to this by producing a correct contrasting term: "No, it's an animal!" In semantic contrast, then, the "foil" (i.e., plant) implies a frame of a particular *level of inclusion* (e.g., superordinate level). The child's response allows us to infer that the child views plants and animals as contrast classes, with the object an exemplar of the latter (though strictly speaking, we cannot be sure that the child views animal as a superordinate class of dinosaur).

The experimenter also demonstrated writing with the crayon, upon which children often remarked, "It's a crayon!" Demonstrating the function provides new information about the object: typically children first name the appearance aspect of the object; subsequent demonstration elicits comment on the functional aspect.

There are several noteworthy features of this procedure. First, after eliciting labels, the experimenter asks the child to verify every pairwise combination of words produced, for example, "Is this a crayon and a dinosaur?" "Is this a dinosaur and an animal?" and "Is this an animal and a crayon?" An equal number of foil pair questions (e.g., "Is this a dinosaur and a pencil?") were interspersed to test for response bias. Pair questions were intended to verify that the subject believed both words applied (because simply asserting that dinosaurs are a kind of animal is not equivalent to asserting that *this* object is an animal). Also, pair questions provide a stricter test of children's willingness to co-extend multiple words. Second, because the objects were unfamiliar, many of the pairs of labels would never previously have been coextended by children--for example, "crayon" and "dinosaur," or "car" and "book." This tests the assertion (Markman & Wachtel, 1988) that children need evidence to override the ME bias. Third, and most importantly for current purposes, by eliciting several labels through specific semantic or demonstration contexts, we can establish something about the conceptual relationships between items. For example, the production of hierarchically-related pairs (e.g., "dinosaur" and "animal") as well as orthogonal pairs (e.g., "dinosaur" and "crayon"), suggests that children can represent both kinds of relationships (inclusion and overlap). It also indicates that children suspend ME not only for hierarchical words (see Waxman & Hatch, 1992), but also for non-synonymous basic level words.

The second task is briefly mentioned to provide converging evidence for polynomy. It was a *story task* in which subjects were told several vignettes about characters (e.g., Ann), including information on gender, daily routine (including occupation), and family role (e.g., parenthood). Children were then asked, for example, "Is Ann a woman?" "Is Ann a person?" "Is Ann a doctor?" and "Is Ann a mother?" Note that the first two words are hierarchical, whereas the last two (roles) are orthogonal. Children were also asked a number of foil words (e.g., "brother," "nurse"). Finally, children were asked about all possible pairs of words, and an equivalent number of foil pairs. The main differences between tasks are the use of objects versus people, and production versus acceptance of words.

In both Experiments children produced a mean of 2.4 words per object (labeling task; see Figure 1). 90% and 95% children (Experiments 1 and 2, respectively) produced two or more words for six or more (of eight) objects.

Figure 1

Experiment	Mean words/object	SD	Range
1	2.4	0.4	1.5 - 3.2
2	2.4	0.3	2.0 - 3.0

Children in both Experiments accepted most hierarchical and orthogonal word pairs (see Figure 2, percentages of pairs accepted). In contrast, children rejected most foil pairs.

Figure 2

Experiment	Orthogonal	Hierarchical	Foil
1	90	93	3
2	90	92	28

In the story task, children accepted a mean of 2.7 out of three (90%) words per character in Experiment 1, and a mean of 3.5 out of four (87%) words per character in Experiment 2. Children uniformly rejected foil words. The mean percentage of word pairs accepted is shown in Figure 3.

Figure 3

Experiment	Orthogonal	Hierarchical	Foil
1	50	80	4
2	72	73	24

It is clear that preschoolers readily applied several words to an object or story character, and they believed that these words *simultaneously* applied. These findings have implications for children's word learning and naming biases, as detailed in Deák and Maratsos (in review). Briefly, they suggest that Mutual Exclusivity is not a general reluctance to apply multiple words to an entity. In the labeling task, preschoolers applied words that they would not previously have learned to coextend (e.g., "crayon" and "dinosaur"). Thus, preschoolers seem to apply an ME bias only in word learning situations. The findings also have implications for children's representational abilities (see below).

Children's rejection of foil labels, and production of appropriate labels, indicates selective application of words to objects. This suggests that children's productions reflect their representations. This is due to procedures for establishing frame (via semantic contrast), and introducing new information (via demonstration). Both rely on the pragmatic tendency for speakers to comment when introducing new topics or shifting topic. For example, the experimenter prefaced demonstrations of object function (new information) by saying, "Let me show you something." Subsequently, many children spontaneously exclaimed, "It's a crayon!" The introduction of new information elicited comment; the context likely clarifies which aspect of the demonstration was commented on.

Semantic contrast also relies on pragmatics because speakers typically stay in a "frame" through an exchange, or alert the listener to a change. For example, when the experimenter asks "What kind of thing is a dinosaur? Is it a plant?", two cues establish local frame: the phrase "kind of," which implies a superordinate relationship, and the term "plant," which contrasts with "animal." Children are sensitive to these cues (see Au & Markman, 1987; Deák & Bauer, 1995; but see Callanan, 1989), and typically respond by rejecting the foil term and producing an appropriate term at the same level of inclusion. Semantic contrast also might be used to make more precise inferences about the child's representation of a word. For example, in the story task in Experiment 2 we chose foil terms that more precisely contrasted with appropriate terms (e.g., if a character was a police officer, we asked whether he was a pilot). By selecting foils similar to the appropriate terms, and by incorporating multiple foils, we can make more precise inferences about the child's word meaning.

Obviously these procedures are not effective in every situation (for example, they might not shed light on the representational underpinnings of children's pointing gestures), but naming tasks can be tailored to take advantage of one or both (see Waxman & Hatch, 1992, for an example of the use of semantic contrast). Nor are these procedures exhaustive; there are other methods that allow well-grounded inferences about the underlying representation of a word. Finally, we stress that the inferential nature of these interpretations will require additional converging evidence.

Illustration of an additional procedure. A third procedure is testing the extension of a word by having children judge whether various items are valid exemplars. This method has been used in studies of children's overextensions (e.g., Fremgen & Fay, 1980; Thompson & Chapman, 1977), and more recently in studies of novel noun generalization (e.g., Jones, Smith, & Landau, 1991; Landau, Smith, & Jones, 1987; Smith, Jones, & Landau, 1992). The difficulty of the procedure is in the selection of relevant contrast items to precisely determine the word's extension.

An example of the effective use of this method is a study in progress by Loulee Yen (Vanderbilt University), on teaching preschoolers new words for the representational objects used in the experiments reported above. Half of the children learn new subordinate terms for the representational aspects of several object (e.g., *biped* for upright-walking dinosaurs); the other half learn new subordinate terms for functional aspects (e.g., *spuffet* for hand-puppet). Moreover, half of the children in each group are given defining information for the novel words; the others are taught by ostension. Children then complete the labeling task, as above, to ascertain whether learning a new word affects children's production of known words (i.e., correction effect; see Merriman & Bowman, 1989). The relevant procedure is a posttest of the child's representation of the novel word. Children are shown objects with the same or similar functions and/or representations as the first exemplar, to test the accuracy of induced meanings of the novel words. For example, children taught "biped" are shown the original exemplar, toy dinosaurs varying in appearance and posture (biped versus quadruped), a quadruped crayon dinosaur, crayons, and non-dinosaur animals. By asking children to find the bipeds, we can ascertain whether they have induced all, some, or none of the defining features of the new word, and whether those features are restricted to the representational aspects of the objects. The ostensive teaching condition serves as a control, to determine what is learned from the definitions. Initial pilot data suggest that some children given defining information nevertheless choose non-defining items (i.e., they overgeneralize), however, they seem to choose the defining items first, suggesting that order of choices reflects prototypicality or graded membership (see Armstrong, Gleitman, & Gleitman, 1983, for evidence from adults). This is further supported by the observation that at least a few children can recall the definitions, suggesting that item choice and verbal memory are not well-coordinated (see Zelazo & Reznick, 1991).

This study will provide information about children's acquisition of subordinate terms, lexical gap filling, correction and rejection effects, and other phenomena. For current purposes several design factors should be noted. First, sufficient test cases are included to cover many possible meanings of the learned word. Second, we record not only *which* objects are chosen but also the *order* of choice, because some children overgeneralize. Third, to minimize pragmatic causes of overgeneralization, children are given a choice whether or not to pick additional objects: "Is there another [X] here, or was that the [only/last] one?" These features maximize our chances of eliciting meaningful information about children's representations.

Conclusion. We do not claim to have presented a comprehensive list of techniques for grounding inferences about representations based on children's referential acts. Nor do we claim that all of these methods are novel (extension testing has been widely used, though perhaps not as effectively as is desirable). We hope, though, that there is merit in initiating an explicit discussion of methodology for assessing representations through referential acts (analogous to discussion in the cognitive literature of interpreting priming and reaction time data, e.g., McNamara, 1992).

In the illustrative research described, fairly simple procedures reveal detailed information about children's representations of multiple categories subsuming a single entity, and the relations among those categories. Children's responses to probe questions using semantic contrast indicate an awareness of hierarchically-related classes, and their responses to demonstrations of function indicate an awareness of orthogonal functional aspects of objects. These findings suggest that children as young as three years represent an entity as belonging not to a single category, nor to merely one or two hierarchically-related categories. Instead, children can construct and maintain an articulated representation of an entity, consisting of as many categories as there are distinct and meaningful aspects. These aspects may encompass both distinct domains (appearance and function), and different levels of inclusion. Thus, the evidence from referential acts indicates that preschoolers' conceptual networks are more articulated and sophisticated than has long been believed.

References

Armstrong, S.L., Gleitman, L., & Gleitman, H. (1983). What some concepts might not be. *Cognition*, 13, 263-308.

Au, T.K. & Markman, E.M. (1987). Acquiring word meanings via linguistic contrast. *Cognitive Development*, 2, 217-236.

Brown, R. (1958). *Words and things.* Glencoe, IL: Free Press.

Butterworth, G.E. (1991). The ontogeny and phylogeny of joint visual attention. In A. Whiten (Ed.), *Natural theories of mind.* Oxford, England: Blackwell.

Butterworth, G. & Jarrett, N. (1991). What minds have in common is space: Spatial mechanisms serving joint visual attention in infancy. *British Journal of Developmental Psychology*, 9, 55-72.

Callanan, M.A. (1989). Development of object categories and inclusion relations: Preschoolers' hypotheses about word meanings. *Developmental Psychology*, 25, 207-216.

Carey, S. & Bartlett, E. (1978). Acquiring a single new word. *Papers and Reports on Child Language Development* (Department of Linguistics, Stanford University), 15, 17-29.

Clark, E. (1973). What's in a word? On the child's acquisition of semantics in his first language. In T. Moore (Ed.), *Cognitive development and the acquisition of language.* New York: Academic Press.

Clark, E.V. (in review). *Speakers, perspectives, and words in acquisition.*

Deák, G. (1995). *The development of flexibility in children's inductive inferences about novel objects.* Doctoral Dissertation, University of Minnesota (available DAI).

Deák, G. & Bauer, P.J. (1995). The effects of task comprehension on preschoolers' and adults' categorization choices. *Journal of Experimental Child Psychology*, 60, 393-427.

Deák, G. & Maratsos, M. (in review). *Preschoolers produce multiple words for unfamiliar objects: Lexical cross-categorization and early dual-encoding ability.*

Dunn, L.M. & Dunn, L.M. (1981). *Peabody Picture Vocabulary Test - Revised.* Circle Pines, MN: American Guidance Service.

Flavell, J.H., Green, F.L. & Flavell, E.R. (1986). Development of knowledge about the appearance-reality distinction. *Monographs of the Society for Research on Child Development*, 51 (1, serial no. 212).

Frake, C.O. (1963). The ethnographic study of cognitive systems. In T. Gladwin & W.C. Sturtevant (Eds.), *Anthropology and human behavior.* Washington: Anthropological Society.

Fremgen, A. & Fay, D. (1980). Overextensions in production and comprehension: A methodological clarification. *Journal of Child Language*, 7, 203-211.

Heibeck, T.H. & Markman, E.M. (1987). Word learning in children: An examination of fast mapping. *Child Development*, 58, 1021-1034.

Jones, S. S., Smith, L. B., & Landau, B. (1991). Object properties and knowledge in early lexical learning. *Child Development*, 62, 499-516.

Landau, B., Smith, L. B., & Jones, S. S. (1987). The importance of shape in early lexical learning. *Cognitive Development*, 3, 299-321.

McNamara, T.P. (1992). Priming and constraints it places on theories of memory and retrieval. *Psychological Review*, 99, 650-662.

Malt, B. C. (1991). Word meaning and word use. In P.J. Schwanenflugel (Ed.), *The psychology of word meanings*. Hillsdale, NJ: Lawrence Erlbaum Associates.

Markman, E.M. (1992). Constraints on word learning: Speculations about their nature, origins, and domain specificity. In M.R. Gunnar & M. Maratsos (Eds.), *The Minnesota Symposium on Child Psychology*: Vol. 25. Hillsdale, NJ: Lawrence Erlbaum Associates.

Markman, E.M. & Wachtel, G.F. (1988). Children's use of mutual exclusivity to constrain the meanings of words. *Cognitive Psychology*, 20, 121-157.

Merriman, W.E. & Bowman, L.L. (1987).The mutual exclusivity bias in children's word learning. *Monographs of the Society for Research on Child Development*, 54 (3-4, serial no. 220).

Nisbett, R.E. & Wilson, T.D. (1977). Telling more than we can know: Verbal reports on mental processes. *Psychological Review*, 84, 231-259.

Ogden , C.K. & Richards, I.A. (1949). *The meaning of meaning* 10th ed. London: Harcourt, Brace and Co.

Olson, D.R. (1970). Language and thought: Aspects of a cognitive theory of semantics. *Psychological Review*, 77, 257-273.

Quine, W.V.O. (1960). *Word and object*. Cambridge, MA: MIT Press.

Reber, A.S. (1993). *Implicit learning and tacit knowledge: An essay on the cognitive unconscious*. New York: Oxford University Press.

Smith, L.B., Jones, S.S., & Landau, B. (1992). Count nouns, adjectives, and perceptual properties in children's novel word interpretations. *Developmental Psychology*, 28, 273-286.

Thompson, J.R. & Chapman, R.S. (1977). Who is 'Daddy' revisited: The status of two-year-olds' over-extended words in use and comprehension. *Journal of Child Language*, 4, 359-375.

Tomasello, M. & Farrar, J. (1986). Joint attention and early language. *Child Development*, 57, 1454-1463.

Waxman, S.R. & Hatch, T. (1992). Beyond the basics: Preschool children label objects flexibly at multiple hierarchical levels. *Journal of Child Language*, 19, 153-166.

Zelazo, P.D. & Reznick, J.S. (1991). Age-related asynchrony of knowledge and action. *Child Development*, 62, 719-735.

From Adam('s) and Eve('s) to Mine and Yours in German Singletons and Siblings

WERNER DEUTSCH, ANGELA WAGNER, RENATE BURCHARDT, KAREN JAHN, & NINA SCHULZ

Technische Universität Braunschweig, Germany

1. Visiting the past: The Stern diaries

When Hilde Stern was born on the 7th of April 1900, her parents, Clara Stern and her husband, the German psychologist and philosopher William Stern, began keeping a record in the form of a diary of their daughter's development. At intervals of two and one and a half years respectively Hilde acquired a younger brother Günther, born on the 13th of July 1902, and sister Eva, born on the 29th of December 1904. The adult Sterns' diary extended over a period of 18 years. Initially, the entries were regular and very detailed; later these became more sporadic and abbreviated.

The Stern diaries have a true Odyssee behind them. They started in Breslau (today Wroclaw) in Silesia where Stern took up a lecturing post at the university. They were continued and closed in Hamburg, where William Stern became an internationally acclaimed scientist and highly respected university professor. When the Nazi era had arrived with a vengeance, William Stern, his wife and the three children were able to leave Germany timeously. As the diaries were included in their scientific baggage, they arrived in Durham, North Carolina. After William Stern's death in 1938 the diaries were taken first to Harvard University and later to the Hebrew University in Jerusalem where they gathered dust, until between 1984 and 1988, as a result of a co-operative effort between the Max–Planck Institute for Psycholinguistics in Nijmegen in the Netherlands and the Technical University of Brunswick in Germany, the diaries were rediscovered and made more freely available via the CHILDES–project (Stern & Stern, 1900 – 1918; see also Behrens & Deutsch, 1991).

What can we learn about the development of personal reference in German child language, when we look into the Stern diaries? What were the very first instances of reference to the self? Are there important differences among the three children regarding the first forms of personal reference and their functions? Answers to these questions can be discovered in two diary entries.

> Diary entry from the 20th of November 1901
> Yesterday evening I showed Hilde her own photograph and asked, "Who is that then?" Answer: "Hilde". Hilde has hardly seen this small picture, although we have often shown her our portrait photograph, in which she appears together with us, and told her to point to "Papa" and "Mama". She has been able to indicate us accurately for some time but has never reacted to her own image despite our repeated gestures and mentioning of her name. Today this occurred for the first time.

> Diary entry from the 8th of February 1904
> If something is happening which involves the others, if for example Hilde is being given some tasty morsel or having her nose blown, the funny little fellow comes over at once and demands, "I au, i au", which means "Ich auch, ich auch" (i. e. "Me too, me too"). On these occasions "I" (or "me") has made its initial appearance, if somewhat indistinctly. This is somewhat odd as the "I" has not been preceded by any mention of his own name. Generally speaking "I" appears much later.

Clara Stern described in her diary entries how her first and second-born children expressed themselves as individuals for the first time. Hilde, the oldest child, began as might be expected with a nominal form, i.e. her own name. However Günther proceeded differently, and interestingly enough, he was at a later stage to actually call himself "Günther Anders" ("anders" in German means "different" in English). When she made the relevant diary entry, Clara Stern was astonished to find her second child developing a means of personal reference by using a pronoun form to indicate himself. Generally speaking, nominal personal references are supposed to precede pronoun forms in the process of language development: The reason for this is that while the nominal form expresses a stable relationship between a person and his name, the pronoun form is dependent upon a given situation and connects the speaker to both his communicative role and his speech designation. Later Clara Stern was able to observe that her third child, Eva, likewise used first pronouns and then her own name to indicate herself. By this stage she was naturally less surprised at this reversal of the expected pattern than she had been in Günther's case.

The Sterns are perhaps the first psychologists to have noted this individual variation in the patterns of speech behaviour of children who have grown up in one family environment. We have called this variation the sibling-effect in the development of personal reference (Wagner, Burchardt, Deutsch, Jahn & Nakath, 1996). The Sterns' diary entries are most helpful in providing parameters for this sibling-effect, although far reaching conclusions cannot really be drawn from their notes. The diary entries represent individual observations and not controlled test cases. In the latter instance a series of children who have grown up with at least one sibling who is a year or two older than they are, needs to be studied and contrasted. The situations described in the diary entries are not comparable with one another. In Hilde's case, her first reference to her own person has a descriptive function: she names a picture of herself. Günther's reference to himself has a volitional function: he wishes to bring about a change in the existing situation thereby.

2. The sibling effect revisited

Some 90 years after the Sterns did their pioneering work in this field, we find ourselves involved in a developmental project on personal reference which aims to produce more concrete and verifiable results pertaining to the sibling-effect than a series of diary entries could hope to do. We have collected test cases including subjects who are siblings and those who are only children. We have furthermore taken into account the constellation of each family group, the sexes of the children concerned, and the exact times at which testing was carried out.

Table 1: Sample of the study

	Singletons		Siblings	
	male	female	male	female
	N = 16	N = 11	N = 9	N = 11
Age ($\bar{x}$) start	1;10.10	1;10.15	1;11.11	2;00.06
end	2;06.20	2;06.19	2;07.02	2;07.18

A total of 47 families took part in our investigations. The studies were conducted during 3 different periods with a gap of approximately 3 months between each of these. The venue in each case was the home of the family being tested. The persons performing the experiments were the children's parents (usually the mother but in some instances the father). The experimenters had attended a training course held by our research group to familiarise them beforehand with the methods they were to apply. In other words our records of the development of personal reference were not based upon observations made in entirely natural surroundings. They were instead based upon more or less standardised tasks which were similar to those situations described in the Sterns' diary entries which we have already discussed. In one of these tasks, called possessor naming, the experimenter showed his or her child two photographs. The two photographs had been taken in the family's home a day or two before the test. One of the photographs was of something belonging to the child, the other of something belonging to the mother. She then asked the child 'Tell me whose this is?'. The child had to name the owner of the photographed object. We believe that this task can be used to determine the range of the sibling–effect in the development of personal reference fairly accurately, given that complete accuracy is difficult to achieve using observations made in more or less natural surroundings. The naming of the possessor has a descriptive function. In other words the child uses language to indicate a specific relation and not, as would be the case in a volitional context, because he/she wishes to bring about a change in his current surroundings.

Furthermore this task involves a fixed division of roles. The experimenter asks questions which the child is supposed to answer. When it comes to the designation of the possessions depicted in the photographs, the child takes on the role of speaker and the parent that of addressee. Motives pertaining to relationships outside of the dyad thus do not feature.

This pre–determined arrangement (involving one parent and one child) is advantageous because it makes it possible to test singletons and children with siblings a year or two older under identical conditions.

Does the sibling–effect still apply? The situation we have discussed has led us to conclude that at the outset the vast majority of children express personal reference – because of its descriptive function – nominally (cf Deutsch, Wagner & Masche, 1994). This phenomenon does not appear to be influenced by their being singletons or not. The critical questions to be dealt with by our investigation are hence:

- Does the transition from nominal to pronominal reference occur more rapidly in the case of siblings than where singletons are concerned?
- Is the sibling–effect observable at self–reference only or can it also be seen during the addressee reference?
- Does the task of designating possessions provoke earlier and more frequent pronominal personal references than other tasks. e.g. naming persons in pictures?

We transcribed the dialogues (some short, some quite long) which occurred during the tasks in CHILDES (MacWhinney, 1991) and coded them in accordance with a coding system for personal references which we had developed. To enable us to analyse the statistics using log–linear models, we compiled the evaluation categories so that every personal reference was rated three times.

At the first stage it was decided whether a verbal personal reference was present or not, at the second if the verbal personal reference was semantically correct in terms of the target language, and at the third if a semantically correct personal reference was also expressed pronominally. As far as the results of all this are concerned we will limit ourselves to those results which are directly related to the sibling–effect. The following two figures make it quite clear that there *is* a sibling–effect even under the controlled conditions of our study.

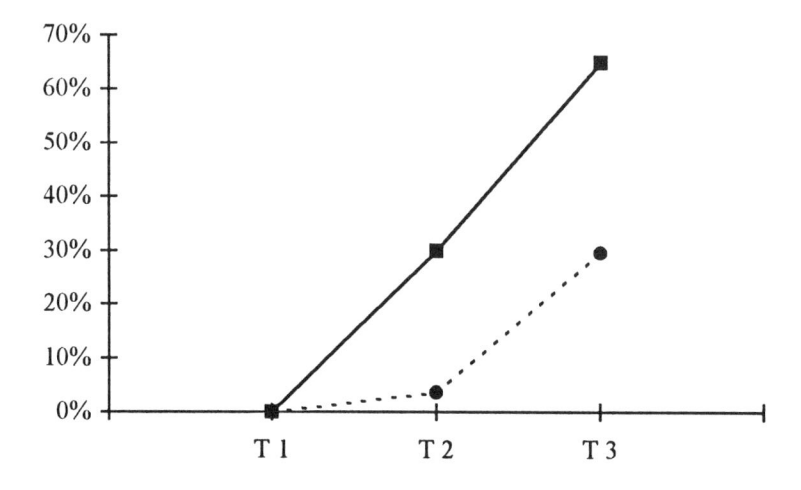

Figure 1: Percentage of correct pronoun use for self as possessor in 27 singletons (broken line) and 20 siblings (solid line) at T 1, T 2 and T 3.

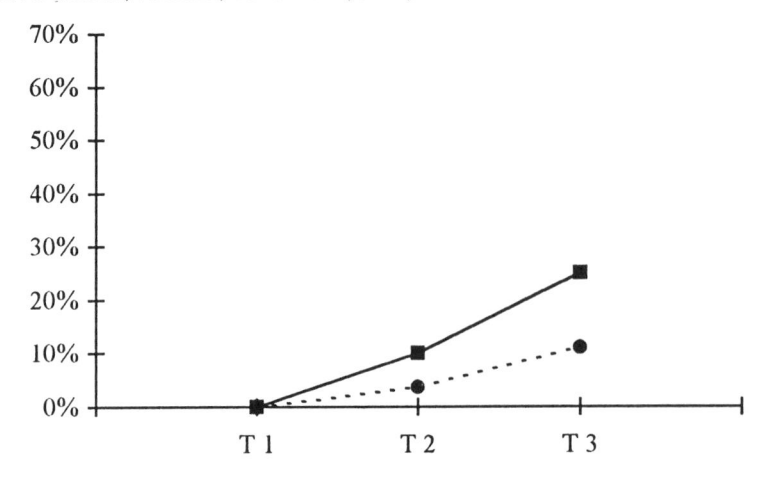

Figure 2: Percentage of correct pronoun use for other as possessor in 27 singletons (broken line) and 20 siblings (solid line) at T 1, T 2 and T 3.

At T 1, neither singletons nor siblings used (semantically correct) pronouns to indicate a possessive relation between the depicted possessum and the (to be inferred) possessor. This result supports the claim that possessive (or personal) pronouns are initially not used when childrens utterances fulfill a descriptive function, whereas volitional utterances of the same children already may contain pronominal references (see for example Budwig & Deutsch, 1983, Kolodziej, Deutsch, & Bittner 1991). In contrast, at T 2 both singletons and siblings have begun to apply pronominal possessive references for the possessor of the depicted object. There is a remarkable difference between the two groups of children, since the approximation toward target-like use of possessive references is speeded up considerably in siblings compared with singletons. This 'sibling-effect' appears in both conditions of the task, reference to self as reference to other (mother). However, between the two conditions differences are evident. Pronominal references are more frequent where 'self'- as opposed to 'other–references' are concerned.

The same picture of results can be found when the task involves naming a photograph of the child itself or its mother (Wagner et al, 1996).

The sibling–effect as well as the asymmetry between self and other are present in the person–naming task too. However, the two tasks differ in so far as pronominal references in both siblings and singletons are more frequent when possessors of depicted possessions are being named compared with naming persons depicted in pictures. This asynchrony was already found in a study by Deutsch & Budwig (1983) where alienable possession appeared to be the first semantic domain in which pronominal expressions occurred in child language. The sibling–effect appears to be relatively far–reaching, in that it is not limited to natural interactions where the volitional function of reference to persons is at center. The sibling–effect is also present in tasks where the descriptive function of personal references is elicited. Our results point to the fact that progress in the transition from child language to target language is domain–specific. Obviously children do not actually discover rules inherent in a target language at some point in development, but they stepwise grow into an adult–like use of personal deixis from an egocentric, speaker–based vantage point (cf Clark, 1978). Having said that the sibling–effect is far–reaching, we must add here that it also has definite limits. It is tied to particular linguistic forms, i.e. pronouns. A summary of the results of the statistical analysis using log–linear models is shown in Table 2. Here, the difference between siblings and singletons only becomes statistically significant, when the correct pronoun use is compared. No significant differences were detected in the categories of semantically correct or missing references. The other effects reported in Table 2 support that the possessor naming task is sensitive to capture the growth into target–like personal reference at the relevant time in development.

Table 2: Results of the statistical log–linear analysis in the possessor naming task.

main effects	semantics correct LR	df	signif.	pronouns correct LR	df	signif.	missing LR	df	signif.
sing vs sib	1.12	1	n.s. (.290)	10.70	1	s**	3.51	1	n.s. (.061)
self vs other	3.96	1	s*	8.86	1	s**	1.46	1	n.s. (.226)
t1, t2, t3	25.32	2	s**	46.77	2	s**	32.77	2	s**
t1 – t2	11.82	1	s**	14.43	1	s**	25.42	1	s**
t1 – t3	22.95	1	s**	45.52	1	s**	19.92	1	s**
t2 – t3	2.04	1	n.s. (.153)	12.09	1	s**	.43	1	n.s. (.514)

3. Explaining the sibling–effect

Our project is of course (and happily) not the only one currently concerned with the sibling–effect on the development of personal reference. The methods and the languages used in the available studies are complementary, so that the results fit together like the pieces of a jigsaw puzzle to provide a more complete picture of the whole. While our project is chiefly concerned with determining the range of the sibling–effect under controlled conditions, other investigations, like for example the studies by Oshima–Takane (1988) and Oshima–Takane, Cole & Yarembo (1993), have analysed the differences ascertainable in the interaction of children with and without older siblings in natural circumstances. In the latter instance, singletons are disadvantaged in that they experience dyadic speech from the outside (as spectators) less often than siblings do. Such (observer) situations can serve to provide a model of shifting reference in personal deixis which is supposed to repress the equal treatment of names and pronouns in personal reference. Our data provide us with evidence for this interpretation. In our possessive and in our personal reference tasks, siblings were less prone to semantically confusing pronoun uses than singletons were.

The Sterns (1907) also mention a further reason that siblings find it easier to master pronominal reference, namely the occurence of competitive situations in which older siblings resort to the use of pronouns such as "my" or "mine" and are soon copied by their younger sisters and brothers (see Clara Stern's diary entry pertaining to Günther). Children who interact with older siblings experience exposure to speech input which differs from that which singletons hear. The sibling–effect makes it clear that this different input leaves traces, which become effective during the transition from child language to target language.

Our study examined only one of many possible sibling constellations. The evaluation of other sibling constellations might well provide answers to various questions like: does the sibling–effect vanish if the age gap between the siblings is more (than two years)? Does it make any difference if the siblings concerned are of the opposite sex, as opposed to their being same sex? Etc.

Our group chose not to take up these and related issues, interesting as they are. Instead, we began a project to investigate the development of personal reference in a very special sibling constellation, 23 pairs of (mono– and dizygotic) twins.

Our twin–project does enable us to conclude at this juncture that twins are not a homogenous group when it comes to the development of personal reference. In fact their heterogeneity is greater than that of children growing up on their own. In addition it appears that genetic similarity is not the only key to the variations within and between twin dyads – at least not in the area we studied.

4. Conclusions

First language acquisition crucially depends on natural input provided by speakers who are more proficient and advanced than the language learning child. Without such an initial gap, language acquisition cannot proceed toward target stages. How important is the social relationship between the child and his (or her) advanced interlocutor? Our studies show that progress is possible under different social settings. Even if linguistic input is limited to just one parent or older sibling, this may suffice to become a native speaker in a natural language. However, our comparisons between singletons and siblings (with an older brother or sister) point to differences in the developmental course from child language to target language. Both, qualitative and quantitative differences appeared. Not only were siblings faster than singletons to replace nominal possessives in favour of (adult–like) pronominal possessives. Siblings also are less prone to semantic errors in terms of pronoun reversals. Twins form a special, but nonetheless heterogeneous category within the population of siblings. Certain phenomena such as the use of new nominals or proper names as duals were never observed in non–twins. However, even these twins become target–oriented, though at a later point in development compared with non–twins. What can we conclude from these specific observations on more general features of the acquisition process? On the one hand, this process appears to be fairly robust, tolerating a variety of (social) input conditions as sufficient for moving toward target language. On the other hand, the speed and smoothness of the acquisition process is sensitive to particularly favourable social settings like growing up with older siblings. Thus, the combination between robustness and sensitivity explains why common trends can go hand in hand with patterns of individual variations.

5. Acknowledgements

We thank the German Research Foundation for generous financial support of our projects on 'Person' (De 338/4–1/ 4–2), the 47 families in our longitudinal study for their most enjoyable cooperation, the photographer of our institute, Rolf Toch, for taking numerous pictures, our research assistants, especially Claudia Böcker, Thorsten Brants, Torsten Fricke, Zorana Gavranovic, Ingrid Kirchner, Gowert Masche, Jörg Nakath, Cornelius Pawlak, Michael Schiewe and Markus Wenglorz, for their help with the collection, transcription, coding and statistical analysis of the data.

6. References

Behrens, Heike and Werner Deutsch. 1991. Die Tagebücher von William und Clara Stern, in W. Deutsch, ed., *Über die verborgene Aktualität von William Stern.* Frankfurt: Peter Lang.

Clark, Eve. 1978. From gesture to word: On the natural history of deixis in language acquisition, in J. S. Bruner and A. Garton, eds., *Human growth and development: Wolfson college Lectures 1976.* Oxford: Oxford University Press.

Deutsch, Werner and Nancy Budwig. 1983. Form and function in the development of possessives. *Papers and Reports on Child Language Development* 22. 36-42.

Deutsch, Werner, Torsten Fricke and Angela Wagner. 1994. Ist die Sprachentwicklung von Zwillingen etwas Besonderes?, in K.-F. Wessel and F. Naumann, eds., *Kommunikation und Humanontogenese.* Bielefeld: Kleine.

Deutsch, Werner, Angela Wagner and Gowert Masche. 1994. Vom Nomen zum Pronomen: Eine experimentelle Untersuchung zur Entwicklung der Personreferenz bei deutschen Kindern im zweiten und dritten Lebensjahr. *Sprache und Kognition* 1. 41-51.

Kolodziej, Petra, Werner Deutsch and Christian Bittner. 1991. Das Selbst im Spiegel der Kindersprache. *Zeitschrift für Entwicklungspsychologie und Pädagogische Psychologie* XXIII (1). 23-47.

MacWhinney, Brian. 1991. *The CHILDES project: Tools for analyzing talk.* Hillsdale, NJ.: Lawrence Erlbaum.

Oshima-Takane, Yuriko. 1988. Children learn from speech not addressed to them: the case of personal pronouns. *Journal of Child Language* 15. 95-108.

Oshima-Takane, Yuriko, Elizabeth Cole and Rosalie L. Yaremko. 1993. Pronominal semantic confusion in a hearing-impaired child: a case study. *First language* 13II, (38). 149-168.

Stern, Clara and William Stern. 1900-1918. *Die Tagebücher. Elektronische Abschrift der unveröffentlichten Tagebücher aus dem Nachlaß.* Nijmegen: Max-Planck-Institut für Psycholinguistik.

Stern, Clara and William Stern. 1907. *Die Kindersprache.* Leipzig: Barth.

Wagner, Angela, Renate Burchardt, Werner Deutsch, Karen Jahn and Jörg Nakath. 1996. Der Geschwistereffekt in der Entwicklung der Personreferenz. Eine Längsschnittstudie mit 27 deutschsprachigen Einzel- und 20 Geschwisterkindern im zweiten und dritten Lebensjahr. *Sprache und Kognition* 1/2.

Is the Simultaneous Acquisition of Two Languages in Early Childhood Equal to Acquiring Each of the Two Languages Individually?

SUSANNE DÖPKE
Monash University

1. Introduction

The second half of this century has seen a turn-around in attitudes towards bilingualism from condemning it as harmful to the mind and the soul of the child (Jespersen 1922; Schmidt-Rohr 1933; Weisgerber 1966) to acknowledging intellectual and educational benefits (Peal and Lambert 1962; Bain and Yu 1980; Katchan, 1985). The question now is: how is the simultaneous acquisition of two languages (2L1) during the process of primary language acquisition realised? The issue is complicated by the fact that we are not even too sure yet of the mental operations involved in acquiring one first language (L1) and are still debating various theoretical alternatives (Pinker 1984; Clark 1987; Bates and MacWhinney 1989; Radford 1990; Clahsen 1991).

A first general hypothesis regarding the simultaneous development of two languages in early childhood was proposed by Taeschner (1983) and based on her own two German-Italian bilingual children. These children's mixed structures during their third year of life led Taeschner to propose the "three-stage hypothesis" suggesting that bilingual children progress from not being able to differentiate between their two languages to differentiating them on the lexical but not the structural level to fully differentiating them on both the lexical and the structural level. The "three-stage hypothesis" has since come under criticism (Genesee 1989; Meisel 1989; De Houwer 1990; Schlyter 1990; Döpke 1993). The major drift of the criticism was that young children are quite able to differentiate between the two languages in their environment in spite of some mixing.

As a reaction to the "three-stage-hypothesis" and congruent with its critics, De Houwer (1994) proposed the "separate development hypothesis" for simultaneous bilingualism (2L1). She argued that simultanoeusly bilingual children develop the grammatical structures in each of their two languages based on the language specific input. She based this hypothesis on empirical evidence from her own study of an English-Dutch bilingual child between the ages of 2;7 and 3;4 (DeHouwer 1990, this volume).

A stronger version of the "separate development hypothesis" can be attributed to Meisel and his colleagues (1990, 1994). This group is involved in a longitudinal study of seven French-German bilingual children, whose development was followed from before the children entered the two-word stage. They are suggesting that children growing up with two languages simultaneously acquire each of their two languages like monolingual children. This is congruent with theoretical assumptions of the Unique Entry Principle (Pinker 1984) and Lexical Learning (Rizzi 1989; Clahsen and Penke 1992) according to which the syntactic structures in the respective languages should become available to bilingual children without cross-linguistic errors because of the association of particular lexical items with their language-specific structures.

However, numerous anecdotal reports from parents of bilingual children as well as accounts published by linguists (Leopold 1939-49; Redlinger & Park 1980; Saunders 1988) confirm that cross-linguistic structures are a normal feature of bilingual children's speech productions. In my own longitudinal data from German-English bilingual children, cross-linguistic structures also abound.

In this paper I will attempt some psycholinguistic explanations for the cross-linguistic structures I have found in my data. After a contrastive sketch of the syntactic structures of German and English, I will review the structural development of my bilingual informants as analysed so far (Döpke 1992, 1993, 1995a,b, in preparation) and compare it with reports on the structural development of German and English monolingual children. In the Discussion section I will attempt a theoretical conceptualisation of the children's cross-linguistic structures which is congruent with theoretical assumptions regarding primary language acquisition as made by the Principle of Contrast (Clark 1987) and the Competition Model (Bates & MacWhinney 1989). This interpretation will suggest that a degree of comparison and contrast of the two languages is operative during the simultaneous acquisition of two languages in early childhood. I will argue that the acquisition of two languages during the primary acquisition process is not principally different from the acquisition of only one language but that the increased processing complexity is responsible for the generation of child structures which are not found in monolingual acquisition.

2. Structural Contrasts and Similarities between German and English

The study of the simultaneous acquisition of German and English is made particularly interesting by the fact that, on the surface, these two languages have a number of syntactic structures in common, but the underlying structures are vastly different and result in different surface structures in more complex sentences (Chomsky 1982, 1986; Deprez & Pierce 1993; Haider 1993).

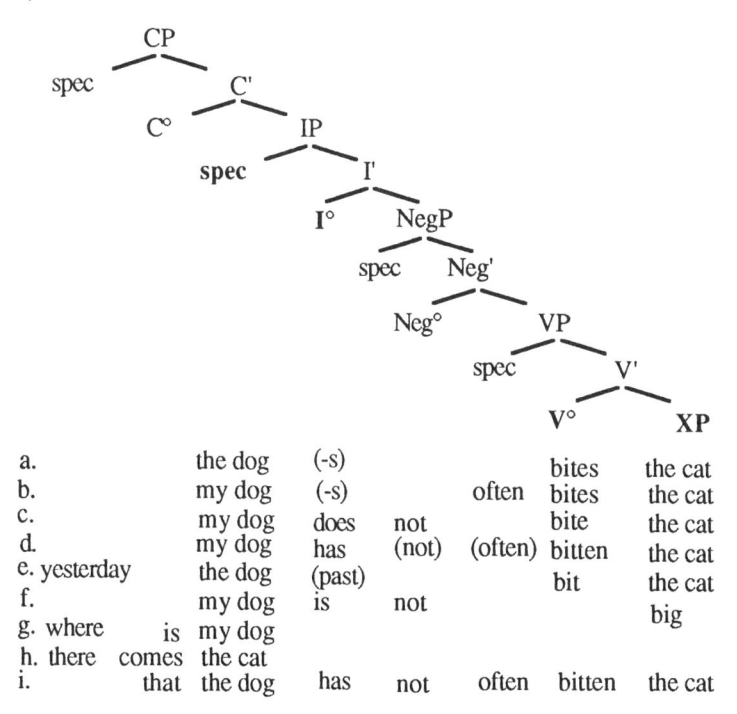

```
                         CP
                      /      \
                   spec       C'
                            /    \
                          C°      IP
                                /    \
                             spec     I'
                                    /    \
                                  I°      NegP
                                        /      \
                                     spec      Neg'
                                              /    \
                                           Neg°     VP
                                                  /    \
                                               spec    V'
                                                      /  \
                                                    V°    XP
```

a.		the dog	(-s)			bites	the cat
b.		my dog	(-s)		often	bites	the cat
c.		my dog	does	not		bite	the cat
d.		my dog	has	(not)	(often)	bitten	the cat
e.	yesterday	the dog	(past)			bit	the cat
f.		my dog	is	not			big
g.	where	is	my dog				
h.	there	comes	the cat				
i.|	that	the dog	has	not	often	bitten	the cat

Figure 1: *English sentence structure*

Within the Principle and Parameter framework, English can be described as having head-initial verb phrases (Fig.1, d) and head-initial but weak tense and agreement functions (IP). Therefore main verbs are not raised to I°, but remain in their original position in the verb phrase, and in the absence of modals or auxiliaries in I°, inflection affixes are discharged onto the verb

98 / SUSANNE DÖPKE

(Fig.1, a). Prove for that comes from sentences with adverbs in preverbal position (Fig.1, b). The negation, however, blocks affix lowering. In the absence of modals or auxiliaries, do-support is necessary for tense and agreement to be realised in negated sentences (Fig.1, c). In sentences with complex verb structures (Fig.1, d), both finite and non-finite verb components precede the verb complements (XP). In the case of topicalisation, the specCP position is filled (Fig.1, e), and the finite verb is in third or even fourth position. Only copulas are raised to I° (Fig.1, f), and since verb fronting is only possible for raised verbs (Fig.1, g), main verbs are never found in C°. The only exception are stereotypical expressions (Fig.1, h). In subordinate clauses, the conjunction takes up the C° position, which does not affect the word order in the rest of the clause in any way (Fig.1, i).

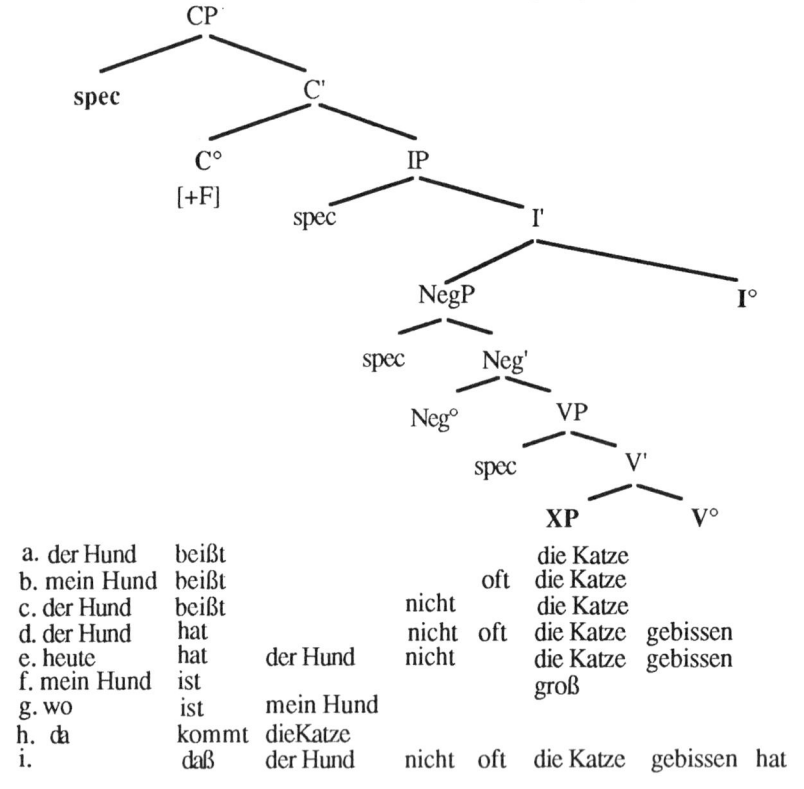

```
                    CP
                   /  \
                spec   C'
                      /  \
                    C°    IP
                   [+F]  /  \
                       spec  I'
                            /  \
                         NegP   I°
                         /  \
                       spec  Neg'
                            /  \
                         Neg°   VP
                               /  \
                             spec  V'
                                  /  \
                                XP    V°
```

a. der Hund   beißt   die Katze
b. mein Hund   beißt   oft   die Katze
c. der Hund   beißt   nicht   die Katze
d. der Hund   hat   nicht oft   die Katze   gebissen
e. heute   hat   der Hund   nicht   die Katze   gebissen
f. mein Hund   ist   groß
g. wo   ist   mein Hund
h. da   kommt dieKatze
i.   daß   der Hund   nicht oft   die Katze   gebissen hat

Figure 2: *German sentence structure*

In German, verb phrases are head-final (Fig.2, d) and the inflection parameter (IP) is head-final as well. In order to receive tense and agreement marking, verbs are first raised to I° and then to C°, because C° attracts finite verbs if it is empty. Topicalisation is obligatory in German. In unmarked cases the subject is topicalised and raised to the specCP position. Thus SVO is achieved through double raising of the verb as well as raising of the subject from specIP to specCP (Fig.2, a). Prove for verb raising comes from sentences with adverbs or negation in postverbal position (Fig.2, b,c). In sentences with complex verbs, the finite and non-finite verb components are separated by the verb complements (Fig.2, d). In the case of marked topicalisation, the subject remains in the specIP position and the constituent to be topicalised is raised into specCP. Consequently the finite verb component always remains in second position in main clauses (Fig.2, e). Thus main verbs, copula, auxiliaries and modals all behave in the same way with respect to verb raising, and examples f. to h. in Figure 2 are possible with all types of verbs and not restricted with respect to the type of constituent which can be topicalised in specCP either. If, however, the C° is filled with a conjunction, as is the case in subordinate clauses, the finite verb is only raised once and remains in the head-final I° position, which produces the verb-last structures in such clauses. Thus subordinate conjunctions and verb-second are mutually exclusive, and main clause word order is believed to be structurally impossible in subordinate clauses.

This short description of German and English has shown that sentences like those in examples a, f, g and h have identical surface structures in German and English. In examples b and c, the relative position of verbs and negation or adverbs differentiates between the languages. In the d. examples, Ger-man and English differ with respect to the word order in the verb phrase, and in the e. examples with respect to the position of the finite verb component. The i. examples represent most directly the differences in underlying structures in German and English.

3. Method

3.1 Subjects

The present study is based on longitudinal data from three bilingual German-English children: two boys, JH and CW, and one girl, NS. All three children are first-born The families live in Australia and have adopted the 'one parent–one language' approach. The children have been spoken to in German by their mothers, and in English by their fathers and nearly everyone else in their environment, from birth on. The language of communication between the parents is English in each family. The mothers are tertiary educated native speakers of German and have made a strong commitment to speaking German with their children at all times. The mothers did not mix German and English on either the lexical or the structural level.

All three children were fully able to understand utterances addressed to them in both languages and to express themselves spontaneously in both languages before recording commenced. This plus the daily exposure to both languages was considered appropriate independent evidence that the children were simultaneous bilinguals. The children's ability to express themselves spontaneously in both languages continued to develop throughout the recording period and beyond, and to date, all children are able to communicate in both languages at a level appropriate for their age.

There was no interruption in the children's exposure to German except during the few days when NS's anf JH's mothers were in hospital for the birth of their second children, but all three children experienced temporary interruptions of their English during visits to Germany with their mothers. However, as we will see later, the independent development of the children's English is not the issue, but the development of their German. Hence the temporary interruptions in their exposure to English have no theoretical implications regarding the children's status as simultaneous bilinguals.

3.2 Procedure

The children were recorded once a month from 2;0, CW and JH, and 2;2, NS, respectively. Data collection took place in the children's homes. Each month the children were tape recorded with audio and video equipment in free play or other spontaneous interaction for two sessions of 45 minutes to one hour, one session each with their German-speaking mother and an English-speaking caregiver. The English recordings were done with the father of CW, predominantly the grandmother of JH, and various babysitters of NS. The length of the period for which the children were included in the study was dictated by availability.

The recordings were transcribed by a research assistant and checked for accuracy by myself. Discrepancies were resolved in discussions.

3.3 The Data

The analysis is based on the children's spontaneous utterances, that is utterances which were not modelled within the immediate vicinity of the child's utterance. So far close analyses have been done concerning the positioning of non-finite and finite verbs in matrix clauses (Döpke 1995a, 1995b), verb morphology (Döpke 1995b), word order in subordinate clauses (Döpke 1992) and the development of negation (Jacobsen 1993; Döpke, in preparation).

The data is presented with respect to phases of development as defined by mean length of utterance (MLU) (Phase II 1.75–2.74, Phase III 2.75–3.74, Phase IV 3.75–4.74, and Phase VI 5.75+). Utterance length was calculated in words rather than morphemes (cf. Brown 1973; Clahsen, Penke & Parodi 1993/94) because of the differences in morpheme complexity in German and English and the difficulties with deciding when a morpheme has actually been acquired. For the same reason contractions were counted as two words.

4. Results

In this section the structure of the children's utterances is described phase by phase and compared to monolingual development as reported in the literature (Mills 1985; Fletcher 1985; de Villiers & de Villiers 1985; Clahsen 1986,

1991; Radford 1990; Clahsen & Penke 1992; Clahsen, Penke & Parodi 1993/93)

L1-German	2L1-German	2L1-English	L1-English
• preference for (S)_XP_V	• preference for (S)_**XP_V**	• preference for (S)_V_'XP	• predominantly (S)_V_XP
• finite verbs predominantly in precomplement position but some *finite* verbs in final position	• finite verbs predominantly in pre-complement position but some *finite* verbs in final position	• some XP_V	• hardly any XP_V
• pre-verbal negation always being NEG_XP_V	• pre-verbal negation, with *preference* for **NEG XP V**	• preverbal negation always being **NEG_V_XP**	• preverbal negation always being NEG_V_XP

Table 1: *Phase I and II*

In Phases I and II (Table 1) the development of 2L1 was very similar to the development of L1 for both languages. Most noticeably the bilingual children were differentiating appropriately between head-final structures in the German verb phrase (XP_V) and head-initial structures in the English verb phrase (V_XP).

In German, the bilingual children also produced some utterances with finite verbs in final position. While this is not a feature of adult-German matrix clauses, such structures have been taken as an indication that the theoretical assumption of the inflection parameter being head-final and verb-second structures being a result of double raising of the verb is in fact correct (Meisel & Müller 1992). Thus initially, these bilingual children appear to have assumed the correct head-final position for both the verb and the inflection. In English monolingual development, verb-last structures are hardly ever found. The very few examples that have been reported in the literature could convincingly be interpreted as topicalisation structures (Radford 1990:79f). In the bilingual children's English, verb-last structures were also rare, but frequent enough to have been encountered in the data from all three informants during monthly 45-minute recording sessions. An interpretation of these structures as topicalisation structures is impossible (Döpke 1995b).

In Phase III (Table 2), considerable variation between L1 and 2L1 started to emerge in the children's German. While monolingual German speaking children clearly differentiate between non-finite verbs in sentence-final position and finite verbs in non-final position (Clahsen & Penke 1992; Clahsen, Penke & Parodi 1993/94), the bilingual children moved verbs from the sentence final position to the mid-sentence position irrespective of finiteness (S_V$_{nonfin}$_XP and V$_{nonfin}$_NEG). In particular the movement of non-finite verbs past the negation is never done by monolingual German speaking children. Weissenborn (1990) argued that -en affixes on the verb cannot necessarily be taken as non-finiteness markers, but simply be due to incorrect agreement choices. However, that verb movement was truly independent of finiteness in the cases of these bilingual children is convincingly indicated by complex verb constructions involving head-initial verb phrases (S_aux/mod_V$_{nonfin}$_XP) and pre-verbal negations with verbs preceding the complements (NEG_V$_{nonfin}$_XP).

L1-German	2L1-German	2L1-English	L1-English
• S_V$_{fin}$_XP	• S_V$_{fin}$_XP *and* S_**V$_{nonfin}$**_XP	• S_V$_{nonfin}$_XP	• S_V$_{nonfin}$_XP
• S_aux/mod_ XP_V	• S_aux/mod_ V_XP *more than* S_aux/mod_ XP_V	• S_aux/mod_ V_XP *and rarely* (S_aux/mod_ **XP_V**)[a]	• S_aux/mod_ V_XP
• pre-verbal negation always NEG_XP_V	• pre-verbal negation NEG_XP_ V$_{nonfin}$ *and* NEG_**V$_{nonfin}$_XP**	• pre-verbal negation *always* NEG_V_XP	• pre-verbal negation *always* NEG_V_XP
• cop/mod/aux _NEG • V$_{fin}$_NEG	• cop/mod/aux _NEG • V$_{fin}$_NEG *and* **V$_{nonfin}$_NEG**	• cop/mod/aux _NEG • (**V_NEG**)	• cop/mod/aux _NEG
• agreement system acquired rapidly	• acquisition of agreement system protracted • non-finite **-n** widely overgeneralised	• occasional use of 3rd ps.sg -s • (some German affixes)	• 3rd ps.sg. -s

[a] Brackets indicate that a structure was only used in isolated instances, but nevertheless by all three children.

Table 2: Phase III

The bilingual children's English hardly differed from that of monolingual English speaking children. Typical German structures like head-final verb phrases (S_aux/mod_XP_V$_{nonfin}$) and post-verbal negation (V_NEG) were only occasionally found.

While all of the five German agreement affixes on the verb appeared within three to five months, most of them were not used correctly or consistently for a year or longer. Instead -en affixes were overgeneralised extensively. The slow development of the agreement system contrasts with its rapid acquisition by monolingual German speaking children (Mills 1985; Clahsen 1986). The -en affix appeared to have had the additional function of marking verbs as German, which was indicated by English verbs in the German context at times marked with -en. As the agreement system developed, occasionally person markers were also used on English verbs in the German context, in particular 1st ps.sg -e.

In English, none of the bilingual children used 3rd ps.sg -s consistently during the period of recording. Interestingly, there was some overgeneralisation of German agreement affixes to English. It thus appears that the acquisition of subject-verb agreement was protracted in both languages.

L1-German	2L1-German	2L1-English	L1-English
• 2nd ps.sg -st productive and consistent => agreement system falls into place	• 2nd ps.sg -st productive but not consistent; **no trigger effect** • 1st ps.sg -Ø or -e consistently correct • S_aux/mod_ XP_V *less than* S_aux/mod_ V_{nonfin}_XP *and* S_aux/mod_ V_{fin}_XP • V_{fin}_NEG/ADV *and* V_{nonfin}_NEG/ADV		
• XP_V_{fin}_S	• XP_V_{fin}_S *and* XP_V_{nonfin}_S	• stereotypical verb fronting • (XP_V_{fin}_S) *and* XP_V_{nonfin}_S)	• stereotypical verb fronting only
	• XP_S_V	• XP_S_V	• XP_S_V

Table 3: *Phase IV*

The characteristic achievement of monolingual German speaking children during Phase IV (Table 3) is the attainment of 2nd ps.sg -st inflection (Clahsen 1986). As soon as this form is used productively, it is also used consistently (Clahsen & Penke 1992; Clahsen, Penke & Parodi 1993/94). Correlating with the use of 2nd ps.sg -st, the rest of the agreement system falls into place (Clahsen & Penke 1992; Clahsen, Penke & Parodi 1993/94). This, in turn, supposedly triggers the verb-fronting rule in German (X_V$_{fin}$_S) (Clahsen & Penke 1992; Clahsen, Penke & Parodi 1993/94) because of the underlying structural relationship between C^o and finiteness [+F].

The bilingual children started to use 2nd ps.sg -st more frequently and definitely productively during Phase IV, but not consistently so. The only person agreement which was applied correctly and consistently as of Phase IV was 1st ps.sg. -Ø or -e. Most interestingly, all three children frequently double marked person agreement in complex verb constructions if the main verb was in head-initial position in the verb phrase (S_aux/mod_V$_{fin}$_XP).

In spite of the agreement system not being attained yet, all three children used the verb fronting rule for German (XP_V$_{fin}$_S) productively. Consequently non-finite verbs were fronted alongside finite verbs (XP_V$_{nonfin}$_S). But the children also topicalised in the English way (XP_S_V). Thus subject-verb inversion was acquired as an option during Phase IV, not as a structural necessity as in monolingual German development.

In English, the bilingual children began to use 3rd ps.sg affixes productively, but not yet consistently. Stereotypical verb fronting was the most frequent, but not the only type of verb fronting. All children occasionally produced (XP_V$_{fin}$_S) utterances with obligatory post-verbal arguments being topicalised, a structure which seems to have been motivated through the exposure to German since it is not found in the English of monolingual children.

L1-German	2L1-German	2L1-English	L1-English
	• S_aux/modal_XP_V		
	• attainment of agreement system		
• conj$_{sub}$_S_XP_V$_{fin}$	• conj$_{sub}$_S_V$_{fin}$_XP and conj$_{sub}$_S_aux/mod_XP_V$_{nonfin}$	• conj$_{sub}$_S_V_XP	• conj$_{sub}$_S_V_XP

Table 4: Phase V

During Phase V (Table 4), the bilingual children finally settled for the correct word order in sentences with complex verbs in German. They also mastered most of the agreement system and the verb fronting rule. The remaining difference to monolingual German speaking children was with respect to subordinate clauses. In Phase V, monolingual German speaking children consistently fill the conjunction slot in subordinate clauses and immediately produce the appropriate word order for subordinate clauses which leaves the finite verb in its underlying clause final position (conj$_{sub}$_S_XP_V$_{fin}$) (Mills 1985; Clahsen 1986).

Once again the German output of the bilingual children did not conform with the theoretical assumptions of the Principle and Parameter Theory in the way monolingual development of German does. Bilingual children, too, fill the conjunction slot consistently in Phase V, but they strongly favour main clause word order after subordinating conjunctions. This structure is maintained for an extended period. It suggests that any assumption regarding a head-final IP, which the bilingual children may have held during Phase II, was thoroughly discarded during Phases III and IV. While main clause word order in subordinate clauses has recently been attested in individual cases of monolingual German speaking children (Gawlitzek-Maiwald, Tracy and Fritzenschaft 1992) and some of the bilingual children in the Meisel study (Müller 1994), for the German-English bilingual informants this seems to be a regular feature of their acquisition of German.

In the final phase of structural development, the correct word order for subordinate clauses is eventually attained. From now on the two languages sound appropriately "native" on the syntactic level. Cross-linguistic structures still occasionally appear, as they also do in bilingual adults, but they are rare and less a matter of grammatical knowledge than of momentary performance.

Discussion

In spite of the cross-linguistic structures in both language environments, one cannot say that the children had only one system of structures for German and English. German and English verb phrases were indeed structurally differentiated since both head-initial and head-final verb phrases were used in German, but head-final verb phrases in English remained the exception. The same is valid for negation structures: In German the children produced pre-verbal as well as post-verbal negation, but in English post-verbal negations were rare. Moreover, the children appeared to be sensitive to German using -en affixes and used them as a means of marking their lexical choices as German. This suggests that they were actively concerned about using separate structures for German and English.

This means that the data in this study does not support the "three-stage-hypothesis". The "separate development hypothesis" is supported in its weaker form, that is, the children never appeared to assume that German and

English are identical in structure. Nevertheless, the bilingual development presents itself as significantly different to monolingual development, at least in German. Thus the stronger version of the "separate development hypothesis" is not supported. This needs to be accounted for.

I am not going to take issue with Principle and Parameter theory and its adequacy for the description of the mature grammar. Rather I want to contemplate the process of data aggregation which precedes the setting of the parameters to their language-specific values. This process is often referred to, but not much explored. I believe that the processes of language acquisition described by the Competition Model (Bates and MacWhinney 1989) and the Principle of Contrast (Clark 1987) can make a contribution to explaining what happens during the bilingual children's data aggregation stage.

In Phases I and II, the development in German 2L1 proceeded in very similar ways to German L1. The children's processing abilities were limited, and they predominantly parsed the end of sentences (Slobin 1973). Thus they recognised XP_V structures in German and V_XP structures in English. This created a binary contrast between the two languages.

English: V_XP ——————— German: XP_V

In Phase III, differences between German L1 and German 2L1 started to appear. With increasing processing abilities both bilingual and monolingual children become aware of elements preceding the verb phrase, in particular of subjects. For monolingual German speaking children, verbs in final position now compete with verbs in second position, and the phenomena distinguishing between them are the verb endings: -en in final position and a range of finiteness markers in second position. This creates a binary contrast between finite and nonfinite verbs and leads monolingual German speaking children to use nonfinite verbs in final position and finite verbs in second position. Plural referents are very uncommon at this age and the -en affix as an agreement marker for 1st and 3rd person plural is therefore not important yet.

German: V_{fin}_XP ——————— German: XP_V_{nonfin}

Bilingual children of the German–English combination find the task of differentiating between finite and nonfinite verbs in German more complex than do monolingual German speaking children. The now perceivable contrast between nonfinite–final verbs and finite–second verbs breaks up the original contrast between final verbs in German and non-final verbs in English. Due to competing cues from English, finite and nonfinite verbs in German do not present themselves as a simple dichotomy since non-final verbs in German also have to be contrasted with non-final verbs in English.

English verbs

German nonfinite verbs

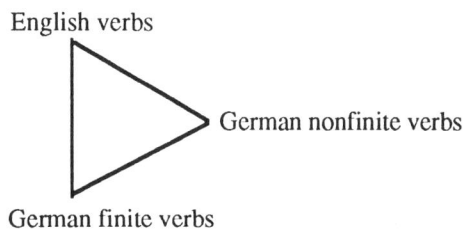

German finite verbs

The difference between German and English verbs is tied up with their structural status. Thus the triangular relationship can only be resolved via the successful differentiation between German and English verbs in the pre-complement position. During Phases III and IV the children are obviously not yet able to do that and temporarily conclude that English verbs are always nonfinal and German verbs can be final or nonfinal.

What is left as a distinguishing phenomenon between German and English are the -en endings on German verbs, which are widely overused at this stage. Finiteness markers in German only slowly take on the function of differentiating between German and English verbs since the first grammatical person to develop, 1st ps.sg, has a -Ø allomorph, which once again threatens the clear differentiation between German verbs and English verbs.

Thus the triangular relationship sketched above is a good example of high cue cost: although the cues are frequent, they are not reliable; verbs in pre-complement position are found in German as well as in English, and German verbs as well as English verbs may have -Ø affix. The structural challenge is thus more demanding in the bilingual acquisition of German and English than in German monolingual development. The high cue costs surrounding verb placement in non-final position has the predictable effect of delaying the acquisition of the finite–nonfinite distinction of verbs in German 2L1, which happens so smoothly and rapidly during the monolingual development of German.

The cue competition between English verbs and German verbs in non-final position is resolved once the children's processing abilities enable them to pay sufficient attention to mid-sentence differences in German and English. This allows them to parse the relative order of verbs, negation and adverbs in the two languages and effectively reduces the complexity of the triangular relationship between German and English verbs in non-final position and German verbs in final position to a new binary contrast between German and English in mid-sentence position.

English: NEG/ADV_V ——————— German: V_NEG/ADV

That the competition between English verbs and German verbs in non-final position is indeed resolved through the NEG/ADV_V vs. V_NEG/ADV contrast and initially not due to the understanding of finiteness is evident from the bilingual children's use of non-finite verbs in V_NEG structures, a feature of bilingual language acquisition which is nonexistent in the monolingual development of German. The issue of finiteness in German is not being resolved during Phase IV, which is indicated by the on-going use of head-initial verb phrases in German as well as the frequent marking of head-initial verbs with person agreement.

During the period of mid-sentence differentiation between V_NEG/ADV in German and NEG/ADV_V in English in Phases III and IV, the possibility for auxiliary fronting and verb fronting becomes available in Phase IV. Again, verb fronting appears originally to be due to word order contrasts in German and English rather than the contrast between finiteness and non-finiteness in German as the bilingual children fronted verbs irrespectively of their finiteness status. The children's attention to AUX_S and V_S structures in German and only AUX_S in English strengthens the V_NEG/ADV vs NEG/ADV_V contrast in Phase IV.

English: AUX=MOD=COP ——————— German: V=AUX=MOD=COP

The children were now able to realise the extent of the structural difference with respect to mid-sentence verbs in German and English: In English auxiliaries, modals and copulas can precede negation and subject; in German verbs can precede negation and subject well.

Due to the realisation that German verbs behave like auxiliaries, modals and copulas, the bilingual children were now able to contrast German verbs in final position with German verbs, auxiliaries and copulas in second position and pay attention to finiteness as the differentiating feature.

        aux, mod, cop
verbs in nonfinal position ——————— verbs in final position
    + Finite   – Finite

By Phase V, non-final verbs in German and English were successfully disassociated. They were usually marked as finite in German with the appropriate person affix, and S_aux/mod_V_XP structures were the exception in German. Thus, German and English could now be differentiated by the AUX_VP complexes in both languages.

English: AUX_ V_XP ——————— German: AUX_ XP_V

The attainment of correct word order in German matrix clauses with complex verb forms (S_aux/mod_XP_V) seemed to be an important achievement for the bilingual children as they maintained this word order throughout Phase V. This was in spite of the fact that subordinate clauses became more frequent during Phase V, the C° position was consistently filled with a conjunction and the finite verb should theoretically have stayed in its underlying head-final position.

The appropriate structures are eventually attained in their full complexity during Phase VI:
        <u>English</u>: [CP [C°][IP [I°][NegP [Neg°][VP [V°][XP]]]]]
        <u>German</u>: [CP [C°/+**Fin**][IP [NegP [Neg°][VP [V° [**XP**]I°]]]]]

Conclusions

The comparison of data from monolingual German and English speaking children with data from children acquiring German and English simultaneously during the process of primary language acquisition clearly disfavours the "three stage" hypothesis as the bilingual children did not show evidence of generating sentences from one common grammar in both languages at any time. To the contrary, right from the earliest stages of word combinations they seem to have intended to differentiate between the two languages.

Nevertheless, cross-linguistic structures were a regular occurrence in German during Phases III and IV. In English cross-linguistic structures were rare but not entirely absent. Thus the "separate development" hypothesis is only supported in its weaker form.

The evidence from the German-English bilingual children in this study points towards the two languages in the 2L1 situation being processed in comparison with and contrast to one another. The English input enhances the 'verb-before-object' cue for German and generates cue conflict as to where the nonfinal verb is structurally located: V^o or C^o. This seems to slow the acquisition process down relative to the children's utterance length. The cue conflict between German and English is eventually resolved through the contrast of lexical adjacencies in the middle field of the sentence.

The swiftness with which cross-linguistic cue conflicts are resolved might well depend on a child's memory capacity. To the degree with which bilingual children operate from stored concrete examples when generating new sentences they might in fact give the impression of developing both languages totally separately from one another. However, those children who have to rely on whatever syntactic regularities they have identified when generating new sentences will provide the researcher with more direct evidence of the cognitive processes which lead to the acquisition of language-specific grammatical structures. It is therefore important that we do not just select apparently fast or efficient language learners as informants.

The study of simultaneous bilingualism (2L1) has the potential of enhancing our understanding of the cognitive principles involved in primary language acquisition by introducing an additional factor: two languages instead of one. The present study supports the theoretical conceptualisations regarding primary language acquisition made by the Competition Model and the Principle of Contrast in showing that cross-linguistic cue competition affects the path of syntactic development. Just as "different types of languages pose different types of acquisition problems" (Slobin 1985:4) the simultaneous acquisition of two languages during primary language acquisition creates particular acquisition challenges of its own.

References

Bain, B. and A. Yu 1980. Cognitive Consequences of Raising Children Bilingually: 'One Parent–One Language'. *Canadian Journal of Psychology* 34.304–313.

Bates, E. and B. MacWhinney 1989. Functionalism and the Competition Model. In B. MacWhinney and E. Bates, eds., *The Crosslinguistic Study of Sentence Processing*. Cambridge: C.U.P.

Brown, R., 1973. *A First Language: The Early Stages*. Cambridge, MA: M.I.T. Press.

Chomsky, N., 1982. *Some Concepts and Consequences on the Theory of Government and Binding*. Cambridge, MA: MIT Press.

Chomsky, N., 1986. *Barriers*. Cambridge, MA: MIT Press.

Clahsen, H., 1986. *Profilanalyse*. Berlin: Marhold.

Clahsen, H., 1991. *Child Language and Developmental Dysphasia*. Amsterdam: Benjamins.

Clahsen, H. and M. Penke, 1992. The Acquisition of Agreement Morphology and its Syntactic Consequences: New Evidence on German Child Language from the Simone-Corpus. In Meisel, ed., *The Acquisition of Verb Placement*. Dordrecht: Kluwer.

Clahsen, H., M. Penke, T. Parodi, 1993/94. Functional Categories in Early Child German. *Language Acquisition* 3.395–429.

Clark, E., 1987. The Principle of Contrast: A Constraint on Language Acquisition. In B. MacWhinney and E. Bates, eds., *The Crosslinguistic Study of Sentence Processing*. Cambridge: C.U.P.

De Houwer, A. 1990. *Two At a Time: An Exploration of How Children Acquire Two Languages From Birth*. Cambridge: Cambridge University Press

De Houwer, A. 1994. The Separate Development Hypothesis: Method and Implications. In Extra, G. and L. Verhoeven, eds., *The Cross-Linguistic Study of Bilingual Development*. Amsterdam: Royal Netherlands Academy of Arts and Science.

Deprez, V. and A. Pierce 1993. Negation and Functional Projections in Early Grammar. *Linguistic Inquiry* 24.25–647.

de Villiers, J.G. and P.A. de Villiers 1985. The Acquisition of English. In D.I. Slobin ed., *The Crosslinguistic Study of Language Acquisition*. Erlbaum.

Döpke, S. 1992. Approaches to First Language Acquisition: Evidence from Simultaneous Bilingualism. *Australian Review in Applied Linguistics* 15.137–150.

Döpke, S. 1993. A Bilingual Child's Struggle to Comply With the 'One Parent–One Language' Rule. *Journal of Multilingual and Multicultural Development* 14.467–485.

Döpke, S. 1995a. Competing Language Structures: The Acquisition of Verb Placement in Bilingual German-English Children. ms.

Döpke, S. 1995b. The Development of Verb Morphology and the Position of the Finite Verb in Bilingual German-English Children. ms.

Döpke, S. The Development of Negation by Bilingual Children: Contrasting Lexical Adjacencies as a Cue to Structural Differences Between Languages. In preparation.

Fletcher, P. 1985. *A Child's Learning of English*. Oxford: B.Blackwell.

Gawlitzek-Maiwald, R. Tracy and A. Fritzenschaft 1992. Language Acquisition and Competing Linguistic Representations: The Child as Arbiter. In J. Meisel, ed.,*The Acquisition of Verb Placement*. Dordrecht: Kluwer.

Genesee, F. 1989. Early Bilingual Development: One Language or Two? *Journal of Child Language* 16.161–180.

Haider, H. 1993. *Deutsche Syntax Generativ*. Tübingen: Narr.

Jacobsen, V. 1993. The Acquisition of Negation. in an English-German Bilingual Child. MA thesis, University of Melbourne.

Jespersen, O. 1922. *Language, Its nature, Development and Origin*. London: Allen and Unwin.

Katchan, O. 1985. Early Bilingualism: Friend or Foe? In J. Kurcz, G.W. Shugar and J.H. Danks, eds., *Knowledge and Language*. North Holland: Elsevier.

Leopold. W.F. 1939-49. *Speech Development of a Bilingual Child*. Evanston, Illinois.

Meisel, J. 1989. Early Differentiation of Languages in Bilingual Children. In K. Hyltenstam and L. Obler, eds., *Bilingualism Across the Lifespan*. Cambridge: C.U.P.

Meisel, J., ed., 1990. *Two First Languages*. Dordrecht: Foris.

Meisel, J., ed., 1994. *Bilingual First Language Acquisition. French and German Grammatical Development*. Amsterdam: Benjamins.

Meisel, J. and N. Müller 1992. Finiteness and Verb Placement in Early Child Grammars: Evidence from Simultaneous Acquisition of French and German in Bilinguals. In J. Meisel, ed., *The Acquisition of Verb Placement*. Dordrecht: Kluwer.

Mills, A.E. 1985. The Acquisition of German. In D.I. Slobin, ed., *The Crosslinguistic Study of Language Acquisition*. Hillsdale, NJ: Erlbaum.

Müller, N. 1994. Parameters Cannot Be Reset: Evidence from the Development of COMP. In J. Meisel, ed., *Bilingual first Language Acquisition*. Amsterdam: Benjamins

Peal, E. and W.E. Lambert 1962. The Relation of Bilingualism to Intelligence. *Psychological Monographs* 76.246–281.

Pinker, S. 1984. *Language Learnability and Language Development*. Cambridge, MA: Harvard University Press.

Radford, A. 1990. *Syntactic Theory and the Acquisition of English Syntax: The Nature of Early Child Grammars of English*. Oxford, UK/Cambridge, MA: Blackwell.

Redlinger, W.E. and Park, T. 1980. Language Mixing in Young Bilinguals. *Journal of Child Language* 7.337–352.

Rizzi, L. 1989. On the Format of Parameters. *The Behavioural and Brain Sciences* 12.355–356.

Saunders, G. 1988. *From Birth to Teens*. Clevedon: Multilingual Matters.

Schlyter, S. 1990. Is the Weaker Language Like L1 or L2? Some Properties of the Weaker Language in Bilingual Swedish–French Children. In V. Adelswärd and

N. Davies, eds. *På väg mot ett nytt språk.* Rapport från ASLA's höstsymposium, Linköping, 9–10 Nov. 1989. Linköping.

Schmidt-Rohr, G. 1933. *Muttersprache. Vom Amt der Sprache bei der Volkwerdung.* [Mother tongue. About the role of language in creating national unity] Jena.

Slobin, D.I. 1973. Cognitive Prerequisities for the Development of Grammar. In C.A. Ferguson & D.I. Slobin, eds., *Studies of Child Language Development.* NewYork: Holt, Rinehart and Winston.

Slobin, D.I. 1985. Why Study acquisition Crosslinguistically? In D.I Slobin, ed., *The Crossliguistic Study of Language Acquisition.* Vol.1. Hillsdale, NJ: Erlbaum.

Taeschner, T. 1983. *The Sun is Feminine: A Study on Language Acquisition in Bilingual Children.* Berlin: Springer.

Weisgerber, 1966. Vorteile und Gefahren der Zweisprachigkeit. [Advantages and dangers of bilingualism] *Wirkendes Wort* 16.73–89.

Weissenborn, J. 1990. Functional Categories and Verb Movement: The Acquisition of German Syntax Revisited. In M. Rothweiler, ed., *Spracherwerb und Grammatik. Linguistische Untersuchungen zum Erwerb von Syntax und Morphologie.* Linguistische Berichte, Sonderheft 3.

Codas, Word Minimality, and Empty-Headed Syllables

HEATHER GOAD
McGill University

1. Introduction*

In this paper, I argue that children's first word-final consonants are not codas. Instead, they are syllabified as onsets of empty-headed syllables.[1] Following from this, augmentation of CVC words to CVCV at the earliest stages in acquisition is motivated solely by the desire to avoid codas. This is counter to the hypothesis put forward in Fee (1992), that augmentation is driven by word minimality, the idea that words must minimally contain one foot (see McCarthy & Prince 1986, et seq.). The data that I discuss all come from the CV stage in acquisition. As will be seen, however, some of the words at this stage are in fact CVCV or CVC in shape. I will argue that *all* of these patterns are representative of the CV stage, henceforth called the 'subminimal stage'.

I conclude by discussing some of the problems that the subminimal stage in acquisition causes for current linguistic theory. The solution that I

---

* This research was supported by a McGill Humanities Research Grant.
[1] For all intents and purposes, we may equate the status of being the onset of an empty-headed syllable with extraprosodicity (but see Piggott 1991 for some differences; see also Kaye 1990).

put forth may be considered to be a hybrid position. I opt for a constraint-based approach to linguistic theory, as advanced in the Optimality-theoretic literature (Prince & Smolensky 1993). However, if we accept the standard view in the acquisition literature which stems from this work, that children's grammars contain the same constraints as do adult languages and that constraints are initially ranked in an order which yields unmarked structures (Demuth 1995, Gnanadesikan 1995, Pater & Paradis 1996), it becomes impossible to account for the subminimal stage in a straightforward manner. To resolve this problem, I suggest that some prosodic categories — namely the foot — mature, as has been argued for in non-optimality works such as Fikkert (1994) and Demuth & Fee (1995).

2. Extraprosodicity

The proposal that, in early stages of acquisition, children's final consonants are not syllabified as codas is not, I suggest, particularly radical. On the contrary, it is consistent with cross-linguistic observations. For example, many languages allow a wider range of consonants to appear word-finally than word-internally; the standard analysis, following Itô (1986) and others, is that the word-final consonants are not codas, but are instead licensed as 'extraprosodic'. For example, in Diola Fogny, word-internal codas are restricted to nasals and liquids that are homorganic with the following consonant, (1a) (data from Itô 1986; original source Sapir 1965). Word-finally, however, any consonant can appear, as revealed by the examples of final obstruents and glides in (1b).

(1)   **Extraprosodicity in Diola Fogny:**

    a. *Word-internal codas:*
       kaŋkan   'made'
       ninennen   'I placed'
       salte   'be dirty'

    b. *Word-final consonants:*
       kunilak   'children'
       lekujaw   'they won't go'
       /ujuk-ja/ → ujuja, *ujukja   'if you see'
       /jaw-bu-ŋar/ → jabuŋar, *jabuwŋar   'voyager'

Following Piggott (1991), I hypothesize that licensing by extraprosodicity is the unmarked case (cf. Itô 1986). Two things motivate this decision. One, codas are cross-linguistically marked constituents. Two, if the child were learning a language where word-final consonants were extraprosodic (onsets of empty-headed syllables), s/he would need to rely on indirect negative evidence to determine that final consonants are not codas. (Indirect negative evidence would not be needed for the Diola Fogny case, as the language displays morphophonemic alternation, as implied by (1b).) For example, if the child were learning Language A in (2a), but s/he had assumed that it was instead like Language B, s/he would have to notice the *absence* of words like *tepda in (2a) to realize that s/he had misanalysed the language as having word-final codas. In other words, the only way that the child could come to realize that word-internal consonants are in fact a subset of word-final consonants would be through indirect negative evidence.

(2) **No Indirect Negative Evidence:**

a. *Language A: No Word-final Codas:*

```
  σ  σ         σ  σ         σ   σ
 /|\ /\       /\  /         /|\ /\
 t e m p a    t e p         *t e p d a
```

b. *Language B: Word-final Codas:*

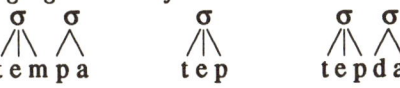

```
  σ  σ         σ            σ   σ
 /|\ /\       /|\           /|\ /\
 t e m p a    t e p         t e p d a
```

3. Augmentation and Word Minimality

Consistent with the discussion thus far, I will argue that augmentation of CVC words to CVCV is motivated solely by a constraint which prevents final consonants in the target from being syllabified as codas (NOCODA in optimality-theoretic terms). As mentioned earlier, this is counter to the hypothesis put forward in Fee (1992), that augmentation is motivated by the minimal word constraint, the idea that words must minimally contain one foot (μμ or σσ). Fee puts forward this idea to account for the fact that children's early words are commonly CVCV in shape, and often reduplicated. If the child must learn that codas are weight-bearing in English, before this point, words like 'dog' must be augmented to meet the bimoraic requirement, e.g. [dɑɡɑ] or [dɑdɑ].

Among English-speaking children, there are two common ways to augment consonant-final words. One pattern, dimunitives, is shown in (3a): a final [i] is added. The second pattern, reduplication, is exemplified in (3b): the vowel (or sometimes the entire first syllable) is copied.

(3) **Augmentation:**

a. *Dimunitives:*
Jennika at 1;4 (Ingram 1974)
'up' [api]
'out' [awti]

b. *Reduplication:*
Padmint at 1;9 (Ross 1937)
'pot' ['pɔtɔ]
'bird' ['bə:də]

Both of these patterns can be analysed as epenthesis of an empty position. This position is then filled in either by default, (3a), or by copying material already present in the root, (3b). (See Yip 1987 for discussion of the source of diminutive -y in English as epenthetic [i].)

The data for the present analysis are drawn primarily from Mollie Holmes at 18 months (Holmes 1927). From these data, we can conclude that augmentation of the type exhibited in (3) is not motivated by the need to satisfy word minimality, but instead by the prominent role that NOCODA plays in children's early grammars.

4. Mollie Holmes' Data

According to Holmes, the list of words that he provides for Mollie at 18 months is more or less complete. It contains 47 words, 32 (68%) of which correspond to monosyllabic targets (in the adult language) and 15 (32%) of which correspond to bisyllabic targets.

4.1 NOCODA in Mollie's Grammar

In Mollie's grammar, CVC targets, which make up 27 (57%) of the words attempted, can be realized in the three ways in (4): as truncated CV, as augmented CVCV, and as something akin to CVC (which we will return to in Section 4.3).

(4) **CVC Targets:**
    a. *Truncation* (CV)   b. *Augmentation* (CVCV)
       [ko] 'come'   [bɪbi] 'bib'
       [dɔ] 'dog'   [wåki] 'walk'
    c. *Final C is an Onset* (CV·C:)   d. CV *or* CV·C:
       [bæ·d:] 'bad'   [bɛ], [bɛ·t:] 'bed'
       [ke·k:] 'cake'   [gu], [gu·d:] 'good'

                                              CVCV *or* CV·C:
                                              [buki], [bu·k:] 'book'

It might appear that the CVCV and CV·C: patterns satisfy word minimality, but the persistence of the CV pattern, which is clearly subminimal, is inconsistent with this analysis. CV forms account for 50% of Mollie's outputs for CVC targets. The fact that, for some targets, CV is in free variation with CV·C: confounds the word minimality account as well; see (4d). I suggest instead that augmentation, along with truncation, is due to the inability of Mollie's grammar to syllabify final consonants as codas.

4.2 Stress and Foot Binarity in Mollie's Grammar

The word minimality account of augmentation is further complicated by the stress patterns of Mollie's words. Holmes (1927:221) observes that in all of Mollie's two-syllable words, each syllable has *equal* stress:

> There were no intervocalic consonants. The few two-syllable words which did exist were treated as *two words* — with a distinct though slight break between the two syllables. Each of these syllables received an *equal* stress; e.g. 'kitty' [tɪ-ti], 'baby' [bɛ-bɛ]. [emphasis original; glosses added]

From this description, we can conclude that Mollie's augmented words do not constitute one (left-headed) binary foot as in (5a). Her bisyllabic words must instead either be represented as in (5b), as two monomoraic feet in violation of foot binarity; or as in (5c), where the foot has not been projected. We will come back to (5b) versus (5c) in Section 6 at which point I will suggest that (5c) is the correct representation.

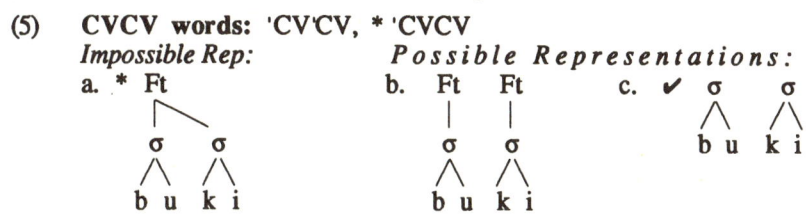

(5) **CVCV words:** 'CV'CV, * 'CVCV
Impossible Rep: *Possible Representations:*
a. * Ft   b. Ft Ft   c. ✔ σ σ
      σ σ   σ σ   b u k i
      b u k i   b u k i

4.3 Word-final Consonants in Mollie's Grammar

Thus far, I have argued that augmentation and truncation are due to the fact that Mollie's grammar does not tolerate codas. If this is true, how do we account for the presence of the final consonant in the CV.C: pattern in (4c)? I suggest that, in these forms, the final consonant is not a coda. Mollie's [bu·k:], for instance, does not have the representation in (6b). The final [k] is instead syllabified as the onset of an empty-headed syllable as in (6a).

(6) **Word-final Consonants:**
'book' [bu·k:]
a. σ σ   b. * σ
    b u k   b u k

Evidence in favour of the representation in (6a) is provided below. First, Holmes describes the production of [k]-final words as follows.

> Final *k* was definitely used, though a vowel sound was felt to be necessary after it. As a consequence the explosion of the *k* was either prolonged (almost equal to a *schwa*), or began a second syllable *ki;* e.g., [bu·k:] or [buki] (Holmes 1927:221).

Second, the lengthening pattern is always found in words which maintain their final consonant, while the augmentation and truncation patterns are never realized with length; see (7). Lengthening, I suggest, is the phonetic manifestation of the syllabification in (6a).

(7)

	Target	Licit Output	Illicit Output
a.	CVC	✔ CV·C:	* CVC
b.	CVC	✔ CVCV	* CV·C:V * CV·CV
	CVC	✔ CV	* CV·

Finally, recall from (4d) that, for some words, the CV·C: pattern is in free variation with truncation (CV) and with augmentation (CVCV), both of which I have argued are motivated by NOCODA. To conclude, all of the patterns in (4) are exemplars of the subminimal stage in acquisition.[2]

5. Optimality Theory, Maturation and Truncated Outputs

Before turning to the question of how to formalize the subminimal stage, I will begin with a brief outline of Optimality Theory (OT). OT is a research program developed by Prince & Smolensky (1993) in which rules and derivations are rejected in favour of constraints only. Inputs (underlying representations) and outputs (surface representations) are related through a set of universal, violable constraints. Individual grammars are constructed from this set of constraints only. Cross-linguistic variation is thus due to differences in constraint ranking.

The standard view in the OT literature on acquisition is that children's grammars contain the same constraints as do adult languages (Demuth 1995, Gnanadesikan 1995, Goad 1995, Pater & Paradis 1996). The differences between child language and the adult target language are handled exactly as is cross-linguistic variation: through differences in constraint ranking.

In the unmarked case, feet are binary in adult languages. Thus, to account for the truncated outputs in the subminimal stage in acquisition, we might be tempted to hypothesize that the foot has not yet matured, as illustrated in (8a). In principle, however, this should not be necessary in Optimality Theory. An important consequence of this theory is that there should be no need for maturation. The entire prosodic hierarchy is present from the outset, but constraints which are initially undominated (inviolable) force the edges of certain categories to coincide. Truncated outputs should therefore fall out of independently-motivated constraints on prosodic structure: NOCODA, in combination with constraints which force the left and right edges of a CV syllable to coincide with the left and right edges of the foot and prosodic word; see (8b).

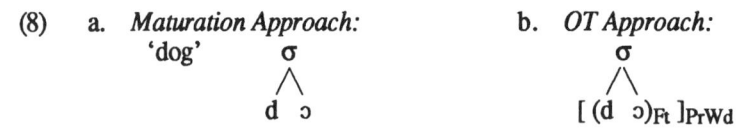

(8) a. *Maturation Approach:* b. *OT Approach:*
'dog' σ σ
 /\ /\
 d ɔ [(d ɔ)Ft]PrWd

---

[2] The data in Fey & Gandour (1982) are consistent with the analysis provided here. However, they represent the next stage in development, when codas are possible, but when they are restricted to nasals and voiceless fricatives. Stops are still syllabified as onsets: voiceless stops are released as aspirated, a highly marked feature for coda position, e.g. 'drop' [dapʰ]; voiced stops are produced with a nasal release, enabling the stop to be syllabified as an onset, e.g. 'stub' [dabm̩]. Fey & Gandour provide prosodic evidence to support the heterosyllabic status of the latter words. Thanks to Carolyn Johnson for directing me to this source.

Pater & Paradis (1995) provide an analysis along these lines for the minimal word stage, the stage during which the child's words are minimally and maximally one foot. As we will see, however, the situation is less straightforward for the subminimal stage. The constraints which are needed to obtain the result in (8b) are given in (9). (Other analyses are possible.)

(9) **Constraints for Truncated Outputs:**
Undominated Constraints:
   a. NOCODA: Codas are forbidden
   b. FILLMORA: A mora not present in the input cannot be added to the output
   c. ALIGNLEFT: Align (Ft, L, PrWd, L): The left edge of every foot must be aligned with the left edge of the prosodic word

Dominated Constraints:
   d. FTBIN: Feet are binary (at some level of analysis, µ or σ)

NOCODA, (9a), must be undominated to yield truncated forms. FILLMORA, (9b), is a member of the FILL constraint family which militates against the addition of material not present in the input (UR). This constraint yields two effects. One, it prevents the child from lengthening the vowel in a CV form to satisfy foot binarity. This is consistent with the claims made in Fee (1992) and Fikkert (1994), that in early acquisition, vowel length is not contrastive. FILLMORA will also prevent augmentation of a CVC form to CVCV.[3] ALIGNLEFT, (9c), will prevent each syllable in a candidate output from being parsed into separate feet. Finally, FTBIN in (9d) must crucially be dominated by the other constraints in (9).

Candidate outputs for /dɔg/ → [dɔ] are given in (10a-e). The optimal form is (10e), as indicated by ✔. It violates only the lower ranked FTBIN.

(10) /dɔg/ → [dɔ]	NO CODA	FILL MORA	ALIGN LEFT	FTBIN
a. [(dɔg)Ft]PrWd	*!			
b. [(dɔ:)Ft]PrWd		*!		
c. [(dɔgɔ)Ft]PrWd		*!		
d. [(dɔ)Ft (gɔ)Ft]PrWd		*!	*	**
✔ e. [(dɔ)Ft]PrWd				*

---
[3] Here, I am only concerned with Mollie's truncated forms, and not with augmented outputs which clearly violate FILLMORA. CV:, which seems to be genuinely absent at this stage, can be independently ruled out by NOLONGVOWEL. To capture the fact that there is more than one possible output for a given input in Mollie's grammar, that FILLMORA (and ALIGNLEFT) is variably violated, we can appeal to the notion of floating constraint as in Reynolds (1994).

All of the other candidates, however, violate one or more of the undominated constraints in (9a-c). Constraint violations are marked by asterisks; an exclamation mark indicates a fatal violation, the point where a candidate loses out to at least one other candidate. Solid lines separate constraints which are crucially ranked, while dotted lines separate constraints for which the ranking is indeterminate.

6. Problems

While with this analysis we obtain the desired result, there are two problems. The first concerns the role of markedness in Optimality Theory. The second concerns foot binarity and CVCV outputs at the subminimal stage. Each is addressed in turn.

6.1 Markedness in Optimality Theory

As mentioned earlier, the standard assumption in the OT acquisition literature is that, in early child language, constraints are ranked in an order which yields *unmarked* structures. Together with ONSET, both NOCODA and FTBIN reflect unmarked structures in adult languages. In child language, this should translate into an early preference for $(CVCV)_{Ft}$ words over $(CV)_{Ft}$. However, virtually all children initially show a high tolerance for CV words, including Mollie as we have seen. Recall that 50% of her CVC targets are realized as CV.

Three possible solutions to this problem are outlined below. The first is to abandon the premise that constraints are initially ranked in an order which yields unmarked structures. This severely reduces the explanatory power of the theory, and ceases to make acquisition data interesting vis-à-vis adult grammars. This should, therefore, be a last resort option.

The second option is to suggest that the subminimal stage is pre-phonology. As this stage seems to be characteristic of the child's first 50 words, this solution is reasonable to entertain. Children's grammars undergo several qualitative changes at the 50 word point, one of which could conceivably be the onset of phonology proper. One piece of evidence in support of the first 50 words as pre-phonology is that, for many children, words at this stage are of two shapes: CV and VC, but not CVC. Given that VC syllables are cross-linguistically very marked (they violate both ONSET and NOCODA), it might be the case that there is no adult-like prosodic structure available at this stage, and that words are merely composed of trough + peak (CV) or peak + trough (VC). This analysis, however, is not well-supported when we consider Mollie's productions at this stage. They seem to be governed by phonological principles typical of those we find in adult languages. Specifically, NOCODA seems to motivate not only the CV outputs of CVC words, but also the co-occurring patterns, CV·C: and CVCV.

The last option is to adopt a hybrid position, that the subminimal stage falls out of unmarked constraint ranking *and* certain prosodic constituents (specifically, the foot) mature. If the foot is initially not available, then any constraint which refers to this constituent (e.g. FTBIN) will be satisfied vacuously.

6.2 Foot Binarity and the Subminimal Stage

We turn now to the second problem for the optimality-theoretic analysis provided in (10) for truncated forms such as [dɔ]: Mollie's bisyllabic forms. As we will see, supporting evidence for the position that the foot matures comes from these forms. Recall from Section 4.2 that Holmes remarks that each syllable in Mollie's bisyllabic outputs has equal stress. If the foot has been projected, Mollie's bisyllabic forms must be parsed as follows: $(bu)_{Ft}(ki)_{Ft}$ 'book', $(kæ)_{Ft}(kæ)_{Ft}$ 'cracker'. However, these forms will never be selected as optimal; no matter how low FTBIN is ranked, is will always be better to parse [buki] as $(buki)_{Ft}$ and [kækæ] as $(kækæ)_{Ft}$. If the Foot has not yet been projected, as in (5c) above, however, the monotonic stress pattern described by Holmes is exactly what we would expect.

7. Final Remarks

In summary, I have argued that the child's first word-final consonants are not codas; they are instead syllabified as onsets of empty-headed syllables. Augmentation in CVC words is not motivated by word minimality (FTBIN) at the earliest stages in acquisition; it is instead motivated solely by NOCODA. The three patterns in (4) — where CVC targets are realized as truncated (CV), augmented (CVCV), and with the final consonant being syllabified as an onset (CV·C:) — are *all* exemplars of the subminimal stage. At this stage in development, the foot has not yet been projected.

As a final comment, it has been proposed by Gnanadesikan (1995) that structural constraints (e.g. NOCODA) outrank faithfulness constraints (specifically PARSE) in early child language. The data from Mollie reveal that this position must be reassessed. Through syllabifying the final consonant in CVC words as an onset as well as through augmentation, Mollie is faithful both to the input and to markedness considerations.

References

Demuth, Katherine. 1995. Markedness and the Development of Prosodic Structure. *NELS* 25:13-25.

Demuth, Katherine and E. Jane Fee. 1995. Minimal Words in Early Phonological Development. Ms., Brown University and Dalhousie University.

Fee, E. Jane. 1992. Exploring the Minimal Word in Early Phonological Acquisition. *Proceedings of the 1992 Annual Conference of the Canadian Linguistic Association.*

Fey, Marc and Jack Gandour. 1982. Rule Discovery in Phonological Acquisition. *Journal of Child Language* 9:71-81.

Fikkert, Paula. 1991. *On the Acquisition of Prosodic Structure.* Holland Institute of Generative Linguistics.

Gnanadesikan, Amalia. 1995. Markedness and Faithfulness Constraints in Child Phonology. Ms., Rutgers University.

Goad, Heather. 1995. Consonant Harmony in Child Language: An Optimality-theoretic Account. To appear in S.J. Hannahs and Martha Young-Scholten, eds., *Generative Studies in the Acquisition of Phonology.* Amsterdam: John Banjamins.

Holmes, Urban T. 1927. The Phonology of an English-speaking Child. *American Speech* 2:219-225.

Ingram, David. 1974. Phonological Rules in Young Children. *Journal of Child Language* 1:49-64.

Ingram, David. 1978. The Role of the Syllable in Phonological Development. In Alan Bell and Joan B. Hooper, eds., *Syllables and Segments.* Amsterdam: North-Holland, pp. 143-155.

Itô, Junko. 1986. *Syllable Theory in Prosodic Phonology.* Doctoral dissertation, University of Massachusetts, Amherst.

Kaye, Jonathan. 1990. 'Coda' Licensing. *Phonology* 7:301-330.

McCarthy, J. and A. Prince. 1986. Prosodic Morphology. Ms., University of Massachusetts, Amherst and Brandeis University.

Pater, Joe and Johanne Paradis. 1996. Truncation without Templates in Child Phonology. To appear in *Proceedings of the Boston University Conference on Language Development.*

Piggott, Glyne L. 1991. Apocope and the Licensing of Empty-headed Syllables. *The Linguistic Review* 8:287-318.

Prince, Alan and Paul Smolensky. 1993. Optimality Theory: Constraint Interaction in Generative Grammar. Ms., University of Massachusetts, Amherst and Rutgers University.

Reynolds, William. 1994. *Variation and Phonological Theory.* Doctoral dissertation, University of Pennsylvania.

Ross, A.S.C. 1937. An Example of Vowel-Harmony in a Young Child. *Modern Language Notes* 52:508-509.

Yip, Moira. 1987. English Vowel Epenthesis. *Natural Language and Linguistic Theory* 5:463-484.

Pronominal Reference in 3-Year-Olds' Narratives

NORMA JEAN GOMME & CAROLYN E. JOHNSON
University of British Columbia

1. Introduction

The general purpose of our study was to investigate the way 3-year-old English-speaking children use pronouns to refer to characters in a narrative. Our study essentially replicates part of Michael Bamberg's (1987) study of German-speaking children, using a form:function approach to explore the forms children use to refer to the protagonists in Mercer *Mayer's Frog, where are you?* (1969). Like Bamberg, we were interested in children's development of narrative coherence and their use of specific linguistic forms to demonstrate their knowledge of narrative structure. Our research fits within the more general contexts of the crosslinguistic study of children's development of narrative coherence, as described by Ruth Berman and Dan Slobin (1994), and a functional approach to children's acquisition of linguistic forms.

With respect to narrative development, experimental evidence demonstrates that children use a narrative schema in comprehension and recall tasks by the time they are 3 to 4 years old (Hudson & Shapiro, 1991). On the other hand, the stories 3-year-olds tell do not exhibit this level of knowledge when they are evaluated in terms of either story grammar components or conventional use of linguistic forms to indicate story structure. Like Bamberg, we reason that a child who has a conceptual representation of narrative structure is likely to express it in some way, using linguistic forms within her control in ways that may not fit the adult system.

One way to make a story coherent is to organize it around a character. The story is about that character's problems, emotional and intentional states, actions, whereabouts, and so on. Within this organization, all references to this character signal his stable identity through the narrative, starting with a first identification and followed with reference-maintaining devices. Once the protagonist is identified at the beginning of the story, maintaining reference is a means of expressing the thematic development of the story and creating the cohesion in the text that shows it is a unified whole. An adult typically introduces a protagonist using a full nominal expression, such as "a boy," and subseqently refers to him with the anaphoric pronoun, "him"; if introduction of a new character intervenes between mentions, the protagonist would be called "THE boy" to avoid ambiguity. A major motivation for looking at this particular way to anchor and organize a narrative is that children can use pronouns anaphorically by the time they are three (Ervin-Tripp & Miller, 1977).

Bamberg found that the 3 1/2-year-old German-speaking children in his study used what he called a "thematic advancement strategy." Once they had identified the boy as the main protagonist, they tended to refer to him with a pronoun, regardless of whether they were maintaining reference to him or switching reference back to him after mentioning another character. This use of anaphora sounds incompetent and ambiguous to adult ears, but is systematic, intentional, and persistent. Bamberg interprets it as a "global strategy," because "the function of referring devices is established for the text as a whole" (p. 97). The children used the pronominal form to advance the thematic progression; they used nominal forms for characters who interrupted the advancement of thematic progress. Because the specific linguistic forms used to mark narrative structure may vary across languages, we judged that it would be interesting to investigate whether English-speaking children used pronouns the same way the German children did. This provides the first specific goal of our research:

1. To determine whether the English-speaking children in our study used the same thematic advancement strategy as the 3-year-old German-speaking children Michael Bamberg (1987) studied.

Further specific goals were:

2. To compare the children's referential use of pronouns before and after they were familiar with the story, and

3. To compare our results with Annette Karmiloff-Smith's (1980, 1981), especially to resolve differences between her study and Bamberg's regarding (a) the age at which children move from deictic to referential use of pronouns, and (b) the precise nature of the thematic advancement strategy.

Karmiloff-Smith studied both English- and French-speaking children, using a much shorter and simpler story. She concluded that children used a thematic advancement strategy at age 6, with only deictic use of pronouns before that age. She also posited a "thematic subject strategy"; the 6-year-olds used pronouns only in utterance-initial position and only to refer to the main protagonist.

2. Method

We designed our study to replicate Bamberg's and to fit the methodology described in Berman and Slobin's (1994) book, *Relating Events in Narrative*. It involves the analysis of *Frog, where are you?* narratives told by ten 3-year-olds.

The six girls and four boys--all monolingual speakers of English from the UBC Child Study Centre preschool--ranged in age from 3;2 to 3;9, as shown in Table 1. After getting to know the children in their classrooms, the experimenter invited each child out to a space outside the room to tell the story. She encouraged the children to become familiar with

TABLE 1. Age of Subjects at Time of First Story Elicitation (T_1)

Girls	Age at T_1	Boys	Age at T_1
S1	3;8.12	S5	3;9.12
S2	3;5.17	S7	3;3.5
S3	3;8.5	S8	3;4.22
S4	3;6.2	S9	3;6.18
S6	3;6.2		
S10	3;2.3		

Age range: 3;2.3-3;9.12

the book before telling the story and invited them to tell the story more than once. The book was then sent home with each child for a week, during which the parents had agreed to read the book with the child at least four times.

The child was audio and video recorded telling the story after this week, again invited to tell the story more than once. This part of the data collection is consistent with Bamberg but differs from the Berman and Slobin methodology. We agreed with Bamberg that this was an important step, because young children need the opportunity to cognitively organize the sequenced pictures into a narrative schema before they can provide a narrative text. Unlike Bamberg, however, we analyzed the stories recorded at both the first and second sessions, choosing the best version of the story told during each session. What counted as "best story" was the one most complete in terms of Berman's (1988) six basic story schema elements: (1) the Initial Event Chain (which is the onset of the problem) including (a) the frog leaving the jar, and (b) the protagonists discovering that the frog was gone; (2) the Search Motif (or goal), where the protagonists search for the escaped frog; and (3) the 3-part End, or resolution of the problem, which includes (a) the boy finding the frog, (b) the boy taking the frog, and (c) the frog being the same as or a substitute for the missing frog.

3. Analyses and Results

To test our first hypothesis, which was that our 3-year-olds would use a global thematic advancement strategy in their narratives, we coded all instances of anaphoric reference to the two main characters of the story (the boy and the dog) according to their form (pronominal, full nominal, or ellipsis) and their function (switch reference or maintain reference) at each of Time 1 and Time 2. "Switch reference" refers to introduction of a character into the story, or reintroduction of a character after other characters or events intervene. "Maintain reference" refers to a subsequent mention of a character after his introduction or reintroduction with no interruption by mention of other characters. The raw counts for each pairing of form and function are shown in Table 2. The columns in and out of parentheses differ by inclussion or exclusion of joint reference to the boy and dog. We separated these because we wanted to include them, but we also wanted to compare our results with Bamberg, who did not include joint reference.

In Table 2, the summed data excluding joint reference show that, out of 166 references exclusively to the boy or the dog, 92 (or 55%) referred to the boy and 74 (or 45%) referred to the dog at Time 1. At Time 2, 61% of the 207 references were exclusively to the boy and 39% to the dog. The trend in the data to refer to the boy more often than to the dog is consistent with Bamberg's data, which also showed that--although the boy and the dog are depicted in approximately the same number of pictures--there is a greater tendency to refer to the boy. This may reflect and support the children's apparent decision to choose the boy as the protagonist of the story.

The summed data in Table 2 also show that, regardless of inclusion of joint reference, the children strongly preferred to use pronouns to refer to

TABLE 2. Number of Nominal, Pronominal, and Elliptical References to the Boy and the Dog at T_1 and T_2, Joint Reference Included (and Joint Reference Excluded)

	Switch T1	Switch T2	Maintain T1	Maintain T2	Sum T1	Sum T2
To the boy:						
Nominal	14 (13)	10 (10)	-- (--)	1 (1)	14 (13)	11 (11)
Pronominal	56 (46)	88 (67)	35 (26)	42 (36)	91 (72)	131(103)
Ellipsis	3 (3)	4 (4)	4 (4)	9 (8)	7 (7)	13 (12)
Sum	73 (62)	102 (81)	39 (30)	53 (45)	112(92)	155(126)
To the dog:						
Nominal	40 (39)	24 (24)	-- (--)	3 (3)	41 (41)	27 (27)
Pronominal	25 (15)	40 (19)	26 (26)	41 (41)	51 (51)	81 (81)
Ellipsis	-- (--)	-- (--)	3 (3)	3 (3)	3 (3)	3 (3)
Sum	65 (54)	64 (43)	29 (20)	47 (38)	94 (74)	111(81)
Sum to the boy and dog	138(116) 166(124)		68 (50) 100 (83)		206(166) 266(201)	

the boy at both times (81% at Time 1 and 85% at Time 2 when joint reference is included, 78% at Time 1 and 82% at Time 2 when joint reference is excluded). This is also consistent with Bamberg's results, although our results show an even greater preference for pronominal reference to the boy. Bamberg found only 53% of references to the boy were pronominal.

For reference to the dog, the children did not show a clear preference to use either nominal or pronominal forms. When joint reference is excluded, there was a slight preference for the nominal form at Time 1 (53%), but there was a preference for the pronoun at Time 2 (64% in this case). This contrasts with Bamberg's results, which showed a preference for referring to the dog with nominal expressions (61%). The children used pronominals to refer to the dog more often when joint reference to the boy and dog is included. This may indicate that, when they referred to the boy and dog jointly, the children were adhering to the strategy reserved for reference to the boy, overriding the strategy for referring to the dog.

The next analytic step was to determine the distribution of form with respect to function for the boy and the dog. Going beyond Bamberg's study, we subjected the group data to parametric statistical tests using the standard normal distribution (z distribution) and setting the level of significance at 0.05 to test hypotheses that involved proportions (Triola, 1992).

At both Time 1 and Time 2 significantly more than half of the expressions used to switch reference to the boy were pronominal in form, supporting Bamberg's proposal of preferred use of the pronoun to refer to the chosen protagonist of the story. On the other hand, the children did not make as clear a distinction between use of pronominals and nominals (which they preferred at Time 1 but not Time 2) to switch reference to the dog as the German-speaking children did. (This may be due to a difference between the languages or the fact that the average age of the children in our study was lower than in Bamberg's. The youngest child in his study was 3;6.) However, our children did use significantly more pronouns to switch reference to the boy than to the dog, supporting the notion that they were treating the two characters differently.

Next we looked at the maintain reference function and the forms used to fill it for the boy and the dog. Our expectation was that the children would use pronominal forms to maintain reference to all characters. In other words, once a character was established or reestablished by a switch reference, the children should have strongly preferred to use pronouns to make further reference, regardless of the character involved. Our results are consistent with our expectation. According to Bamberg, this usage may be how children learn to select the form that is most appropriate to avoid amibiguity at the local level. Overall, our results support our hypothesis and are like Bamberg's.

Our next set of measurements was designed to determine whether and how performance changed from Time 1 to Time 2, when the children were more familiar with the story. First we examined the proportion of pronominal reference used to switch reference to the boy for change between Time 1 and Time 2. This is a key element of the thematic advancement strategy, so should reflect any change in the children's application of the strategy in their storytelling. Although there was an increase at Time 2, this did not reach significance. Looking at the maintain reference function, there was no significant difference between Time 1 and Time 2 in the preference for pronouns to refer to the boy and the dog, but the use of pronouns in this function was already very high at Time 1.

We used three other measures to indicate the children's ability to tell a "good" story at both Time 1 and Time 2: (1) the percentage of clauses contributing to thematic advancement, (2) mean length of clause (based on just those clauses that contributed to thematic advancement), and (3) the presence or absence of Berman's six basic story elements. The percentage of thematic advancement clauses showed a wide range across all subjects (14% to 60% in the first telling, and 46% to 79% in the second telling), as shown in Table 3. For all the children but Subject 1, the percentage of thematic advancement clauses was higher on the second telling. When the data was summed for all subjects, there was a significantly higher percentage of clauses contributing to thematic advancement at Time 2. Further, except for two subjects (1 and 3) the total number of clauses at Time 2 was lower that at Time 1. This means that for the most part children were telling shorter, more focused stories at Time 2.

The mean length of clause (MLC) for each subject at each time is shown in Table 4. Again there is variation among subjects. Seven subjects

TABLE 3. Total Number of Clauses and Number of Thematic Advancement Clauses at Each Telling; Percentage of Total Clauses Contributing to Advancement of the Story Theme at T_1 amd T_2

Subject	# Clauses T_1	# Clauses T_2	# Thematic adv. clauses T_1	# Thematic adv. clauses T_2	% Thematic adv. clauses T_1	% Thematic adv. clauses T_2
S1	73	97	44	48	60	49
S2	45	34	18	20	40	59
S3	69	141	30	78	43	55
S4	82	46	43	35	52	76
S5	56	42	20	27	36	64
S6	69	29	10	23	14	79
S7	62	37	17	17	27	46
S8	66	51	29	27	44	53
S9	60	44	13	33	22	75
S10	57	40	24	19	42	48
All subjects	639	561	248	327	40	58

TABLE 4. Mean Length of Clause (Words)* at T_1 and T_2

	S1	S2	S3	S4	S5	S6
T_1	4.1	3.8	4.9	5.7	6.2	5.4
T_2	4.4	6.7	5.4	5.8	4.7	6.2

	S6	S7	S8	S9	S10
T_1	5.4	6.2	5.2	4.4	4.9
T_2	6.2	5.2	5.7	5.4	4.4

*Measured over clauses that contributed to thematic development

increased their mean length of clause from Time 1 to Time 2, and three decreased their MLC. Overall there is a trend toward longer clauses at Time 2, a rough indication that the children used more complex language when they were familiar with the story.

The final measure is shown in Table 5. The six story elements considered basic to a "good" story are listed below the table. We expected that children should include more of these elements at Time 2, after hearing

TABLE 5. "Goodness" of Stories, as Determined by Presence/Absence of Six Basic Story Elements* at T_1 and T_2

	\multicolumn{7}{c}{T_1 Story elements}	\multicolumn{7}{c}{T_2 Story elements}
	1	2	3	4	5	6	T	1	2	3	4	5	6	T
S1	√	√	√	√	–	√	5	√	–	√	–	√	√	4
S2	√	–	√	√	–	–	3	√	–	√	√	√	√	5
S3	√	√	–	√	–	–	3	√	√	√	√	√	√	6
S4	√	√	√	√	–	–	4	–	√	√	√	√	√	5
S5	√	–	√	√	–	–	3	√	√	√	√	√	–	5
S6	√	–	–	√	–	–	2	√	–	√	√	–	–	3
S7	√	–	–	√	–	–	2	√	–	√	√	–	–	3
S8	√	–	√	√	–	–	3	√	√	√	√	√	–	5
S9	√	–	–	√	–	–	2	√	√	√	√	√	–	5
S10	–	√	–	√	–	–	2	√	√	√	√	√	–	5

*Story schema elements:
1. Frog leaves jar
2. Protagonist(s) discover frog's absence
3. Protagonists search for frog
4. Boy finds frog
5. Boy takes frog
6. Frog is same or substitute frog

an adult model over the week between recordings. This held true for all but one child (again, S1). Three children increased their number of elements by three, three children by two, and three children by one. This indicates that the children were generally able to produce more complete stories after being exposed to an adult model.

Overall, we see a trend toward children telling more developmentally advanced stories at Time 2. They produce longer clauses, more efficient thematic advancement, and more story schema elements, although there was no correlation among these measures (Pearson correlation coefficient). This supports the proposed idea that with exposure to an adult model, children have a greater opportunity to reveal in their productions what they know about stories. It also can be taken to support other research conclusions that young children tell better stories in a story retelling task than a story generation task (Merritt & Liles, 1987), where our Time 1 is equivalent to story generation and our Time 2 is story retelling. However, as we noted earlier, the children did not change their pronominal reference strategy from Time 1 to Time 2. Indeed, Bamburg found that the thematic advancement strategy persisted over several years in his cross-sectional sample of German children.

Our last measures allowed us to compare our results with Karmiloff-Smith's. Karmiloff-Smith interpreted her data to indicate that children under the age of 6 were using pronouns deictically, not anaphorically. Her main argument was that most utterances that contained pronouns were isolated statements, static picture descriptions with no apparent intention on the part of the child to link them linguistically. The only evidence she offered was (1) high frequency of spatial deictic forms, and (2) high frequency of pointing accompanying pronoun use. Because most of our subjects were video taped as well as audio taped, we can use our data to address Karmiloff-Smith's claim.

Simply counting the number of pronouns accompanied by point is not informative due to the nature of the experimental task, which promoted the accompaniment of utterances with point. So we compared the points that accompanied pronouns with the number of points that accompanied nouns. We also compared the number of deictic expressions that were and were not accompanied by pointing. These included *this, that, these, see, look, I see, there's* and *(right) there*. The data are from the seven of our children who were video taped at both sessions.

The results are telling, showing that there was no significant difference in the distribution of point with pronouns and full nominals at either time. In contrast, at both times, significantly more deictic terms were accompanied by point than were not. We conclude that pronouns are not being treated as deictic terms, but rather as referential terms. We do not mean to say that pronouns do not have a deictic in addition to referential function, and a study by Tomasello and colleagues (1984/85) shows that children even younger than ours point with pronouns more frequently than nouns when adults feign noncomprehension of a child's request. The difference between the results of our study and theirs can be taken as support for the proposal central to this study--that the pronouns found within the context of the narrative task are serving functions constrained and guided by global aspects of the narrative, that is, the creation of coherence within the text.

Karmiloff-Smith's other proposal is that when children using the thematic advancement strategy utter a pronoun in clause-initial position, it is reserved for reference to the protagonist. In our study, even when the pronominal references in initial position to the boy alone are summed with the joint pronominal references to the boy and the dog, these only constitute 105 of 204 (or 51%) of all pronouns in initial position. This contrasts dramatically with Karmiloff-Smith's claim. An interesting related result, which we do not have space to go into in detail, is that many of the remaining initial pronouns maintain reference in a very local way when a character *other* than the boy has been mentioned with a full nominal and there are no intervening characters.

When we limited our look at clause-initial pronouns to those from the perspective of reference to the boy, we found that 86% of the pronouns were in clause-initial position. In addition, 56% of the pronouns used to switch reference to the boy were in initial position. This shows that the clause-initial position was in fact special for the protagonist of the story, even if not to the extent Krmiloff-Smith predicted. We attributed our overall lower figures to the complexity of the frog story, which includes a number of episodes in which the boy was not the main focus and the children chose another character as the agent of the act, often with the boy as patient, so grammatical object.

4. Conclusion

Our study gives credit to these young children for their developing abilities to manage the narrative production task from a variety of perspectives. In particular, it provides evidence that 3-year-old English-speaking children do pay attention to aspects of local cohesion and textual coherence in their narratives. What is more, these children were able to demonstrate their knowledge of narratives and linguistic structure and function while telling a story, a task that is far from simple.

This study demonstrates the importance of form:function approaches in examining the development of the referential system and, indeed, language development in general. Investigation of the functions served by referential forms in the narratives allowed us to demonstrate 3-year-olds' relatively sophisticated strategy for creating both local cohesion and textual coherence. It also allows us to account, in a principled way, for the children's use of the referential system, which in a purely formal framework would look highly variable and immature.

References

Bamberg, Michael. 1987. *The Acquisition of Narratives*. Berlin: Mouton de Gruyter.

Berman, Ruth. 1988. On the Ability to Relate Events in Narrative. *Discourse Processes* 11:469-497.

Berman, Ruth and Dan Slobin. 1994. *Relating Events in Narrative*. Hillsdale, NJ: Lawrence Erlbaum.

Ervin-Tripp, Susan and Wick Miller. 1977. Early Discourse: Some Questions about Questions, in M. Lewis & L.A. Rosenblum, eds., *Interaction, Conversation, and the Development of Language*. New York: Wiley.

Hudson, Judith and L. Shapiro. 1991. From knowing to telling: The Development of Children's Scripts, Stories and Personal Narratives, in A. McCabe & C. Peterson, eds., *Developing Narrative Structure*. Hillsdale, NJ: Lawrence Erlbaum.

Karmiloff-Smith, Annette. 1980. Psychological Processes Underlying Pronominalisation and Non-pronominalisation in Children's Connected Discourse, in J. Kreiman & A. E. Ojeda, eds., *Papers from the Parasession on Pronouns and Anaphora*. Chicago: Chicago Linguistic Society.

Karmiloff-Smith, Annette. 1981. The Grammatical Marking of Thematic Structure in the Development of Language Production, in W. Deutsch, ed., *The Child's Construction of Language*. London: Academic Press.

Mayer, Mercer. 1969. *Frog, Where Are You?* Hong Kong: South China Printing Company.

Merritt, D. and B. Liles. 1987. Story Grammar Ability in Children With and Without Language Disorder: Story Generation, Story Retelling and Story Comprehension. *Journal of Speech and Hearing Research* 30:539-552.

Tomasello, Michael, D. Anselmi, & M. J. Farrar. 1984/85. Young Children's Coordination of Gestural and Linguistic Reference. *First Language* 5:199-210.

Triola, M.S. 1992. *Elementary Statistics*, 5th ed.. Reading, MA: Addison-Wesley.

The Acquisition of Controlled PRO: A Crosslinguistic Perspective

HELEN GOODLUCK, ARHONTO TERZI, & GEMA CHOCONO DÍAZ
University of Ottawa, CUNY-Lehman, & Ortega y Gasset Institute, Madrid

1. PRO and pro in Greek and Spanish

Greek and Spanish are both pro-drop languages with nonlexically realized subjects in main and subordinate tensed clauses. They also both have controlled PRO, namely, the subject empty category that is obligatorily associated with an argument of the main clause.

Greek and Spanish differ in the distribution of pro and PRO, however. Greek has no infinitives. Some verbs, such as *thelo* meaning WANT[1], select a subjunctive complement which licenses a pro subject; thus, the embedded empty subject can be interpreted as referring either to the main clause subject or to an entity not mentioned in the sentence, as shown by the indices in (1a). By contrast, verbs such as *prospatho*, meaning TRY, select for a subjunctive complement whose subject is PRO; the latter obligatorily refers to the main clause subject, as shown in (1b) (see Terzi 1992, 1996; Varlokosta and Hornstein 1993 on the bipartition of subjunctive clauses with respect to whether their subject is pro or PRO.)

(1) a. I Maria$_i$ theli pro$_{i/j}$ na tragoudisi.
    Mary wants pro SUB sings
    'Mary wants (him/her) to sing.'

   b. I Maria$_i$ prospathi PRO$_{i/*j}$ na tragoudisi.
    Mary tries PRO SUB sings
    'Mary tries to sing.'

In Spanish a distinction in the selection of pro and PRO is made according to whether the complement is subjunctive or infinitival. Subjunctives license a pro subject, which is *obligatorily* disjoint in reference from the subject of the main clause, whereas infinitives license PRO with obligatory control by an argument of the main clause. Although there are lexically-based restrictions on the distribution of PRO and pro in Spanish, the verbs *querer* (WANT) and *intentar* (TRY) are not distinguished in this regard, as illustrated by the examples in (2a-b):

(2) a. María$_i$ quiere/intenta PRO$_i$ cantar.
    Mary wants/tries PRO sing-INF
    'Mary wants/tries to sing.'

   b. María$_i$ quiere/intenta que pro$_j$ cante.
    Mary wants/tries Comp pro sings-SUB
    'Mary wants/tries (for) someone else to sing.'

The central issue addressed here is how sensitive to the above distinctions children's grammars are. By comparing the performance of children learning the two languages, we hoped to shed light on the relative force of the lexical semantics of the matrix control verb vs. the morphology (tense/mood) of complement clauses in the development of PRO.

We concentrated on the verbs meaning WANT and TRY because these verbs represent core cases of non-obligatory vs. obligatory control. To an English or Greek speaker it very often seems that the meaning of TRY should mandate obligatory control; however the facts of Spanish show otherwise, since only when TRY is construed with an infinitival complement is there obligatory control. Although the Spanish case demonstrates that the meaning of TRY does not mandate obligatory control, there is long-standing debate concerning the contribution of semantic factors to the distribution of PRO. The agentive role of the subject of TRY plausibly promotes the selection of PRO for that verb (for pertinent discussion see, for example, Jackendoff 1972: 207-226, and Williams 1989, the latter as reported and discussed in Vanden Wyngaerd 1994). Given that the meaning of TRY may promote obligatory control in a manner that the meaning of WANT does not, it might be hypothesized that there is a general stage in which lexical semantics determine control. One consequence might be for Spanish-speaking children to go through a stage in which there is disjoint reference of the main and subordinate clause subjects for WANT but not for TRY. A combination of lexical and morphological factors (see the next paragraph) might also lead to a delay in the acquisition of disjoint reference in subjunctive complements to TRY in Spanish.

With respect to subordinate clause morphology, controlled PRO has traditionally been associated with infinitives rather than finite clauses, an observation formalized in Chomsky's (1981) PRO theorem. Thus, controlled PRO in subjunctive clauses in Greek can be regarded as a marked case. Accepting that PRO is standardly licensed in infinitival clauses, it might be hypothesized that controlled PRO in Greek subjunctives will be a relatively late acquisition.

2. Experiments

Twenty-three 4-5 year old Greek-speaking children and thirty-three 4-7 year old Spanish-speaking children were each tested on two experiments. The first test was a picture verification task, in which subjects were read a short (two or three sentence) story, the last sentence of which involved the verb WANT or TRY followed by an embedded complement clause. The subject's task was to say whether the picture fitted the story they had heard. The embedded clause verb was in the subjunctive in Greek (3) and was either a subjunctive or an infinitive in Spanish, (4) and (5).

(3) O Yiannis pige me to skilo tou stin agora. O Yiannis agorase lahanika. O skilos tou *ithele/prospathise* na agorasi ena kokalo.

(4) Juan y su perro fueron al mercado. Juan compró verdura. Después su perro *quiso/intentó* que comprase un hueso.

(5) Juan y su perro fueron al mercado. Juan compró verdura. Después su perro *quiso/intentó* comprar un hueso.[2]

'John and his dog went to the market. John bought vegetables. Then his dog *wanted/tried* buy-INF/SUB a bone.'

Subjects were asked to judge the acceptability of a sentence-external interpretation of the complement subject, viz. of an interpretation in which the action of the subordinate clause was performed by an individual other than the individual that was the subject of the WANT/TRY sentence.[3] Such a situation is illustrated by the picture in (6),

(6)

The correct answer in adult Greek was to say that the picture fitted the sentence when the main verb was WANT, as this verb allows for external reference of the embedded subject (cf. the indices in (1)) but that the picture did not fit when the main verb was TRY (cf. (2)).[4] In the case of Spanish, by contrast, the correct answer was to say that the picture fitted the sentence when the complement of either WANT or TRY was in the subjunctive and to say that the picture did not fit when the complement was infinitival. Each child received four stimuli with WANT and four with TRY; in the Spanish version of the experiment, two stimuli for each verb were in the subjunctive and two were infinitival.

The second experiment was an act-out task, in which subjects acted out with a doll family WANT and TRY sentences with the subjunctive in Greek (7) and, in the case of Spanish, with both subjunctive (8) and infinitival complements (9).

(7) a. O babas theli na fai ti banana. (Greek)
'Daddy wants (him/her) to eat the banana.'

b. I Maria prospathi na krifti piso apo ton tiho.
'Mary tries to hide behind the wall.'

(8) a. Papá quiere que de una voltereta. (Spanish)
'Daddy wants him/her to do a somersault'

b. Papá intenta que lea un libro.
'Daddy tries that he/she reads a book.'

(9) a. María quiere ir a dormir.
'Mary wants to go sleep.'

b. María intenta beber una coca cola.
'Mary tries to drink a coke.'

Subjects responded to three tokens each of the sentence types in (7), (8) and (9).

3. Results

A total of 17 out of the 23 Greek-speaking 4-5 year olds showed a sensitivity to the WANT/TRY distinction on one or both tasks in the sense that they allowed external reference for the complements of WANT sentences more frequently that for those of TRY.[5] In the act-out, there was 70% choice of the main clause subject as complement subject for WANT, as compared to 98% for TRY. However, although this distinction was made, the Greek children favored internal reference for the pro subject of the WANT complement sentences. That is, children showed a tendency for internal reference in both tasks, patterning with the adult interpretive preference in this respect (see Goodluck and Terzi 1996 for more details of the Greek results).

Tables 1 and 2 present the results of the Spanish experiments, which have not been reported before. At age 4-5 (N=15), Spanish-speaking children performed poorly on both tasks. Unlike adults, they tended to incorrectly accept external interpretation of the complement subject in infinitival clauses on the picture verification task (83% acceptance for WANT and 67% acceptance for TRY) and to incorrectly act out the embedded subject of subjunctive clauses as coreferential with the main clause subject (89% of responses for WANT and 96% of responses for TRY).

At age 6-7 (N=18), performance on the picture verification task moves down to 56% and 30% acceptance of external construal of the embedded subject in infinitival clauses for WANT and TRY respectively (acceptance is incorrect). On the act-out task, the 6-7 year olds correctly selected an external referent for the embedded subject of a subjunctive clause in 54% of their responses to WANT sentences and in 44% of their responses to TRY sentences, as compared to virtually no external act-outs at age 4-5. The difficulty Spanish-speaking children have with obligatory disjoint reference replicates the results of Padilla (1990).

Anovas performed on the scores for acceptance of the external reading of the embedded subject in the picture verification task and on the number of sentence internal interpretations of the embedded subject in the act-out task revealed a clear difference in the effects of subordinate clause morphology and verb semantics. On both tasks there was a highly significant effect of subjunctive vs. infinitival

Table 1
SPANISH PICTURE VERIFICATION TASK
PERCENTAGE ACCEPTANCE OF EXTERNAL READING OF
THE EMBEDDED SUBJECT

	WANT-sub	WANT-inf*	TRY-sub	TRY-inf*
Child 4-5 (n=15)	80%	83%	87%	67%
Child 6-7 (n=18)	89%	56%	86%	30%
Adult (n=8)	88%	19%	75%	19%

* Acceptance is incorrect

Table 2
SPANISH ACT OUT TASK
PERCENTAGE INTERNAL AND EXTERNAL CONSTRUAL OF
THE EMBEDDED SUBJECT[!]

	WANT-sub I* / E	WANT-inf I / E*	TRY-sub I* / E	TRY-inf I / E*
Child 4-5 (n=15)	89% / 9%	100% / 0%	96% / 4%	100% / 0%
Child 6-7 (n=18)	46% / 54%	98% / 2%	56% / 44%	100% / 0%
Adult (n=8)	0% / 100%	100% / 0%	4% / 96%	100% / 0%

! Percentages of I and E do not always total 100, due to unscorable responses
* Incorrect response

morphology, and on neither task was there a significant effect of WANT vs TRY (morphology/picture verification: (F(1,31)=33.63, p<.0001; morphology/act-out: F(1,31)=26.40, p<.0001; WANT-TRY/picture verification: F(1,31) = 2.06, p>.16; WANT-TRY/act-out: F(1,31)=3.17, p >.08). Age group fell short of significant as a main effect for the picture verification task (F(1,31)=3.93, p<.06), but interacted significantly with infinitive vs. subjunctive morphology for that task (F(1,31)=15.93, p <.0004). In the act-out, there was a main effect of age (F(1,31) =16.00, p <.0004) as well as a significant interaction of age with infinitive vs. subjunctive morphology (F(1,31)=13.59, p <.0009). In the picture verification test there was a significant interaction between subjunctive/infinitive morphology and WANT-TRY (F(1,31)=6.77, p <.02), reflecting the fact that performance was better for the TRY-infinitive condition than for the WANT-infinitive condition.

While the stimuli were highly similar or identical (language differences aside) in the Greek and Spanish experiments, there was a difference in the training we gave Greek and Spanish children on the act-out task. In piloting in Greek, we found it very difficult to get even adult speakers of that language to "see" the external reference reading for the subject of the complement to WANT. In the final version of the experiments, three sentences with the verb meaning ORDER, without a direct object (i.e. the equivalent of "John ordered to go") were presented for act-out immediately before the three sentences with WANT, which were then followed by the three tokens with TRY. Such sentences with ORDER are semi-ungrammatical in Greek (as they are in English). Maratsos (1974) found that English-speaking children tend to act out sentences lacking a main clause object that normally controls PRO with sentence-external reference of the complement subject. By including such sentences with ORDER in the Greek experiment immediately before the three WANT sentences, we intended to point children towards the possibility of external reference, and we were successful in doing so, to the extent that the difference in proportion of internal reference for the subject of the complement to WANT and TRY was highly significant for the Greek children. That is, although the Greek children preferred internal reference for both WANT and TRY, they did give significantly less internal reference for WANT than for TRY. When we tested Spanish adults, these speakers had no problem (aside from a smallish proportion of errors on the picture verification task) in giving external reference for the subject of subjunctive complements, with no special training required (see the last row of Tables 1 and 2). We presented the act-out materials to the children as we had to the Spanish adults, in three blocks of one token of each sentence type tested. We considered the possibility that the poor performance of the Spanish children on obligatory disjoint reference might be ameliorated if children were given more training to go outside the sentence. In a follow-up with 14 4-5 year olds, we administered the picture verification and act-out experiments again, with a modification in the presentation of the act-out materials. The child was presented with three ORDER sentences with no object (as in Greek and English, a marginal construction at best), followed by the three WANT subjunctive sentences, followed by the three TRY subjunctive sentences, next the three WANT infinitive sentences and finally the three TRY infinitive sentences.

The results of the follow-up are given in Tables 3 and 4. This group of 4-5 year olds did rather better on the picture verification task than those in the first experiment, although the two groups of 4-5 year olds did not differ significantly in terms of number of correct responses on that task. The infinitive-subjunctive difference misses significance ($F(1,13)=4.37$, $p<.06$) but the WANT-TRY distinction reaches significance ($F(1,13)=5.03$, $p<.05$), reflecting a lesser willingness to accept external reference for TRY; there was no significant interaction between morphology and WANT-TRY. On the act-out performance improved considerably in comparison to the 4-5 year olds in the first act-out experiment. The percentage internal and external reference for the PRO/pro subject is given in Table 4. Both WANT and TRY exhibit over 25% external reference in the subjunctive and less than 10% external reference in the infinitive. As in the first act-out experiment, there was a significant effect of subjunctive vs. infinitive ($F(1,13) = 8.11$, $p <.02$), but not of WANT vs. TRY ($F(1,13)= 1.68$); there was no significant interaction between morphology and WANT/TRY.[6]

Table 3
SPANISH PICTURE VERIFICATION TASK: FOLLOW-UP
PERCENTAGE ACCEPTANCES

	WANT-sub	WANT-inf	TRY-sub	TRY-inf
Child 4-5 (n=14)	82%	64%	61%	46%

Table 4
SPANISH ACT-OUT TASK: FOLLOW-UP
PERCENTAGE INTERNAL AND EXTERNAL RESPONSES

	WANT-sub I	WANT-sub E	WANT-inf I	WANT-inf E	TRY-sub I	TRY-sub E	TRY-inf I	TRY-inf E
Child 4-5	62%	31%	95%	5%	74%	26%	93%	7%

4. Conclusion

The main goal of this study was to look at the relative force of lexical semantics and subordinate clause morphology (tense and mood) in driving children's hypotheses concerning the existence and distribution of controlled PRO. Based on the semantics of TRY and WANT, we hypothesized that the acquisition of the obligatory disjoint reference requirement in subjunctives in Spanish might be delayed for TRY. Based on the assumption that PRO is found in non-finite clauses in the unmarked case, we hypothesized that the acquisition of controlled PRO might be delayed in Greek, which has no non-finite clauses.

We found little or no evidence either for a general (cross-linguistic) stage in which lexical semantics dictates the distribution of PRO subjects or for extended delay in the acquisition of PRO in finite clauses. This summation is argued for by a comparison of the performance on the act-out task of the Greek-speaking children and their follow-up Spanish peers. For the Greek children we found a significantly smaller proportion of internal reference for the embedded subject of WANT than for TRY; for the Spanish children we found no significant difference between WANT and TRY, but a significant effect of infinitive vs. subjunctive morphology.

Although we did not find a general stage where lexical semantics alone determine control, the performance of the Spanish-speaking children is not completely free of lexical effects. As noted above, in the first picture verification task children were more able to reject an external interpretation of the embedded subject of an infinitive when the verb was TRY, and in the follow-up children were generally (regardless of morphology) more willing to accept internal reference for TRY than for WANT. These effects suggest that we are correct in assuming that the semantics of WANT and TRY promote non-obligatory and obligatory control, respectively. Since such effects in Spanish were confined to picture verification, the Spanish results call for caution in interpreting the data from those Greek children who showed a WANT/TRY distinction for that task only (nine children); we cannot tell if the WANT/TRY distinction such children drew was driven by the experimental task rather than by knowledge of the grammar of Greek.

Notes

1. Small capitals are used to represent a core of meaning which we assume to be shared by the verbs in the different languages we discuss.

2. The same story is used in (4) and (5) for expository purposes; in the test a given story had a subjunctive or infinitival complement, with WANT and TRY alternated between two questionnaires.

3. Only an external interpretation of the embedded subject was presented, due to the difficulty that adult Greek speakers have in getting that interpretation.

4. It is perhaps not entirely accurate to say that *the* correct answer in the WANT condition of the picture verification test in Greek was to say that the picture fitted the sentence; if the subject had mentally selected a sentence internal construal for the subject of the complement clause prior to verifying the picture, then s/he could be driven to say the picture did not fit.

5. Additionally, one Greek child showed conflicting results on the two tests.

6. The ORDER sentences had infinitival complements; more external interpretation for WANT/TRY might have been found with subjunctive training.

Acknowledgements

This research was supported by Social Sciences and Humanities Research Council of Canada grant no 410-94-0707. Students in course L72 in winter 1995 at the Ortega y Gasset Institute helped greatly in planning the Spanish study.

References

Chomsky, Noam. 1981. *Lectures in Government and Binding.* Dordrecht, Holland: Foris.
Goodluck, Helen and Arhonto Terzi . 1996. Controlled PRO and the Acquisition of Greek. *Proceedings of the 20th Annual Boston University Conference on Language Development.* Brookline, Ma: Cascadilla Press.
Jackendoff, Ray. 1972. *Semantic Interpretation in Generative Grammar.* Cambridge, Mass: MIT Press.
Maratsos, M. 1974. How Preschool Children Understand Missing Complement Subjects. *Child Development,* 45: 700-706.
Padilla, J. 1990. *On the Definition of Binding Domains in Spanish: Evidence from Child Spanish.* Dordrecht, Holland: Kluwer.
Terzi, Arhonto. 1992. *PRO in Finite Clauses. A Study of the Inflectional Heads of the Balkan Languages.* Doctoral dissertation, CUNY Graduate Center.
Terzi, Arhonto. 1996. PRO and Null Case in Finite Clauses. To appear in *The Linguistic Review.*
Vanden Wyngaerd, Guido. 1994. *PRO-legomena: Distribution and Reference of Infinitival Subjects.* Berlin: Mouton de Gruyter.
Varlokosta, Spyridoula and Norbert Hornstein. 1993. Control in Modern Greek. *Proceedings of NELS* 23: 507-521.
Williams, Edwin. 1989. Human PRO. Unpublished ms.

Evidence in Phonological Acquisition: Implications for the Initial Ranking of Faithfulness Constraints

MARK HALE & CHARLES REISS

Concordia University

This contribution to the study of phonological acquisition is predicated on a fundamental acceptance of a modular approach to the study of language, arguing that the bulk of research on phonological aspects of children's speech, which attributes the peculiarities of their output to 'child phonology', fails to properly maintain the performance/competence contrast in the evaluation of acquisition data.

The study of phonology involves a characterization of mental representations and computation involving these representations. Alternative views include the characterization of 'tendencies' and 'trends' sometimes subsumed under the ill-defined notion of 'markedness,' e.g., "The goal of phonology is the construction of a theory in which **cross-linguistically common** [but not necessarily universal — mh & cr] and well-established processes emerge from very simple combinations of the descriptive parameters of the model" (McCarthy 1988). We take as our goal the development of a theory of possible/impossible human languages, not "common" (statistically preponderant) human languages. "Common" features are artifacts of the sampling process, phonetic factors grammaticalized through historical change, etc., some of which are interesting and important domains of inquiry, but which are, strictly speaking, extra-grammatical.

The study of acquisition includes a characterization of the initial state of the grammar, S_0, and a theory of a learning path from S_0 to a subsequent state S_n. Our approach is strongly innatist, but adopts a performance-based account of many of the peculiarities of children's speech production. The competence/performance contrast is, of course, accepted in phonological circles in the study of adult phonology, where it is used to determine which aspects of adult output phonological theory needs to concern itself with and which aspects it does not.

Our arguments can be placed in the context of the following pairs of opposing hypotheses:

i) The nature of child phonology
  a. The Strong Identity hypothesis, which holds that child phonology is governed by the same principles as adult phonology
  b. The view that child phonology is fundamentally distinct from adult phonology — licensing processes unattested in adult language, dependent on a series of developmental stages, etc.

ii) The nature of the evidence
  a. Deviations from target forms — in children's as well as adults' grammars — are to be attributed to performance effects, including non-linguistic cognitive and motor processing
  b. Deviations from target forms are the result of 'child phonology' (i.e., the child's phonological competence) — grammatical effects for which the target language provides no evidence

We propose that both empirical evidence and learnability considerations favor the (a) hypotheses.

We believe, contra Smolensky 1996 and most other work on phonological acquisition since Jakobson, that the supposed parallels between child and adult patterns of 'markedness' are illusory. One of the best described phenomena of 'child phonology,' consonant harmony (responsible for the realization of 'duck' as 'guck'), has long been known to have no parallels in adult phonological systems (Drachman 1978). Another widely discussed phenomenon in children's speech is coda devoicing, which is often compared to similar processes in languages such as German and Russian. Supposed parallelism between acquisition and cross-linguistic tendencies constitutes the basis of much of the literature on markedness theory, from Jakobson, to Stampe and current Optimality Theory. But children's tendency to neutralize VOT contrasts in onset consonants has no parallel in the world's languages and is not widely discussed in the child phonology literature. The opportunistic nature of appeals to 'markedness' indicates that the practice of ascribing the existence of parallels between child and adult phonological output to an underlying mechanism of the grammar, rather than (in the case of child phonology) to performance effects, is questionable. For example, the total absence of across-the-board initial stop neutralization and place harmony, in adult phonological systems indicates that such processes may not be possible in human phonological systems. Attributing them to children would thus be seriously misguided.

If the peculiarities of children's speech are attributed to the performance system, why are these effects sometimes paralleled by clearly *phonological* phenomena? *Pseudophonological (i.e., performance-related) effects* (like coda devoicing) have been documented among populations other than children. Johnson, Pisoni, and Bernacki (1990) report on the intoxicated speech of the captain of the *Exxon Valdez* around the time of the accident at Prince William Sound, Alaska. They note, as do other studies of intoxicated speech, that the realization of segments may be affected by intoxication. They include among their list of observed effects

- misarticulation of /r/ and /l/
- final devoicing
- deaffrication

The accurate articulation of /r/, /l/, and affricates, as well as the existence of a voicing contrast in final position, all represent 'marked' features of English whose presence in the grammatical output is attributed, within Optimality Theory (Prince and Smolensky 1993), to relatively high-ranked faithfulness constraints regarding the features of the segments in question and by the non-application of neutralizing rules in other theories. To account for Captain Hazelwood's output we have two options: either these instances of the 'emergence of the unmarked' are to be attributed to the impairment of his *performance system* by alcohol, or the consumption of alcohol in sufficient quantities leads to constraint re-ranking or rule addition in adult grammars. We must recognize that the presence of 'unmarked' patterns in children's bodily output does not permit us to attribute these patterns to the effects of the grammar, rather than to the 'impairment' of their performance system by immaturity. Of course, this does not prove that none of the cited cases of 'child phonology' are due to the grammar. It does, however, demonstrate that other explanations are potentially available. It is an empirical question, whether or not in each case the data which forms the basis for such analyses represents output of the grammar or output of the 'body'.

A serious look at the evidence for child phonology reveals considerable variability in production. For example, Ferguson (1986) cites the following attempts at producing adult [pʰẽn] 'pen' collected from a 15 month old child in a thirty minute period: [mã.], [ṽ], [deᵈⁿ], [hɪn], [ᵐbõ], [pʰɪn], [tʰn̩tʰn̩tʰn̩], [baʰ], [dhauɴ], [buã]. The situation is actually worse than this case suggests since the transcriptions are also 'patched' by being filtered through the grammar of the adult listener who is also a speaker of English. *Any* use of production evidence will have to selectively cull the data (i.e., recognize the important role of 'performance' factors in children's output).

The conclusion we would hope to derive from the arguments given above is that it is not at all obvious that a competence-only account for children's speech output is a desirable goal. Children's output is actually not very parallel to so-called 'unmarked' aspects of adult languages when considered *in toto*. Furthermore, children's output can be demonstrated to parallel systematic, yet unambiguously non-grammatical, performance effects, as seen in intoxicated speech. It is also well-known that children's non-grammatical abilities, such as physiological aptitude at articulation and short-term memory capacity, are limited. Even when their performance appears to parallel that of adults, for instance, their control of respiration and voicing differs qualitatively from that of adults. Occam's razor demands attributing 'peculiar' aspects of their speech output to these factors as the null hypothesis.

The existence of 'chainshifts', a type of apparent counterfeeding rule-ordering, in child speech, is often cited as incontrovertible evidence of the grammatical basis of child 'phonology'. In fact, shifts such as child [ʃu] for *chew*, but [su] for *shoe* pose a much greater challenge to competence-only accounts. Note that the child must construct an opaque phonology (given the assumption that s/he stores the correct adult forms in the lexicon) for which the target language provides no evidence, only to revert later to a non-opaque grammar upon successful acquisition of the target grammar. We propose that chainshifts arise at the level of implementation: given the command from the grammar to produce a [tʃ], the processor implements a [ʃ]-like sound. Given the command to produce [ʃ], the processor implements a [s]-like sound. Such consistent mappings are typical of many physical tasks where targets are consistently over- or undershot.

Smolensky 1996 and others have also cited children's improved production of target forms when encouraged to imitate adult speech as evidence for the grammatical basis of children's speech patterns. As far as we can tell such data only provides further support for a performance and competence model, rather than a competence-only model. There are at least two distinct accounts for what has been labeled 'imitation': (1) increased performance skill under concentration and (2) parroting. Under our account it is during concentration on the act of performance that the child will perform better in carrying out the instructions provided by the grammar. Parroting clearly has no grammatical basis: a speaker of English can parrot a Cree sentence fairly well without acquiring a Cree grammar.

Under Smolensky's competence-only approach, neither of these types of 'imitation' can be accounted for. In the first type, since Smolensky assumes the *grammar* is responsible for, e.g., realization of /ʃ/ as [s], increased attention to performance should lead only to a clearer hit of the target [s]. In the second case, to account for an English speakers' ability to imitate Cree, Smolensky would have to assume instantaneous acquisition of Cree constraint rankings or rules.

If, as we hope to have shown, 'markedness' considerations, chainshifts, imitation and production behavior tell us almost nothing about the state of children's phonology, is there any way in which we can bypass the performance system and get a glimpse at the child's grammar? We believe that we do have access to more reliable evidence concerning the nature of children's phonological competence from sources such as perception and comprehension studies. We also believe that several learning theoretic arguments favor our claims about the learning path in phonological acquisition over that proposed by Smolensky and most other researchers in the field.

Children's advanced comprehension abilities, as compared to their production, is well documented. Faber and Best 1994 describes one type of evidence for children's abilities, their rejection of adult speech which mimics the output of their mouth, and not the output of their grammar:

> "...these studies show that by the time infants are starting productive use of language they can already discriminate almost all of the phonological contrasts of their native language. While they cannot yet produce adult-like forms, they appear, in many respects, to have adult-like representations, which are reflected, among other things, in their vociferous rejections of adult imitations of their phonologically impoverished productions " (Faber and Best 1994: 266-7).

The passage also alludes to the well-known evidence for children's apparent innate categorical perception—the tendency to perceive sounds on an acoustic continuum as falling into discrete categories corresponding to contrastive categories in human language. Further evidence for a dissociation between childrens' speech output and the output of their grammars can be seen in the results of Dodd (1975) who demonstrated that children are often not able to parse their own output when it is played back to them.

Smolensky (1996, henceforth S) provides an ingenious solution to a long-standing problem in the acquisition of phonology. He demonstrates that a single Optimality Theoretic (OT) grammar can in principle, without appeal to children's performance systems, account for both adult-like comprehension and degenerate, 'unmarked' child production with the assumption that all faithfulness constraints are initially low ranked. (We refer readers to S's paper and to foundational works in OT, such as Prince and Smolensky 1993 for background.) S's model also allows for the acquisition of a lexicon, though only because he departs from most work on phonological acquisition in implicitly assuming (we believe correctly) that children have access to the full set of universal features in constructing underlying representations (see Hale and Reiss 1996). S's model is intuitively satisfying: the production of phonological forms represents the OT-grammar's selection of the most 'harmonic' output for a given input (the set of candidates being generated by GEN); the comprehension of phonological forms, on the other hand, represents the (same) OT-grammar's selection of the most harmonic *input* for a given output (again with the candidate set being generated by GEN). As S demonstrates, the two algorithms will not always converge upon the same input-output link, thus accounting for a difference in production and comprehension.

The difference is demonstrated by S's example of competing forms for the production and perception of underlying /kæt/. Assuming that W-constraints are all ranked above F-constraints gives rise to the following production situation: in selecting the most harmonic output for underlying /kæt/, only something maximally 'unmarked' like *ba* will succeed (since *kæt* violates numerous W-constraints, such as NOCODA, *DORS, *æ...). On the other hand, the comprehension process is rather different: assuming an adult output *kæt* the markedness of the *input* (the lexical entry which the child will posit) is quite irrelevant, since the W-constraints evaluate *output* representations, which will be *kæt* for any posited input in this example, by definition. Since the same W-constraints are violated by *kæt* for any input, it is left to the F-constraints to determine the best input representation, favoring /kæt/. It is thus consistent with an OT-grammar, assuming S's model of production and comprehension, that the child's output should be maximally unmarked while her comprehension is adult-like.

A simple and well-known example will reveal that S's proposal faces empirical difficulties. In fact, any example which shows the effects of a phonological merger (or chainshift) would do the trick. German has two clearly distinct lexical items, a noun *Bund* 'union' and an adjective *bunt* 'multi-colored'. The phonological process of final devoicing (or in OT terms the high ranking of a constraint against voiced coda obstruents) leads to a surface neutralization of the two words as [bunt] in their citation form. When combined with phonologically identical suffixes the two roots reveal their underlying difference: *Bund* surfaces with a voiced stop, and *bunt* surfaces with a voiceless stop: *Bundes* [bundəs] (gen.sg.) vs. *buntes* [buntəs] (nt. n/a strong). Many pairs of German roots are neutralized when stem final obstruents occur in coda position, thus displaying surface ambiguity — that is, a speaker will react to [bunt] with the clear knowledge that it represents an appropriate realization of *both* underlying /bund/ 'union' and /bunt/ 'multi-colored'. Any model of comprehension which fails to account for this fact is clearly missing something fundamental.

However, if we run these forms through S's model of comprehension a clear problem arises. Given an output [bunt], the candidate underlying representation /bund/, with an egregious violation of FAITHFULNESS not shared with its competitor /bunt/, will invariably lose to that competitor. (This parallels S's example of /skæti/ as a possible, but unsuccessful comprehension match for output *kæt*.) The result will not be the desired ambiguity, but rather invariable comprehension of [bunt] as being the realization *only* of underlying /bunt/. Note that this flaw in S's comprehension model is independent of the issue of acquisition — i.e, the model produces the wrong result both for children (who, according to S, have low-ranked F-constraints) and adults (who have elevated selected F-constraints). See Hale and Reiss (forthcoming) for a fuller discussion.

S's proposed resolution of the 'comprehension'/'production' dilemma thus gives rise to an unresolvable empirical problem — in any case of surface phonological merger, only the more 'unmarked' underlying lexeme will be capable of comprehension. This is contraindicated by a wealth of evidence from virtually every human language. We argue that the perception/comprehension evidence, along with some fundamental learnability considerations, allows us to explore the initial state of the phonological computational and representational system in interesting ways.

This involves confronting the difficult problem of distinguishing, in children as we do in adults (in keeping with the Strong Identity Hypothesis), between an output of the phonology (a mental representation) and a real-time output of the body under some particular circumstances (those in effect at the time of utterance). The phonology represents a mapping relationship between the underlying representation, X, and the output of the phonology for the string in question, Y (where Y may be equal to X if the relevant F-constraints outrank the potentially relevant W-constraints). The performance system of the adult, responsible for directing the body to "hit" the output target in question, converts the mental representation Y to a set of articulatory commands which, filtered by contingent environmental factors (including accidental features of the body in question as well as contingent features of the context in which the body finds itself at the moment of utterance) generate an acoustic output, Z. As the study of adult phonetics shows, Z is highly variable (e.g., multiple articulations of /æ/ from the same speaker in the same phonological environment will still differ acoustically). Given the complex set of factors determining its form (physical attributes, stable and accidental, of the speaker as well as numerous environmental effects) this is to be expected. Note that Z cannot, under any circumstances, be the same as Y: Y is a mental representation and Z is an acoustic (or articulatory) event.

Each of these relationships represents a mapping: the grammar is responsible for the mapping of lexical entries onto output representations, the production system (and environmental factors) for mapping the output representation onto an acoustic realization. It is to be expected that these relationships, therefore, will be relatively systematic and regular; indeed, such systematicity is implicit in the notion of 'mapping relationship.'

Given the discrepancy between children's performance and comprehension capabilities, we would not be surprised if the effects of an immature production system on Y were more dramatic than the effects of the adult production system are. That is, we would predict from general considerations such as these that Z should be more distant from Y (and more variable in its realization of a given Y) in children than it is in adults. This, indeed, is the definition of immature control of the production system.

We demonstrate more fully elsewhere (Hale and Reiss 1996, forthcoming) that this conception of the speech output system, which lacks the empirical shortcomings of other proposals (e.g., Gnanedesikan 1995) leads to the necessary assumption that the initial state of the grammar is one in which children's grammars store adult-like representations and output them unchanged. That is, the phonology initially contains no rules, or, in OT terms, F-constraints are initially ranked high, above W-constraints.

Given the empirical failings of Smolensky's view of the comprehension process, we propose instead a model in which comprehension involves searching the lexicon for representations which, when run through the grammar will generate the observed surface form. If F-constraints are ranked low initially, the child will face what is essentially the famous 'ba-problem' in reverse. Given a surface form [kæt] and a grammar in which all W-constraints are ranked above all F-constraints, there is no UR which could possibly have [kæt] as an output. Such a grammar, by hypothesis, initially generates only maximally unmarked utterances. Our theory holds, instead, that the child hears [kæt], stores /kæt/, and outputs [kæt]. This **grammatical** output is then mangled by an immature performance system.

An additional implication of our theory concerns the acquisition of the set of representations found in the lexicon. One of the standard arguments for the 'marked' nature of certain segments is that they emerge late in the acquisition process (e.g., Jakobson 1941, Kenstowicz 1994). Such observations provide the background for a conception of phonological acquisition as moving from a relatively small inventory of unmarked segments to a larger inventory containing increasingly marked segments (e.g., Rice 1996). We argue that if one assumes the existence of a Universal Feature Set as a component of UG and that the child has no access to negative evidence, then the opposite conception of the acquisition of phonological competence follows. UG provides for free combination of features (in principle, the maximal inventory) and learning consists of the rejection of various combinations, with concomitant shrinking of the inventory. As shown above, the late emergence of a feature contrast in the 'bodily output' is irrelevant to the presence of this contrast in the grammar.

As mentioned above, the perceptual system of children appears to be very well-developed. Indeed, it is crucial that children be sensitive to any distinction which could be used by the phonological system of any human language since, without such sensitivity, acquisition of the hypothetically 'imperceptible' distinctions could not occur. If we assume, with most acquisitionists, that children correctly store the phonetic details (to the degree necessary to license acquisition of any human language) of adult output forms, we need to ask why they do not simply feed these stored, accurate representations into their production systems, thereby producing accurate output to the extent possible, given their immature control of their output devices. Put another way, why assume a phonology at all? We will adopt the traditional answer to this question. The lexicon, at this stage (with full phonetic specification of acquired adult output forms), contains two types of information which turn out to be eliminable from underlying representations with no loss in output accuracy. First, some phonetic features found on particular segments turn out to be predictable on purely distributional grounds (e.g., aspiration on voiceless stops in English). Second, after the child has achieved some morphological parsing, the existence of morphophonemic alternations licenses the further elimination of redundancy in the lexicon. For example, the voiceless /s/ of 'cats' and the voiced /z/ of 'dogs' can be reduced to a single underlying representation. We will refer to these processes as 'lexicon optimization.' Lexicon optimization results in a phonology.

Both these processes, the stripping of allophonic features from the adult phonetic forms stored in the lexicon, and the reduction of phonologically conditioned allomorphs to a single representation, are consistent with the Subset Principle. The child appears to be going from 'bigger' to 'smaller' when it decides to leave the aspiration feature off of the /p/ in [pʰat], but this is misleading. The representation that contains just the specifications for voiceless labial stops is LESS restrictive than that which contains the specifications for aspirated voiceless labial stops.

We believe that assiduously maintaining the competence/performance distinction is as crucial in the study of phonological acquisition as it is in the study of adult phonology. Taken together with the empirical evidence cited above, the acquisition of phonological *competence* (as well as the successful acquisition of a lexicon) requires that F-constraints start out ranked high, if an OT model of grammar is to be adopted.

References

Dodd, Barbara. 1975. Children's Understanding of their Own Phonological Forms. *Quarterly Journal of Experimental Psychology* 27:165-172.

Drachman, Gabarell. 1978. Child Language and Language Change: a Conjecture and Some Refutations, in J. Fisiak, ed., *Recent Developments in Historical Phonology*. The Hague: Mouton.

Faber, Alice and Catherine T. Best. 1994. The Perceptual Infrastructure of Early Phonological Development, in S. Lima, R. Corrigan, and G. Iverson, eds., *The Reality of Linguistic Rules*. Philadelphia: Benjamins.

Ferguson, Charles. 1986. Discovering Sound Units and Constructing Sound Systems: It's Child's Play, in J. Perkell and D. Klatt, eds., *Invariance and Variability in Speech Processes*. Hillsdale, NJ: Erlbaum.

Gnanadesikan, Amalia. 1995. Markedness and Faithfulness Constraints in Child Phonology. ms., Rutgers Optimality Archive.

Hale, Mark and Charles Reiss. (forthcoming) How to Parse (and How Not to) in OT Phonology. *Proceedings of NELS 27*. University of Massachusetts Graduate Linguistics Association, Amherst.

Hale, Mark and Charles Reiss. 1996. The Comprehension/Production Dilemma in Child Language: A Response to Smolensky. ms., Rutgers Optimality Archive.

Hale, Mark and Charles Reiss. 1995. On the Initial Ranking of OT Faithfulness Constraints. ms., Rutgers Optimality Archive.

Jakobson, Roman. 1941. Kindersprache, Aphasie und allgemeine Lautgesetze. Selected Writings, vol. 1, 328-401. The Hague: Mouton, 1971.

Johnson, Keith, David Pisoni, and Robert Bernacki. 1990. Do Voice Recordings Reveal Whether a Person is Intoxicated? A case study. *Phonetica* 47:215-237.

Kenstowicz, Michael. 1994. *Phonology in Generative Grammar*. Oxford: Blackwell.

McCarthy, J. 1994. Remarks on Phonological Opacity in OT. ms. UMass, Amherst.

McCarthy, J. 1988. Feature geometry and dependency: a review. *Phonetica* 45, 84-108.

Prince, Alan and Paul Smolensky. 1993. Optimality Theory: Constraint Interaction in Generative Grammar. Technical Report Rutgers Center for Cognitive Science, Rutgers University, New Brunswick, N.J.

Rice, Keren 1996. Phonological Variability in Language Acquisition: a Representational Account. ms., University of Toronto.

Smolensky, Paul. 1996. On the Comprehension/Production Dilemma in Child Language. To appear in *Linguistic Inquiry* 27.

The Role of Input in the Acquisition of Past Verb Forms in English and Dutch: Evidence from a Bilingual Child

ANNICK DE HOUWER
Belgian National Science Foundation/University of Antwerp[1]

1. Introduction

Dutch and English often express past time reference by means of verb forms. As such, there exists a grammaticalized meaning-form relationship in both languages as far as past time reference is concerned. Furthermore, Dutch and English past verb phrases (VP's) exhibit strong structural similarities: the past VP's most commonly used in informal conversation in both languages, namely the simple past and present perfect forms, are more similar in form than that they are different. Finally, both Dutch- and English-speaking adults make use of simple past and present perfect forms in speaking to young children and thus provide children with appropriate learning opportunities.

Given the fact that monolingual Dutch- and English-speaking children are confronted with formally very similar structural possibilities to express basically the same semantic notion one might expect young children

---

[1] This paper was prepared while the author was a Resident VNC-Fellow at the Netherlands Institute for Advanced Study (NIAS) in Wassenaar, the Netherlands. The support of NIAS is hereby gratefully acknowledged. Thanks are also due to Rens Bod and Alex Housen for useful pointers to some of the literature.

acquiring Dutch and English to take similar acquisitional paths as far as the use of past VP's is concerned. Surprisingly, this does not appear to be the case: preschoolers acquiring American English as their only language typically start out using the simple past when referring to anteriority by means of verbs (Brown 1973, Gathercole 1986), whereas from very early on Dutch-speaking monolingual children use the Dutch present perfect for this purpose (Schaerlaekens and Gillis 1987).

These cross-linguistically different routes in acquisition cannot easily be explained by reference to comparative differences or similarities in the structural complexity of the forms under consideration: in both Dutch and English, the single-unit simple past can be seen as being less structurally complex than the dual-unit present perfect. Yet Dutch-speaking children start out with the dual-unit form that is arguably more complex than the single-unit form.

The interpretative problem is not aided by the fact that the cross-linguistically different routes in acquisition observed here might be due to non-language related differences between Dutch- and English-speaking monolingual children that cannot be controlled for, such as level of cognitive and psychosocial development, cultural background, and the like.

The primary goal of cross-linguistic research is to help rule out undue influence from one specific language-in-acquisition on explanations of the acquisition process in general (cf. Slobin 1985). An obvious concomitant of this goal is that to the extent possible, 'language exposed to' should be the only dependent variable. Monolingual populations acquiring different languages often differ on many more dimensions than just the languages they are exposed to. This makes it methodologically difficult to isolate the precise role of the variable 'language exposed to': in cross-linguistic comparisons of monolingual children, any observed differences or similarities in the acquisition of two languages may not necessarily be due to factors relating only to the acquisition of these languages, but possibly also to non-language related differences between the two populations.

Rather than comparing two monolingual groups with each other, cross-linguistic research can perhaps be carried out more profitably using children who have been simultaneously exposed to two languages from birth. These children, after all, form their own ideal matched pair, since all their language-independent characteristics are identical regardless of what language is being used. Using simultaneously bilingual children who have been regularly and frequently exposed to two languages from birth up to the time of investigation permits a more solid basis for studying the relative importance in the acquisition process of factors such as input, cognitive style, and linguistic complexity.

This paper presents a cross-linguistic study of the early use of past VP's in Dutch and English by an ideal matched pair, i.e., by a child simultaneously exposed to standard Dutch and American English from birth. It will be shown that this bilingual child, Kate, combines within her the acquisition patterns found for English- and Dutch-speaking monolingual children. In the search for possible explanations of this state of affairs an analysis of some characteristics of the input provided to Kate proves to be especially instructive.

2. Simple Past and Present Perfect in Dutch and English: Some Structural Characteristics

Dutch and English use basically two kinds of verb forms to refer to past events: one that consists of a single lexical item, the simple past (e.g. Dutch ZONG/English SANG), and one that consists of a finite auxiliary in the present and a past participle, i.e., the present perfect (e.g. Dutch HEB GEDANST/English HAVE DANCED).

In both languages, the exact shape of the simple past and the past participle in the present perfect depends on the type of verb that is being used, i.e., a lexical verb, a modal or the copula (since past modals hardly ever featured in the corpus analyzed in this paper they will be left out of consideration). Within the class of lexical verbs, both languages distinguish between regular and irregular verbs. Irregular simple past and past participle formation shows similar patternings in both languages in that various 'schemas' (Bybee and Slobin 1982) involving vowel changes can be identified that lie at the root of particular forms. Regular simple past and past participle formation is quite similar across the two languages, except that the Dutch past participle contains both a prefix GE- and a suffix -D (note that the prefix is not present when the verb stem begins with a syllable that looks like a prefix, such as VER-, BE- and the like), whereas the English past participle does not have any prefix.

Dutch and English differ to the extent that English uses a single lexical item for the simple past only in the affirmative: English past negatives and interrogatives are formed using DID in combination with the base or infinitive form. Dutch simple pasts always consist of a single form regardless of mood. Another structural difference is that in the present perfect, Dutch uses one of two auxiliaries, HEBBEN or ZIJN, whereas English always uses HAVE.

Using stability of form across moods, number of words and morphemes needed for a form, and, related to this, length as criteria for determining levels of structural complexity, the Dutch simple past would appear to be the least complex, with the English simple past in second place, the English present perfect in third place, and the Dutch present perfect in fourth place as the most complex.

3. A Bilingual Child's Early Use of Dutch and English VP's to Refer to the Past

The data presented below are based on a corpus of utterances produced by Kate, a girl simultaneously exposed to standard Dutch and American English from birth. Kate was studied between the ages of 2;7 and 3;4. Spontaneous interactions between Kate, either of her parents and/or the investigator were audio-recorded in the home and subsequently transcribed. A comprehensive morphosyntactic analysis of the data including an analysis of language-alternation in the corpus can be found in De Houwer (1990). The data have been made available through CHILDES (MacWhinney and Snow 1990, MacWhinney 1991).

For the analysis of Kate's use of past VP's all utterances containing a verb were extracted from the corpus. Using contextual clues, all utterances with a verb clearly referring to a past event, state or action were then isolated. The verbs in these utterances were then classified in terms of their morphological form. It should be noted that nearly all utterances in the corpus that contained a verb to refer to the past in effect used a past VP, i.e., a simple past, present perfect, past perfect or past continuous form. There was only one exception to this, viz. an English utterance with a verb in it that clearly referred to the past while the verb inappropriately appeared in the base or infinitive form.

Table 1 shows which and how many past verb forms Kate used in English and Dutch. It so happens that over the 8-month period of observation Kate produced nearly the same token number of past VP's in both languages. The distribution of the various forms, however, is quite distinct for each language: English simple past forms of lexical verbs appear with virtually the same frequency (44) as Dutch present perfects of lexical verbs (43). Dutch simple past forms of lexical verbs appear very infrequently, and English present perfect forms are entirely absent. The simple past copula appears with virtually the identical frequency in English and Dutch. For lexical verbs, then, the picture is the reverse in the two languages, with the present perfect as the preferred form to refer to anteriority in Dutch, and the simple past as virtually the only form to refer to anteriority in English. In both languages, past VP's that are not in the present perfect or simple past form occur very infrequently indeed.

Table 1. *Kate's past verb forms*

	DUTCH	ENGLISH
present perfect lexical verb	43	-
simple past lexical verb	5	30
DID + base form	-	14
simple past copula	14	12
past continuous/perfect	1	6
TOTAL	63	62

It is crucial to establish that as was found for all the other morphosyntactic categories investigated in the Kate corpus, there is no sign of any 'amalgamation' of the two language systems for the expression of anteriority by means of verb forms (cf. the analyses in De Houwer 1990). As such, there is no application of form elements from one language to the other, and no sign of any comparison procedures across languages in the sense that a formally more complex form in one language might be avoided in favor of a related, but formally less complex form in the other. In effect, there is overwhelming evidence at all levels of morphosyntactic functioning for what I have termed the Separate Development Hypothesis, which states that under regular and frequent bilingual exposure conditions, early morphosyntactic development in bilingual first language acquisition proceeds in a language-specific manner, without reference to the other language that is being acquired (De Houwer 1990, 1994). As such, young simultaneously bilingual children look like two monolingual children in one as far as the structural properties of their language use are concerned.

In effect, the past verb forms used by Kate in each of her languages greatly resemble those used by her monolingual peers (cf. De Houwer 1990). Thus, Kate combines within her the cross-linguistically different paths found in monolingual Dutch- and English-speaking children as outlined in the introduction. Since Kate is always at the same level of cognitive and psychosocial development regardless of what language she is using, the different routes that she is taking for Dutch and English past VP's cannot be attributed to factors not directly related to language but must somehow be explicable through factors that do relate to language. One such possible factor, i.e., differential levels of structural complexity, seems not to be applicable in this case. A more viable one might be input frequency.

4. Dutch and English Past VP's in Adult and Child Speech

In order to explore the possibility of an input frequency bias that might help explain the acquisition data, the use of past VP's in the input to Kate was analysed employing a method similar to the one used for Kate's own speech production.

Using a combination of CLAN programs (MacWhinney 1991), all adult utterances addressed to Kate that contained a past VP were isolated. This set of utterances was then divided into English utterances (as produced by Kate's American mother) and Dutch utterances (mostly as produced by the investigator; some of these were also produced by Kate's father). After a basic frequency count, these two data sets were then coded in terms of the type of past VP's they contained.

A first and quite basic finding is that past VP's are used quite regularly in the input in both languages. The frequency counts over time of both Kate's and the adults' past VP's further show that with one exception (English at child age 2;7) the number of adult past VP's present for any observed month is higher than the number of child past VP's (Table 2).

Table 2. *Raw frequencies of past VP's (Kate corpus)*

age Kate	2;7	2;9	2;10	2;11	3;0	3;1	3;2	3;3	totals
English									
child	4	-	8	0	3	41	6	-	62
adult	1	-	26	6	13	117	22	-	185
Dutch									
child	4	4	3	0	2	14	4	32	63
adult	28	12	53	13	8	79	42	76	306

The child data show a very clear developmental picture for both languages in terms of frequency of occurrence: 47 out of 62 English past VP's and 50 out of 63 Dutch past VP's occur after age 3;1 (as observed in De Houwer 1990, the number of past VP's as used by Kate is independent of the total number of utterances for any recording session). Indeed, 78% of all Kate's past VP's occur after age 3;1,0, i.e., more than three quarters of the child's past VP's occur in the final 3 months of an 8-month observation period.

The adult data show a somewhat similar picture (although here of course it is rather odd to speak of 'development'). That picture is rather more clear for English than it is for Dutch, though: 75% of all English adult past VP's vs. only 64% of all Dutch adult past VP's occur after Kate has reached the age of 3;1.

There appears to be some evidence indicating that frequencies of use of past VP's by child and adult are somehow connected to each other (cf. the finding that for both the child and adult corpus the bulk of the past VP's occur after child age 3;1,0). For the English data set it appears that in the time between child ages 2;10 and 3;3, adult and child frequencies of use of past VP's are correlated with each other, but since only 5 out of 8 data points show such a correlation the evidence is not very strong. The Dutch data set shows no correlation between child and adult frequencies of use of past VP's across time. On the whole, then, the frequency of use of a past VP by Kate for any month of observation is not strongly determined by its frequency of use by an adult (nor the other way round!). Thus, whether Kate uses a past VP at all seems to have little to do with the number of past VP's that the adults around her use in talking to her.

In contrast, the frequency distribution of the types of past VP's that adults use with Kate does seem to have a very strong influence on the types of past VP's that Kate ends up producing.

Both simple past and present perfect forms are present in the input in both languages (Table 3). As such, there are learning opportunities for both forms for both English and Dutch (cf. also the very first paragraph of this paper). The distribution of these learning opportunities is quite different across the two languages, though. As is shown in Table 3, lexical verbs referring to the past primarily appear in the present perfect form in the Dutch input, whereas in the English input they primarily appear in the simple past (including the form with DID). Dutch present perfect forms and English simple past forms of lexical verbs each account for ca. 70% of the past VP's used by the adults in each input language. Contrastingly, Dutch simple past forms and English present perfect forms of lexical verbs each account for respectively 10.5 and 8.1% of the past VP's used by the adults in each input language. Thus, the picture is reversed for both languages.

Table 3. *Past verb forms as used in the input (Kate corpus)*

	DUTCH	ENGLISH
present perfect lexical verb	72.2%	8.1%
simple past lexical verb	10.5%	44.9%
DID + base form	-	24.3%
simple past copula	15.4%	15.7%
other	3.6%	7.0%
TOTAL	306	185

Note that the proportional use of the simple past of the copula in the input is the same for both languages. In addition, present perfect and simple past are the primary verb forms used to refer to the past rather than other past VP's.

When Tables 1 and 3 are compared to each other, it is clear that the same cross-linguistic results hold for the child and adult data: (1) English lexical verbs referring to the past occur primarily in the simple past, (2) Dutch lexical verbs referring to the past occur primarily in the present perfect, (3) the proportion of use of the simple past copula is the same across languages, and (4) present perfect and simple past occur much more frequently than other past VP's.

A closer examination of the adult and child data for both languages separately reveals a very strong correlation between the distributions of the various forms between the input and the child data within each language. As Table 4a shows for Dutch, the rank order with which past VP's are used by Kate and the Dutch-speaking adults is the same. Similarly, Table 4b shows that for English the rank order with which past VP's are used by Kate and the English-speaking adult is virtually the same as well. At the same time, the rank orders are quite different for Dutch and English (compare a and b in Table 4).

It is possible that the frequency effects demonstrated in the above comparisons between the Dutch and English child and adult data are not crucially related to different categories of past VP's (simple past vs. present perfect) but rather to the specific lexical realizations of past VP's. In order to explore this possibility a comparative analysis was made of the lexical realizations of English affirmative simple past and Dutch present perfect forms as used by Kate and in the input. Space does not permit the detailed presentation of the results of this analysis [2]. The major finding was that there was relatively little overlap between child and adult lexical realizations of English simple past forms. The same was true for Dutch present perfect forms. As such, there is little reason to assume on the basis of the data available in the transcripts that Kate's use of past VP's in either language is a primarily lexically driven, directly imitative process that by implication leads to the sorts of frequency distributions as shown in Table 4. Rather, the main result still holds, i.e., it is the frequency distributions of the categories 'simple past' and 'present perfect' that are correlatable between child and adult speech.

Table 4. *Past verb forms: child and adult data per language*

	KATE raw frequency	rank	ADULT raw frequency	rank
a. DUTCH				
present perfect	43	1	221	1
simple past copula	14	2	47	2
simple past lexical verb	5	3	32	3
other	1	4	11	4
TOTAL	63		306	
b. ENGLISH				
simple past lexical verb	30	1	83	1
DID + base form	14	2	45	2
simple past copula	12	3	29	3
present perfect	-	5	15	4
other	6	4	13	5
TOTAL	62		185	

5. Discussion and Conclusion

The central focus in this article has been the search for an explanation of cross-linguistically divergent patterns in the use of Dutch and English past verb phrases by young children. As a methodological decision, data were analysed of a simultaneously bilingual child, thus sharply reducing the number of dependent variables that might help account for particular acquisitional paths observed across monolingual populations.

The cross-linguistic study of a Dutch-English simultaneously bilingual child presented in this paper shows that her use of lexical VP's to refer to the past is quite different for each language. Results of analyses of the past verb forms used in the input show very clear correlations between the frequency distributions in the Dutch input data and the Dutch child data on the one hand, and between those in the English input data and the English

---

[2] Interested readers may obtain the information directly from the author.

child data on the other. The most frequently occurring adult usage patterns are the ones appropriately used by the child.

Taking this a step further, it can be hypothesized that the frequency of occurrence of syntagmatically defined morphosyntactic categories in the input is a strong guiding factor in the child's own use of these categories [3]: no additional explanations besides the child's close attention to frequency characteristics of the input within each language are required here to interpret her language-adequate use of past VP's in Dutch and English [4]. As I have suggested earlier, differences in the formal complexity of the past VP's under consideration cannot serve as an explanation for the acquisition data, since forms of different complexity occur simultaneously. It could be argued that aspectual factors play an important role in the early use of past VP's in English and Dutch. Whereas it may indeed be possible that aspectual, meaning-based categories play a role as well, the strong influence of input frequency on the forms used by the child makes it doubtful that aspectual categories play a primary, decisive role at the stage of development investigated here. For the areas and age range investigated the data can be adequately explained without having to take into account aspectual categories. Naturally, an additional analysis focusing on aspectual categories might be quite valuable. A major methodological problem for such a cross-linguistic aspectual analysis, however, would be the lack of cross-linguistically valid and useable tools to code aspect in English and Dutch.

Frequency of input has not been a popular explanation for past VP acquisition in child language studies (but see Gathercole's 1986 proposal based on a cross-variety study that for English-speaking children frequency of input plays a major role in the timing and order of acquisition of the present perfect). Lately, however, there have been specific proposals that children's early use of past verb forms is at least to some extent determined by distributional frequencies in the input (Shirai and Andersen 1995, Krasinski 1995). Since frequency tagging as an automatic process has been shown to play a role in many different areas of cognition, including that of language (for an overview, see Hasher and Zacks 1984), it indeed makes sense to suggest that input frequencies could play quite a major role in

---

[3] It is striking that Dutch-speaking children take a very long time to learn irregular past participle formation, whereas the appropriate combination of the auxiliary ZIJN or HEBBEN with particular past participles seems hardly to be an issue. This leads me to suggest that paradigmatic relationships may be less sensitive to frequency characteristics of the input than syntagmatic ones. After all, the discovery of paradigmatic relationships involves the comparison across time of elements that do not occur side by side. Syntagmatic relationships would seem to be more accessible to frequency tagging since they present themselves more clearly as things that belong together.

[4] It is obvious, of course, that in order to be able to use past VP's appropriately, the child must have discovered a link between various past VP forms and their meanings. In this learning process, the role of input frequency might be far less significant.

determining the particular paths that children take in acquiring certain aspects of language. The findings from the present study show that particular distribution frequencies of morphosyntactic categories in the input are an influential factor that can help explain the data where other accounts fail.

6. References

Brown, Roger, 1973. *A First Language. The Early Stages.* Cambridge, Massachusetts: Harvard University Press.

Bybee, Joan, and Dan Slobin, 1982. Rules and Schemas in the Development and Use of the English Past Tense. *Language* 58: 265-289.

De Houwer, Annick, 1990. *The Acquisition of Two Languages from Birth: a Case Study.* Cambridge: Cambridge University Press.

De Houwer, Annick, 1994. The Separate Development Hypothesis: Method and Implications, in G. Extra & L. Verhoeven, eds, *The cross-linguistic study of bilingualism.* Amsterdam: North-Holland.

Hasher, Lynn and Rose Zacks, 1984. Automatic Processing of Fundamental Information. The Case of Frequency of Occurrence. *American psychologist* 39: 1372-1388.

Gathercole, Virginia, 1986. The Acquisition of the Present Perfect: Explaining Differences in the Speech of Scottish and Americam Children. *Journal of child language* 13: 537-560.

Krasinski, Emily, 1995. The Development of Past Marking in a Bilingual Child and the Punctual-Nonpunctual Distinction. *First language* 15: 277-300.

MacWhinney, Brian, 1991. The CHILDES Project. Tools for Analyzing Talk. Hillsdale, NJ: Lawrence Erlbaum Associates.

MacWhinney, Brian and Catherine Snow, 1990. The Child Language Data Exchange System: an Update. *Journal of child language* 17: 457-472.

Schaerlaekens, Anne-Marie and Steven Gillis, 1987. *De taalverwerving van het kind. Een hernieuwde oriëntatie in het Nederlandstalig onderzoek.* Groningen: Wolters-Noordhoff.

Shirai, Yasuhiro and Roger Andersen, 1995. The Acquisition of Tense-Aspect Morphology: a Prototype Account. *Language* 71: 743-762.

Slobin, Dan, 1985. Introduction: Why Study Acquisition Crosslinguistically?, in D. Slobin, ed, *The crosslinguistic study of language acquisition.* Hillsdale, New Jersey: Lawrence Erlbaum Associates.

The Role of Prosody in the Acquisition of Grammatical Morphemes

RICHARD F.S. HUNG
University of Hawaii at Manoa

1. Introduction

The Chinese languages have virtually no inflectional devices that indicate tense, aspect, voice, number, gender, or case relations. Almost all the markers that serve these functions are free morphemes. In addition to four full lexical tones, MC has a neutral tone, which mainly occurs on suffixes and particles which serve grammatical functions. The occurrence of the neutral tone can thus be regarded as a phonological feature that helps distinguish MC closed-class items from open-class items. In fact, neutral-toned syllables are a close phonological analogue to reduced syllables in English, since in addition to having no assigned tone, they share with the English syllables shorter durations and lenited vowel qualities (Beckman 1986:104). The MC neutral-toned functor syllables are shorter in length and less tonally distinctive than full-toned lexical syllables. Sequences of full-toned lexical syllables followed by neutral-toned functor syllables help to impart a stress-timed sort of rhythm to MC utterances. In other words, in MC the tonal domain is analogous to the stress domain (i.e., foot) (Duanmu 1990; Hsiao 1991). Lexical syllables simultaneously have higher pitch, longer and fuller vowels, and greater loudness than functor syllables. Hence, the interplay of changes in four acoustic properties: pitch, duration, rhythm, and intensity, coincides in MC.

Among the Chinese languages, TW offers interesting contrasts. TW has seven distinctive lexical full tones. The tonal nature of grammatical morphemes in TW contrasts sharply in complexity with that for MC. TW functors may carry any of the seven full tones as well as neutral tone; moreover, those with full tones are subject to the same sandhi changes as are full-toned lexical syllables. Although TW functors are more often full-toned, there is a tendency for them to lose their distinctive pitch patterns in phrase-final position. On the other hand, the environments for the occurrence of the neutral tone are frequently the same as those for tone spreading. As a result, neutral tones on these function words are often replaced by the tones of preceding content words, greatly reducing the likelihood of function words undergoing tonal neutralization in phrase-final position.

For these distributional reasons, and because there is neither reduction of vowels in functor syllables nor lengthening of vowels in lexical syllables, TW functors are more likely to carry full tones than their MC counterparts. In general, since prosodic prominence in TW is imparted through intensity, pitch, duration, and/or vowel quality, its functors are not so likely to be less prominent than its lexical syllables. It thus appears that TW is a language where syllable-based rhythm is predominant (Tseng 1995). Here the prosodic characteristics of pitch, duration, rhythm, and intensity operate separately rather than in concert. These characterizations are consistent with the results of several acoustic and perceptual experiments which reveal that there is no stress in TW as far as linguistic significance is concerned (Du 1988:225).

These differences in the prosodic structures of MC and TW led me to propose the following hypothesis concerning children's perception of salient prosody that may coincide with grammatical morphemes:
- The timing/rhythm difference in MC and TW affords different acquisition paths (i.e., a foot path vs. a syllable path) for children learning grammatical morphemes.

This hypothesis makes two predictions that can be investigated by comparing the early productions of grammatical morphemes in MC and TW:
1. The segmentation strategies employed by MC- and TW-speaking children will differ from the earliest stages of language acquisition, with MC children paying attention to metrical feet, and TW children paying attention to individual syllables.
2. There will be a significant difference in the patterns of realization and omission of grammatical morphemes between the two groups of children, with full tones expected to be more salient than reduced ones.

2. The Study

I tested my hypothesis and predictions by longitudinally studying the early grammatical development of six children, three learning MC and three learning TW as their first language. In each language I tracked the appearance of a set of highly frequent grammatical morphemes, focusing on toneless syllables in MC and on full-toned syllables in TW. Table 1 shows the morphemes which I tracked in each language.

Table 1. Grammatical morphemes selected for the study

function	MC	TW
DIMinutive	-zi	-a2
CLassifier	ge	e5*[a]
NOMinalizer/GENitive	de	e5
COMpletive	le	(a)
DURative	zhe	leh4
PLural	men	—
LOCative	zai4	ti7
PROGressive	zai4*	teh4

[a] * distinguishes one of a homonymous pair of morphemes.

I had to make a few adjustments, however. Because TW does not have an equivalent for the MC plural *men*, and because *a*, the TW equivalent for the MC completive aspect *le*, almost always remains neutral-toned in utterance-final position, I chose to focus on the locative *ti*7 and the progressive aspect *teh*4 instead. To further preserve functional equivalence across the two lists, I also kept track of the patterns of realization and omission of two full-toned markers in MC, the locative *zai*4 and the homophonous progressive aspect marker *zai*4*.

3. Experiment

3.1 Subjects

For each language group, three children of normal intelligence from monolingual families living in Taiwan were selected. Overall, the mean age was 20 months, 26 days for the MC group and 20 months, 7 days for the TW group at the time of the first transcribed recording. The average age of the two groups differed by 19 days. Each child's MLU was calculated from the spontaneous speech he or she produced during each experimental session. The mean MLU was 1.85 for the MC group and 2.04 for the TW group.

3.2 Procedure

Spontaneous utterances were tape recorded twice a month for each child over a period of six months. Each recording session lasted for about 60 minutes. Usually, the children were interacting with their mother.

3.3 Transcription and Coding

All the data input were in CHAT format (MacWhinney 1991). Since it was not always possible to determine from the context whether a grammatical morpheme would have been obligatory in the child's speech, and which grammatical morpheme a child should have used, it was decided to code only those functor omissions signaled by a caregiver's repetition with correction.

4. Results

Neither group produced a significantly larger proportion of functors in their spontaneous speech, $t = .546$, $p = .6140$, two-tailed.

Table 2 shows the total number of content morphemes, target functors, and utterances produced by MC and TW caregivers in 12 hours of tape-recorded spontaneous speech.

Table 2. Number of content morphemes, target Functors, and utterances in input

	MC Caregivers	TW Caregivers
content morps	105,275	70,835
target functors	8,252	6,780
utterances	26,976	21,932
content/utts	3.903	3.232
functors/utts	0.306	0.309
functors/content	0.078	0.096

The similarity of these ratios suggests that differences in input rates do not contribute to the differences in the omission of grammatical morphemes between MC and TW children.

Table 3 presents, for each of the target neutral-toned functors in MC (plus two zai4 morphemes), the percentages omitted in all three MC children's spontaneous speech.

Table 3. Percentages of functors omitted in the spontaneous speech of MC children

Mo.	de	ge	-zi	le	men	zhe	zai4*	zai4
1st	-	-	-	-	-	-	-	-
2nd	33%	-	-	-	-	-	-	-
3rd	8%	-	-	-	-	-	100%	-
4th	11%	-	-	-	-	-	-	-
5th	17%	3%	-	-	-	-	-	-
6th	27%	5%	-	-	-	-	-	-
M	16%	2%	-	-	-	-	23%	-

The proportions of functor omissions were very low for the MC children. The nominalizer/genitive marker *de* was more susceptible to omission than any other neutral-toned functor in spontaneous speech. We will return to this later. The diminutive marker *-zi*, the completive aspect marker *le*, the plural marker *men*, the durative aspect marker *zhe*, and the locative marker *zai4* were never omitted in the children's spontaneous speech. The progressive aspect marker *zai4** was frequently omitted in the third month of data collection but virtually never afterwards.

Table 4 presents, for each of the target full-toned functors in TW, the percentages omitted in the three TW children's spontaneous speech.

Table 4. Percentages of functors omitted in the spontaneous speech of TW children

Mo.	teh4	e5	e5*	ti7	-a2	leh4	a
1st	100%	65%	-	-	22%	-	-
2nd	100%	64%	44%	7%	17%	-	-
3rd	88%	29%	18%	28%	7%	-	32%
4th	91%	36%	-	26%	2%	-	16%
5th	92%	32%	20%	34%	-	-	4%
6th	92%	15%	-	-	-	-	-
M	93%	33%	18%	16%	9%	-	9%

Regardless of their pitch value (full-toned or neutral-toned), grammatical function (semantic and syntactic complexity), frequency in input, and/or position in which they occurred in an utterance, all seven grammatical morphemes studied were susceptible to omission in the TW children's spontaneous speech. In comparing functors omitted in spontaneous speech between the two language groups, we can find that the TW children omitted significantly more functors than the MC children did, $t = 2.243$, $p < .05$, two-tailed.

5. Imitation tests

5.1 Subjects

An imitation test was conducted for both groups of children when their MLUs, calculated from spontaneous utterances, reached above 1.90. For the MC children, their ages ranged from 23 to 26 months and their MLUs from 1.93 to 2.15. For the TW children, their ages ranged from 22 to 25 months and their MLUs from 1.91 to 2.42.

5.2 Stimuli

MC children were asked to imitate a set of 14 sentences. Each test sentence had four syllables, of which three were lexical and one was one of the seven neutral-toned grammatical morpheme from the set I tracked longitudinally. In all, there were 56 syllables in the test -- 42 lexical syllables and 14 neutral-toned functor syllables. Each functor appeared twice in the test, with nominalizer de and genitive de treated as separate. The 14 test sentences are listed in Appendix A.

The TW children were also asked to imitate a set of 14 sentences. Each test sentence had four syllables, of which three were lexical and one was one of the seven full-toned grammatical morphemes from the target set. Again, there were 56 syllables in the test -- 42 lexical syllables and 14 full-toned functor syllables. Each functor appeared twice in the test, with nominalizer, genitive, classifier e5 treated as separate. The 14 test sentences are listed in Appendix B.

5.3 Transcription and Coding

Imitations were coded for the number of functor or content elements omitted. Two scores were calculated: (1) number of functors omitted (out of a total of 14), (2) number of content words omitted (out of a total of 42).

Table 5 gives the percentages of functors and content words omitted by the MC children in imitation.

Table 5. Functors and content words omitted by the MC children in imitation

Child	Age	MLU	Content omissions	Functor omissions	de (4)	men (2)	zhe (2)
Jie	1;11	1.95	14%	14%	25%	50%	0%
Lon	1;11	1.93	12%	14%	50%	0%	0%
Ron	2;2	2.15	0%	21%	50%	0%	50%

For the MC group, the proportions of functor omissions were not significantly higher than those of content word omissions, $t = -1.172$, $p = .3619$, two-tailed. That is, the MC children, overall, did not show a significant difference in the omission of full-toned content words and neutral-toned grammatical morphemes. As in spontaneous speech, the nominalizer/genitive marker *de* was more vulnerable to omission than any other neutral-toned functor in imitation. Although the plural marker *men* and the durative aspect marker *zhe* were rarely produced in the children's spontaneous speech, they were infrequently omitted in their imitative speech.

Table 6 gives the the percentages of functors and content words omitted by the TW children in imitation.

Table 6. Functors and content words omitted by the TW children in imitation

Child	Age	MLU	Content omissions	Functor omissions
Mao	2;1	1.91	21%	57%
San	1;10	2.42	10%	50%
Xii	1;10	1.96	14%	57%

teh4 (2)	leh4 (2)	e5* (2)	e5 (4)	ti7 (2)
100%	50%	50%	75%	50%
100%	100%	50%	50%	0%
100%	100%	100%	50%	0%

For the TW group, the proportions of functor omissions were significantly higher than those of content word, $t = 18.965$, $p < .003$, two-tailed. That is, the TW children did demonstrate a significant difference between the omission of full-toned content words and full-toned grammatical morphemes. As in their spontaneous speech, nearly all the grammatical morphemes were susceptible to omission in the TW children's imitative speech. The diminutive marker -$a2$ was the only grammatical morpheme that was not omitted by the children in imitation, and the locative marker $ti7$ showed relatively strong resistance to omission in imitation. The progressive aspect marker $teh4$ and the durative aspect marker $leh4$ were rarely produced in spontaneous speech, and very frequently omitted in imitation.

In comparing functors omitted in imitation between the two language groups, I found that the TW children omitted significantly more functors than the MC children did, $t = -16.085$, $p < .004$, two-tailed. The proportions of content word omissions were low for both groups of children, and the TW children did not omit significantly more content words than the MC children did, $t = 1.1310$, $p = .3026$, two-tailed.

6. Discussion

The first prediction the proposed hypothesis makes is: The segmentation strategies characteristically employed by MC children and TW children will differ from the earliest stages of language acquisition, with MC children paying attention to metrical feet, and TW children paying attention to individual syllables. Although children's early speech typically shows a high frequency of content words, the appearance of neutral tone is no later than that of the full tones in MC children's productions. MC children thus learn to use the neutral tone early -- as soon as they begin to produce nouns which contain the diminutive marker -zi. In addition to the diminutive -zi, neutral-toned functors such as the classifier ge, the nominalizer/genitive marker de, and the completive aspect marker le also appear quite early. The relevant features of grammatical morphemes in MC and TW are compared in Table 7.

Table 7. Features of grammatical morphemes in MC and TW

Feature	MC	TW
1. Closely follow content words and in syntactic construction with them	Yes	Yes
2. Associate regularly with a pitch pattern (i.e., neutral tone)	Yes	No
3. Almost always contain a short, central vowel (i.e., schwa)	Yes	No
4. Frequently produced with preceding content words as prosodic units	Yes	No

In MC, speech rhythm has a characteristic pattern which is expressed in the opposition of strong versus weak syllables. Strong syllables bear primary stress and contain full vowels, whereas weak syllables are unstressed and contain short, central vowels such as schwa. A child encountering a strong syllable in spontaneous MC conversation would have a good chance of finding that strong syllable to be the onset of a new content word. A weak syllable, on the other hand, would be most likely to be a neutral-toned grammatical morpheme. It would appear, therefore, that MC speech indeed provides a good basis for the implementation of a segmentation strategy which assumes that full-toned lexical syllables followed by neutral-toned functor syllables constitute strong-weak trochaic feet.

Segmentation of nonstress languages like TW does not have such an obvious rhythmic basis, since in such languages there is no opposition between strong and weak syllables; all syllables contribute equally to the linguistic rhythm. Although grammatical morphemes in TW share with content words the phonological property of being tonal, they do not have the transparent semantic meanings of major content words. Grammatical morphemes do not refer to anything concrete. The concepts they express (e.g., progressiveness, possession) are more abstract than those expressed by the content words, and are therefore expected to be more difficult to acquire. TW children's difficulty in learning grammatical morphemes is reflected in their retention of content words and their deletion of grammatical ones in both spontaneous and imitative speech.

The second prediction is: There will be a significant difference in the patterns of realization and omission of grammatical morphemes between the two group of children, with full tones expected to be more salient than reduced ones. To the extent that the trochaic foot functions as a segmentation unit for MC children, while the syllable acts as a segmentation unit for TW children, we would expect to see a significant difference in the patterns of realization and omission of grammatical morphemes between the two groups of children, and this is indeed what I found: in the spontaneous and imitative speech of MC children, neutral-toned grammatical morphemes that fit a strong-weak template are frequently preserved, whereas grammatical morphemes are much more frequently omitted in the spontaneous and imitative speech of TW children.

What was unexpected about my findings is the direction of the difference. Intuitively one might expect full-toned functors of TW to be more salient than the neutral-toned ones of MC, but this does not seem to be the case. Rather it is the neutral-toned grammatical morphemes that participate in strong-weak templates that are earlier reproduced. This conclusion is reinforced by the finding that in MC the two most vulnerable of the neutral-toned functors were de and ge. A consideration of the position in which de was omitted reveals that out of 31 de omissions, 28, or 90%, occurred when de was followed by a noun phrase. As for ge, all three omission occurred in a single child's speech, when ge was followed by a noun phrase. These data suggest that this metrically more problematic phrase-medial positon is much more vulnerable than phrase-final position.

7. Conclusion

The results from the between-language comparisons suggest that rhythmic characteristics of languages can affect segmentation by providing different kinds of prosodic "handles" for the child to grasp at. Metrical feet may offer MC children one kind of segmentation handle because neutral-toned grammatical morphemes that closely follow full-toned content words are in position to be "picked up" as parts of unopened packages. In TW, however, since there is no opposition between full- and neutral-toned syllables, all syllables contribute equally to the linguistic rhythm, and the syllable more likely functions as a segmentation unit for TW children. In this language, it is the lexical syllables which have the perceptual advantage because of their semantic salience. This advantage is reflected in TW children's retention of content words and deletion of grammatical morphemes in spontaneous and imitative speech.

Appendix A

1. kan4 zhe ma1 ma1
   see DUR mother
   "looking at mommy"
2. hao3 duo1 che1-zi
   very many car-DIM
   "many cars"
3. san1 ge wan2 ju4
   three CL toy
   "three toys"
4. hong2 se4 de qiu2
   red color NOM ball
   "a ball that is red"
5. ma3 de wei3 ba1
   horse GEN tail
   "the tail of the horse"
6. zuo4 zhe chang4 ge1
   sit DUR sing song
   "sitting there singing"
7. Mao1 chi1 le yu2
   cat eat COM fish
   "The cat has eaten the fish."
8. da4 de fei1 ji1
   big NOM airplane
   "an airplane that is big"
9. mao1 mi1 shui4 le
   cat sleep COM
   "The cat has fallen asleep."
10. ya1-zi you2 shui3
    duck-DIM paddle
    "The duck is paddling."
11. san1 ge ping2 guo3
    three CL apple
    "three apples"
12. ma1 ma1 de shu1
    mother GEN book
    "mother's book"
13. xiao3 peng2 you3 men
    little friend PL
    "little friends"
14. wo3-men lai2 wan2
    I- PL come play
    "Let's play."

Appendix B

1. kau2-a2 chin1 koai1
   dog-DIM very good
   "good dog"
8. poe1-a2 u7 chui2
   cup- DIM have water
   "There is water in the cup."

2. che7 <u>leh4</u> chia1 sng2
   sit DUR here play
   "sitting here playing"
3. u7 sā1 <u>e5</u> lang5
   have three CL people
   "There are three persons."
4. ng5 <u>e5</u> kin1 chio1
   yellow NOM banana
   "a banana that is yellow"
5. ma1 ma1 <u>ti7</u> chia1
   mother LOC here
   "Mommy is here"
6. niau1 mi1 <u>teh4</u> khun3
   cat PROG sleep
   "The cat is sleeping."
7. pa1 pa1 <u>e5</u> chheh4
   father GEN book
   "father's book"
9. be2 <u>teh4</u> chiah8 chhau2
   horse PROG browse
   "The horse is browsing."
10. chheh4 khng3 <u>ti7</u> chia1
    book put LOC here
    "Books are placed here."
11. che7 <u>leh4</u> sia2 gi7
    sit DUR write character
    "sitting there writing"
12. sā1 <u>e5</u> ko3 su7
    three CL story
    "three stories"
13. goa2 <u>e5</u> bak8 chiu1
    I GEN eye
    "my eyes"
14. ang5 sek4 <u>e5</u> hoe1
    red color NOM flower
    "a flower that is red"

References

Beckman, Mary. E. 1986. *Stress and Non-stress Accent*. Dordrecht, The Netherlands: Foris Publications Holland.

Du, Tsai-Chun. 1988. *Tone and Stress in Taiwanese*. Doctoral dissertation, University of Illinois at Urbana-Champaign.

Duanmu, San. 1990. *A Formal Study of Syllable, Tone, Stress and Domain in Chinese Languages*. Doctoral dissertation, MIT.

Hsiao, Yu-Chao. 1991. *Syntax, Rhythm and Tone: a Triangular Relationship*. Taipei: The Crane Publishing Co., Ltd.

Hung, Feng-Sheng. 1996. *Prosody and the Acquisition of Grammatical Morphemes in Chinese Languages*. Bloomington: Indiana Linguistics Club.

MacWhinney, Brian. 1991. *The CHILDES Project: Tools for Analyzing Talk*. Hillsdale, NJ: Erlbaum.

Peters, Ann M. 1996. Language Typology, Prosody, and the Acquisition of Grammatical Morphemes. In press, Dan I. Slobin ed, *The Crosslinguistic Study of Language Acquisition*, Vol. 5. Hillsdale, NJ: Erlbaum.

Tseng, Chin-Chin. 1995. *Taiwanese Prosody: An Integrated Analysis of Acoustic and Perceptual Data*. Doctoral dissertation, University of Hawai`i at Manoa.

Scope and Distributivity in Child Mandarin*

THOMAS HUN-TAK LEE
Chinese University of Hong Kong

1. Introduction

It is well known that sentences containing quantifier phrases in subject and object positions show scope-dependent interpretations. A sentence such as (1a) has the scope-dependent readings given by Logical Form representations in (2a-b). (2a) stands for the subject wide scope interpretation, and (2b) the object wide scope interpretation, the meanings of which are shown in (3a) and (3b) respectively. These readings reflect a referential dependency in that the choice of objects corresponding to one quantifier phrase (QNP) depends on that corresponding to the the other QNP. Thus, on the subject wide scope reading, the choice of the binary set of umbrellas depends on which boy one chooses. Likewise, on the object wide scope reading, the selection of the three-member set of boys covaries with that of the umbrellas.

(1) a. Three boys are holding two umbrellas.
　　b. All the boys are holding two umbrellas.
(2) a. [three boys$_1$ [two umbrellas$_2$ [t$_1$ be holding t$_2$]] (subject wide scope)
　　b. [two umbrellas$_2$ [three boys$_1$ [t$_1$ be holding t$_2$]] (object wide scope)
(3) a. There are 3 x=boy, such that for each x, there are 2 y=umbrella, x is holding y.　　　(subject wide scope)
　　b. There are 2 y=umbrella, such that for each y, there are 3 x=boy, x is holding y.　　　(object wide scope)
　　c. There is a set of 3 boys and there is a set of 2 umbrellas such that each member of the boy set is holding at least an umbrella, and each member of the umbrella set is held by at least a boy.
　　(scope-independent)

---

*This research was supported by RGC grant CUHK 335/95. I wish to express gratitude to Xie Jun for her help in running the experiments, and to No.2 Nursery of the Chinese Academy of Science, Beijing, for allowing me to carry out child language experiments at the school. I have benefited from discussions on scope with Stephen Crain, Feng-hsi Liu, William Philip, and Kenneth Wexler. Please address correspondence to T. Lee, Dept of English, Chinese University of Hong Kong, Shatin, Hong Kong. Email: thomasLee@cuhk.edu.hk.

It has long been observed that in addition to scope-dependent readings, scope-independent or branching readings may also be available in QNP interpretation (cf. Barwise 1979, Kempson and Cormack 1981, Liu 1990, Beghelli, Ben-Shalom and Szabolcsi 1993). Thus, in addition to the readings (3a-b), (1a) has also the interpretation given in (3c), in which the sets of objects corresponding to the two QNPs are taken independently and a variety of connections are set up between members of the two sets. If each member of one set is connected with all members of the other set, this would be called, following (Sher 1990), the each-all reading. If each member of either set is connected with at least one member of the other set, this would be called the cumulative reading, since the totality of one set is cumulatively related to that of the other by the predicate. The scope-dependent and scope-independent readings of (1a) are depicted in (4).

(4) Scope-dependent and scope-independent readings of "Three boys are holding two umbrellas" (B=boy; U=umbrella)

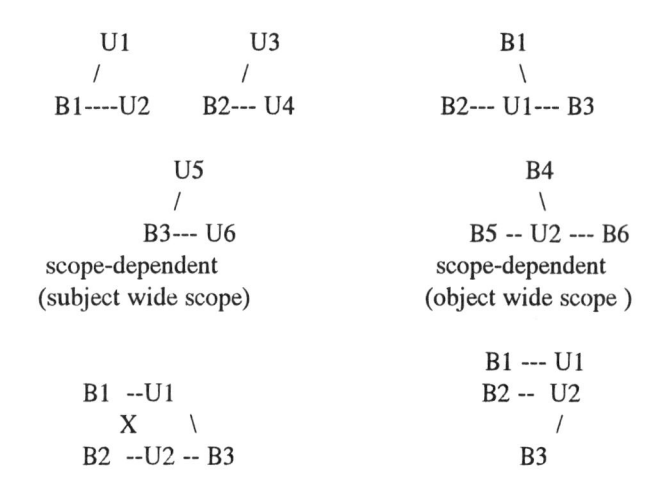

```
      U1         U3                    B1
      /          /                      \
  B1----U2   B2--- U4            B2--- U1--- B3

             U5                         B4
             /                           \
         B3--- U6                  B5 -- U2 --- B6
    scope-dependent              scope-dependent
   (subject wide scope)          (object wide scope)

                                     B1 --- U1
      B1 --U1                        B2 -- U2
       X   \                            /
      B2 --U2 -- B3                    B3
```

scope-independent (each-all)   scope-independent (cumulative)

The above analysis of the numeral phrases in (1a) can be extended to sentences containing the universal quantifier, as in "All the boys are holding two umbrellas" (1b). Assuming that we have a set of three boys, the subject-wide-scope, each-all, and cumulative readings pictured in (4) are also available in (1b).

2 Previous acquisition studies on scope

Studies on the acquisition of quantifier scope have largely looked at children's interpretation of sentences containing a universal QNP and a singular indefinite NP, e.g. "A boy is holding every umbrella" (see for example, Lee 1986, 1991, Chien and Wexler 1989, Philip 1995, Crain et al to appear). Researchers have explored the nature of the LF representations of children, specifically whether they involve quantification over events or individuals. Based on the apparent tendency for young children to pair entities in a one-to-one fashion, some researchers (cf. Philip 1995) have argued for a stage of development in which young children prefer event quantification. This view, however, has been challenged in Crain et all (to appear) on empirical and methodological grounds. Researchers have also shown that for languages like Chinese, which permits scope ambiguity in more restricted ways than English (see Aoun and Li 1991), young children may not map scope order isomorphically from surface hierarchical relations in the same way as adults do (cf. Lee 1991, Chien and Wexler 1989). That is to say, young Chinese children tend to regard sentences containing QNPs in subject and object positions as having both subject and object wide scope, when Chinese adults will only permit a subject wide scope reading. A third type of finding relates to children's early knowledge of quantifier types. It has been shown that four-year-olds respond differently to sentences containing QNPs than those with bare noun phrases (e.g. Philip 1985:119-122). Thus the percentage of non-adult interpretations differed greatly between sentences like "Is every boy riding a pony?" and sentences like "Are boys riding ponies?".

The issue of scope independent interpretations has not been systematically studied. Given the availability of both scope-dependent and scope-independent readings, it is natural to ask which type of interpretation is more basic. On the basis of typological evidence, it has been suggested that with respect to the relative scope of numeral phrases, the scope-independent readings are unmarked (cf. Gil 1992). On the other hand, Hornstein (1984) conjectured that children would initially assume all QNPs to have operator status. That is children would assign scope dependency readings right from the beginning. An understanding of how children interpret the relative scope of numeral phrases would be crucial for settling this issue.

3. Aims of the present study

This study explores Chinese children's understanding of quantifiers in the following five types of sentences, which involve the adverb *dou*, a distributor which is obligatory when the subject is a universal quantifier:

I. (Universal quantifier subject; numeral phrase object)
souyoude shushu dou   tiaozhe   liang tong shui
all   uncle   each carry-on-shoulder two bucket water
"All the men are carrying (on their shoulder) two buckets of water"

II. (Universal quantifier subject; bare NP object)
souyoude shushu dou tiaozhe   shuitong
  all   uncle each carry-on-shoulder water-bucket
"All the men are carrying (on their shoulder) water-buckets"

III. (Numeral phrase subject; numeral phrase object)[1]
you sange shushu tiaozhe   liang tong   shui
exist three uncle carry-on-shoulder two   bucket water
"Three men are carrying (on their shoulder) two buckets of water"

IV. (Conjoined NP subject; numeral phrase object; *without* distributor)
Xiaoliang he   Xiaoma nazhe liangge qiqiu
Xiaoliang and Xiaoma hold two   balloon
"Xiaoliang and Xiaoma are holding two balloons"

V. (Conjoined NP subject; numeral phrase object; *with* distributor)
Xiaoliang he   Xiaoma **dou** nazhe liangge qiqiu
Xiaoliang and Xiaoma each   hold two   balloon
"Xiaoliang and Xiaoma are both holding two balloons"

We would like to address the following issues: (a) whether young children interpret sentences with subject universal quantifier and object numeral phrase (Type I) in the same way as they do corresponding sentences with bare NP objects (Type II); (b) whether children permit scope-dependent readings and allow the subject numeral phrase to take wide scope over the object numeral phrase (cf. Type III); (c) whether young children are sensitive to the properties of the distributor *dou* when the latter is not preceded by the universal QNP (cf. whether they distinguish Type IV and Type V sentences). This issue is important for Mandarin, since universal quantifiers in subject position always require the presence of the distributor *dou* 'each'. It is therefore unclear whether a subject wide scope reading of a Type I sentence is due to the universal quantifier itself or the distributivity signalled by *dou*. The role of the distributor must be isolated from that of the subject universal quantifier.

4. Method

An experiment employing truth-judgement tasks was carried out in Beijing with 13 four-year-old and 14 five-year-old children, as well as 14 adults. Each of the Type I-III sentences was paired with 6 interpretations depicted by pictures: *distributive, each-all, cumulative, extra theme object, unrelated theme, non-exhausted agent*. The *distributive* situation corresponds to the subject wide scope reading, a scope-dependent reading. The *cumulative* reading represents unambiguously a scope-independent interpretation. The *each-all* situation can be taken as a scope-independent reading or a scope-dependent

---

[1] The existential verb *you* 'exist/have' is needed at the beginning because of the definiteness restriction on the subject position in Chinese.

reading. The *unrelated-theme* and the *non-exhausted agent* conditions are situations which falsify the sentences. The *extra-theme* condition differs from the *distributive* situation in having two extra theme objects, and serves to test the proposal of Philip (1995). A child preferring symmetric interpretations would say no to the *extra-theme* picture while saying yes in the distributive condition. Below is a schematic representation of the test pictures for Type I-III sentences, illustrated by "All the men are carrying two buckets".

(5) Interpretations for Type I-III sentences
    (M=person, W=water bucket, S=stone)

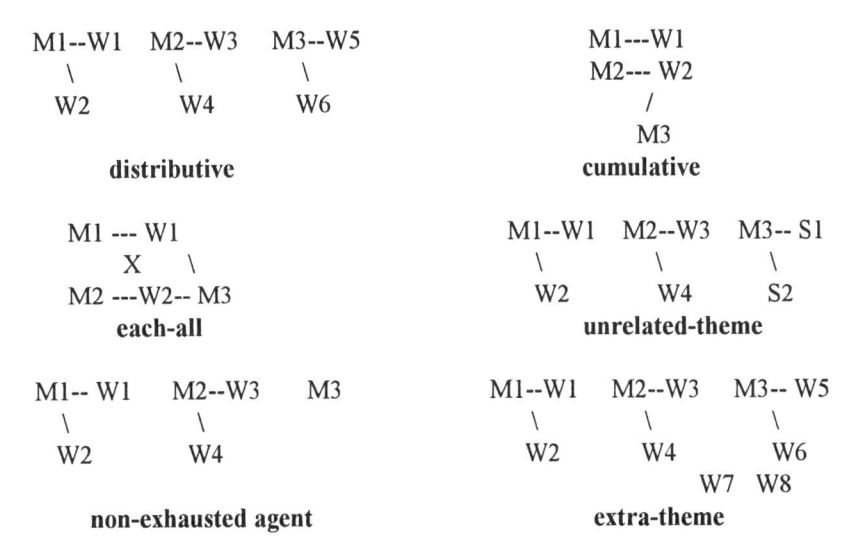

M1--W1   M2--W3   M3--W5   M1---W1
  \   \   \   M2--- W2
  W2   W4   W6   /
                                  M3
    distributive   **cumulative**

M1 --- W1   M1--W1   M2--W3   M3-- S1
  X   \   \   \   \
M2 ---W2-- M3   W2   W4   S2
    each-all   **unrelated-theme**

M1-- W1   M2--W3   M3   M1--W1   M2--W3   M3-- W5
  \   \   \   \   \
  W2   W4   W2   W4   W6
                                                  W7 W8
    non-exhausted agent   **extra-theme**

Sentence types IV-V were paired with three readings: *distributive*, *cumulative* and *each-all*, illustrated by "Xiaoliang and Xiaoma are (both) holding two balloons". The referents of the conjoined subject were, respectively, a short, fat boy called Xiaoliang and a tall, skinny boy identified as Xiaoma. A schematic representation of the test pictures is given in (6). Without the distributor *dou* 'each', as in Type IV sentences, all three situations should be compatible with the test sentence. With the distributor present, as in Type V sentences, the cumulative interpretation should be ruled out.

(6) Interpretations for Type IV-V sentences
    (XL= Xiaoliang; XM= Xiaoma; BL=balloon)
XL--BL1   XM--BL3   XL--BL1   XL---BL1
  \   \   X
  BL2   BL4   XM--BL2   XM-- BL2
    distributive   **cumulative**   **each-all**

Each of the sentence types I-III had three versions using different verbs and arguments (boys holding umbrellas; men carrying water buckets; dogs chewing bones). Thus a total of 54 items (3 x 3 x 6 sentence-situation pairings) were used for Types I-III. As for Types IV-V, each test sentence was paired with three versions varying in verbs and arguments (Xiaoling and Xiaoma holding balloons, spraying water over pots of plants, and drinking water from glasses). Thus a total of 18 items (2 x 3 x 3 sentence-situation pairings) were used for Types IV-V. The sentences were audio-recorded. Each child was tested in three separate sessions, in which some other items were also tested, with successive sessions separated by at least half a day or a day. A session lasted about 20 minutes.

5. Results

As can be seen from Figures 1 and 2, 4- and 5-year-olds behaved like adults in accepting the distributive and each-all readings of Type I and Type II sentences (approximately 70% or more of the time). They also correctly rejected the non-exhausted agent and unrelated-theme interpretations, as reflected in the low acceptance rate for these interpretations (15% or lower).

A glance at the two figures shows that adults clearly differentiated a numeral phrase object from a bare NP object in sentences with a subject universal quantifier. While adults allowed distributive and each-all readings for both Type I and Type II sentences, they accepted cumulative readings only for Type II sentences but not for Type I sentences (90% acceptance in Fig. 2 vs 10% in Fig. 1). Children by five years old differentiated numeral NPs and bare NPs in interpreting their scope relative to a universal QNP. About half of the four-year-olds and around 80% of the five-year-olds rejected the cumulative reading for sentences with object numeral phrases (see Fig. 1), but accepted the same reading for sentences with bare NP objects (with approximately 65-75% acceptance, see Fig. 2).

Figure 3 gives the results on the relative scope of numeral phrases. Chinese adults generally did not accept a distributive reading (ie the subject wide scope reading) in assigning scope to numeral phrases (only 20% acceptance). However, they allowed a cumulative reading as well as an each-all reading, which could be taken in this case as a scope-independent interpretation since the canonical scope-dependent reading (ie the distributive reading) was strongly disfavored. A surprising finding of our study is that unlike adults, 4- and 5-year-olds overwhelmingly favored the distributive interpretation. The preponderance of distributive readings cannot be attributed to a task bias, since the children did not reject all sentences paired with non-distributive contexts. sentences. For example, they correctly rejected the unrelated-agent and the non-exhausted agent pictures, and showed different levels of acceptance for the cumulative reading in Type I and Type II sentences.

Fig. 1: Interpretation of Type 1 sentences: universal QNP subject and numeral phrase object.

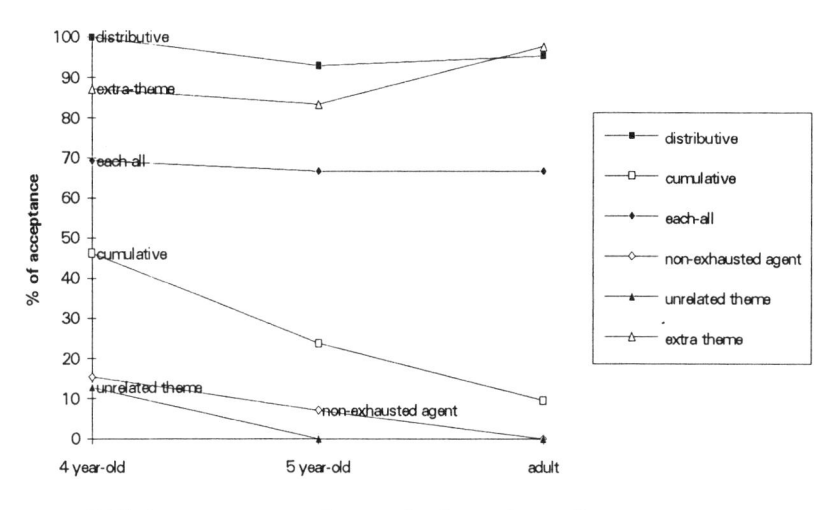

"All the men are carrying two buckets of water"

Fig. 2: Interpretation of Type II sentences: universal QNP subject and bare NP object.

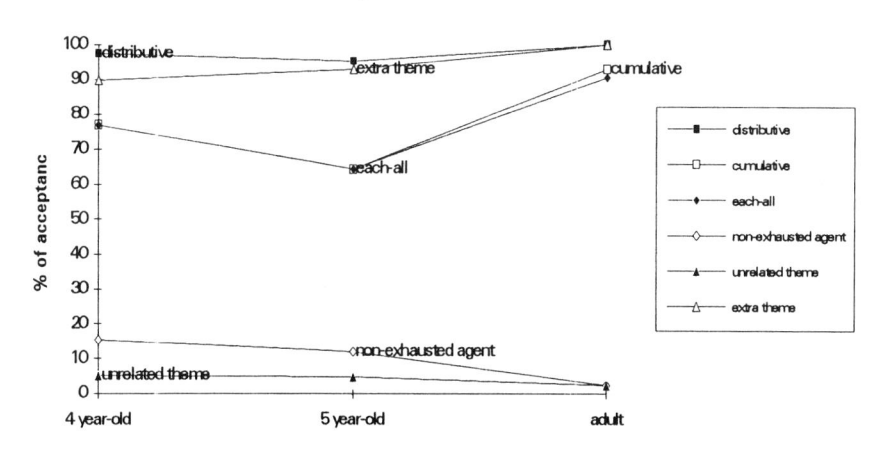

"All the men are carrying water-buckets"

Fig. 3: Interpretation of Type III sentences: numeral phrase subject and numeral phrase object

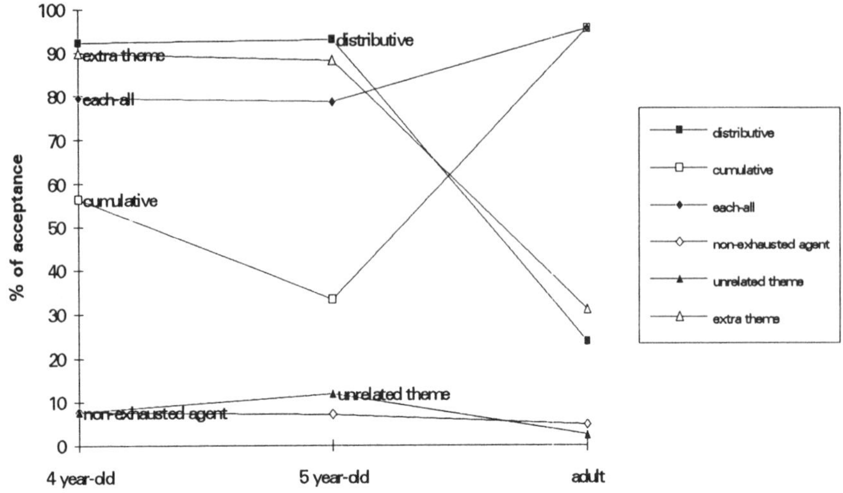

"Three men are carrying two buckets of water"

Figures 4 and 5 reflect subjects' knowledge of the distributive properties of *dou* 'each'. In the absence of the distributor *dou*, adults mostly refused to distribute the conjoined subject NP (with only 40% acceptance, see Fig. 4). At the same time, they accepted the each-all and cumulative readings around 70% or more of the time. On the other hand, with the distributor *dou* present, adults accepted the distributive and each-all readings around 70% or more of the time (cf. Fig. 5). In addition, they rejected the cumulative reading overwhelmingly (with less than 10% acceptance), since this reading is incompatible with the distributive property of the *dou*. Our data show that the four- and five-year-olds were not sensitive to the distributive property of the *dou*. They accepted the cumulative reading for sentences with conjoined proper noun subjects, irrespective of the presence of *dou*, between 65 and 80 % of the time.

On the issue of whether young children give symmetric interpretations when extra objects are presented in the picture, Figures 1-3 show that Mandarin-speaking children did not behave differently on the ***distributive*** and ***extra-theme*** conditions. Figures 1-3 show that the level of the distributive reading was not hampered at all by the presence of extra theme objects (witness the 85-90 % acceptance rate for the extra-theme condition). The symmetric readings reported in Philip (1985) failed to be replicated in the present study.

Fig. 4: Interpretation of Type IV sentences: conjoined NP subject and numeral phrase object; without distributor.

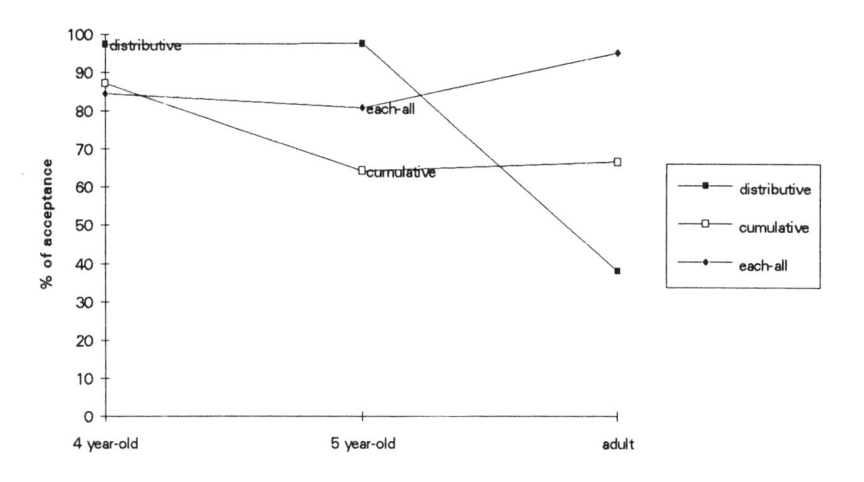

"Xiaoliang and Xiaoma are holding two balloons"

Fig. 5: Interpretation of Type V sentences: conjoined NP subject and numeral phrase object, with distributor

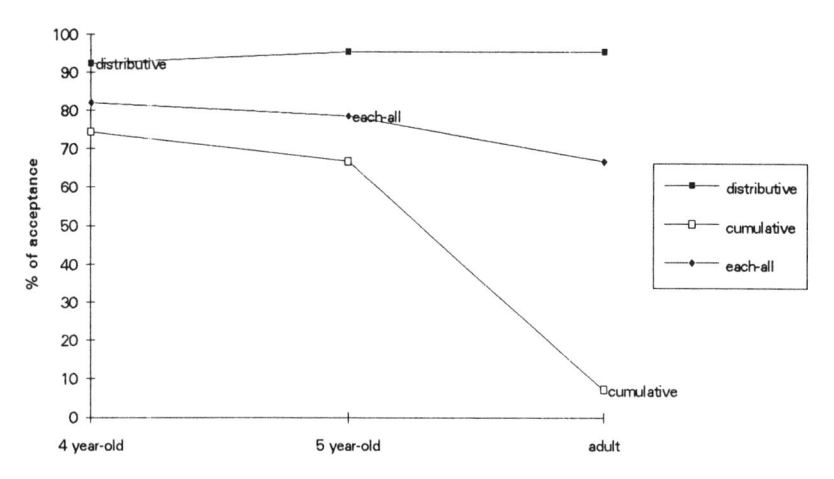

"Xiaoliang and Xiaoma are both holding two balloons"

6. Conclusions

Our study has shown that young children are sensitive to the distinction between a QNP and a bare NP vis-a-vis a subject universal quantifier. They allow a cumulative reading only for the bare NP but not for a QNP. The findings show that children prefer to give a distributive reading to sentences with numeral phrases in subject and object position. This runs counter to the typologically based predictions of Gil (1992), and lends support to Hornstein (1984)'s proposal that scope dependency between quantity-denoting NPs is unmarked. The results on *dou* 'each' show that children's knowledge of the adverb's distributivity is acquired late. Thus the assignment of subject wide scope by Chinese children cannot be due to the distributivity of the adverb, but must be attributed to scope interactions between the QNPs. Lastly, our children did not give symmetric readings even when presented with extra theme objects, suggesting that data from Chinese do not warrant the event quantification accounts given by Philip (1995).

References

Aoun, J. and A. Li. 1991. *The Syntax of Scope*. MIT Press.
Barwise, J. 1979. On branching quantifiers in English, *Journal of Philosophical Logic* 8: 47-80.
Beghelli, F., D. Ben-Shalom and A. Szabolcsi. 1993. When do subjects and objects exhibit a branching reading?, in E. Duncan, D. Farkas and P. Spaelti eds. *Proceedings of the Twelfth West Coast Conference on Formal Linguistics*. pp. 501-516.
Chien, Y. and K. Wexler. 1989. Children's knowledge of relataive scope in Chinese, *Papers and Report in Child Language Development* 28:72-80.
Crain, S., R. Thornton, C. Boster, L. Conway, D. Lillo-Martin and E. Woodams. (to appear) Quantification without qualification, *Language Acquisition*.
Gil, D. 1992. Scopal quantifiers: some universals of lexical effability, in J. van der Auwera, ed., *Meaning and Grammar: crosslinguistic perspectives*. Mouton de Gruyter.
Hornstein, N. 1984. *Logic as Grammar*. MIT Press.
Kempson, R. and A. Cormack. 1981. Ambiguity and quantification, *Linguistics and Philosophy* 4: 259-310.
Lee, T. 1986. *Studies on Quantification in Chinese*. Ph.D. dissertation. UCLA.
Lee, T. 1991. Linearity as a scope principle for Chinese: evidence from first language acquisition, in D. Napoli and J. Kegl, eds., *Bridges between Psychology and Linguistics*. Lawrence Erlbaum.
Liu, F. 1990. *Scope Dependency in English and Chinese*. Ph.D. dissertation, UCLA.
Philip, W. 1995. *Event Quantification in the Acquisition of Universal Quantification*. Ph.D. dissertation, University of Massachusetts at Amherst.
Sher, G. 1990. Ways of branching quantifiers, *Linguistics and Philosophy* 13: 393-422.

Vertical Path in Tzotzil (Mayan) Early Acquisition: Linguistic vs. Cognitive Determinants[1]

LOURDES DE LEÓN
Reed College

1. Introduction

When Lupa, a nineteen month old Tzotzil Mayan girl wants to be picked up by a caregiver she uses the verbs

pet! 'carry in arms' or

kuch! 'carry on back'

depending on whether she just wants to be held for a short time in her mother's arms or whether she wants to sleep or rest on her mother's back. In a similar situation, an English speaking child of the same age might say *up!*

When Lupa wants her mom to adopt a lower position so as to nurse her she tells her

kej ! 'kneel down'

---

[1] Tzotzil is a Mayan language spoken in the highlands of Chiapas by about 300,000 speakers. Data for this study were obtained in the hamlet of Nabenchauk, Zinacantan. See Haviland (1991) for a grammatical description.

Or when she wants her playmate to sit down by her side she uses a Baby Talk verb that means 'sit down'

pepex 'sit down'

In both situations an English speaking child of her age might say *down!*

Why is the Tzotzil child not using words denoting UP or DOWN in these particular requests if her language provides the verbs *muy* 'ascend', *yal* 'descend' and the directional particles *muyel* 'going up' and *yalel* 'going down'? If these are among the first words learnt by an English speaking child supposedly as a result of the influence of a prelinguistic spatial concept encoding vertical motion why do they fail to appear in Lupa's speech? (Bloom 1973, Choi and Bowerman 1991, H. Clark 1973, McCune-Nicolich 1981, Nelson 1974).

The present study shows that the expression of vertical path *per se* is apparently not an early concern for Tzotzil children. It evaluates the acquisition of path in relation to linguistic type and language-specific semantics. The research is based on the longitudinal study of two Tzotzil children, plus supplementary data from a third child.

I will start with a brief review of research on the development of spatial language and previous cross-linguistic findings regarding the acquisition of path. Tzotzil path resources will be sketched briefly; this is followed by a section on how vertical motion is expressed in early one word utterances and early two word combinations in Tzotzil. The Tzotzil early acquisition data will be used to evaluate the possible influence of a non linguistic notion of vertical motion against typological and language-specific determinants.

2. Background

Spatial notions such as containment, support, contact, and vertical motion have been considered to precede developmentally and to guide the acquisition of spatial language (E. Clark 1973a, b, H. Clark 1973, Johnston and Slobin 1979, Sinha et al. 1994, Slobin 1985). Of the basic spatial notions, verticality and gravity have been included among candidates for semantic primitives, associated with innate perceptual processing mechanisms (H. Clark 1973). In a recent study, based on the cross-linguistic acquisition of spatial morphemes, Sinha et al. (1994:82) conclude that when spatial meanings are encoded in closed-class forms "basic morphemes," they may follow an order of acquisition where vertical motion will appear among the set of the early spatial forms acquired. In fact, several researchers have stated that English speaking children learn the words *up* and *down* at an early age and extend them to many events involving vertical motion because they are mapping them directly to nonlinguistic notions of motion "downward" and "upward" (Bloom 1973, Bowerman 1995, Choi and Bowerman 1991, Gruendel 1977 in Bowerman in press: 5, McCune-Nicolich 1981, Nelson 1974).

From a typological perspective, "motion events" have been analysed as consisting of a moving object (the *Figure*), a reference object (the *Ground*), and the trajectory of the Figure with respect to the Ground (the *Path*) (Talmy 1985, 1991). The lexicalization of path displays different patterns across languages, dividing them roughly into "verb-framed" and "satellite-framed" languages (Talmy 1985). The distinction is based on whether path is encoded in the verb, as in Romance languages like Spanish: *subir* 'ascend', *bajar* 'descend', *entrar* 'enter', *salir* 'exit.' Here Manner is expressed separately from the verb. In the satellite framed type, Path is encoded in separate particles that may merge with prepositions such as English (*in, on, off, out).* In this type, of which Germanic languages are typical, Motion and Manner are characteristically encoded in the verb:

Verb-framed:

La niña $_{Figure}$ entró $_{Motion, Path}$ (a la casa $_{Ground}$) brincando $_{Manner}$

Satellite-framed:

The girl $_{Figure}$ jumped $_{Motion, Manner}$ in $_{Path}$ (to the house$_{Ground}$)

The interaction between the typology of path and language development has been a recent topic of reflection. Berman and Slobin (1994) have examined the development of narrative in languages differing in where they encode path. More recently, Slobin[2] (to appear) has proposed a learning theory based on typological patterns as a guide for acquisition (c.f. Bowerman 1993). In a pioneering study, Choi and Bowerman (1991) examined the development of path in Korean, a "verb-framed" language, and English, a "satellite framed language." They showed that the typological differences between the two languages in where they encode path guide the children in how to express it, and that a non linguistic spatial concept of say, motion on a vertical axis, or topological path, does not dominate over the language specific ways of encoding such concept. In fact, Korean children learn path specific verbs first, learn the motion verbs for *go up* and *go down* at a slower pace, and do not generalize the latter verbs to all kinds of vertical motion.

With the same typological concern in mind Bowerman, de León and Choi (1995) brought Tzotzil, a Mayan language, into the same cross-linguistic comparison.[3] This language does not fall neatly into Talmy's typology but

---

[2] Slobin (to appear) argues quite justifiably that the distinction between open and closed classes is not striclty applicable to grammatical and lexical form classes. Verb subclasses can be considered "closed" on the basis of syntactic and semantic particularities. For Slobin's recent review of Talmy's typology, see *The Max Planck Institute 1995 Annual Report*, p. 83.

[3] Tzotzil is a morphologically ergative VOS language with relatively few roots but with high morphological derivation of words.

presents a situation intermediate between verb-framed and satellite-framed languages:

(i) in common with "verb-framed languages" it encodes path in the verb together with other semantic dimensions such as Manner, shape, geometry of Figure and Ground, etc. (Haviland, 1994 a, b), as in Table 1.

Insertion	tik'	'insert loosely'
	xoj	'put in pole/ring'
	paj	'insert with force'
Extraction	tas	'take out from container'
	mas	'take off of liquid'
	botz'	'pull out'
Gravity	p'aj	'fall vertically from height' (e.g. falling off cliff)
	lom	'topple over' (e.g. tree, lightpost)
	jach'	'slip and fall on base'(e.g. person on mud, ice)
	jin	'fall over and roll down (e.g. chair, pot, pile of rocks)

Table 1. Tzotzil path-conflating verbs

As a verb-framed language Tzotzil also has high frequency of intransitive verbs for motion denoting 'ascend,' 'descend,' 'enter,' 'exit,' 'pass.'

(ii) But Tzotzil also behaves as a "satellite-framed language." It encodes path in directional particles derived from the intransitive motion verbs that resemble Germanic particles meaning *in, out, up, down*. Table 2 presents Tzotzil resources encoding path of the kind encoded by the English particles *in, out, up, down*.

English	Tzotzil gloss	Intransitive	Transitive	Directional
in	'enter'	och	otes	ochel
out	'exit, off, remove'	lok'	lok'es, lok'	lok'el
up	'ascend'	muy	muyes	muyel
down	'descend'	yal	yales	yalel

Table 2. English path particles and Tzotzil motion verbs and directionals.

The directional particles are stressed and often occur sentence-finally. They combine freely with virtually any predicate (Haviland 1991). For example:

pit' ochel   'jump into'
p'aj yalel   'fall vertically downward'
jip lok'el   'throw out'
xuj muyel   'push upwards'

They can also occur with path-conflating verbs, and with stative predicates:
botz' lok'el   'pull off removing'

tik' ochel   'insert loosely into'
tz'ukul yalel   'falling head down' (be upside-down downwards)
latzal muyel   'stacked upwardly' (e.g. having been stacked upwardly)

Given the typological particularities of Tzotzil and the cognitive predictions about the acquisition of spatial language, in this paper we will evaluate the following hypotheses:

(i) guided by a non linguistic spatial notion such as containment or verticality and having the option to use the general motion verbs and particles over the specific verbs, children would choose general verbs and/or particles and apply them across different contexts (cf. Bowerman in press:5).

(ii) spatial notions encoded in closed classes may be acquired earlier than open class forms. Among these notions containment, support, and verticality are supposedly the first ones to be acquired (Sinha et al. 1994).

(iii) like Germanic speaking children, Tzotzil children will acquire particles at an early age because they are stressed and sentence final (Slobin 1973, Bowerman, de León, Choi 1995: 104).

However, data obtained from my Tzotzil longitidunal study and from cross-sectional tasks eliciting spatial actions designed by Bowerman and Choi (Bowerman in press, Bowerman and Choi, in preparation) revealed that Tzotzil children do not use the directional particle denoting IN before the semantically richer Path verbs for topological actions. They use the intransitive motion verbs but they do not generalize them to refer to abstract spatial situations of the kind IN/ON, UP/DOWN as research on spatial linguistic development might predict.

The collection of path conflating verbs used by the children revealed an early concern with topological actions involving insertion, attachment, separation, and division. This finding showed evidence for the influence of a nonlinguistic topological notion as predicted by Johnston and Slobin (1979). However, it also clearly showed attention to Tzotzil semantics of topology: the verb for putting something loosely in a container (*tik'*) is different from the verb used for putting a finger in a ring (*xoj*), or from the verb for putting on clothes (*lap*), and these differences are clear to a two-year-old Tzotzil child.

A similar pattern of dispreference for pure path forms appeared also in early the expression of vertical path among Tzotzil youngsters. In this case, we observed a tendency not to express vertical path until topological path was well established. When the vertical motion verbs appeared they were used strictly for intransitive vertical or inclined motion. Vertical path particles did not appear at all until the production of multi-word utterances. Children showed instead an early profusion of posture verbs expressing canonical and non-canonical position and Figure/Ground configuration, much like to the Korean children in Choi and Bowerman's study (1991).

3. Expression of Vertical Path in Three Tzotzil Children

The data come from a longitudinal study of a girl (Lupa), and two boys (Xun and Palas). Lupa's data come from a six month period (19- 25 months old) of weekly three hour visits starting with one-word utterances and continuing through early word combinations appearing by the 24th month. The examples reported here come from videotaped and audiotaped sessions of the weekly visits, a total of around 50 hours of analyzed material.

Data from Xun and Palas are based on monthly one hour audio recordings over a period of two years starting when they were two years old with three to multiple word combinations. Videotaped recordings were made every two to three months for the two year period. Data from Palas will be used here to supplement findings. Materials were transcribed by the researcher and her assistant in consultation with the parents. The data rely exclusively on the researcher's notes and recordings. Information through interviews or questionnaires to parents is impossible to obtain in this fieldwork situation in which caregivers are basically illiterate and show little explicit interest in the child's linguistic development (Pye 1992: 242-244). Our main two subjects (Lupa and Xun) are first children and first grandchildren. They spend more time with adult caregivers and less with younger children than many other Zinacantec youngsters. Palas is the fourth child and lives in a compound with six children, his parents, aunts, uncles and grandparents.

3.1 Findings

In general, the three children of the study did not use directional particles before verbs.[4] They learnt path conflating verbs and some intransitive motion verbs before directionals. This paralleled findings reported in Bowerman, de León and Choi (1995) where the IN directional particles was absent and the path conflating verbs denoting topological relations were preferred.

The use of pure motion verbs in our three subjects developed in a similar pattern which may be divided in two broad stages. The first stage included the verbs *bat* 'go', *la`* 'come' (imperative form), *och* 'enter', *lok'*, 'exit', *lok'es* 'take out', *kom* 'stay'. The motion verbs 'ascend' (*muy*) and 'descend' (*yal*) appeared at a later stage and were used in very low frequency in contrast to the previously acquired motion verbs.

Our youngest subject, Lupa, by her 25th month--still at a one word stage-- used the verb root *muy* 'ascend' to mean both 'ascend' and 'descend' on a vertical line, basically referring to a child climbing up corn bags. This verb was late and highly infrequent in comparison to other motion verbs previously

---

[4] The deictic directional *tal* 'come' is the only directional that appears in earlier combination with a main verb. However, it does not seem to be productive at this stage but appears in amalgam with a small number of verbs.

acquired. Our records show that our two other subjects--Xun (at 4.3 MLU) and Palas (at 3.5 MLU), used the verb *yal* 'descend' initially to mean 'go downhill'. This use is consistent with one of the meanings of the verbs in adult Tzotzil *yal* 'go downhill' and *muy* 'go uphill' (cf. Brown and Levinson 1993 for Tzeltal, de León 1994 for Tzotzil). In the case of these two boys, reference to the local slope of the domestic space seemed to dominate over reference to motion on a vertical axis. Of course, we don't know if at an earlier stage they started as Lupa did, referring to motion on a vertical axis in a restricted way.

We observe neither generalization of the motion verbs to other motion situations nor overgeneralization of intransitives to transitive use.

We do observe the production of vertical path conflating verbs. In Tzotzil, there is a large collection of verbs that refer to "falling." Among the more frequent are *p'aj* 'falling from height' used for objects falling off from a high surface, i.e. table, cliff, roof, vs. *lom* 'toppling over' used to refer to vertically standing objects that fall, such as trees, lamp posts, sticks, or even a drunk man. The verb *jach'* 'slipping and falling' applies basically to animated beings that fall in motion. The verb *jin* 'fall over and roll down' is applied to objects that have a canonical position and fall over such as a chair, a pot, or a bycicle. It can also be used to refer to a pile of rocks that collapses and rolls over. Several of these verbs appear earlier than the pure vertical motion verbs in our three subjects.[5]

The early acquisition of these "falling" verbs obviously reflects the child's concern for the effects of gravity, but it also reflects attention to how this semantic domain is organized in Tzotzil.

Tables 3 and 4 show the developmental progression (by months after birth) of "falling" verbs' in Lupa and Xun.

Gravity	19	20	21	22	23	24
'fall from height'	p'aj					
'topple over'					lom	
'slip and fall'						jach'

Table 3. Lupa's acquisition of "falling" verbs.

Gravity	25	26	27	28	29
'fall from height'	p'aj				
'topple over'					
'slip and fall'					jach'

Table 4. Xun's acquisition of "falling" verbs.

The late acquisition of the vertical motion verbs contrasted noticeably with an early profusion of verbs denoting posture changes, change of location, or

---

[5] Longitudinal data from a child currently studied at her one word stage shows the early production of *p'aj* 'fall down vertically', vs. *jach'* 'slip and fall' vs. *jin* 'fall over'.

change of state used in many cases to request transitive actions or to indicate location. Table 5 reproduces the verb forms as they were produced by Lupa, basically with no verb inflection and an incipient morphology, mainly positional roots.[6]

	19	20	21	22	23	24	25
POSTURE							
'sit'	pepex			chotol			
'kneel down'	kej						
'face down'	nuj				nujp'ij		
'stand up'		va`al					
'stand on all fours'			kotol				xkotet
'face up'					javk'uj		
'flip over'					valk'uj		
'lying face down'							patal
SUPPORT							
'on high surface'	kaj						
'on ground'			pak'al				
'hanging'	jok'						
'perched'		luchul					
'piled up'				busul			
'bowl on surface'						pach	
'on base/ mouth up'							vuch

Table 5. Lupa's early posture and change of location verbs

Table 6 shows Xun's early verb roots. By the time of the study he had some derivational morphology which is not included in the chart.

---

[6] Positional roots are a typical class of verbal roots with a specific derivational morphology in Mayan languages where they play a central role in conveying location. They range over several notional domains that encode notions of shape, geometry, position and collocation, surface, material, visual appearance (Haviland 1994a: 727). In Tzotzil they constitute about 30% of the verbal raw material (Haviland 1992, 1994 a, b). See Brown (1994) for Tzeltal positional roots.

	25	26	27	28	29	30
POSTURE						
'stand on all fours'			kot			
'sit'	pepex	chot				
'stand upright'			va`			
'face up'						jav
SUPPORT						
'stack'		latz				
'on ground'				pak'		
'on high surface'				kaj		
'hanging'				jok'		
'perched'						noch'

Table 6. Xun's early posture and change of location verbs

A close look at Lupa's and Xun's verbal productions reveals an early attention to canonical position, fine anatomic contrasts, shape, and the geometry of Figure and Ground. The production of these verbs demonstrates an early grasp of Tzotzil semantic contrasts to denote change of posture and change of location on a vertical axis, consistent with the adult semantic categories.[7]

Table 7 shows the context of use of utterances containing Lupa's early verbs associated with change of posture and change of location on a vertical axis. These verbs were produced at her one word utterance stage and in her early word combinations.

Verbs	
Change of posture	**Context of production**
pepex (Baby Talk) 'sit down' (19)	(to request people to sit by her, to describe people and dolls sitting)
chotol 'on sitting position' (22)	(to describe people, dolls on sitting position)
va`al 'standing position' (20)	(after standing up two thread spools, after standing doll)
nuj 'face and belly down' (20)	(referring to a child 's posture on ground, to doll facing down.)
valk'uj 'flip over' (23)	(referring to a child sudden change of posture)

---

[7] The early appearance of these verbs is guided not only by the semantics of the language but also by the morphological saliency of the verbal class of positional roots in Tzotzil grammar (de León, in preparation).

(Table 7, continued)

javk'uj 'belly up' (23)	(referring to a child sudden change of posture, to doll lying face up)
patal 'lying face down' (25)	(referring to dog, cat, toy, lying face down with stretched limbs)
Change of location verbs **(i) High/low placement**	
kaj 'place on raised surface' (19)	(requesting to place ring, bag on table)
pak'al 'lying on ground' (21)	(describing objects lying on the ground such as cloth, bag, coin)
(ii) Canonical orientation	
pach 'bowl on surface' (24)	(to request for bowl of soup or beans to be placed on table)
vuchul 'on base, long standing object' (i.e. bottle, jar) (25)	(to refer to a container of powdered soap, to a clay pot standing on ground)
(iii) Form of attachment	
luchul 'perched on top' (20)	(referring to person/object perched on top of base; bird on tree, girl on top of piles of corn bags, two thread spools on top of each other).
jok' 'hang' *(19)*	(asking for help to hang a cloth from a branch, or for hanging a balloon from a ceiling lamp)
(iv) Arrangement	
busul 'piled up' (22)	(to refer to multiple objects piled up on a surface: beans, stones, small toys)

Table 7. Contexts of use of change of posture and change of location verbs by Lupa.
Note: the one word utterances were produced just before, during, or just after the events indicated. Numbers in parenthesis refer to age in months.

In sum, the posture and change of location verbs of these children show

(i) awareness of change of posture and canonical orientation. This may suggest perception of a main axis and its canonical or non-canonical orientation. Visual determinants of this kind may reflect an early predisposition to perceiving a main axis as suggested by Landau (1995). Even if that is the case, our Tzotzil subjects' early productions indicate an awareness of the orientation of the main axis always consistent with the particular semantics of the verb root class in Tzotzil which draws fine anatomical distinctions such as being 'face up', 'mouth up', 'belly down', 'down with stretched limbs', 'lying on one's side', etc..

(ii) expression of change of location involving a vertical axis, (i.e. ground vs. raised surface, hanging, perched, etc.). In this case again attention to Figure and Ground configuration, shape, form of attachment, etc., is central to Tzotzil specific semantics.

The relatively earlier acquisition of the specific verbs over the general vertical motion verbs and directionals, the lack of generalization of the vertical motion verbs, and the absence of vertical directionals clearly indicate the power of language-specific determinants over cognitive ones.

3.2 A Comparative Look at English and Tzotzil

Context	English[a]	Tzotzil[b]
Standing up	up (e.g. in crib, car)	va`al 'stand upright' (e.g. in corral, on ground) kot 'stand on all fours'
Asking adult to lift child up	up	pet 'carry on arms' kuch 'carry on back'
Climbing on raised surface	up (e.g. on highchair, counter)	luch 'perch on top' (e.g. on tree, bags of corn)
Putting object on raised surface (i.e table)	up	kaj 'put object on surface' pach 'put bowl on surface'
Putting object on pile of objects	up	busul 'set on piles'
Asking adult to sit down	down	chot 'sit down' kej 'kneel down'
Setting objects on floor, ground	down	pak' 'set on ground carelessly' vuch 'set standing object on base' (e.g. bottle)
Describing a person or animal's head down	down (putting cat head's down)	nuj 'face down' (describing a child or doll) patal 'lying face down' (animal)

Table 8. Examples of English and Tzotzil utterances used in similar contexts involving motion or change of location on a vertical axis.

Note: Examples for both languages are taken from utterances that were produced just before, during, or just after the events indicated.

[a] English examples are from Bowerman's daughters C and E presented in Choi and Bowerman (1991:101-102). Ages in months: 16 to 21. Only those utterances that matched in context with the Tzotzil utterances were included here.

[b] Examples from Tzotzil come from the author's case studies of Lupa (19-25) in her one word utterance and early word combination stage and Xun (25-30) starting at his early word combination.

A comparative look at English and Tzotzil utterances produced by two-year-olds (see Table 8) shows similarity in contexts invoking change of posture and change of location on a vertical axis. However, according to the literature, English speaking children at the one word utterance and early word combination stage (16 to 24 months of age) use the particles *up* and *down* across all change of posture and change of location contexts. Tzotzil toddlers, by contrast, having the choice between the vertical path particle, the pure motion verb and the path conflating verb, prefer to use the latter ones.

By contrast to English speakers, Tzotzil children, like the Korean children reported in Choi and Bowerman (1991), use particular verbs that either do not necessarily encode verticality or conflate it with other semantic information.

4. Conclusions

At the beginning of this paper we raised cognitive, morphological, and typological arguments to evaluate the acquisition of vertical path in Tzotzil. Let's start with the cognitive ones. In recent papers, Haviland (1992, 1994a, b) and Brown (1994) have pointed out the difficulty in isolating spatial notions such as those conveyed by the English prepositions *in* and *on* in languages such as Tzotzil and Tzeltal. They argue that it is unreasonable to postulate the spatial concepts as prelinguistic guides to acquisition in these languages. Both authors notice that predicates in these two Mayan languages encode cross-cutting semantic notions that cannot be grouped under such general notions as containment, support, attachment, etc.. Nevertheless, as predicted by Johnston and Slobin (1979) and as shown in Bowerman, de León and Choi (1995), verbal reference to topological actions seems indeed to be an early concern for Tzotzil children. In contrast to English speaking children who express such actions with the early use of the prepositions *in* or *on*, Tzotzil children express topological notions in complex semantic packages that encode geometry, the nature of attachment, contact etc., together with path.

With respect to the early expression of vertical motion and its supposed early generalization, we find no early preoccupation with motion on a vertical axis *per se*. We do observe a strong bias for expressing notions involving gravity. It is reflected in the early expression of nonvolitional downward motion conflated with manner of falling and certain distinctions in both Figure (i.e shape, anatomy, canonical orientation) and Ground (i.e. 'slippery'). Notions involving volitional upward and downward motion are not expressed until much later. Tzotzil children instead begin quite early to acquire change of posture verbs.

Predictions that spatial notions encoded in closed class morphemes are earlier acquired do not seem to apply to Tzotzil in the case of vertical path (Sinha et al. 1994). Tzotzil children started with the open class of posture verbs and later acquired the verbs and directionals meaning 'ascending' and 'descending'.

As for typological predictions, our findings regarding vertical path confirm findings reported in Bowerman, de León and Choi (1995). Tzotzil children did not follow the vertical particle option as the "satellite-framed" language child would have done, apparently guided both by prosodic and cognitive determinants. In spite of the availability of the satellite and of the vertical motion verbs--both of which belong to a coherent and closed class--these children showed instead an early elaboration of semantically complex packets that, in some cases, may imply vertical path but that do not lexicalize it. These early verbs display some patterns of semantic packaging which resemble those used by the Korean children reported by Choi and Bowerman (1991). Further research on the typology of semantic packaging in early verbs of path-conflating languages may throw light on the patterns of their early acquisition.

In sum, language specific, cultural, and ecological factors seem to override cognitive, typological, morphological, and prosodic features which may favor the early acquisition of vertical path in Tzotzil.

Acknowledgments

Research for this study was supported by NSF Grant # SBR-9222394, awarded to the author together with John B. Haviland. I am grateful to John B. Haviland for comments on an earlier draft, and to Melissa Bowerman for inspiration and feedback. I acknowledge help and support from my compadres Tinik, Loxa, Xun and Romin Vaskis, and from my god-daughter Lupa. A longer version of this paper will appear in Bowerman and Levinson (eds.) (to appear).

REFERENCES

Berman, R. A. & D. I. Slobin (1994). *Relating events in narrative: A crosslinguistic developmental study*. Hillsdale, NJ: Lawrence Erlbaum.

Bloom, L. (1973). *One word at a time: The use of single word utterances before syntax*. The Hague: Mouton.

Bowerman, M. (1989). Learning a semantic system: What role do cognitive predispositions play? In M.L. Rice & R.L. Schiefelbusch (Eds.). *The teachability of language*. Baltimore: Brooks.

Bowerman, M. (1993). Typological perspectives on language acquisition: Do crosslinguistic patterns predict development? *The proceedings of the 25th Annual Child Language Research Forum*. Stanford: Center for the Study of Language and Information.

Bowerman, M. (in press). Learning how to structure space for language--A crosslinguistic perspective. In P. Bloom, M. Peterson, L. Nadel, & M. Garrett (Eds.) *Language and space*. Cambridge, MA: MIT Press.

Bowerman, M., de León, L. and Choi, S. (1995). Verbs, particles, and spatial semantics: Learning to talk about spatial actions in typologically different languages. *The Proceedings of the 27th Annual Child Language Research Forum*. Stanford: Center for the Study of Language and Information.

Brown, P. (1994). The Ins and Ons of Tzeltal locative expressions: the semantics of static descriptions of location. *Linguistics* 32:743-790.

Brown P. and S. Levinson (1993). "Uphill" and "Downhill" in Tzeltal. *Journal of Linguistic Anthropology* 3(1): 46-75

Choi S. & M. Bowerman (1991). Learning to express motion events in English and Korean: The influence of language-specific lexicalization patterns. *Cognition* 4:83-121.

Clark, E.V. (1973a). Nonlinguistic strategies and the acquisition of word meanings. *Cognition* 2: 161-182.

Clark, E.V. (1973b). What's in a word? On the child's acquisition of semantics in his first language. In T.E. Moore (Ed.), *Cognitive development and the acquisition of language* (pp. 65-110). New York: Academic Press.

Clark, H.H. (1973). Space, time, semantics, and the child. In T.E. Moore (Ed.), *Cognitive development and the acquisition of language.* New York: Academic Press.

de León, L. (1993). Shape, geometry and location: The case of Tzotzil body part terms. In K. Beals *et al.* (eds). *Proceedings of the 29th regional meeting of the Chicago Linguistic Society.* CLS: University of Chicago.

de León, L. (1994). Exploration in the acquisition of geocentric location by Tzotzil children. *Linguistics* 32 4/5: 857-885.

de León, L. (in preparation). Tzotzil (Mayan) early verbs.

Haviland, J. B. (1981). Sk'op Sotz'leb: El tzotzil de San Lorenzo Zinacantán. México: UNAM. (English translation in http:www.zapata.org).

Haviland, J. B. (1992). Seated and settled: Tzotzil verbs of the body. *Zeitschrift fur Phonetik, Sprachwissenschaft und Kommunikationsforschung* 45.6: 534-561. Berlin: Akademie Verlag.

Haviland, J.B. (1994a). "Te xa setel xulem" [The buzzards were circling]: categories of verbal roots in (Zinacantec) Tzotzil. *Linguistics* 32: 791-743

Haviland, J.B. (1994b). Verbs and shapes in (Zinacantec) Tzotzil: The case of "insert." *Función 15-16*: 83-117. Número especial sobre Estudios sobre lenguas mayas, editado por Roberto Zavala Maldonado. Universidad de Guadalajara.

Johnston, J. and Slobin, D.I (1979). The development of locative expressions in English, Italian, Serbo-Croatian and Turkish. *Journal of Child Language* 6: 529-245.

Landau, B. (1995) Multiple representations of objects in languages and language learners. In P. Bloom, M. Peterson, L. Nadel, & M. Garrett (Eds.) *Language and space.* Cambridge, MA: MIT Press.

Landau, B. and R. Jackendoff (1993). "What" and "where" in spatial language and spatial cognition. *Behavioural and Brain Sciences* 16: 217-238.

The Max Planck Institute for Psycholinguistics Annual Report (1995). Nijmegen: The Netherlands.

McCune-Nicolich , L. (1981). The cognitive bases of relational words in the single-word period. *Journal of Child Language* 8: 15-34.

Nelson, K. (1974). Concept, word, and sentence: Interrelations in acquisition and development. *Psychological Review* 81: 267-285.

Pye, C. (1992). The acquisition of K'iche Maya. In D. I. Slobin (ed.) *The crosslinguistic study of language acquisition* Vol. 3. Hillsdale, N.J.: Lawrence Erlbaum Association.

Sinha, C., Thorseng, L.A., Hayashi, M., Plunkett, K. (1994). Comparative spatial semantics and language acquisition: Evidence form Danish, English and Japanese. *Journal of Semantics* 11, 253-287.

Slobin , D. (1973). Cognitive prerequisites for the development of grammar. In Ch. A. Ferguson and D. I. Slobin, eds., *Studies of child language development.* New York: Holt, Rinehart & Winston.

Slobin, D. (1985). Crosslinguistic evidence for the language-making capacity. In D.I. Slobin (Ed.), *The crosslinguistic study of language acquisition* Vol. 2: *Theoretical issues.* Hillsdale, NJ: Lawrence Erlbaum.

Slobin, D. (to appear). Why are grammaticizable notions special?--A reanalysis and a challenge to learning theory. In M. Bowerman and S. Levinson (eds.) *Conceptual and linguistic development.* Cambridge: Cambridge University Press.

Talmy, L.(1985) Lexicalization patterns: Semantic structure in lexical form. In T. Shopen (Ed.). *Language typology and syntactic description.* Vol. 3: *Grammatical categories and the lexicon.* Cambridge, UK: Cambridge University Press.

Are English-Speaking One-Year-Olds Verb Learners, Too?

LETITIA NAIGLES
Yale University

1. Introduction

One-year-old language learners are reknowned for, among other things, their burgeoning noun vocabulary (especially of object words), their growing proficiency with social-interaction terms (e.g., HI, BYE-BYE, MORE, NIGHT-NIGHT), and for their intriguing overextensions (e.g., when they call the moon "ball"). But are one-year-old children <u>verb</u> learners, too? The evidence is far from straightforward.

1.1. Evidence that one-year-olds are not verb learners

Intensive diary studies of children learning English or Hebrew have found that very few verb types are produced during the second year, especially in relation to the number of nouns, or object words (Nelson, 1973; Dromi, 1987). Furthermore, cross-sectional studies of vocabulary size and content in children acquiring English or Italian, as assessed by checklists, have also yielded many fewer verbs than nouns in one-year-olds' production vocabularies (Caselli et al., 1995; Reznick & Goldfield, 1990). Finally, experimental studies in which young children are taught nonsense words have shown convincingly that one-year-olds can easily learn words for novel objects (e.g., Waxman & Markow, 1995); in contrast, there has been little evidence that children this age can learn words for novel motions (Echols, 1994).

It has also been argued that verbs <u>should</u> be relatively late acquisitions, for several reasons: First, the patterns of mapping verbs onto events vary across languages and so must themselves be acquired (Gentner, 1982). For example, English verbs of motion overwhelmingly encode the manner of motion in the event (<u>run</u>, <u>walk</u>), whereas Spanish motion verbs are more likely to encode the path of motion instead (<u>entrar</u>, <u>salir</u>). Until English and Spanish learners discover their language-specific pattern, they may be at a loss to determine, for example, whether a verb uttered in the presence of running out of a house means *running* or *exiting*.

Second, verbs are particularily dependent on grammar (syntax and morphology) for aspects of their meaning; especially, for distinguishing which aspect of an event is the referent of the verb (Gleitman, 1990; Naigles, 1990). For example, if I throw a pen and say "I blicked the pen", then "blick" is likely to refer to *throw*, whereas if I say "the pen blicked", then "blick" is more likely to refer to *fall* or *land*. Until children have acquired enough syntax to represent frames such as these, verb learning may proceed fairly haphazardly. And third, verbs (or their actions/motions/ relations) may appear less often as the target of joint attention or other pragmatic focus in early parent-child interaction (e.g., Tomasello & Akhtar, 1995; Baldwin, 1991), and so may be either less frequently used and/or less salient to young children.

In sum, much of the available evidence suggests that one-year-olds should not be proficient verb learners; that verb learning is more characteristic of children in their third year of life, when they can exploit syntax and pragmatics in the service of verb acquisition (Naigles, 1996; Tomasello, 1995). However, some recent data from other languages and other tasks suggests that the situation is more complicated.

1.2. Evidence that one-year-olds are verb learners

Recent cross-sectional research on the acquisition of Korean and Mandarin Chinese has revealed that one-year-olds learning these languages produce at least as many verb types as noun types in their spontaneous speech, and sometimes even more verbs than nouns (Choi & Gopnick, 1996; Tardif, in press). A recent diary in English, too, has found considerable verb learning in the second year: Inspection of Tomasello's (1992) corpus of his daughter's verb development reveals that before this child reached 24 months of age, she had produced some 60-70 English verbs. It may be interesting to note that in this diary, most of the verbs (67%) made their first appearance after the child was 18 months of age.

The adaptation of the preferential-looking paradigm to the study of language development (Golinkoff et al., 1987) has enabled researchers to investigate one-year-olds' language comprehension independently of their production. In some preliminary work, Golinkoff et al. (1987) found some verb comprehension (of wave, eat, and bounce) in 17-month-olds. Similarly, Huttenlocher et al. (1983) found some limited verb comprehension (i.e., of bounce) in a group of children who ranged in age from 1 to 2, but the performance of one-year-olds in this study was not analyzed separately. These findings are not conclusive, however, because stimulus salience was not rigorously controlled in either study. That is, the children may have looked longer at bouncing rather than pushing when they heard "bouncing" because they found *bouncing* to be more interesting, not because they thought it was the referent of the verb.

Finally, a recent dissertation using the preferential-looking paradigm (Koenig & Naigles, 1996) has found that there are situations where 15-month-olds will prefer to map a new word onto a new action instead of a new object. Specifically, when the new word was in a separate prosodic unit from the words referring to the actors (e.g., "there's the doggie and the kitty!

And look, there's (the) toopen"), children preferred to look at what the dog and cat were doing rather than at the accompanying novel puppet.

In sum, a more comprehensive look at the research in this area indicates that the status of verb learning in the second year is not clear. ARE English-speaking one-year-olds verb learners? The time is ripe for another test of English-learning one-year-olds' verb comprehension. In this study, I compared verb comprehension in children just over and under 18 months of age and included rigorous controls for stimulus salience. The class of verbs studied depicted motion events (e.g., CRAWL and ROLL), and included both common verbs (RUN, WALK) and uncommon ones (SLIDE, JUMP).

2. Method

A total of 35 children participated. They ranged in age from 14 to 19 months, with a mean age of 17.5 months. All of the children were being raised in English-speaking homes, 18 were girls. At the time of participation, the children's production vocabulary was assessed via a checklist their mothers filled out; they produced an average of 83 words (range 2 to 307) and 8 verbs (range 0 to 36). This is a typical sample of one-year-olds, then, in that they vary widely in their language use.

The preferential-looking paradigm was used, in which the children sat on their mothers' laps and watched two videos on side-by-side TV screens. The audio, coming from a center speaker, matched only one of the screens, and the assumption was that if the children understood the audio, they would look longer at the matching screen. The children's eye movements were recorded on videotape for later coding. The mother wore a visor throughout the duration of the videotapes to prevent her from seeing the videos and influencing the child.

The layout of the videos is shown in Table 1. One screen came on showing one of the motion events (in this case, a boy walking up a hill), accompanied by an attention-getting but neutral audio ("what's he doing?"). The other screen was blank. Then the first screen went blank and the second screen came on with the other motion event (the boy crawling up the hill), again with a neutral audio. These first two trials were the ones that familiarized the child with the events. Then both screens came on simultaneously, showing both events, and the audio was again neutral. This trial served as the <u>control</u> for stimulus salience: without any distinguishing language, which event did the child prefer to watch? Finally, the two events appeared simultaneously two more times, now paired with the <u>test</u> audios ("where's he walking?" or "where's he crawling?").

TABLE 1: Layout of verb comprehension videotapes

TAPE 1	AUDIO	TAPE 2
Boy WALKS uphill	"What's he doing?"	Black
Black	"What's happening?"	Boy CRAWLS uphill
Boy WALKS uphill	"What is he doing?"	Boy CRAWLS uphill
Boy WALKS uphill	"Where's he walking?"	Boy CRAWLS uphill
Boy WALKS uphill	"Find him walking!"	Boy CRAWLS uphill

There were four such motion event pairs shown and a total of 6 verbs tested, as presented in Table 2. Notice that the actor, setting, and path of the motion event pairs were kept constant; all that differed was the manner of motion. Nineteen of the children (10 girls) saw the videos and heard the WALK-first audio (WALK, ROLL, CRAWL, SLIDE), while the other 16 children (8 girls) heard the CRAWL-first audio (CRAWL, RUN, WALK, JUMP).

TABLE 2: Pairs of motion events

WALK-first audio	CRAWL-first audio
Boy WALKS uphill	Boy CRAWLS uphill
Girl ROLLS downhill	Girl RUNS downhiill
Boy CRAWLS across sidewalk	Boy WALKS across sidewalk
Girl SLIDES into water	Girl JUMPS into water

The children's visual fixations were coded off of the videotape. Reliability between coders was high, averaging 93% for the test trials. The measure of interest compared the children's preferences during the control trial with their subsequent preference during the test trials. If they significantly shift their preference from control trial to test trial, we conjecture that they understood the verb in the test audio.

3. Results

The results will be presented in several waves, from less to more detailed. First, across all 6 verbs, did the children shift their looking preferences significantly from the control to test trials, displaying verb comprehension? Second, for each individual verb, did the children significantly shift their looking preferences? Third, did the childrens' shifts in looking preferences (i.e., their verb comprehension) vary by their gender, age, or language measures?

3.1. Across verbs, was there significant verb comprehension?

Across all 6 verbs, the children showed a preference of -0.32 seconds to the matching screen during the control trials, and 0.08 seconds to the matching screen during the test trials. While this shift in preference from control to test is in the right (matching) direction, its magnitude is too small to reach significance (t(34) = 1.56, p > .10).

3.2. Was there significant verb comprehension for any individual verb?

The children's looking preferences by verb are shown in Table 3. For WALK, the children preferred the nonmatch during both control and test, so that there was no significant change of preference from control to test (t(34) = 1.34, p > .10). For RUN, the children preferred the match during both control and test; somewhat more so during the test trials, but again not significantly so (t(15) < 1). For CRAWL, the children preferred the match during both control and test; interestingly, they seemed to look less to the match during the test trials, but not significantly so (t(34) = -1.11, p > .10). For ROLL, there was a significant shift from control to test trials, and in the predicted, matching direction (t(18) = 4.11, p < .01). For JUMP, the children preferred the nonmatch for both control and test (no significant shift, t(15) < 1), and for SLIDE, the children preferred the match for both control and test trials; again, there was no significant shift with the presentation of the verb (t(18) < 1).

TABLE 3: Children's mean matching screen preferences (in seconds) during the control and test trials

VERB	CONTROL	TEST
WALK	-1.48	-0.90
RUN	0.26	0.87
CRAWL	0.94	0.52
ROLL	-1.50	0.63
JUMP	-1.05	-1.00
SLIDE	0.79	0.81

In sum, the children showed reliable comprehension for only one of the 6 verbs, ROLL. Interestingly, this was neither one of the most common verbs of the set (e.g., WALK, RUN), nor one of the most uncommon (e.g., SLIDE). Notice that if control and test trials had not been compared in assessing comprehension, it would have appeared that the children understood RUN,

CRAWL, and SLIDE as well; however, the control trials indicate that for these verbs, the matching preference was there before the verb was heard.

Another way to look at the verb differences is to consider the children's looking preferences for each PAIR of verbs/motion events--RUN and ROLL, SLIDE and JUMP, CRAWL and WALK. The RUN/ROLL comparison is the clearest (Figure 1), and corroborates the earlier finding: All children preferred to look at RUNNING during the control trials, but those who heard ROLL significantly shifted their preference towards ROLLING during the test trials. Those who heard RUN did not look even more at RUNNING.

The JUMP/SLIDE comparison is clearcut in a different way (Figure 2): All children preferred to look at SLIDING during the control trials, and more or less maintained that preference during the test trials (no greater looking to SLIDING for the "slide" children). So here, the presentation of the word had no effect for either verb.

The third pair shows yet another pattern (Figure 3): All children preferred to look at CRAWLING during the control trials, and then looked LESS (but not significantly so) at CRAWLING during the test trials. I will return to this pair of verbs in the next analyses, when we consider subgroups of the children.

3.3. Did children's verb comprehension vary by gender?

Because numerous studies of early language comprehension have found that girls show earlier or better comprehension of object words and phrases than boys (Hirsh-Pasek & Golinkoff, 1996; Fernald et al., in press, Naigles, 1996), I next considered the control-to-test shifts for each verb for girls and boys separately. For ROLL, the one verb that showed significant comprehension, both boys and girls showed the significant control-to-test shift towards the matching screen in their looking preferences. In contrast, for RUN, JUMP, and SLIDE, neither boys nor girls showed significant verb comprehension. Finally, with WALK and CRAWL I found an effect of gender, in a rather surprising pattern: The boys showed a significant shift from control to test for both WALK and CRAWL ($t(16) = 2.08$, $p < .05$ and $t(17) = -1.86$, $p < .10$), but the girls did not.

Before making the claim that with verbs, boys may be ahead of girls, it is necessary to look more closely at the effects. It turns out that during the control trials, the boys all preferred to look more at crawling. During the test trials, their preference shifts more towards walking, but for both verbs, CRAWL and WALK! That is, when the boys heard a verb, they did shift their motion event preference away from their earlier preference; however, this happened regardless of whether the verb was CRAWL or WALK. This may indicate

Figure 1: RUN vs. ROLL

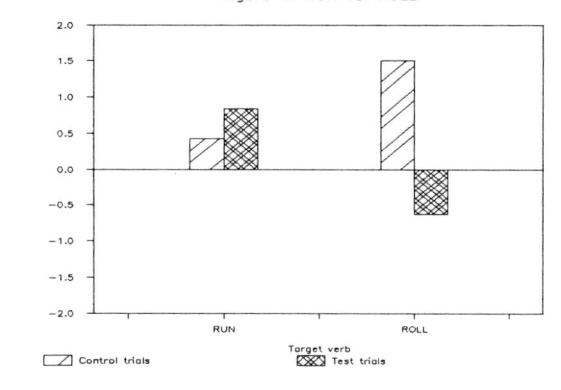

Figure 2: SLIDE vs. JUMP

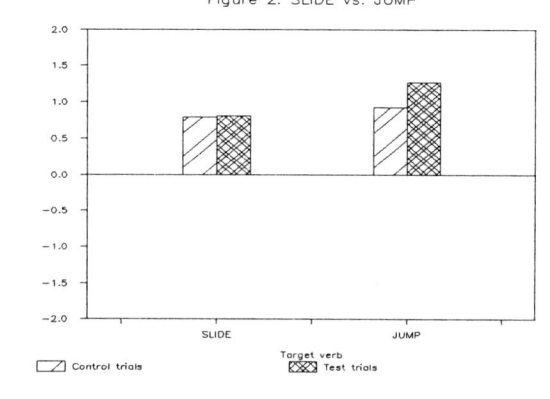

some very rudimentary understanding of the function of a heard lexical item to redirect attention, but it is hard to argue that it signals understanding of the event referent of the verb.

3.4. Did children's comprehension vary by age or language measure?

I first performed correlations of the children's age, number of words, and number of verbs, with their degree of control-to-test shift for each verb separately (the larger the control-to-test shift is, the more the children shifted towards the matching screen during the test trials). T-tests were then performed between groups of children divided by age (over or under 18 months), number of words (over or under 60 words), and number of verbs (over or under 4 verbs).

For WALK, JUMP, and ROLL, none of the correlations was significant, but for different reasons. For WALK and JUMP, none of the subgroups showed significant verb comprehension. Regardless of whether older or younger, with large or small vocabulary, the children did not shift their looking preferences from control to test. In contrast, for ROLL, all of the subgroups showed significant verb comprehension (ts range from 2.07 to 6.86, all $p < .05$). This verb's comprehension seems quite stable and robust very early on, and is not subject to age, gender, or language production factors.

The correlations with CRAWL, RUN, and SLIDE all yielded significant effects; for all three verbs, the children's number of verbs and (marginally) number of words (but not age) significantly predicted their degree of shift towards the matching screen during the test trials. The most conventional effect occurred with RUN: Children's number of verbs was positively correlated with their degree of control-to-test shift ($r = .52$), and those who produced more than 4 verbs (by maternal report) tended to look more towards RUN during the test trials ($t(5) = 2.17$, $p < .10$; 5 out of 6 children did this).

With CRAWL, the children's number of words was also positively correlated with their degree of verb comprehension, $r = .38$. However, the t-tests with the subgroups revealed that it was not the children with over 60 words or 4 verbs that were preferring the matching screen more, but the children with fewer than 60 words or 4 verbs who were preferring the matching screen LESS ($t(17) = -1.69$, $p < .10$; $t(19) = -1.76$, $p < .10$). That is, these were the children who were looking at crawling less during the test trials, when it was requested, than they had during the control trials, when it was not. With SLIDE, the children's number of verbs was negatively correlated with their degree of verb comprehension, $r = .47$. That is, the children with more than four verbs tended to look away from sliding during the test trials ($t(7) = -2.02$, $p < .10$).

Finally, I also directly asked each child's parent whether their child said or understood each of the 4 verbs the child was about to hear. I then divided the children according to whether they were reported to understand each verb or not, and then calculated the mean control-to-test shift for each group, as well as the percent of children in each group who shifted towards the matching screen. The results, as shown in Table 4, indicate that across verbs, there was little relation between maternal report concerning a specific verb and comprehension of that verb in this task. For example, most of those children who were reported to say or understand JUMP did shift towards the matching screen when asked for "jumping", and most of those who were not reported to say or understand JUMP shifted away from the matching screen. The opposite pattern was found for RUN, however: Children who were reported to say or understand RUN performed poorly during preferential looking, and those reported to not say or understand RUN performed well. And finally, no parent said her child said or understood ROLL, yet this verb yielded the best comprehension performance of all. It seems likely that, while mothers are quite good at estimating their child's overall vocabulary size, they are less reliable at assessing their child's knowledge of specific verbs.

TABLE 4: Comparison of maternal report and task comprehension

	By maternal report			
	Understanders		Non-understanders	
VERB (N)	Mean shift in preference to matching screen	(%)	Mean shift in preference to matching screen	(%)
WALK (27)	0.42	55	1.12	67
JUMP (6)	1.53	83	-1.00	38
RUN (7)	-0.39	33	1.22	86
SLIDE (9)	0.58	33	-0.47	50
CRAWL (11)	0.32	64	-0.71	45

4. Discussion

This study was designed to investigated the extent to which English- learning children in the middle of the second year understood 6 verbs of motion. The results suggest that substantial verb comprehension is not present in English learners this young. Specifically, when stimulus salience was controlled, only ROLL elicited significant verb comprehension in the 17-month-old subjects. Because ROLL was not one of the most common verbs in the set, this is a somewhat surprising finding; however, it is not without precedent. Tomasello's corpus (1992) indicates that his child produced ROLL before either RUN or WALK. The verb RUN also elicited significant comprehension from a subset of the children; namely, children with more than 4 verbs in their production vocabulary already (Note that RUN did not have to be one of those verbs, by maternal report). The comprehension of WALK by the boys was only apparent, and can be attributed to a general shift in attention when a lexical verb (i.e., CRAWL or WALK) was heard. In summary, these children's motion verb knowledge did not appear to be very extensive.

Before discussing why these findings may have occurred, I will briefly mention some qualifications that must be made to the above conclusion. First, although little verb comprehension was found, it must be noted that verb comprehension in this study was assessed with only one foil per verb. That is, it is possible that comprehension of RUN or WALK might have been found if these motions had been presented with more divergent pairs (e.g, jumping or dancing horizontally). Second, the motion events were performed by actors, not by the children themselves, and Huttenlocher et al. (1983) present some evidence that understanding of some verbs emerges first in reference to actions performed by oneself, and is only later transferred to actions performed by others. This explanation fails with ROLL, though, because "roll" is typically acquired with reference to the motion of objects (e.g., balls), yet the children apparently had no trouble extending it to the motion of an unfamiliar person. Third, it is worth while asking whether older children would show significant verb comprehension with this task and these videos. Accordingly, I have run 6 28-month-olds on these videos, and found robust verb comprehension. In the composite score, the children's matching screen preference during the control trials was -0.16 seconds; this shifted to a matching screen preference of 1.0 during the test trials ($p < .05$).

Then, WHY didn't the one-year-olds children show better comprehension of the other five verbs? The lack of verb comprehension was not obviously attributable to vocabulary size, as the one-year-olds varied greatly on this variable and even those with the largest vocabularies did not display consistent verb comprehension. There was a hint that verb vocabulary size predicted verb comprehension, but as this held for only one verb (RUN), it was hardly conclusive.

I would like to suggest that the theory of syntactic bootstrapping, that children need and use syntax to help acquire verbs (Gleitman, 1990; Naigles, 1996), might provide an explanation. If these children were not very sophisticated yet, grammatically, then their verb knowledge might not be very sophisticated and distinctive, either. If grammar is needed to help pick out and distinguish the referents of verbs, then a less-sophisticated grammar might yield less distinctive and elaborated verb meanings. Thus, while one-year-olds' linguistic knowledge might well be elaborate enough to distinguish whether a new word refers to an action or an object, supporting Koenig's findings, it is entirely reasonable to suppose that their syntactic (possibly also pragmatic) knowledge is not yet sophisticated enough to make fairly subtle distinctions between aspects of actions as the referents of new verbs.

To make this concrete, consider the verbs RUN and JUMP. Because these verbs differ primarily on only one aspect of meaning, their manners of motion, it might take a good deal of input (of all kinds) to fully distinguish them. How might syntax help? Although it is true that most English verbs of motion share a large percentage of their broad syntactic priviledges of occurrence, recent work on maternal input to one-year-olds has revealed that even highly similar verbs have distinct syntactic frame profiles (Naigles & Hoff-Ginsberg, 1995). In our study of the frames 57 mothers used with 25 common verbs, Hoff-Ginsberg and I found that RUN and JUMP shared two frames (utterance-final and PP) and diverged on three more: RUN appeared with adverbs (e.g., "run quickly) but JUMP did not, and JUMP appeared with verb particles ("it's jumping around") and coordinate sentences ("let's jump and see what the pillow feels like") but RUN did not.

Notice that I am not suggesting that one-year-old English learners have any particular trouble conceptualizing motion events, or finding some words in the input to designate them--one has only to look at the frequent use of in, on, out, off, up, and down in one-year-olds' speech to dispell this notion. Rather, what I am suggesting is that mapping those events onto what will become verbs in English is what is perhaps beyond the reach of young one-year-olds, because performing this mapping requires some syntactic (and probably also pragmatic) proficiency that these one-year-olds have not yet fully acquired. Why do children learning other languages seem to acquire more verbs earlier? My conjecture would be that these other languages may facilitate the earlier development of the syntactic (and pragmatic) information needed to acquire an initial set of verbs.

At this point, there is no direct evidence for the proposal that English learners' relatively late verb acquisition is tied to their syntactic development. In the current study, there were no precise measures of the children's grammatical abilities to enable a correlational analysis. Future studies might collect at-home assessments of MLU for comparison with the preferential-looking results. Furthermore, a slightly older sample of children (e.g., 18-21 months of age) might generate more positive results. Overall, I must conclude that this study of verb comprehension has corroborated the diary and checklist data on the age at which significant verb learning in English begins to take place; namely, not before the second half of the second year. That is, unlike children learning

Korean and Mandarin, English speakers in the middle of their second year have NOT shown themselves to be verb learners, too.

5. References

Baldwin, D. (1991) Infants' contribution to the achievement of joint reference. Child Development 62, 875-890.

Caselli, M., Bates, E., Casadio, P., Fenson, J., Fenson, L., Sanderl, L., & Weir, J. (1995) A cross-linguistic study of early lexical development. Cognitive Development 10, 159-200.

Choi, S. & Gopnick, A. (1996) Early acquisition of verbs in Korean: A cross-linguistic study. Journal of Child Language.

Dromi, E. (1987) Early lexical develoment. Cambridge: CUP.

Echols, C. (1994) An influence of labelling on infants' attention to objects and consistency: Implications for word-referent mappings. Unpublished manuscript, University of Texas at Austin.

Fernald, A., McRoberts, G., & Herrera, C. (in press) Effects of prosody and word position on lexical comprehension in infants. Journal of Experimental Child Psychology.

Gentner, D. (1982) Why nouns are learned before verbs: Linguistic relativity versus natural partitioning. In S. A. Kuczaj (Ed.), Language Development (Volume 2): Language, Thought, and Culture. Hillsdale, NJ: Erlbaum.

Gleitman, L. (1990) The structural sources of verb meanings. Language Acquisition 1, 3-55.

Goldfield, B. & Reznick, R. (1990) Early lexical acquisition: Rate, content, and the vocabulary spurt. Journal of Child Language 17, 171-183.

Golinkoff, R., Hirsh-Pasek, K., Cauley, K., and Gordon, L. (1987) The eyes have it: Lexical and syntactic comprehension in a new paradigm. Journal of Child Language 14, 23-45.

Huttenlocher, J., Smiley, P., & Charney, R. (1983) Emergence of action categories in the child: Evidence from verb meanings. Psychological Review 90, 72-93.

Koenig, P. & Naigles, L. (April, 1996) Prosody affects meaning: 15-month-olds interpret a novel word as an action. International Society of Infancy Studies. Providence, RI.

Naigles, L. (1990) Children use syntax to learn verb meanings. Journal of Child Language 17, 357-374.

Naigles, L. (1996) The use of multiple frames in verb learning via syntactic bootstrapping. Cognition 58, 221-251.

Naigles, L. and Hoff-Ginsberg, E. (1995) Input to verb learning: Evidence for the plausibility of Syntactic Bootstrapping. Developmental Psychology 31, 827-837.

Nelson, K. (1973) Structure and strategy in learning to talk. Monographs of the Society for Research in Child Development, 38.

Tardif, T. (in press) Verbs are not always learned after nouns: Evidence from Mandarin. Developmental Psychology.

Tomasello, M. (1992) First verbs. Cambridge: Cambridge University Press.

Tomasello, M. (1995) Pragmatic contexts for early verb learning. In M. Tomasello & W. Merriman (Eds.) Beyond Names for Things (pp. 115-146). Hillsdale, NJ: Erlbaum.

Tomasello, M. & Akhtar, N. (1995) Two-year-olds use pragmatic cues to differentiate reference to objects and actions. Cognitive Development 10, 201-224.

Waxman, S. & Markow, D. (1995) Words as invitations to form categories: Evidence from 12-13-month-old infants. Cognitive Psychology 29, 257-302.

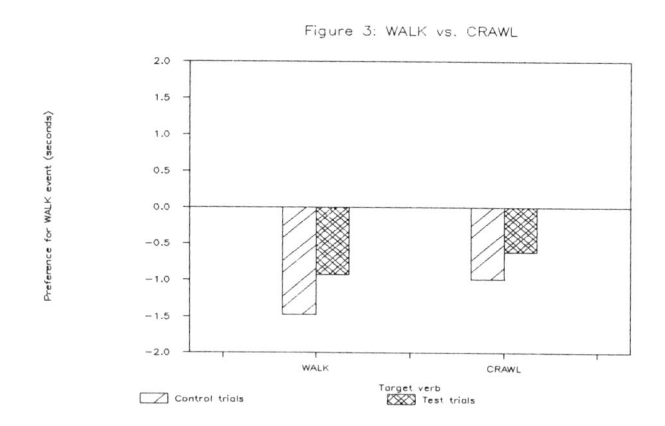

Figure 3: WALK vs. CRAWL

Gender-Based Differences in the Language of Japanese Preschool Children: A Look at Metalinguistic Awareness

KEI NAKAMURA
University of California, Berkeley

Introduction

One of the most fascinating aspects of the Japanese language is the wide variety of gender-based linguistic distinctions. This topic has been well-documented by researchers such as Ide (1979), Ide and McGloin (1990) and Shibamoto (1985). Even from brief dialogue, it is usually possible to guess whether the speakers are men or women. Some of these differences are phonological. For example, Japanese women usually speak in a higher pitch and use more intonational contours than men. In addition, women are also more likely to use phonetic forms which approach the standard language or have higher prestige.

Lexical differences also play a prominent role. Men and women often use different terms for self-reference (e.g., *boku/ore* for men and *atashi* for women) and second-person reference (e.g., men use terms such as *omae/kimi*) in informal contexts. In addition, men and women can also use distinct male and female forms for specific lexical items (e.g., men can use *'hara'* for 'stomach). Women also tend to use more polite and honorific prefixes, such as *'o-'* and *'go-'*, which make their language sound more polite. Furthermore, despite the fact that men tend to use more slang and colloquial expressions during informal speech, in general, they also tend to use more Sino-Japanese compound words than women, making them sound more 'educated'. Finally, women tend to use more exclamatory interjections such as *'ara'* (oh my) and *'maa'* (dear me) which have a softening effect, while men often use expressions such as *'che'* (shucks) which are harsher.

In addition to phonological and lexical differences, there are also morphosyntactic differences. Men often use sentence-final particles that express assertion, such as *yo, ze, zo* and *na*, while women tend to use particles that express uncertainty and indirectness, such as *wa, no, kashira* and *ne*. Women also tend to be less conservative than men in their use of certain morphosyntactic rules. Women use more repetition, subject-noun phrase-deletion, ellipsis of case-marking particles, unfinished sentences and postposing. In general, women tend to use more honorific and polite forms than men.

Lastly, there are differences in conversational style. Women often use pragmatic devices such as softening requests, backchannelling and polite expressions which make them sound more supportive and less assertive.

Many of these gender-based differences are similar to those found in other languages. As in other languages, usage of gender-based linguistic distinctions seems to vary greatly according to a variety of factors including dialect, educational background and setting (e.g., urban/rural). Furthermore, it is important to note that gender differences in Japanese have changed in recent years as a greater degree of equality in language has emerged. Standards are constantly changing.

One of the myths of the Japanese language is that there are many linguistic features used exclusively by one sex. However, these days, most Japanese tend to use a wide range of styles according to the nature of the conversational context. For example, there are occasions when men use a softer, more empathetic 'feminine' style (e.g., when talking to babies), and times when women use a more blunt, 'masculine' style (e.g., at work).

Gender Differences in Child Language

According to Schieffelin and Ochs (1986), in becoming linguistically competent, the child learns to become a male or female member of the speech community. Conversely, when children adopt gender-appropriate linguistic behaviors, they perpetuate the social order which creates such gender distinctions. Research on Japanese, a language which has a multitude of gender-based differences, is a rich source of information regarding children's acquisition of gender-based language. Surprisingly though, studies on gender differences in Japanese child language are relatively rare. The majority of these studies only focus on two aspects of the language, namely sentence-final particles and addressee/reference terms.

Methodology

This study is part of a project to examine the acquisition and development of language that reflects pragmatic and social knowledge in young Japanese children. The data is based on naturalistic observations in the homes of 24 boys and girls, ages 2-6, living in the Tokyo area. Efforts were made to observe the same groups of children across a wide range of activities (e.g., snacktime, role-play, object construction) while interacting with various people such as their mothers, siblings, peers and unfamiliar adults. Monthly visits, each approximately 2 hours, were conducted with each child over the course of 18 to 24 months.

Results

Even 2-year-olds were able to use gender-appropriate language. The children modified their speech in various ways: such as using appropriate sentence-final particles, addressee/reference terms, lexical items, different types of requests and polite/honorific forms. (Please refer to Martin, 1975, for an explanation of these language features.)

1. Sentence-final Particles

As reported by researchers such as Sakata (1991) and Takahashi (1969), girls and boys as early as age 2 use gender-appropriate sentence-final particles. Female particle usage is reported to be related to women's tendency to caretake and respond to the needs of others, while male particle usage often seems to reflect an aggressive or assertive stance. Girls used particles which express uncertainty and indirectness, such as *wa, no* and *kashira*, while boys use particles which express assertion, such as *zo, ze* and *na*.

Particles used predominantly by girls:
1. *wa*: This particle is a feminine marker which is often used to indicate mild insistence and/or affective intensity. In addition, *wa* sometimes expresses the speaker's intimacy or friendliness. Used alone, it has a softening effect, as seen in the following example. Yukako (3;7), pretending to be a nurse, says that she will bandage the patient:

watashi ga yaru wa. I'll do it.

Wa can also be used in combination with other particles in order to show the speaker's concern, as seen in this example, during lego construction:

Mother: *o-hana tsukechaoo ka naa.* Maybe I'll attach a flower.

Yukako (3;1): *hai...ii wa yo.*   OK, that's fine.

Here Yukako uses *yo* to express her opinion and *wa* to soften her statement, while expressing her concern. *Wa* rarely appeared in girls' spontaneous speech, but frequently appeared during role play, when children assumed female roles. Boys never used *wa* spontaneously.

2. *kashira:* This particle expresses a speaker's uncertainty about a proposition. While pretending to be a customer in a restaurant, Mika (4;0) whispers softly:

nani ni shiyoo kashira?   I wonder what I should have?

This particle was only used by girls, and by boys taking the roles of girls and women.

Particles used predominantly by boys:

1. *zo:* This particle expresses extremely strong insistence, assurance or assertion, such as "I tell you", or "believe me". Here we see Akira (3;0) arguing with his brother Yutaka (4;1) over the rights to a key lego piece. Yutaka has taken it and used it in the construction of his house.

Akira: *zurui!*   (You're) unfair!

Yutaka: *zuruku nai zo!*   (I'm) not unfair!

Akira: *omae no hoo ga zuruin da zo!*   You're the one who's unfair!

Both of them use *zo* to insist that the lego piece is theirs.

Zo can also be used as an attention-calling marker. Koosuke (3;4), while pretending to be a customer at a store, says:

nai zo!   (I) don't have (it)!

as he checks his wallet when the cashier asks him to pay one thousand yen. With the exception of one girl, most spontaneous uses of this particle were by boys.

2. *ze:* This particle is often used by men in informal contexts among friends, or with listeners of lower status, implying assurance or assertion, as in "you know" or "I'd say". Only a few of the boys used this particle. None of the girls used it, even during pretend play. In this example, Ryota (3;8) assures his mother that there is milk in the refrigerator:

miruku mo haitteru ze.   There's also milk in here.

3. *na:* This particle can indicate confirmation or inspiration when it is attached to informal declarative or invitational sentences. Boys frequently used this particle. Sho (3;11) uses it as he watches his mother clumsily making a plane out of lego blocks:

>   *okaasan hikooki heta da na!*   Mother, (you're) no good at
>   (making) planes!

Na can also be used as a negative imperative marker when used with informal non-past verbs (used with listeners of lower status), as in this example, in which Hiro (5;0) tells his mother not to take away a special lego piece:

>   *sore toru na yo!*   Don't take that!

Na is usually used by men, but can sometimes be heard in self-addressed utterances by women. Girls occasionally used this particle, as in the following self-addressed utterance:

>   *atashi sotchi ga ii na.*   I prefer that one.

in which Yukako (3;1) whispers to herself, attempting to get her mother to exchange toys with her.

Particles used both by boys and girls:
Of the many particles which were used both by boys and girls, two sentence-final particles were particularly noteworthy.

1. *yo:* This particle is used when the speaker is providing new information, while adding moderate emphasis (often to a listener of lower status). It presupposes that the addressee did not already know the information being communicated and is common when making claims, expressing opinions, as well as when giving advice and warnings. Boys used a much larger number of *yo* than girls (with one exception). In many contexts, *yo* was the most frequently-used particle among boys. In the following example, Ryota (3;6) enthusiastically shows his mother a new toy telephone:

>   *zero made aru yo....mite!*   Look it even has a zero!

Girls often used *yo* in statements directed toward their younger siblings, as in the next example:

>   *Yoshi-kun dame yo.*   Yoshi, don't do (that).

in which Yukako (3;1) attempts to be forceful as she tries to stop her brother from chewing on the phone. This particle was often used when children were encountering resistance and they felt a need to impose their will on the addressee.

2. *no*: Much controversy surrounds the usage of this particle. Among its many functions, it has been reported that women and children use *no* when asking or giving an explanation, or to indicate emotive emphasis in informal contexts. While constructing a lego house, Yukako (3;1) asks her mother where she should attach a lego piece:

>   *kore wa doko ni tsukeru no?*   Where should (I) attach this?

Boys also used this particle. Here Ryota (3;6) explains why he needs his mother's help to take a toy stethoscope off:

toru no...o-ryoori yaru kara

(I'm) taking it off, because (I'm) going to cook.

No was used frequently by both boys and girls. However, it is interesting to note that *no* was the most frequently-used particle among girls.

2. First-Person Reference

As reported previously in the literature (e.g., Ide 1978-1979), children were able to use gender-appropriate terms to refer to themselves. Boys used male first-person pronouns such as *boku* and *ore*. Even young children were able to do this:

Mother: *dare ga tsukutte-kureta no?*   Who made this for me?

Ryota (3;6): *boku ga tsukutta no.*   I made it.

Girls were also able to use gender-appropriate first-person pronouns such as *atashi*. When her mother asks her whether she can make a lego house by herself, Yukako (3;1) says:

atashi mo dekiru.   I can also do (it).

Boys and girls start to use sex-appropriate terms for self-reference (e.g., *boku, ore, atashi*) around age 2 and are able to use them consistently around age 3.

3. Second-Person Reference

Most explicit second-person references were made by using the addressee's name (e.g., *Mika-chan*) or occupation/title (e.g., *sensei* 'teacher'). Children often used diminutive markers for their peers (e.g., *-chan*) and honorific markers for adults (*-san*). The older boys were able to use the second-person pronoun *omae* to refer to their peers, but the older girls rarely used *anata*, preferring to use the addressee's name.

While trying to get his younger brother to stop hitting him, Yutaka (5;0) says:

Yamero omae!   You stop (it)!

Here Yutaka uses a command and the second-person pronoun *omae* to create a forceful statement.

4. Male/Female Lexical Forms

Many of the older boys used lexical forms that are used exclusively by men. For example, Hiro (5;2) asks his mother to help him look for a large lego piece:

kono dekkai no nai?   Are there any of these large ones?

Dekkai is an adjective used mainly by men to describe things that are large.

In the next example, Akira (5;10) says:

yabee na! (We're) in trouble!

using a masculine slang form with non-standard pronunciation to express how he and his brother will get in trouble for breaking the VCR. Use of such male lexical forms were used mainly in peer interaction contexts, and increased drastically especially after the children started preschool.

5. Sino-Japanese Compound Words

Some of the boys show bursts in their usage of difficult Sino-Japanese compound words. This sudden increase was often commented on by the mothers. For example, in conversations with their mothers, Yutaka (5;7) used the more difficult term *'sagyoo'* instead of the more common *'shigoto'* for 'work', and Koosuke (4;7) used the expression *"nyuuin suru"* instead of the easier *"byooin ni hairu"* for "to be admitted to a hospital".

6. Requests and Commands

Boys used a large number of commands, especially during rough & tumble play. While pretending to be Ultraman, a superhero, Tooru (4;9) says:

sore kase! Give that (to me)!

totte shimae! Take (it from him)!

In general, girls used more polite requests as well as indirect requests. Most commonly, they used informal request forms instead of commands. Here Yukako (3;1) tries to get her baby brother to answer the phone, using an informal request form:

hai Yoshi-kun moshimoshi shite. Here Yoshi, please say "hello".

7. Polite Language & Honorific/Humble Forms

It has been said that Japanese women are more polite than their male counterparts. Japanese girls seemed to be slightly more formal and polite than the boys. For example, Eri (5;2), pretending to be a store clerk, asks a customer to sign a credit card receipt by saying *"kore ni namae o o-kaki-kudasai"* (please sign your name here), using a polite request form. Girls were able to use a wider variety of honorific/humble forms, and also used them more frequently.

Girls also seemed to be more polite in certain routines, such as when answering the door and answering the phone. For example, Mika (4;) when answering the door, asks:

>   *donata* desu ka?   Who is it?

using; the polite form *'donata'* for 'who'. In another situation, Mayu (4;3) upon entering her friend's house, uses a humble verb form:

>   *ojama itashimasu.*   (Excuse me for) disturbing (you).

Boys rarely used such polite and honorific forms, and if so, only during role-play.

8. Phonological Differences

Boys sometimes used non-standard pronunciation in informal contexts. In the following example, Hiro (5;4) says *"tatenee"* instead of the standard form *"tatenai"* as he tries to get up from the floor.

>   *tatenee yo!*   (I) can't stand up!

In general, girls spoke in a higher pitch. Boys often switched to a higher pitch when playing the roles of women during role-play.

Discussion

It is clear that Japanese children are extremely sensitive to gender differences in their usage of language.

1. The Importance of Context

The data clearly show that usage of gender-based linguistic distinctions varies according to context. Even young children seem to be sensitive to the topic of conversation, as well as speaker/hearer characteristics, such as the familiarity of the listener and the listener's sex and age. For example, boys who usually did not use masculine sentence-final particles such as *zo* and *ze* while interacting with their mothers and other adults, often used them while interacting with male peers, especially when engaged in rough-and-tumble play. Here we find Shin, a 3-year-old boy using the male sentence-final particle *zo* as he runs after another boy with a paper sword.

>   Shin (3;6): *yattsukeru zo!*   (I'm) going to get (you)!

When language use is compared across activity contexts, it becomes clear that boys and girls vary their language across the nature of the activity (e.g., rough-and-tumble play, object construction, pretend play). For example, boys who rarely used used masculine sentence-final particles during object construction frequently used them during rough-and-tumble play. Girls who rarely used feminine sentence-final particles spontaneously often used them while playing the roles of their mothers. When the activity setting was controlled, differences between boys' and girls' speech were reduced considerably.

2. Role-play Based on Gender-Based Language Stereotypes

Children were quite adept at performing role-play based on their gender-based language stereotypes. Role-play contexts gave children the opportunity to use forms which did not appear in everyday interactions. Data from role-play contexts illustrate the fact that even 3-year-olds have a sophisticated understanding of genderlect stereotypes.

For example, Akira (3;6), pretending to be a young woman, wanders into an empty room and comments:

dare mo inai wa nee.   There's nobody in here.

As he walks out of the house into the street, he murmurs:

ushiro kara kuru wa.   (A car) is coming from behind.

using the female sentence-final particle *wa* over several turns. Boys playing the roles of girls and women are able to speak in a higher pitch, using exaggerated intonation patterns. In addition, they can use appropriate addressee/reference terms, as seen in this example taken from a 6-year-old boy:

atashi tsugi kashite.   Lend it to me next.

in which the female first-person pronoun *atashi* is used in combination with a high-pitched voice.

Girls were also able to take male roles, such as those of the father, making changes such as using the appropriate sentence-final particles, male lexical forms and non-standard pronunciation.

3. Self-Correction

Children rarely made errors in their usage of gender-based linguistic features, and when they did, they usually corrected their own mistakes. In one scene, Saeko (3;8) and her sister are playing house. Saeko shows that she is grappling with the difficult task of speaking like a man with her frequent repairs. In this example, she corrects herself, substituting a feminine sentence-final particle with a masculine one:

ii wa yo--> ii zo.   That's fine.

4. Metalinguistic Comments

Finally, children often make metalinguistic comments regarding the gender-appropriateness of the linguistic forms used by their peers. Boys were quick to berate their peers for using "sissy" language, while girls criticized their friends for using "rough" language. During snacktime, Rina (4;5) comments *"umai na!"* ("it's delicious") as she enjoys her snack, using a male lexical form with the masculine sentence-final particle *na*. Immediately her peers criticize her, saying such language is only for boys.

Conclusion

Appropriate usage of gender-based linguistic distinctions is often mentioned as one of the most difficult aspects of Japanese for Japanese returnees and non-native speakers to grasp. However, children acquire these features relatively early and effortlessly. Many factors interact in enabling Japanese children to learn gender-appropriate forms, such as modeling, differential treatment, as well as the influence of siblings, peers and the media (Nakamura, 1996). Metalinguistic data taken from role-play contexts, repairs and metalinguistic comments also illustrate the fact that Japanese children have a sophisticated understanding of gender-appropriate language from an early age.

References

Ide, Sachiko.1978-1979. A Sociolinguistic Analysis of Person References by Japanese and American Children. *Language Sciences* 1.273-292.

Ide, Sachiko. 1979. *Onna no Kotoba, Otoko no Kotoba*, Tokyo: Nihon Keizai Tsuushinsha.

Ide, Sachiko and Naomi Hanaoka McGloin, eds., 1990. *Aspects of Japanese Women's Language*. Tokyo: Kurosio.

Martin, Samuel. 1975. *A Reference Grammar of Japanese*. Rutland, VT: Tuttle.

Nakamura, Kei. 1996. *Gender-Based Differences in the Language of Japanese Preschool Children: A Look at Language Socialization*. Paper presented at the 1996 Conference of the American Association for Applied Linguistics, Chicago, IL.

Schieffelin, Bambi & Elinor Ochs. 1986. Language Socialization, in B. Siegel, ed., *Annual Review of Anthropology*. Palo Alto, CA: Annual Reviews.

Sakata, Minako. 1991. The Acquisition of Japanese 'Gender' Particles. *Language & Communication.* 11:3.117-125.

Shibamoto, Janet. 1985. *Japanese Women's Language,* New York: Academic Press.

Takahashi, Iwao. 1969. *Yooji no Gengo to Kyooiuku,* Tokyo: Kyooiku Shuppan Center.

Thorne, Barrie, Cheris Kramarae and Nancy Henley, eds., 1983. *Language, Gender and Society.* Rowley, MA: Newbury House.

Acknowledgments

This research was supported in part by a University of California Affirmative Action Dissertation-Year Fellowship, an American Psychological Association Minority Fellowship Program Dissertation Support Grant, a National Science Foundation Doctoral Dissertation Improvement Grant, a Fulbright Graduate Research Award and a Woodrow Wilson Women's Studies Grant for Doctoral Candidates.

Rhythm in Newborns' Language Processing

THIERRY NAZZI

Laboratoire de Science Cognitives et Psycholinguistique, CNRS-EHESS, Paris

INTRODUCTION

Learning a language requires recognizing linguistically relevant regularities, while discarding irrelevant variations. In developmental psychology, much attention has focussed on the acquisition of syntax and semantics and, more recently, to the acquisition of phonology. Studies in this domain first explored the acquisition of the phonetic inventory of the native language (Eimas, Siqueland, Jusczyk & Vigorito, 1971). Results have shown that the phonetic classes of the native language begin to influence the perception of vowels and consonants by the sixth month (Kuhl, 1991) and the tenth month of life (Werker & Tees, 1984; Best, McRoberts & Sithole, 1988) respectively. Recently, focus has shifted to prosody, an aspect of phonology that encompasses properties such as intonation and rhythm. Infants have been found to be sensitive to prosodic properties from birth, and to begin to specify the prosodic properties of their native language early in life (from about 7 1/2 months, see Newsome & Jusczyk, 1995).

The present paper will concentrate on the perception of language-specific rhythmic properties. Research has established that adults of different linguistic backgrounds use different segmentation strategies based on the rhythmic unit appropriate to their native language. The discovery of these strategies has prompted further research regarding their acquisition. Two series of experiments are presented, exploring whether newborns are sensitive to the different rhythmic types evidenced in adults' segmentation studies.

RHYTHM AND SPEECH SEGMENTATION

Several studies have shown that in the course of speech processing adult speakers of French, English, and Japanese use segmentation strategies that rely on different rhythmic units. Using a segment detection task, Mehler, Dommergues, Frauenfelder & Segui (1981) have established that the segmentation unit used by speakers of French is the syllable. These speakers were indeed faster to detect a segment (e.g., BA or BAL) when it coincided with the first syllable in the word (e.g., BALANCE or BALCON respectively) than when it was either longer or shorter than this first syllable. However, this syllabic effect could not be obtained with English subjects (Cutler, Mehler, Norris & Segui, 1986). This difference might be explained by the crucial role played by stress in the process of lexical access in English (Cutler & Norris, 1988; Cutler & Butterfield, 1992). The segment detection task has revealed a third pattern of results : Japanese speakers segment speech in a way that is dependent on the moraic structure (in Japanese, syllables are constituted of either one or two morae) of the Japanese language (Otake, Hatano, Cutler & Mehler, 1993).

It was further shown that the use of these three segmentation strategies depend on the language of the subjects, rather than on the language heard. Speakers of different languages indeed behave differently even when they are confronted with the same stimuli. English and French subjects tend to use whichever strategy they developed to process their native languages even when listening to stimuli in a foreign language (Cutler et al., 1986; Otake et al., 1993). Moreover, it has been found that highly proficient French-English bilingual subjects are unable to switch from one processing strategy to the other depending on the language they are processing (Cutler, Mehler, Norris & Segui, 1992), suggesting that one person cannot use more than one type of segmentation strategy.

One way to explain these contrasting results is to refer to the existence of language classes that basically differ in their rhythmic structure. Phonologists have proposed such a classification of languages based on timing properties (Pike, 1945; Abercrombie, 1967; Lehiste, 1977). They have claimed that many romance languages (like French) are syllable-timed, many germanic languages (like English) are stress-timed, while languages like Japanese and Tamil are mora-timed. The strategies used to segment speech could therefore be determined by the rhythmic properties of the speakers' native language.

This hypothesis is corroborated in a study by Mehler, Sebastian, Altmann, Dupoux, Christophe & Pallier (1993). Using a compressed speech adaptation task, they have noted a cross-linguistic adaptation (i.e. enhanced comprehension of compressed sentences in one language after listening to compressed sentences in another language) between two languages belonging to the syllable-timed class (Spanish and Catalan). This was not the case with English and French, two languages that belong to different rhythmic classes.

If natural languages are based on different rhythmic units, it seems important to understand how infants develop the adult rhythmic strategy specific to their native language. One might postulate that they can represent all the rhythmic units used by adults at birth, and select from these the one appropriate to their native language. The following section reports studies that have tested this hypothesis by investigating newborns' abilities to discriminate words according to their number of rhythmic units.

PERCEPTION OF RHYTHMIC UNITS IN NEWBORNS

Bijeljac-Babic, Bertoncini & Mehler (1993) have explored infants' ability to represent the number of syllables in simple consonant-vowel sequences. French-born newborns were first familiarized to a varied list of either bisyllabic or trisyllabic items. They were then either presented again with the same list of stimuli (control group) or presented with a list of items they had not previously heard (experimental condition). Infants were found to discriminate between the bisyllabic and the trisyllabic stimuli, suggesting that they had extracted the number of syllables in the items on the list. This interpretation was supported by the results of two further experiments which allowed to rule out alternative interpretations of a discrimination based on differences in duration and number of consonantic segments between the bisyllabic and trisyllabic stimuli. It must however be pointed out that the number of syllables and the number of vowels were correlated. As vowels seem to play a more salient role than consonants in early speech perception (Bertoncini, Bijeljac-Babic, Jusczyk, Kennedy & Mehler, 1988), these results were also compatible with the notion that infants had represented the number of vowels in the stimuli.

The Bijeljac-Babic et al. result was confirmed by Bertoncini, Floccia, Nazzi & Mehler (1995). They explored whether French-born newborns are sensitive to the number of syllables when presented with words from an unknown language, that is, bisyllabic and trisyllabic Japanese words. French-born newborns were found to react to a change in the number of syllables, generalizing the result obtained with French stimuli to words from another phonological system (see Figure 1, left panel).

2- VS. 3-SYLLABLES

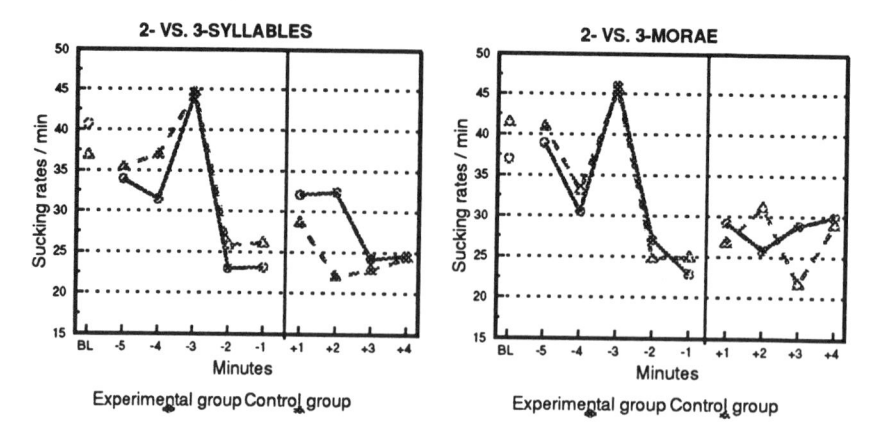

2- VS. 3-MORAE

Figure 1 : Discrimination of Japanese words according to their number of rhythmic units (From Bertoncini et al., 1995). Sucking-rates during baseline (BL), last 5 min of familiarization (-5 to -1) and 4 min of test (+1 to +4) for experimental and control group.

Bertoncini et al. (1995) have also investigated newborns' sensitivity to another rhythmic unit, the mora. They have shown that French-born newborns do not discriminate a varied list of bisyllabic words composed of 2 morae from a list of bisyllabic words composed of 3 morae (see Figure 1, right panel). As the additional mora was a consonant in most of the items (ka-*N*-go), this result again suggests that vowels are more important than consonants. It could be that trimoraic and bimoraic bisyllables were represented in the same way, as two-vowel strings. These results support the view that newborns do not represent the mora, hence, that they do not have access to all the rhythmic units used by adult speakers.

Ooijen, Mehler, Bertoncini & Sansavini (in preparation) have brought new support to this conclusion. They have found that newborns do not discriminate a list of strong-weak English bisyllables from a list of strong-strong English bisyllables. This result suggests that newborns are not sensitive to the difference between strong and weak syllables, the distinction upon which the segmentation strategy used by English speakers is based.

To summarize, we have presented experiments suggesting that adults' segmentation strategies are based on the unit that defines the rhythmic pattern of their native languages, but that newborns are not sensitive to all of these units. Rather the results suggest that newborns might represent words as a sequence of vowels, that might include at least some durational informations (see Mehler, Dupoux, Nazzi & Dehaene-Lambertz, 1996). It is possible that the initial vowel-based representation allows for the perception of differences between the different types of language timing. The following section presents data showing that newborns are sensitive to such differences, despite the fact that they cannot represent multisyllabic words in terms of the rhythmic unit appropriate to the language in which these words are spoken. This evidence comes from experiments exploring newborns' ability to discriminate between languages.

RHYTHM-BASED LANGUAGE DISCRIMINATION IN NEWBORNS

A few studies have explored the ability of infants under six months of age to discriminate between languages. Bahrick & Pickens (1988) have shown that English-born four-month-olds can detect a change between their native language and a foreign language : infants, familiarized to an English utterance, dishabituated more to a Spanish sentence than to a novel English utterance. Mehler, Jusczyk, Lambertz, Halsted, Bertoncini & Amiel-Tison (1988) have studied the ability of French four-day-olds and American two-month-olds to discriminate between two languages when lists of varied utterances were presented. French-born newborns and American 2-month-olds were found to discriminate their native language (French and English respectively) from a foreign language, Russian and Italian respectively. Moreover, it was claimed that both groups of infants had failed to discriminate two foreign languages.

Mehler et al. (1988) have then concluded that language discrimination in young infants is limited to the recognition of their native language. Mehler & Christophe (1995) however challenged this conclusion. They reanalized the data concerning French newborns' discrimination of foreign languages, and suggested that newborns actually discriminated foreign languages. We conducted a new study designed to better understand this ability and to explore the role played by rhythm in language discrimination (Nazzi, Bertoncini & Mehler, submitted).

The study was designed to test the hypothesis according to which infants extract the prosodic, and more specifically, rhythmic properties of fluent speech and use these properties to sort languages into a small number of rhythmic classes. This hypothesis predicts that newborns' ability to discriminate two languages relies on the perception of differences between their respective timing properties. To test this prediction, rhythmic distance between the languages presented was systematically varied. Thus, the contrasted languages belonged either to two different rhythmic classes or to the same class. The prediction was that languages would only be discriminated if they belonged to different rhythmic classes.

In a first experiment, French newborns were tested on their ability to discriminate two languages belonging to different rhythmic classes : stress-timed English and mora-timed Japanese. Stimuli were low-pass filtered with a cutoff frequency of 400 Hz, a transformation that reduces phonetic information while preserving prosodic information. Infants were familiarized to a varied set of sentences in one language or the other, the sentences being taken from the recordings of two native speakers. The infants were then presented either to a varied set of sentences from the other language (experimental group), or to a new set of sentences from the same language, taken from the recordings of two other native speakers (control group). Although infants in both groups heard a change in speakers' voices, only the infants from the experimental group heard a change in language. The results show that only infants in the experimental group increased their sucking rates, and that this increase was significantly different from that of the control group, suggesting that they had discriminated English from Japanese (see Figure 2, left panel). This experiment confirms the fact that newborns can discriminate between foreign languages. It further suggests that prosody is involved, and that the prosodic differences between the languages are more salient than differences between speakers' voices.

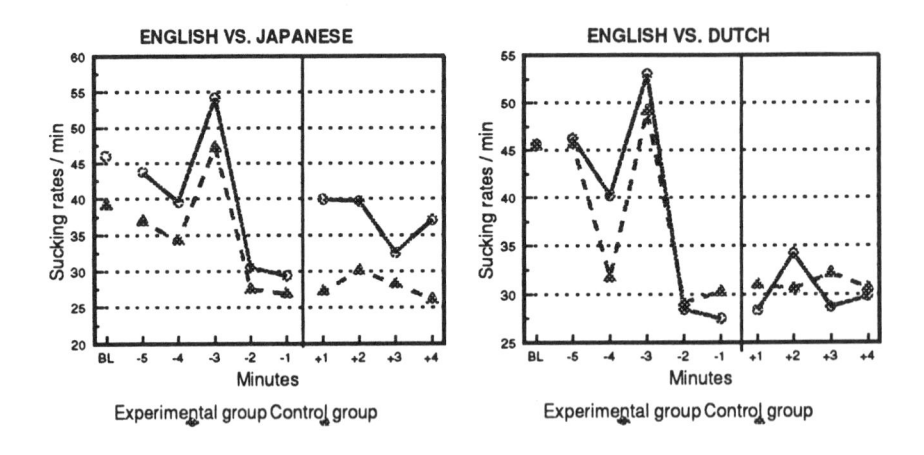

Figure 2 : Discrimination of foreign languages (From Nazzi, Bertoncini & Mehler, submitted). Sucking-rates during baseline (BL), last 5 min of familiarization (-5 to -1) and 4 min of test (+1 to +4) for experimental and control group.

In a second experiment, infants were tested on their ability to discriminate two languages belonging to the same rhythmic class : stress-timed English and Dutch. The procedure was exactly the same as in the previous experiment. The results show that infants in both groups react similarly, suggesting that they cannot discriminate English from Dutch on the basis of prosodic information (see Figure 2, right panel).

These two experiments support the hypothesis according to which languages are discriminated by young infants on the basis of their rhythmic, timing properties. A third experiment was conducted to determine whether French newborns form categories of languages according to the rhythmic classes. Four foreign languages were used : stress-timed English and Dutch, and syllable-timed Italian and Spanish. Infants were familiarized with sentences taken from two different languages, and then changed to the other two languages. For half of the infants (rhythmic group), the languages were combined according to the rhythmic classes (e.g., familiarization with English and Dutch, then change to Italian and Spanish); for the other half (non-rhythmic group), the languages were combined across the rhythmic classes (e.g., familiarization with English and Italian, then change to Dutch and Spanish). The results show a significant increase in sucking rates for the rhythmic group only, the reaction to the language change of the two groups of infants being significantly different (see Figure 3). Infants reacted to the change in languages only when the languages were combined according to their rhythmic class. This suggests that newborns sort utterances according to rhythmic classes, ignoring differences between individual languages that belong to the same rhythmic class.

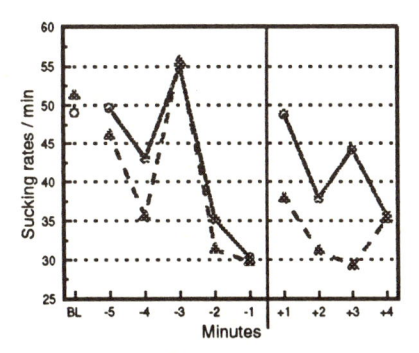

Figure 3 : Discrimination of rhythmic classes (From Nazzi, Bertoncini & Mehler, submitted). Sucking-rates during baseline (BL), last 5 min of familiarization (-5 to -1) and 4 min of test (+1 to +4) for rhythmic and non-rhythmic group.

Taken together, these results suggest that infants are sensitive to differences in the timing properties of fluent speech. Significantly, this early sensitivity to rhythm allows them to classify utterances (languages) according to the rhythmic classes that are found to determine adults' segmentation strategies. It then appears that the newborns' vowel-based representation of speech allows them to notice differences between types of languages varying on their underlying rhythmic unit. This sensitivity could be the prerequisite for the specification of the rhythmic unit on which the timing of their native language is based.

CONCLUSION

This paper presented a review of a series of experiments showing that adults of different linguistic backgrounds use segmentation strategies that are based on different rhythmic units. These differences were interpreted in terms of differences in the underlying rhythmic (timing) properties of their native languages. The aim of this paper was to present experiments exploring how these differences may already influence early speech perception. The first hypothesis was that infants might represent all rhythmic units right from birth, the appropriate unit being selected through infants' exposure to the native language. Results rather indicate that newborns could not represent all rhythmic units, and rather seemed to represent speech as a sequence of vowels. A last series of experiments however suggested that the vowel-based representation could be sufficient to perceive differences between the different types of language timing, an ability that could provide the basis for the specification of the rhythmic unit of the native language and the development of the appropriate segmentation strategy. Regarding these developmental issues, research has shown that the predominant, strong-weak pattern of English words is acquired by American infants between 6 and 9 months of age (Jusczyk, Cutler & Redanz, 1993), and that this pattern might influence speech segmentation in 7.5-month-old American infants (Newsome & Jusczyk, 1995). What allows the specification of the appropriate rhythmic unit of the native language during the second half of the first year of life could be the early sensitivity to language timing that was found by Nazzi, Bertoncini & Mehler (submitted).

REFERENCES

Abercrombie, D. (1967). *Elements of General Phonetics.* Edinburgh: Edinburgh University Press.

Bahrick, L.E. & Pickens, J.N. (1988). Classification of bimodal English and Spanish language passages by infants. *Infant Behavior and Development, 11,* 277-296.

Bertoncini, J., Bijeljac-Babic, R., Jusczyk, P.W., Kennedy, L. & Mehler, J. (1988). An investigation of young infants' perceptual representations of speech sounds. *Journal of Experimental Psychology: General, 117,* 21-33.

Bertoncini, J., Floccia, C., Nazzi, T. & Mehler, J. (1995). Morae and syllables : Rhythmical basis of speech representations in neonates. *Language and Speech, 38,* 311-329.

Best, C.T., McRoberts, G.W. & Sithole, N.M. (1988). Examination of perceptual reorganization for nonnative speech contrasts : Zulu click discrimination by english-speaking adults and infants. *Journal of Experimental Psychology : Human Perception and Performance, 14,* 345-360.

Bijeljac-Babic, R., Bertoncini, J. & Mehler, J. (1993). How do four-day-old infants categorize multisyllabic utterances. *Development Psychology, 29,* 711-721.

Cutler, A. & Butterfield, S. (1992). Rhythmic cues to speech segmentation: Evidence from juncture misperception. *Journal of Memory and Language, 31,* 218-236.

Cutler, A., Mehler, J., Norris, D. & Segui, J. (1986). The syllable's differing role in the segmentation of French and English. *Journal of Memory and Language, 25,* 385-400.

Cutler, A., Mehler, J., Norris, D. & Segui, J. (1992). The monolingual nature of speech segmentation by bilinguals. *Cognitive Psychology, 24,* 381-410.

Cutler, A. & Norris, D. (1988). The role of strong syllables in segmentation for lexical access. *Journal of Experimental Psychology: Human Perception and Performance, 14,* 113-121.

Eimas, P.D., Siqueland, E.R., Jusczyk, P.W. & Vigorito, J. (1971). Speech perception in infants, *Science, 171,* 303-306.

Jusczyk, P.W., Cutler, A. & Redanz, N. (1993). Preference for the predominant stress patterns of English words. *Child Development, 64,* 675-687.

Kuhl, P.K. (1991). Human adults and human infants show a "perceptual magnet effect" for the prototypes of speech categories, monkeys do not. *Perception and Psychophysics, 50*, 93-107.

Lehiste, I. (1977). Isochrony reconsidered. *Journal of Phonetics, 5*, 253-263.

Mehler, J. & Christophe, A. (1995). Maturation and learning of language in the first year of life. In M.S. Gazzaniga (Ed.), *The Cognitive Neurosciences* (pp. 943-954). Cambridge, MA : Bradford Books, MIT Press.

Mehler, J., Dommergues, J.Y., Frauenfelder, U. & Segui, J. (1981). The syllable's role in speech segmentation. *Journal of Verbal Learning and Verbal Behavior, 20*, 298-305.

Mehler, J., Dupoux, E., Nazzi, T. & Dehaene-Lambertz, G. (1996). Coping with linguistic diversity: The infant's viewpoint. In J.L. Morgan and K. Demuth (Eds.), *Signal to Syntax : Bootstrapping from Speech to Grammar in Early Acquisition* (pp. 101-116). Mahwah, NJ: Lawrence Erlbaum Associates.

Mehler, J., Jusczyk, P.W., Lambertz, G., Halsted, G., Bertoncini, J. & Amiel-Tison, C. (1988). A precursor of language acquisition in young infants. *Cognition, 29*, 143-178.

Mehler, J., Sebastian, N., Altmann, G., Dupoux, E., Christophe, A. & Pallier, C. (1993). Understanding compressed sentences : the role of rhythm and meaning. *Annals New York Academy of Sciences*, 272-282.

Nazzi, T., Bertoncini, J. & Mehler, J. (submitted). Language discrimination by newborns : towards an understanding of the role of rhythm.

Newsome, M. & Jusczyk, P.W. (1995). Do infants use stress as a cue for segmenting fluent speech? Paper presented at D. MacLaughlin & S. McEwen (Eds.), 19th Boston University Conference on Language Development, 2 (pp. 415-426). Somerville, MA : Cascadilla Press.

Ooijen, B. van, Mehler, J., Bertoncini, J. & Sansavini, A. (in preparation). The strong-weak syllable distinction in neonate representations.

Otake, T., Hatano, G., Cutler, A. & Mehler, J. (1993). Mora or syllable? Speech segmentation in Japanese. *Journal of Memory and Language, 32*, 258-278.

Pike, K. (1945). *The Intonation of American English*. Ann Arbor, MI: University of Michigan Press.

Werker, J.F. & Tees, R.C. (1984). Cross-language speech perception : evidence for perceptual reorganization during the first year of life. *Infant Behavior and Development, 7*, 49-63.

Overextension of Intransitive Verbs in the Acquisition of Japanese

MASAMI NOMURA & YASUHIRO SHIRAI
Daito Bunka University

1. Introduction

Ito (1990) proposes that there is a stage in children's acquisition of verbs when they use intransitive verbs for situations where transitive verbs are required, such as:

(1)   a.   atui-kara   sameru-n-da
            hot-because   cool.int-Part-Cop
           '(It) will cool because it is hot.'   (3;0)
           (intended meaning 'I'll cool it because it's hot.')

      b. (buranco)   tomat-te
          (swing)   stop.int-Request
          'Please stop.'   (3;11)
          (intended meaning 'Please stop the swing.')   (Ito 1990:69)

The correct form for (1a) is *atui kara samasunda* (*samasu* 'cool,' transitive), and for (1b) is *tomete* (*tomeru* 'stop,' transitive). Ito (1990) ascribes this phenomenon to the cognitive development of children; i.e. children are egocentric, and therefore acquire intransitive expressions first. When transitive forms are not available, they have to use intransitive verbs to refer to situations where transitive verbs are required.

Ito's argument is based on earlier studies on children's verbs such as Greenfield and Smith (1977) and Ingram (1971). He cites Greenfield and Smith (1977:115), who observed that a child (Nicky) expressed the first transitive action at 21 months by the verb *touch,* which is a two-argument transitive verb. He further cites Bowerman (1974), where the child uses intransitive verbs to refer to causative transitive situations, such as *Can you stay this open? I'm gonna fall this on her.*

Based on such examples and his own data, he proposed a four-stage model of acquisition of intransitive and transitive verbs (Ito 1990:69-71):

Stage 1:   Use of intransitive verbs for transitive meaning
Stage 2:   Use of causative suffix *-sase*
Stage 3:   Use of causative suffix *-sase* with *-sa* deleted[1]
Stage 4:   Acquisition of correct transitive form

Although Ito claims that intransitive verbs are acquired first because of the egocentricity of children, he only discusses verbs that constitute transitive/intransitive pairs, as in (1) above (e.g. *sameru* 'cool.int' and *samasu* 'cool.trans'), and does not mention the acquisition of transitive and intransitive verbs that do not constitute pairs.

Despite Ito's claim, Rispoli (1987) notes that in the speech of a Japanese child at 22 to 24 months, he produced more transitive verbs than intransitive verbs (type count), although Rispoli only analyzed dynamic verbs. Morikawa (1989) analyzed a longitudinal corpus of a Japanese child Sumihare between 1;11 and 3;4, and notes that he did make overextension errors in using transitive/intransitive pairs. However, they were minimal in relation to the total correct uses of other transitive and intransitive verbs. Since Ito's (1990) claim is not based on quantified data, but on examples from children's speech, we need to examine his claim using quantified data.

This study investigates the use of intransitive and transitive verbs in a longitudinal corpus of a child (1;4-2;4). It was hypothesized that the child would use both transitive and intransitive verbs early, and that the supposedly unidirectional nature of overextension (intransitive-->transitive) is reflective of the distribution of input to the child.

2. Data Analysis

The data used in the present study consist of a longitudinal corpus of a Japanese boy, Sumihare (Noji 1974-1977). The present study used the Noji data computerized and coded by Hiromi Morikawa (Morikawa 1989). The original Noji corpus records the child's speech as well as adult speech, which starts on the day of his birth and ends on his 7th birthday. Morikawa computerized the data from 1;11 to 3;4. The present study analyzed the data

---

[1] The verb forms by children for stages 2 and 3 that Ito (1990) cites are mostly ungrammatical uses of the causative morpheme. Interestingly, most of them are in request form (*-te*), similar to Allen's (1995) observation in Inuktitut.

from 1;11 to 2;4, during which period errors in the use of transitive/intransitive pairs are frequently observed (Morikawa 1989). In addition, the data from 1;4 to 1;10 were also analyzed using the original Noji corpus. The classification of transitive vs. intransitive verbs in this study follows the coding done by Morikawa (1989).

3. Results

First, to see the general trend in the use of transitive and intransitive verbs, the first 100 tokens of verbs for each month were counted, according to the transitivity type (i.e. transitive vs. intransitive). All verb tokens were counted for the data from 1;4 to 1;7 because there were less than 100 verb tokens. The results are shown in Table 1.

	transitive verbs		intransitive verbs		percentage of intransitive verbs	
	type	token	type	token	type	token
1;4	2	2	2	2	(50%)	(50%)
1;5	0	0	9	38	(100%)	(100%)
1;6	3	6	9	57	(75%)	(90%)
1;7	3	11	10	73	(77%)	(87%)
1;8	8	44	12	56	(60%)	(56%)
1;9	7	42	10	58	(59%)	(58%)
1;10	8	55	13	45	(56%)	(45%)
1;11	6	31	14	69	(70%)	(69%)
2;0	13	38	16	62	(55%)	(62%)
2;1	13	28	26	72	(66%)	(72%)
2;2	17	30	19	70	(53%)	(70%)
2;3	16	35	23	65	(59%)	(65%)
2;4	19	40	24	60	(56%)	(60%)

Table 1. First hundred verbs for each month used by Sumihare by transitivity type

The table shows that intransitive verbs generally outnumber transitive verbs, both in type and token. It also shows that from 1;5 to 1;7, Sumihare's verbs are predominantly intransitive. At 1;5, all verbs used (9 types, 38 tokens) are intransitive. After 1;8, the ratio for intransitive verbs decreases, and ranges between 50% and 70%. This indicates that there may be what Ito called "the intransitive stage" in Sumihare's language development.

Second, regarding the verbs that constitute transitive/intransitive pairs, there is a preponderance of intransitive verbs up to 1;7. Table 2 shows the distribution of the verbs constituting transitive/intransitive pairs. We used Jacobsen (1992:258-268) for a complete list of the verbs constituting the transitive/intransitive pairs. The table shows that Sumihare was using only the intransitive side of the transitive/intransitive pairs, up to 1;7. Starting at 1;8, the child used both sides of the pair, except for 1;11, when his verbs are again all intransitive.

	transitive verbs		intransitive verbs	
	type	token	type	token
1;4	0	0	2	2
1;5	0	0	3	12
1;6	0	0	4	14
1;7	0	0	4	18
1;8	3	8	6	11
1;9	2	2	5	8
1;10	3	6	8	12
1;11	0	0	8	18
2;0	3	5	10	18
2;1	3	6	16	25
2;2	7	9	11	19
2;3	5	8	14	29
2;4	7	10	17	35
total	33	54	95	175

Table 2. Use of verbs that constitute transitive/intransitive pairs among first 100 verbs for each month

One interesting observation is the higher ratio of intransitive verbs for verbs constituting pairs than for verbs in general (see also Table 1). This holds even after 1;8, when the child frequently used transitive verbs. The ratio of intransitive to transitive is approximately 3 to 1, which is higher than that for verbs in general after 1;8, which is approximately 6 to 4.

Thus far, it appears that Ito's claim that children go through an intransitive stage is correct. Next, we discuss the use of the intransitive-transitive pairs. This analysis is not restricted to the first 100 verbs at each month; all verbs constituting intransitive/transitive pairs are counted.

Table 3 shows that the overextension of intransitive verbs to transitive contexts is rare in comparison to the correct use of the transitive-intransitive pairs. First, A% (the ratio of column 5 to column 7) shows that the overextension rate in relation to correct use of transitive-intransitive pairs is very small--1.9% overall, only 6.0% even at the highest period (2;2). This shows that the child was using these verbs quite accurately. Second, B% (the ratio of column 1 to column 8) shows that the overextension of intransitive verbs for transitive contexts are not very high. Although at 2;0 it is 33.3%, overall the percentage of intransitive overextension is only 7.3%.

Table 3 also shows that at age 2;1, transitive verbs are overextended to intransitive contexts; i.e. overextensions in transitive-intransitive pairs are not unidirectional (see also Morikawa 1989, 1990). These include use of transitive *nuku* 'pull out' for intransitive *nukeru* 'come out,' transitive *akeru* 'open,' for intransitive *aku* 'open,' intransitive *katamaru* 'become hard' for transitive *katameru* 'make hard' (see Table 4, which lists all cases of overextension in the use of transitive-intransitive pairs.)

	OVEREXTENSION ERROR						CORRECT USE			
	intr.--->tr.		tr.--->intr.				total	tr. verbs	int.verb	
column	1	2	3	4	5	6	7	8	9	10
	token	(type)	token	(type)	total	(A%)				(B%)
1;4	0	(0)	0	(0)	0	0%	2	2	0	0%
1;5	0	(0)	0	(0)	0	0%	12	0	12	0%
1;6	0	(0)	0	(0)	0	0%	14	0	14	0%
1;7	0	(0)	0	(0)	0	0%	18	0	18	0%
1;8	1	(1)	0	(0)	1	5.0%	20	8	12	12.5%
1;9	0	(0)	0	(0)	0	0%	14	4	10	0%
1;10	0	(0)	0	(0)	0	0%	25	7	18	0%
1;11	1	(1)	0	(0)	1	1.4%	72	8	64	12.5%
2;0	4	(3)	0	(0)	4	5.3%	75	12	63	33.3%
2;1	8	(3)	6	(3)	14	6.0%	232	57	175	14.0%
2;2	6	(4)	0	(0)	6	1.1%	533	111	422	5.4%
2;3	1	(1)	0	(0)	1	0.4%	273	48	225	2.1%
2;4	2	(2)	0	(0)	2	0.7%	275	58	217	3.4%
Total	23	(15)	6	(3)	29	1.9%	1565	315	1250	7.3%

A% = Overextension rate (i.e. overextension as percentage of correct use)
B% = Intransitive overextension rate (i.e. use of intransitive verb in transitive context as percentage of correct use of transitive verb)

Table 3. Substitutions and correct uses of the verbs constituting transitive-intransitive pairs

It should also be noted that even for cases where the child overextended intransitive verbs, he used the correct transitive forms prior to the overextensions. For example, intransitive *aku* 'open,' is overextended for transitive *akeru* at 2;1, and intransitive *noru* 'ride,' for transitive *noseru* 'make something ride,' and intransitive *noku* 'get out of the way' for transitive *nokeru* 'remove' at 2;2. These verbs, however, had already been used in correct transitive forms prior to the overextension error. Moreover, in the case of *akeru* vs. *aku,* not only were intransitive overextensions observed 5 times, but also transitive overextensions were observed 4 times (see Table 4).

intransitive-->transitive			transitive-->intransitive		
(type)		(token count)	(type)		(token count)

[1;11]
okiru for okosu 'wake up' 1

[2;0]
okiru for okosu 'wake up' 1
aku for akeru 'open' 2
deru for dasu 'come/push out' 1

[2;1]
aku for akeru 'open' 5   akeru for aku 'open' 4
sameru for samasu 'cool' 1   nuku for nukeru 'pull/come out' 1
nokoru for nokosu 'remain/leave' 2   katameru for katamaru 'harden' 1

[2;2]
agaru for ageru 'rise/raise' 3
nureru for nurasu 'get/make wet' 1
noru for noseru 'ride/make..ride' 1
noku for nokeru 'get out of the way/remove' 1

[2;3]
sameru for samasu 'cool' 1

[2;4]
okiru for okosu 'wake up' 1
nigeru for nigasu 'run away/let go' 1

Table 4. Overextensions in transitive/intransitive pairs

4. Discussion

The results of this study show that there is a stage (up to 1;7) when Sumihare's verb use was mostly restricted to intransitive verbs. This supports the notion of the intransitive stage. However, the pattern of overextension does not necessarily support Ito's four-stage model, in that (1) the use of transitive-intransitive pair verbs was mostly accurate, (2) use of correct transitive preceded overextension of the intransitive verbs, (3) overextension of transitive to intransitive contexts were also observed.

Furthermore, the causative morpheme *-sase,* which Ito (1990) predicts would occur after the stage of intransitive overextension, did not occur at all between 1;11 and 2;4. According to Ito's four-stage model, this should be observed after 2;0, during which period Sumihare showed the highest ratio of intransitive overextension, but it never did. For example, intransitive *okiru* 'wake up' was overextended for transitive *okosu* 'wake...up' at 2;0, but then Sumihare went on to use the correct transitive form *okosu* at 2;2 without going through the stage of *-sase* attachment. In sum, although there was some support for the notion of the intransitive stage, Ito's four-stage model was not supported by the Sumihare data.

An important question to consider is why Japanese children show overextension of intransitive verbs to transitive contexts, and vice versa. We argue that it is due to processing difficulties. Rispoli (1987) shows that two-year-old Japanese children already have the knowledge of the transitive vs. intransitive distinction, which he claims they acquire based on two semantic cues (theme animacy and plannedness of action). It indeed appears that Sumihare already has a knowledge of the transitive/intransitive distinction, given the small percentage of errors observed. However, even if a child knows this basic semantic distinction at the conceptual level, there may be cases where the child cannot access or retrieve the correct linguistic form for a given verb; and in such cases, it is only natural that the child will access something that is very close in meaning and form. Notice that in Japanese most transitive/intransitive pairs have in common the first few (at least two) phonological segments (e.g. *nuku/nukeru; aku/akeru; katamaru/katameru; noru/noseru*, see Table 4). If our lexical retrieval is organized around the onset of words, as suggested by research on the tip-of-the-tongue phenomenon (Brown & McNeill 1966, Yarmey 1973), it is quite understandable that children make performance errors of incorrectly retrieving a phonologically similar item, which, needless to say, is also semantically similar. (Most transitive/intransitive pairs are semantically identical except for one semantic parameter--causativity.) This processing explanation is consistent not only with the fact that Sumihare overextended the verbs that he had earlier used correctly, but also with the fact that he showed rather random uses of the pair *aku/akeru* 'open' at 2;1. Although Sumihare correctly used transitive *akeru* twice, and intransitive *aku* 6 times, he also overextended transitive *akeru* four times, and intransitive *aku* 5 times at 2;1. This is probably due to the lack of solid control of these two competing verb forms, leading to the utterance of whichever was retrieved or activated first (see also Morikawa 1989:124-131).

What, then, about the direction of overextensions? So far, this issue has been extensively investigated in English (Bowerman 1974, Braine et al. 1990, Maratsos et al. 1987) and Hebrew (Berman 1982, 1993). English data often show that intransitive overextension is more frequent than transitive overextension (Bowerman 1974), but this is not always the case (Lord 1979). Maratsos et al.'s (1987) nonce-word experiment suggests that there is individual variation in the use of innovative causative forms. The issue is far from resolved both at the level of description (whether uni-directional or not) and of explanation (why intransitive overextensions occur) and is still being investigated (Pye et al. 1995, Allen 1995).

Here, we discuss a possible reason for the higher frequency of intransitive overextension observed in this study. We argue that this is partly because intransitive verbs are more frequent in children's language. As discussed above, intransitive verbs in the child's speech are more frequent than transitive verbs.[2] Ito claims that children move from an intransitive stage, when they are egocentric, to a transitive stage. Children's egocentricity may be one contributing factor. However, the ratio may be a reflection of the input frequency. We classified the first 100 verbs[3] in the adult speech addressed to Sumihare at early periods (between 1;5 and 2;1) and found the following frequency distribution (see Table 5).

	transitive verbs		intransitive verbs	
1; 5	11	(22%)	39	(78%)
1; 6	23	(29%)	56	(71%)
1; 7	24	(24%)	76	(76%)
1; 8	20	(39%)	31	(61%)
1; 9	29	(46%)	34	(54%)
1; 10	21	(40%)	32	(60%)
1; 11	41	(41%)	59	(59%)
2; 0	21	(28%)	53	(72%)
2; 1	38	(38%)	62	(62%)
Average		(33%)		(66%)

Table 5. Verbs used by adults by transitivity type (token count)

The table shows that adults also use intransitive verbs more frequently (66%). Interestingly, the average percentage of the transitive verbs used by Sumihare for the periods after initial restriction (1;8 to 2;1) is 60%, which approximates the adult use. It is therefore possible that children come to use intransitive verbs more often because of the distribution in the adult input. Because of this distribution, Sumihare may be more comfortable in using intransitive verbs, and this may also be what the higher ratio of intransitive overextension is reflecting.

5. Conclusion

In conclusion, this study investigated the longitudinal development of transitive and intransitive verbs and found that although the child's use of verbs is initially restricted to intransitive verbs, he soon starts to use both intransitives and transitive, and the overextension rate is very low. The overextension is attributed to retrieval error due to the child's unstable representation of the transitive-intransitive pairs.

Finally, we mention possible future research in this area. First, we need to investigate more data from Japanese children to see whether the

---

[2] The only exception is the token count for age 1;10. This is probably due to the high frequency (37 tokens) of the phrase *Tyoodai* 'Give me (something).' For type count, intransitive verbs are more frequent than transitive verbs.

[3] However, only the periods 1;11 and 2;1 had more than 100 verb tokens.

pattern observed in Sumihare's development is common among Japanese children, especially in view of the individual differences noted by Maratsos et al. (1987). Second, it would be interesting to analyze second language acquisition data to test the validity of the claim based on children's egocentricity. If cognitive factors such as egocentricity are the primary sources of the initial restriction to intransitive verbs and more frequent overextension of intransitive verbs, then in second language acquisition, such tendencies should not be observed. Rather, any preponderance of intransitive verbs may be attributed to more linguistic factors, such as input frequency or the unmarked nature of intransitive verbs. A longitudinal analysis of verb use by second language learners would be a good test case.

Also interesting would be to investigate the possibility that children may be attending to linguistic cues to acquire transitive/intransitive pairs in Japanese, not just learning transitive and intransitive verbs item by item. The pairs are semi-productive, i.e. although there is some regularity, no single rule can capture the formation of transitive from intransitive or vice versa (Jacobsen 1992). However, one salient cue for transitivity in transitive-intransitive pairs is the *-su* ending. In Jacobsen's complete list of the transitive-intransitive pairs in Japanese, close to half of the transitive verbs end in *-su*. (e.g. *kowasu* 'break'; *kaesu* 'return'), whereas no intransitive verbs have the *-su* ending. This in fact may be related in the child's mind (and probably in the adult native speaker's mind) to the productive causative morphemes *-(s)asu* and *-(s)aseru* (e.g. *taberu* 'eat' > *tabesasu* 'make someone eat'; *taberu* > *tabesaseru*).

A preliminary analysis of the verbs used by Sumihare shows from 1;4 to 1;10 there is no token of transitive *-su*. Almost all verbs up to 1;10 end in *-ru* or *-ku*. Sumihare may have created the phonological representation of the category 'verb' as ending only in *-ru* and *-ku*, not *-su*. Verbs ending in *-su* appear only after 1;11, and gradually increase after that. This may be related to the early preponderance of intransitive verbs. In creating the semantic and phonological representation of the category verb, a child may associate it with "semantically, intransitive" and "phonologically, ends in *-ru* or *-ku*." This possibility should be further investigated.

Acknowledgments

We are greatly indebted to Hiromi Morikawa, who generously provided her computerized and coded data of Sumihare. We thank Kevin Gregg and Foong Ha Yap for their helpful comments on the draft of this paper. Usual disclaimers apply. Supported by a grant from the Japanese Ministry of Education, Science, and Culture (no. 06851070) to the second author.

References

Allen, Shanley E. M. 1995. Acquisition of Causatives in Inuktitut, in E. Clark, ed., *Proceedings of the Twenty-seventh Annual Child Language Research Forum*. Stanford, CA: CSLI.

Berman, Ruth. 1982. Verb-Pattern Alternation: The Interface of Morphology, Syntax, and Semantics in Hebrew Child Language. *Journal of Child Language* 9.169-191

Berman, Ruth. 1993. Marking of Verb Transitivity by Hebrew-Speaking Children. *Journal of Child Language* 20.641-669.

Bowerman, Melissa. 1974. Learning the Structure of Causative Verbs: A Study in the Relationship of Cognitive, Semantic, and Syntactic Development. *Papers and Reports on Child Language Development* 8.142-178.

Braine, Martin D. S., Ruth E. Brody, Shalom M. Fisch, Mara J.Weisberger and Monica Blum. 1990. Can Children Use a Verb Without Exposure to Its Argument Structure? *Journal of Child Language* 17.313-342.

Brown, Roger and David McNeill. 1966.. The Tip of the Tongue Phenomenon. *Journal of Verbal Learning and Verbal Behavior* 5.325-327.

Greenfield, Patricia M. and Joshua H. Smith. 1976. *The Structure of Communication in Early Language Development.* New York: Academic Press.

Ingram, David. 1971. Transitivity in Child Language. *Language* 47.888-910.

Ito, Katsutoshi. 1990. *Kodomo no Kotoba: Syuutoku to Soozoo.* Tokyo: Keiso Shobo.

Jacobsen, W. M. 1992. *The Transitive Structure of Events in Japanese.* Tokyo: Kuroshio.

Lord, Carol. 1979. "Don't You Fall Me Down": Children's Generalizations Regarding Cause and Transitivity. *Papers and Reports on Child Language Development* 17.81-89.

Maratsos, Michael, Roxane Gudeman, Poldi Gerard-Ngo and Ganie DeHart. 1987. A Study in Novel Word Learning: The Productivity of the Causative, in B. MacWhinney, ed., *The Mechanisms of Language Acquisition..* Hillsdale, NJ: Erlbaum.

Morikawa, Hiromi. 1989. *Acquisition of Case Marking and Predicate-Argument Structures in Japanese: A Longitudinal Study of Language Acquisition Mechanisms.* Doctoral dissertation, University of Kansas.

Morikawa, Hiromi. 1990. Acquisition of Transitivity in Japanese: Early Use of Transitive/Intransitive Verb Pairs. *Working Papers in Language Development* 15.1-13.

Noji, Junya. 1974-1977. *Yooziki no Gengo Seekatu no Zittai.* Hiroshima: Bunka Hyoron.

Pye, Clifton, Diane Frome Loeb, Sean Redmond and Lori Zobel Richardson. 1995. When Do Children Acquire Verbs? in E. Clark, ed., *Proceedings of the Twenty-sixth Annual Child Language Research Forum.* Stanford, CA: CSLI.

Rispoli, Matthew. 1987. The Acquisition of the Transitive Action Verb Categories in Japanese. *First Language* 7.183-200.

Pronominalization in the Narratives of Turkish-Speaking Children

F. HÜLYA ÖZCAN
Anadolu University

The fact that noun phrases play an important role in constructing a coherent narrative has been indicated in different studies in different languages (Bennett-Kastor, 1983; Wigglesworth, 1990; Peterson and Dodsworth, 1991; Özcan, 1993). It is not only the reiteration of the referents which facilitates coherence but also the introduction and reiteration of these referents by means of appropriate linguistic means. Therefore, another requirement of a coherent narrative is the appropriate use of pronominals.
The lexical realization of the referents is meant to inform the hearer about the certain specifications of the particular referents. The speaker establishes the continuity of the participants through lexical realization meaning that chosen forms code whether this referent has just been introduced or is being maintained or codes a switch from one referent to another (Givon, 1983). According to this, the continuing participants are realized in the form of a pronominal while the discontinuous topics are brought into the consciousness of the hearer by means of full noun phrases. Givon (1983) reported that there is a correlation between the degree of the continuity and the lexical realizations in spoken language. The continuing referents are marked with pronouns and the discontinued entities, mentioned previously in discourse, are marked by NPs. In other words, new and given information is established through lexical forms, with new and given information coded through nominal and pronominal forms (Yule, 1981). In addition to the lexical realizations, the form of a pronominal may have implications for discourse in languages with null subjects. Anaphoric null subjects mark continuing referents while overt pronominals and noun phrases occur when the speaker marks a contrast between the referents (Flashner, 1987).
Thus, the issue of whether children acquiring their first language are aware of this and organize their discourse accordingly has drawn considerable attention and been widely studied. This research has indicated that children's pronominalization is guided by a thematic subject strategy (Karmiloff-Smith, 1980, 1981, 1985; Bamberg, 1987). It has also shown that children's early pronominals are deictic (Karmiloff-Smith, 1980,1981, 1985; Verhoeven, 1986). However, in these studies, the referents were visible to both hearer and speaker. The presence of referents in the extralinguistic context may provide children a context to use pronominals deictically. If this condition changed and the referents were available to neither hearer nor speaker in context, would the pronominals be deictic or anaphoric? The present study investigates whether the input where the referents are not present affects the nature of the pronominals and also aims to delineate the strategies children employ for the pronominalization of referents.

Turkish was chosen because there, if a pronominal is used for the subject of the sentence, it may either be null or overt since Turkish employs both overt pronominal and Ø representations to convey a coreferential relationship with a full NP. The pronominal forms need to be analysed to see which form is used to code the reference to a particular referent. This study is, therefore, guided by the research questions;

"*What governs pronominalization in the narratives of Turkish-speaking children?*"

"*Under what circumstances does a child use overt pronominal subjects and null subjects for the referents in discourse?*"

This study, part of a larger project on coherence in the narratives of Turkish-speaking children, has a cross-sectional design. The subjects were 60 monolingual Turkish-speaking children whose ages ranged from 3 to 7, and 20 adults. The children were divided into three groups by age. The youngest group consisted of children between 3;0 and 3;11 (mean age 3;4); children between 5;0 and 5;11 (mean age 5;4), and the third group was children between 7;0 and 7;11 (mean age 7;4). Each group contained 20 children, with equal numbers of boys and girls, all from middle class and upper-middle class families with sinilar socio-economic backgrounds and with university-graduate parents. The children aged 3 and 5 were nursery-school children, while 7-year-olds were in primary school and had already learned to read and write. University graduate adults comprised the control group.

The data collected for this study consist of narratives told by Turkish-speaking children and adults. These narratives were elicited through a video film. This was a silent film about a little boy living alone with his mother and father in a house in a forest (see Appendix). It was chosen for elicitation because the events were presented in chronological order, and because different characteristics of the referents involved in the events, such as being a protagonist or secondary character, would help to elicit different aspects of narrative development. After watching the video film, the children narrated the story to another person who did not watch the film. The children knew that this person had not watched the film. In the case of adults, subjects watched the film and then told the story to a child who had not seen the film.

For the analysis, the data was transcribed orthographically. Since the overall coherence is maintained by connecting smaller units into a large whole, the narrative texts were divided into clausal units based on Hunt's (1970) T-unit criteria. The present analysis was based on all the noun phrases in these units. In order to examine what governs children's pronominalizations, the introduced and reiterated referents in linguistic units were analysed qualitatively by making a profile of all mentions of each referent. This profile was repeated for each referent and the similarities and differences in pronominalization strategies between different referents were examined, and the results compared across ages to reveal any developmental differences.

RESULTS

We first looked at "**What governs children's pronominalization?**". Two claims have been made concerning this issue: thematic subject strategy and paragraph boundary strategy. In thematic subject strategy, narrators save pronominal uses for the main referent of the story. This main referent is characterized as the thematic subject (Karmiloff-Smith, 1980, 1981, 1985). The child chooses as thematic subject the main character n the story and afterwards this referent is referred by pronominals. Therefore, this referent is lexically realized as a pronominal whether the function is maintaining or switching reference. The referents other than this thematic subject, on the other hand, are introduced and switched to by means of nominals but maintained by means of pronominals. The second strategy considers pronominalization as a semantic process in which 'semantically prominent' information is marked by nominal forms while continuously available information is marked by pronominals, considered as less prominent forms. Therefore, nominal expressions should be preferred over pronominal ones to mark paragraph boundaries (Hinds, 1977, 1979). When a referent is first introduced into the story, or the speaker switches from one referent to another, a nominal form is used to mark the importance of the shift in topic. But, when a recently introduced or switched referent is maintained, a pronominal form is used. So, each referent is mentioned within paragraphs starting with a nominal and continuing with a pronominal regardless of that referent being a protagonist or a secondary character. This strategy is termed a "paragraph boundary strategy". We have analysed our data taking these two strategies into consideration. The analysis will be performed in terms of major referents and minor referents separately.

In our 3-year-old group, we see some individual differences among the subjects. Two out of 20 subjects do not use any pronominal forms at all for any of the referents. Instead, they use full NPs throughout for introducing, maintaining and switching the referents, as in (1).

(1) *Kardan adam yap -t> çocuk/* (3;3)
snowman make PAST boy

Çocu¤ -un baba -s> var -d>/
boy GEN father POSS exist PAST3SG

...

Kardan adam da git -ti/
snowman too go PAST 3SG

...

Sonra eri -mifl kardan adam/
then melt PAST snowman

Çocuk da çok üzül -dü/
boy too very sad PAST3SG

(The boy made a snowman/There was the boy's father/...The snowman went/Then, the snowman melted/The boy was very sad.)

Children at this age treat the major referents, the boy and the snowman, in a different way. Three subjects consider the boy as the thematic subject of the narrative and always pronominalize this referent after the first introduction as seen in (2).

(2)   *Kar -lar yaŋ -dı/*   (3;7)
      snow PLU snow PAST3SG
      Kardan adamᵢ yap -tı çocukⱼ /
      snowman make PAST boy
      Øᵢ Sonra uç -tu/
      then fly PAST3SG...
      Noel baba var -dı/
      FatherXmas exist PAST 3SG
      Øᵢⱼ Git -tik -ler -i yer -de müzik
      go PART PLU ACC place LOC music
      cd- di -ler
      play PAST3PLU
      sonra Øᵢⱼ ev -ler -i -ne dön -dü -ler/
      then house PLU ACC DAT return PAST3PLU
      Øⱼ Uyu -du/
      sleep PAST3SG
      Øⱼ Kalk -ti/
      get up PAST3SG
      ...
      Eri -miş -ti kardan adam/
      melt PAST PAST snowman
      Øⱼ Sonra üzül -dü/
      then become sad PAST3SG
      (It snowed/The boy made (a) snowman/Then, (the snowman) flew/...There was this Father Christmas/ After (the boy and the snowman) had played music at the place (they) went, (they) came back/The snowman had melted/(The boy felt sad.)

As illustrated in (3), seven of the 3-year-olds introduce the referent as a full NP, then use pronominal forms until a new referent is introduced as a full NP. When the boy comes to the focus again, the referent is switched by a full NP and pronominalized afterwards.

(3)   ***Çocuk var -dı/***   (3;3)
      boy exist PAST3SG
      Ø Kardan adam yap -tı/
      snowman make PAST3SG
      ...
      Sonra çocuk uyu -du/
      then boy sleep PAST3SG
      Ø Uyan -dı/
      wake up PAST3SG
      *Ama **kardan adam** eri -miş -ti/*
      but snowman melt PAST PAST

Çocuk hedye -si -ni kardan adam -a ver -di/
boy present POSS ACC snowman DAT give PAST
(There was the boy/(He) made a snowman/.../Then, the boy slept/(He) woke up/But the snowman melted/The boy gave the snowman his present.)

Six of the 3-year-old children employ both these strategies with the same referent. When they first introduce the boy, they treat it as a thematic subject and reserve the pronominal forms for it. After a while, when more referents are introduced, they switch to the boy with a full NP and pronominalize it while maintaining the new referent until that in turn is switched to another referent with a full NP. This is illustrated in (4).

(4)   *Ø Kardan adam yap -tı/*   (3;11)
       snowman make PAST3SG
Kardan adam *yer -i -nde dur -uyor -du*
snowman place ACC LOC stay PROG PAST3SG
Yat -tı   *o /*
go to bed PAST   he (the boy)
Ø Kalk -tı/
   get up PAST3SG
Kardan adam *canlan -dı/*
snowman   become alive PAST3SG
Ø Yürü -meye basla -dı/
    walk INF   start PAST3SG
...

Ø Aç -tı/
open PAST3SG
...
Noel Baba *var -dı/*
FatherXmas exist PAST3SG
Noel Baba -nın ev -i -ne gir -di çocuk/
FatherXmas GEN house POSS DAT enter PAST boy
...

((He) made (a) snowman/ The snowman was standing at his place/ ((The boy) went to bed/(He) got up/ The snowman became alive/ (He) started walking/.../(He) opened/.../There was Father Christmas/The boy went into Father Christmas's house.)

Two of the children in this group do not use pronominals for 'the boy'. This referent is never maintained as one information block as seen in (5).

(5)   **Çocuk** *kardan adam yap -tı/*
       boy snowman make PAST3SG
Kardan adamᵢ *yürü -dü/*
snowman   walk PAST3SG
...
Çocuk *da yürü -dü/*

> boy too walk PAST3SG
> *Øᵢ Uç -tu/*
> fly PAST3SG
> ...
> *Oyna -dı çocuk/*
> play PAST boy
> *Kardan adamᵢ sıcak -da kal -dı*
> snowman hot DAT stay PAST3SG
> *Øᵢ Eri -di/*
> melt PAST3SG
>> (The boy built (a) snowman/The snowman walked/.../The boy also walked/(The snowman) went flying/.../The boy danced/The snowman stayed in the hot/(He) melted.)

Children in this age group treat 'the snowman' in a different way than the boy. Although the snowman is considered as a major referent appearing quite early in the eventline and participating in almost all the scenes throughout the story, none of the 3-year-olds considers the snowman as the thematic subject. They all mention the referent with a full NP both when introducing and switching to it, and they pronominalize subsequent mentions until they switch to another referent. They therefore mark paragraph boundaries by introducing or switching to the snowman by means of full NPs and using anaphoric devices for subsequent mentions until they switch to another referent.

(6) *Kardan adam yap -tı çocuk/* (3;11)
snowman make PAST boy
Ø Çok güzel ol -du/
very beautiful become PAST3SG
...
Ø Sonra uç -tu/
then fly PAST3SG
Kardan adam -la çocuk orman -a git -ti/
snowman with boy forest DAT go PAST
>> (The boy made (a) snowman/(It) was very beautiful/.../Then, (he) flew/The boy and the snowman went to the forest.)

It is difficult to draw any conclusions about minor referents. Children this age normally drop them after the introduction. If they reiterate them, which is rare, they mention them as full NPs initially and then pronominalize until another referent comes on the scene, as in (7).

(7) ...
Çok kardan adam var -dı/ (3;11)
a lot of snowman exist PAST
Onlar dansed -iyor -du/
then dance PROG PAST
Sonra çocuk yat -mış -tı/
then boy go to bed PAST PAST

(.../There were a lot of snowman/They were dancing/Then, the boy went to bed.)

In the 5-year-old group, seven out of 20 children treat the boy as the thematic subject and always use pronominal forms for maintaining and switching to this referent throughout the text. Another seven introduce the boy as a full NP and then maintain the referent with pronominals until another referent comes onto the scene. Six children treat the boy in relation to the other referents. They introduce him as a full NP and pronominalize thereafter. As seen in (8), when they switch to 'the boy' from a minor referent, they still pronominalize, treating this referent as the thematic subject.

(8)   *Çocuk$_i$ yat -ıyor -du/*   (5;3)
       boy   sleep PROG PAST

       ...
       Ø$_i$ Giyin   -di/
       get dressed PAST3SG

       ...
       O$_i$ gid -ip   kardan adam yap -tı/
       he go PART   snowman   make PAST3SG
       ***Anne**   -si   yatır   -dı   o -nu/*
       mother POSS   tuck in PAST he ACC
       Ø$_i$ Yat   -a -ma -dı/
       sleep ABL NEG PAST3SG
       (The boy was in bed/.../(He) got dressed/.../He made (a) snowman/His mum tucked him in bed.)

On the other hand, as illustrated in (9), when they switched from the other major character, the snowman, a full NP is used and the referent is pronominalized afterwards.

(9)   ...
       Ø$_i$ Kalk -tı/
       get up PAST3SG
       *Sonra **kardan adam** eri -miş -ti/*
       then   snowman   melt PAST PAST
       Çocuk$_i$ da çok   üzül -müş -tü/
       boy   PART very become sad PAST PAST
       ((He) could not stay in bed/.../(He) got up/Then, the snowman melted/The boy was very sad.)

When they talk about the snowman, only one child treats it as the thematic subject and pronominalizes it throughout the text after introducing as a full NP. Ten children use pronominals anaphorically to maintain the referent, and seven do not pronominalize the referent at all. This is because they mention the snowman only once as a full NP and then switch to another referent. When they return to the snowman again, they use a full NP.

Five-year-olds have the same tendency as the 3-year-olds for the minor referents. Minor referents are not reiterated very often and when they are, they are pronominalized within the paragraph boundary strategy by switching to these referents by means of a full NP and then maintaining them with pronominals.

The seven-year-old s'data does not differ from the 3-and 5-year-olds'. Six children treat the boy as the thematic subject and pronominalize the agent all the time both when maintaining and switching the referent. Seven of them treat all the characters equally and pronominalize major referents in terms of paragraphs, switching from one reference to another with full NPs. Seven of them regard pronominalization of the boy in relation to the other referents; as in (10), they treat this referent as the central character by the time the snowman appears. By then, the boy is always referred by a pronominal even when it is switched from the other referent. Once the snowman is introduced, they adopt a different pattern of pronominalization. When the boy is switched to from the snowman (the other major character), a full NP is used. But when it is switched to from a minor referent, the boy is still treated as the thematic subject and switched to with a pronominal form.

(10)   **Bir   çocuk$_i$ var -dı/**   (7;10)
       one boy   exist PAST3SG
       Ø$_i$ Sabah   uyan   -dı/
       morning wake up PAST3SG
...
       Ø$_i$ Hemen gid-ip bir kardan adam yap -ı/
       at once go PART one snowman make PAST3SG
       ...anne -si öğlen yemeğ -i -ne çağır -dı/
       mother POSS lunch   POSS DAT call PAST
       ...Ø$_i$ hep pencere -den dışarı bak -ıyor -du
       always window ABL out look PROG PAST3SG
       baba -sı yat -ma saat i -nin   gel -diği -ni
       father POSS sleep INF time POSS GEN come PART ACC
       işaret et -ti/
       point out PAST3SG
       Ø$_i$ Gid -ip pijama -lar -ı -ı giy -di/
       go PART pyjama PLU POSS ACC put on PAST3SG
...
       Kardan adam bir şey -e çok üzül -müş -tü/
       snowman one thing DAT very becomes ad PAST PAST
...
       Çocuk git -ti el   -i -nden tut -tu/
       boy   go PAST hand POSS ABL hold PAST
...
       Kardan adam yer   -i -nde dur -du/
       snowman   place POSS LOC stay PAST
       Çocuk git   -ti kapı -da dur -du/
       boy   go PAST door LOC stop PAST
       (There was a boy/(He) woke up in the morning/.../(He) made a snowman/...(his) mum   called him inside for lunch/...(he) kept

looking out of the window/In the evening, (he) still was looking out of the window/(His) father pointed (him) out that it was bedtime/(The boy) put his pyjamas on/.../The snowman was upset about something/...The boy went (near him) and held (his) hand/.../The snowman stood at (his) place/The boy went and stopped at the door.)

A few children in this group treat the snowman as a thematic subject after the initial introduction. Until the snowman appears, the boy is considered the thematic subject, but once the snowman appears, it is treated as the thematic subject even though the boy is still there. They emphasize that another important referent has taken over the role of thematic subject for that period, and they organize their discourse accordingly.

(11) $Çocuk_i$ *uyan* -*yor*/   (7;5)
         boy   wake up PROG
         ...
         Anne -si "çorap - lar -ı- nı giy" di -yor/
         mother POSS socks PLU POSS ACC wear say PROG
         ...
         $Ø_i$ *Sonra kardan adam -ı -naj bir daha bak -yor/*
         then snowman POSS DAT one time look PROG3SG
         $Ø_j$ *Ozaman arka -sı -nı dön -ip flapka -sı -nı*
         then back POSS ACC turn PART hat POSS ACC
         çıkar -ıyor o -na/
         take off PROG he DAT
         ...
         Kardan adam -a "bin" di -yor çocuk/
         snowman DAT mount say PROG boy
         $Ø_j$ *Bin -iyor/*
         mount PROG3SG

         (The boy wakes up/.../(His) mother said "Put your socks on"/(He) puts (his) socks on/.../Then, (he) looks at (his) snowman one more time/(The snowman) then turns behind and greets him by taking (his) hat off/The boy told the snowman "Mount (on the bike)/(The snowman) mounts (on the bike).)

Since the narratives of 7-year-olds become more sophisticated and longer, and since children this age talk more about minor referents, there is a clear picture of the pronominalization for minor referents: children mainly treat them as paragraph units, and introduce them with full NPs and then pronominalize until a new referent is introduced. When they need to return to the same referent, they do so by switching to a full NP again and then reiterate with pronominal forms.

(12)   ...
         Anne -si o -na söyle -di/   (7;5)
         mother POSS he DAT say PAST
         Ø Giy -dir -di/
         wear PAST3SG

> *Sonra Noel Baba o -nu d -ıp bir*
> then FatherXmas heACC takePARTone
> *yer -e götür -dü*
> placeDATtakePAST
> *ØOra -da kızağı -ı - nı, geyik -ler -i -ni*
> thereLOC sledgePOSS ACC deer PLU POSS ACC
> *göster -di/*
> showPAST
> *ØO -na hediye ver -di/*
> he DAT present give PAST3SG
> ((His) mum told him/(She) dressed (him)/.../Then, Father Christmas took him somewhere/(He) showed (the boy) (his) deers and sledge/(Father Christmas) gave him a present.)

Adults do not follow a single strategy for anaphoric devices, either. Seven adults treat the boy as thematic subject and use pronominals both for switching and maintaining while six prefer full NPs for switching to the referent and pronominals for maintaining it. The remaining seven consider the functions of the other referents in the story. They treat the boy as the thematic subject by mentioning it with pronominals until the snowman is introduced. From then on, reference to the boy is switched with full NPs and maintained with pronominals. None of the adults treats the snowman as a thematic subject. The snowman is always mentioned in the form of paragraphs, switched to and from another referent with full NPs and maintained with pronominals. Like the 7-year-olds, all the adults introduce minor referents with full NPs and then maintain them with pronouns within paragraphs.

We next look at pronominalization from a different angle. Pronominal forms are employed for different mentions of referents. Under what circumstances does a child use an overt pronominal subject in Turkish versus a null subject?

All the subjects, regardless of age, use null subjects 96% of the time when they pronominalize.

Table 1 Distribution of null subject and overt pronominal subjects across the age groups

Age	Null Subject	Pronominal Subject
3-year	95% (N=60)	5% (N=3)
5-year	94% (N=50)	6% (N=3)
7-year	96% (N=68)	4% (N=3)
Adult	98% (N=60)	2% (N=2)
Mean	96%	4%

Table I shows that overt pronominal subjects are rare. Some examples from each age group follow, with interpretations that, because of the small number, can only be tentative.

The 3-year-old group uses overt pronominal subjects mainly in two different contexts. The first context, as illustrated in (14), is to switch the reference from one major referent -*the snowman*- to another one -*the boy*.

(14)   ...Sonra **kardan adam** "hoşçakal" de -di/ (3;4)
then   snowman   good-bye say PAST
O   *da*   "hoşçakal" de -di/

he too   good-bye say PAST
(Then, the snowman said "good-bye"/he (the boy), too, said "good-bye".)

In the second context, the pronominal maintains a referent, but an overt one functions to emphasize the referent being maintained, as in (15).

(15)   *Kardan adam -la çocuk orman -a git -ti/*   (3;11)
snowman with boy forest DAT go PAST3SG
Çok   **kardan adam**   *var -dı/*
a lot of   snowman   exist PAST
Onlar   *dansed -yor -du/*
they   dance PROG PAST
(The snowman and the boy went to the forest/There were a lot of snowmen/They were dancing.)

In a sense, the child tries to emphasize that the action belongs only to other snowmen, with the main snowman and the boy no longer involved in this action.

Five-year-olds also use overt pronominal subjects in the same contexts: when they switch from one major referent to another, as in (16), and to maintain only one major referents, as in (17). They also use overt pronominals to switch to 'snowman and the boy' when they narrate the actions that involve both together.

(16)   *Sonra bir* **kardan adam** *yap -tı/* (5;0)
then   one snowman   make PAST3SG
Kömür *koy -du/*
coal   put PAST3SG
...
Sonra o canlan   -dı/
then he become alive PAST3SG
(Then, (the boy) made a snowman/(He) put (some) coal (on the snowman's eyes/...Then, he (the snowman) became alive.)

(17)   ***Çocuk*** *kalk -tı/*   (5;3)
boy   get up PAST3SG
Ø Bir sey gör -dü/
one thing see PAST3SG
Sonra o gid -ip kardan adam yap -tı/
then he go PART snowman make PAST
(The boy got up/(He) saw something/...Then he went and made an snowman.)

Like the 3 and 5-year-old groups, 7-year-old children employ overt pronominal subjects both to maintain and switch major referents, as in (18), (19).

(18) *Birtane çocuk bir kardan adam yap -ıyor/* (7;9)
one boy one snowman make PROG
Hep kardan adam -a bak -ıyor/
all snowman DAT look PROG
Sonra o ışık saçma -ya basla -dı/
then he light give away PART start PAST
(A boy makes a snowman/(He) looks at the snowman all the time/Then, he (the snowman) starts giving away light.)

Again, the overt pronominal emphasizes the referent just switched to.

(19) *Sonra bir yer -e gel -iyor -lar/*
then one place DAT come PROG 3PLU
Başka kardan adam -lar da var or -da/
other snowman PLU too exist there DAT
Onlar çekil -iyor -lar/
they step aside PROG 3PLU
(Then, (the boy and the snowman) came to a place/There are some other snowmen, too/They stepped aside.)

Adults use pronominal subjects to maintain both major and minor referents. They use overt pronominal subjects to maintain a referent, as in (20) ,or to switch from a minor to a major referent, as in (21).

(20) *Or -da bir de Noel Baba var/*
there DAT one too Father Xmas exist
O çocuğ -a güzel bir atkı hediye ed -iyor
he boy DAT nice one scarf give PROG 3SG
(There was this Father Christmas there, too/ He gave the boy a nice scarf as a present.)

(21) *Sonra baba -sı "hadi, yat -ma vakti" de -di/*
then father POSS come on sleep INF time say PAST 3SG
O da hemen oda -sı -na çık -tı/
he too at once room POSS DAT go up PAST 3SG
(Then, (his) father said (to him) "*it is time to go to bed* "/He (the boy) went to (his) room at once.)

The rate of preferring null subjects to overt pronominal subjects does not show any significant change across the age groups, as indicated in Figure 2. The situations in which children and adults use pronominal subjects remain more or less the same as well.

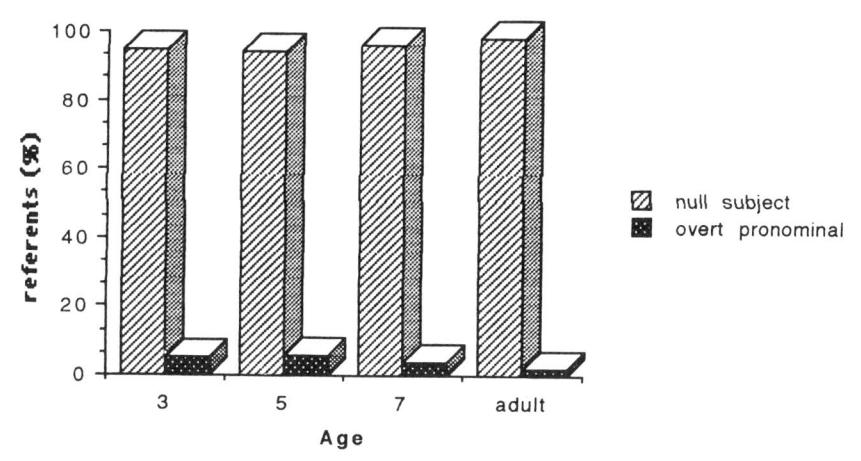

Figure 2 Distribution of null subjects and overt pronominal subjects across the age groups

DISCUSSION

In the analyses for each group, we see that it is not possible to derive a single strategy and that pronominalization of referents in our data is governed by three factors. One factor, with obvious influence on the choice of linguistic expressions, is the type of referent. Major and minor referents are treated differently, and the property of being a major or minor referent influences the choice of pronominal and nominal forms. Major referents, in some instances, are assigned thematic subject status, with pronominals used predominantly for reference maintaining and switching. Pronominal forms, either a null or overt pronominal, are not restricted to major referents. A different strategy, the paragraph boundary strategy, is employed with minor referents. These are pronominalized within paragraphs where the reference is switched with a full NP and then maintained with pronominals.

In addition to the type of the referent, the relation of the referents to each other and the point at which major referents are introduced govern pronominalization. The major referents, 'the boy' who appears at the very beginning of the story and is in every scene until the end; and 'the snowman', who appears after a while and participates in every action thereafter, are treated in a different way by all age groups. In some data, 'the boy' is treated as the thematic subject and referred to with pronominals throughout. Reference to the other major referent, 'the snowman', and to minor referents, is switched with a full NP to attract the listener's attention, and then they are referred to with pronominal subjects to show that the same referent is still in focus. A full NP is used when the focus changes to another referent, thus serving to "*demarcate the 'peaks' of particular discourse segments* " as Hinds states (quoted in Bamberg, 1986: 232-233).

The last factor with considerable effect on pronominalization is age. The difference in handling pronominalization starts after age 5. Until then, children consider the referents individually and adjust their preference for linguistic expressions accordingly. But 7-year-olds and adults rely on the same strategies for the other referents in the discourse as well.

Although we have tried to sum up the pronominalization strategies in our data, there are no clear-cut phases in development for anaphoric devices. Apart from the few 3-year-olds who do not employ pronominal forms at all, children starting at age 3 can use pronouns anaphorically. The findings in this study contrast with Karmiloff-Smith's results (1980, 1981) on English- and French-speaking children, and with Verhoeven's results (1986) on monolingual Turkish-speaking children. Karmiloff-Smith concluded that children around age 4 and 5 use pronouns only to refer to entities in ithe extralinguistic context, accompanied by paralinguistic gestures such as pointing, but not to maintain a referent mentioned earlier. Verhoeven also reported that 5-year-olds use pronominals to refer to the extralinguistic context, but not to the intralinguistic one. For this reason, younger children's pronoun uses are deictic rather than anaphoric. As a result, they claimed that pronominal anaphora is only acquired around age 6, and that the first developmental phase is marked by use of pronouns only for the central protagonist in a narrative. In our study, however, children use pronominal anaphora for other referents as well as the central onet in their narratives. We are not in a position to compare English and French with Turkish, because our methodology was different from that in Karmiloff-Smith's studies. But Verhoeven's results suggest that the reason for our findings is the method of data collection. When the referents are available to the narrator and listener in context, as in picture-narration, pronominals are used deictically at earlier ages. At the same time, children at an early age are aware of the discourse requirement on the choice of pronouns within an intralinguistic context.

As a further step, we looked into pronominalization in terms of overt and null pronominal subjects. Null subjects were very common for children at all ages, and for adults as well. Overt pronominal subjects were relatively rare. There were no significant differences for them across ages. The contexts where overt pronominal subjects were used can be characterised as follows:
1) when reference was switched from one referent to another;
2) when the referents were maintained and emphasized.

These two contexts show slight differences in each age group: 3-year-olds use overt pronominal subjects on switching the reference from one major referent to another, and in maintaining a referent; 5-year-olds use overt pronominal subjects to switch to the boy and the snowman whenever these two act together and can be considered a single referent. This group employs overt pronominals only in maintaining one major referent. Seven-year-olds use overt pronominals only rarely to maintain and switch major referents. The only difference in the adult group is that they employ overt pronominal subjects to switch from a minor referent, and when two main referents act together, as well as for maintaining both major and minor referents.

The analysis showed evidence for anaphoric reference in young children. We therefore conclude that Turkish-speaking children are aware of the discourse requirements and possess the linguistic means to do this linguistically as early as age 3. We stress that anaphoric reference is used here to mark coherence and cannot be interpreted deictically.

REFERENCES

Bamberg, Michael. 1986. *The Acquisition of Narratives: Learning to Use Language.* Berlin: Mouton de Gruyter.

Bennett-Kastor, Tina. 1983. Noun phrases and coherence in child narratives *Journal of Child Language.* 10., 135-149.

Flashner, V. 1987. The grammatical marking of theme in oral Polish narrative. In R. S. Tomlin (ed.), *Coherence and Grounding in Discourse.* Amsterdam: John Benjamins.

Givón, Talmy. 1983. *Topic Continuity in Discourse: A Quantitative Cross-Language Study.* Amsterdam: John Benjamins.

Hinds, J. 1977. Paragraph structure and pronominalization *Papers in Linguistics,* 10, 77-99.

_____ 1979. Organizational patterns in discourse. In T. Givón (ed.), *Syntax and Semantics,* Vol. 12. N. Y.: Academic Press.

Hunt, W. K. 1970. *Syntactic Maturity in Schoolchildren and Adults. Monographs of the Society for Research in Child Development.* Serial No. 134, Vol. 35, No. 1.

Karmiloff-Smith, Annette. 1980. Psychological processes pronominalization in children's connected discourse. In J. Kreiman and E. Ojedo (eds.), *Papers from the Parasession on Pronouns and Anaphora.* Chicago Linguistic Society.

_____ 1985. Language and cognitive processes from a developmental perspective. *Language and Cognitive Processes* 1, 1-86.

_____ 1981. The grammatical marking of thematic structure in the development of language production. In W. Deutsch (ed.), *The Child's Construction of Language.* N. Y.: Academic Press.

Özcan, Fatma Hülya 1993. *Coherence in Narratives of Turkish-speaking Children: The Role of Noun Phrases.* Unpublished PhD Thesis. Reading: University of Reading.

Peterson, Carole, and Pamela Dodsworth. 1991. A longitudinal analysis of young children's cohesion and noun specification in narratives. *Journal of Child Language* 18, 397-415.

Verhoeven, Ludo. 1988. Acquisition of discourse cohesion in Turkish. In Sabri Koç (ed.), *Studies in Turkish Linguistics. Proceedings of the Fourth International Conference on Turkish Linguistics.* Ankara: METU.

Wigglesworth, Gillian. 1990. Children's narrative acquisition: A study of some aspects of reference and anaphora. *First Language* 10, 105-125.

Yule, George. 1981. New, current and displaced entity reference. *Lingua* 55, 41-52.

APPENDIX: Summary of the story presented in the film :
One morning, a boy wakes up and sees that it has snowed. He gets ever so excited and dresses himself up quickly and rushes out to play with snow. After a while, he gets tired and makes a large snowman. In the evening, his mom calls him inside. After eating his dinner, he is sent upstairs to sleep. He cannot sleep since he is too excited about the snowman. When he goes down to the front door, he sees the snowman waved, raised his hat and walked towards the door. He takes the snowman's hand and invites him indoors. They play together in the house and frighten the cat. When they are looking out of the window, they see a motorbike in the garden and decide to play with it. Afterwards, the snowman holds his hand, begins to run across the garden first and then to fly with the boy. They land when they come to the North Pole. There, they meet a lot of snowmen and snowwomen who are having a big party. Father Christmas was there, too. They have a jolly good time eating, playing and dancing. Father Christmas takes the boy to his house, shows him his Reindeers and gives the boy a little present.

Now, it is time to go back home. So the snowman flies the boy back home. The boy goes to bed.

In the morning, he wakes up with great excitement and rushes down the stairs to find his mother and father having breakfast. He does not join them and runs to the window to see the snowman. It has disappeared. And the sun was shining brightly. He rushes into the garden and finds the hat and the scarf of the snowman. He feels very bad. He takes a blue scarf with snowman patterns out of his pocket and kneels down near the melting snowman. This is the scarf Father Christmas gave him the night before.

Acquisition of Past Tense Inflection in Icelandic and Norwegian Children[1]

HRAFNHILDUR RAGNARSDÓTTIR, HANNE GRAM SIMONSEN & KIM PLUNKETT[2]

University College of Education, Reykjavík, University of Oslo, & Oxford University

1. Introduction

Recent research in the acquisition of past tense (PT) morphology has focussed on the role played by input factors such as the phonological properties of verbs and their type and token frequencies (Plunkett & Marchman 1991). This paper reports a cross-linguistic, experimental study of the acquisition of PT inflection of Icelandic and Norwegian, testing the effects of these factors. As little is known about the acquisition of verbal morphology in Icelandic and Norwegian, we also hope to contribute to our current understanding of morphological development in these languages.

Both languages are Germanic, and in many ways their inflectional systems are similar to that of English. For instance, they all honour the basic distinction between weak (regular) and strong (irregular) verbs. Figure 1 exemplifies the paradigms for weak verbs and highlights those points where the three languages differ:

The first difference illustrated here is one of **general morphological complexity**. While English verbs have 4 different forms, Norwegian verbs have 7, and Icelandic verbs have at least 18 in the weak paradigm, and even up to 30 different forms in the strong verbs. Icelandic is more complex not only in the many different suffixes, but also in the vowel changes: while both English and Norwegian keep their stems relatively unchanged all through their weak paradigms, Icelandic incorporates vowel change both in weak and strong verbs. The same type and amount of complexity is also found in the other word classes in Icelandic. Due to such morphological complexity, the Icelandic child seems to face a much more complicated task than the Norwegian (or English) child.

---

[1] This work was supported by NOS-H, Univ. College of Education Research Center, Reykjavík and the Oceania Group, Dept. of Linguistics, Univ.of Oslo.

[2] The two first and main authors are listed in alphabetical order.

Figure 1. Weak verb paradigms in English, Norwegian and Icelandic

ENGLISH	One weak inflectional class	
stem (= inf./pres./imp.)	dance	call
-ing-form	dancing	calling
-s form (3rd p. sg. pres.)	dances	calls
-ed form (past/past part.)	danced	called
NORWEGIAN	Two weak inflectional classes	
	Large	Small
stem (= imperative)	kast	rop
infinitive	kaste	rope
present	kaster	roper
past	kastet	ropte
past participle	kastet	ropt
pres. participle	kastende	ropende
passive	kastes	ropes
ICELANDIC	Two weak inflectional classes	
	Large	Small
stem	kast	dæm
infinitive & pres.ind.3. p.pl.	kasta	dæma
pres.ind. 1.p. sg.	kasta	dæmi
pres.ind.2 & 3 p. sg.	kastar	dæmir
pres.ind.&subj. 1.p. pl.	köstum	dæmum
pres.ind.&subj.2.p. pl.	kastið	dæmið
pres.subj.1.&3.p. sg.; 3.p. pl.	kasti	dæmi
pres.subj. 2.p. sg.	kastir	dæmir
past ind.&subj. 1.&3.p. sg.	kastaði	dæmdi
past ind.&subj. 2.p. sg.	kastaðir	dæmdir
past ind.&subj.1.p. pl.	köstuðum	dæmdum
past ind.&subj.2.p. pl.	köstuðuð	dæmduð
past.ind.&subj.3.p. pl.	köstuðu	dæmdu
imperative sg.	kastaðu	dæmdu
imperative. pl.	kastiði	dæmiði
passive ind. sg./pl .	kastast	dæmast
passive subj. sg./pl.	kastist	dæmist
pres.part.	kastandi	dæmandi
past part. sg.	kastað	dæmt

Another, more specific difference is the **number of weak classes** in the languages. While English has a single weak class, Icelandic and Norwegian have two weak classes. In both languages, the two weak classes are much larger than any strong class. However, one of them is clearly larger than the other, and is generally productive, while the other is smaller and unproductive (or productive only for certain subgroups of verbs). An approximation of the different proportions of the verb classes, based on the most recent dictionaries for Icelandic and Norwegian (Íslensk orðtíðnibók 1991[3], Bokmaalsordboka 1986) are illustrated in Figure 2:

Figure 2

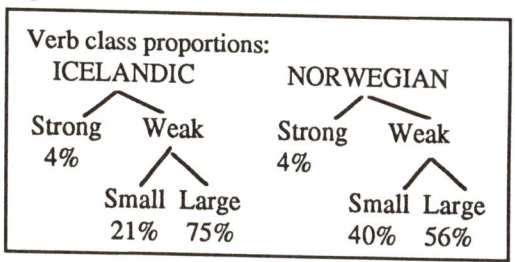

```
Verb class proportions:
   ICELANDIC          NORWEGIAN
   ╱╲                 ╱╲
Strong  Weak       Strong  Weak
 4%     ╱╲          4%     ╱╲
     Small Large        Small Large
     21%   75%          40%   56%
```

It seems clear that with their two weak classes, Icelandic and Norwegian exhibit a less clear dichotomy between regular and irregular categories than the one we find in English. An evaluation of how verbal inflection is acquired in these languages may therefore throw a new light on models that have been previously evaluated on basis of the English PT.

In this paper, we will address the following 2 questions:

i) Do input factors play a role in the acquisition of past tense morphology, and does this change during development?

ii) Is the different morphological complexity of Icelandic and Norwegian reflected in the children's acquisition process?

2. The experiment

We designed parallel experiments for Icelandic and Norwegian, eliciting past tense forms of cognate verbs in the two languages. We used a picture elicitation task similar to that of Bybee and Slobin (1982), where the subject is presented with a picture of someone performing an action, together with the corresponding verb in the infinitive. The child is then prompted to respond orally with the past tense of the verb.

In both languages, 3 groups of children were tested at 4, 6, and 8 years with approximately 30 children in each group and an equal number of boys and girls.

Each subject was tested individually, on 60 verbs. The verbs were carefully chosen according to both *frequency factors* (*type* and *token* frequency) and *phonological properties* of the verbs. For a detailed description of the choice of verbs, see Ragnarsdóttir, Simonsen & Plunkett

---

[3] Thanks to Eiríkur Rögnvaldsson for his unpublished list of Icelandic verbs by classes used in the preparation of this study.

(in preparation). Three main classes may be distinguished in Icelandic and Norwegian, ranked in increasing order of type frequency: Strong verbs (S), the Small Weak class (WS), and the Large Weak class (WL) (cf. Figure 2 above). Verbs from all these classes were included in the test – half of the verbs included were strong, and half were weak, with an equal number from each of the two weak classes. The verbs from the different classes have the same average token frequency.

3. Results

3.1. Correct performance

There is a clear and statistically significant[4] developmental progression in overall correct performance both in Norwegian and in Icelandic, as shown in Table 1 below. At age 4, the Norwegian children do better than the Icelandic ones, but this cross-linguistic difference has disappeared by age 6.

Table 1. Correct PT answers for all verbs by age-group and language

	Age 4	Age 6	Age 8
Icelandic	35%	74%	87%
Norwegian	51%	72%	90%

Different developmental patterns were observed for the three verb groups in both languages, as well as cross-linguistic differences between the Icelandic and Norwegian children, as shown in Tables 2 and 3:

Table 2. Correct answers by verb and age groups: Icelandic children

	S-class	WS-class	WL-class
Age 4	15%	41%	88%
Age 6	71%	82%	87%
Age 8	87%	87%	94%

Table 3. Correct answers by verb and age groups: Norwegian children

	S-class	WS-class	WL-class
Age 4	33%	47%	85%
Age 6	60%	71%	94%
Age 8	86%	91%	96%

---

[4] In testing statistical significance, we used ANOVAs and Tukey-b test for multiple comparisons. Significance level was in all cases less than p .05.

In both languages the children score highest on the verbs from the large weak class (WL), followed by the verbs from the small weak class (WS), with the strong verbs (S) obtaining the lowest overall score of correct answers.

The performance of the Icelandic children already approaches a ceiling for the WL-verbs at age 4 and is stable across age groups (cf. Table 2). The WS-class lags significantly behind WL at age 4, with only 41% correct PT-forms. By age 6, however, correct performance for these verbs has increased significantly to 82%, and continues to improve at age 8. The score on the S-verbs is very low (15%) among the Icelandic 4-year-olds. But the progress between ages 4 and 6 is dramatic, rising to 71%. By 8 years, the children's performance has again improved to 87%. Planned comparisons indicate that improvements in performance on S-verbs from 4 to 6 and from 6 to 8 are all significant.

The Norwegian children perform at a much higher level than their Icelandic peers on the S-verbs at age 4 (cf. Table 3). They continue to make significant progress on S-verbs at 6 and 8 years of age, although their earlier advantage over Icelandic children has disappeared by age 6, where the Icelandic children even outperform the Norwegian children by 11%.

There is no difference in performance between Icelandic and Norwegian children on the WL-verbs, but a cross-linguistic difference is found in the acquisition pattern of the WS-class, where the Norwegian children's progress is much slower than that of the Icelandic ones. At ages 4 and 6 the correct performance for the WS-class clusters with that of the S-verbs in Norwegian, whereas in Icelandic the WS-class is significantly different from the WL-verbs on the one hand and the S-verbs on the other at age 4. The WS-class catches up with the WL-class at age 8 in Norwegian, as compared to age 6 for the Icelandic children.

3.2 Error types

The errors the children made were classified into 6 main types:

1. Generalisation of the default weak pattern (GEN>WL)
2. Generalisation of another weak pattern (GEN>WS)
3. Generalisation of a strong pattern (GEN>S)
4. No change of stem
5. No answer
6. Non-past form

In this paper, the focus will be on the first three error types, each consisting of the generalisations of one of the main past tense patterns As was found to be the case for the correct responses, developmental as well as cross-linguistic differences were observed in the types of errors children make.

The overgeneralisation of the inflectional pattern of the large weak class (GEN>WL) constitutes the most frequent overall error-type in both languages, accounting for 47% of all the errors in Icelandic and 45% of the Norwegian ones. Generalisation of the pattern of the small weak class (GEN>WS) is also frequently observed, especially in Icelandic where 40% of all errors were of this kind as compared to 21% in Norwegian. (The GEN>WS errors occur in all verb-classes, including the WL-class.)

Tables 4 and 5 below show the developmental profiles of the different generalisation errors for the two languages:

Table 4. Generalisation errors by age group: Icelandic children

	GEN>WL	GEN>WS	GEN>S
Age 4	62%	30%	1%
Age 6	22%	61%	12%
Age 8	12%	75%	11%

Table 5. Generalisation errors by age group: Norwegian children

	GEN>WL	GEN>WS	GEN>S
Age 4	44%	12%	2%
Age 6	52%	27%	9%%
Age 8	37%	44%	13%

There are significant developmental differences in the two types of errors of overgeneralisation to the weak classes. In Icelandic, the GEN>WL is the dominant error type at age 4. By age 6, however, it has decreased from 62% to 22% of all errors. As the proportion of GEN>WL errors decreases, the proportion of overgeneralisations to the less productive weak pattern (GEN>WS) increase, the latter being the dominant error-type at ages 6 and 8.

In Norwegian, the developmental profile is delayed relative to the Icelandic. GEN>WL overgeneralisations are the main error type at age 4. These continue to be dominant at age 6 but decrease by age 8. The GEN>WS increases slowly from age 4 through 6, to become the major error-type at age 8, as compared to age 6 in Icelandic.

Errors of overgeneralisation of a strong inflection also occur in both languages. Their number increases with age, although their share in the overall error score is much lower than that of the other error-types.

When the development of error-types is compared to the development of correct performance for the two weak classes, it appears that these are quite synchronised in both languages. In Icelandic (cf. Tables 2 and 4), the 4-year-olds perform best on the WL-class, and the same children overgeneralise predominantly to this class. At age 6, the performance on the WS-class makes a spurt – synchronically, generalisation errors into this class make an upwards leap, while the GEN>WL error decreases substantially. This tendency persists in the 8-year-olds.

A similar pattern is observed in Norwegian, only it develops more slowly (cf. Tables 3 and 5). Interestingly, in a replication of this experiment on adult Norwegian subjects, GEN>WS was found to be the dominant error type, accounting for 45% of the errors as compared to 10% of GEN>WL and 20% GEN>S (Bjerkan & Simonsen 1995).

4. Discussion

The results confirm the view that input factors play an important role in the acquisition of past tense morphology in Icelandic and Norwegian. We also discuss the possible effects of the difference in morphological complexity of the two languages.

4.1. The role of input factors

All three major inflectional classes are acquired in an order reflecting their type frequency in the input: WL>WS>S. The larger the number of verbs in an inflectional class (type frequency), the earlier it is acquired. Thus, by 4 years the large weak class is the only class generally mastered above the 80% level, but by 8 years all verb classes have reached this level of performance.

The overgeneralisation errors children make follow the same pattern as the correct performance; all three classes form bases for overgeneralisations, and to a large extent their relative importance as sources of overgeneralisation reflects the type frequency of the classes in the languages. However, over the course of development, the small weak class becomes increasingly important as a source of generalisation errors in both languages, while errors of overgeneralisations into the large weak class diminish.

These are crosslinguistically valid findings. On the other hand, we also find some important cross-linguistic differences. One of these concerns the small weak class, which is acquired more easily in Icelandic than it is in Norwegian, and overgeneralisations to the small weak class become the most dominant error type much earlier in Icelandic than in Norwegian. This crosslinguistic difference cannot be explained by type frequency: the small weak class has a higher type frequency in Norwegian

(40%) than in Icelandic (21%). Other input factors, such as phonological cues, seem to contribute to the pattern of performance. In the following we suggest some phonological features in the two languages which may help explain these results.

Phonological factors may support suffix segmentation in the large weak class. Suffixes in this class seem to be more salient than the suffixes in the small weak class. In both languages, the WL-class suffixes begin with a vowel – probably making it easier to recognise or separate from the stem than a suffix beginning with a consonant. In Icelandic, the "vowel" suffix is even more salient, having two syllables as opposed to one in the consonant suffixes. In this manner, type frequency and phonological factors work together to make the large weak class the easiest one for the children to acquire.

On the other hand, as already mentioned, the small weak class gains ground in the course of development. And while the WL-class assumes the role of the "default" class in both languages, including verbs of a wide range of phonological patterns, there appear to be certain phonological restrictions on the verbs belonging to the WS-class, probably helping the child to identify it. In Norwegian, for example, there are two subgroups of verbs in this class which are phonologically defined: verbs ending in *-ere*, and monosyllabic verbs. Furthermore, there seem to be some more subtle phonological patterns in the stems of the small weak class. Thus, certain phonological features (e.g. a long vowel combined with certain consonant types) seem to be more common than others in this verb class (cf. Hagen 1994). These are only tendencies, and it is not possible to define clear subcategories on the basis of these phonological patterns. Subtle tendencies of this kind are probably harder for the children to detect than more clearcut ones, and need longer time (and more verbs) for them to discover and generalise from. Similar subtle tendencies may also be found in the verbs stems of the small weak class in Icelandic. The potential role of these patterns in the acquisition process needs further investigation, but they may help explain the developmental profile associated with the small weak class.

To explain the cross-linguistic differences in the rate of acquisition, where the the small weak class was acquired more easily by Icelandic than Norwegian children, certain language specific phonological features may be relevant. In Icelandic, the present tense suffixes are different in the two weak classes. Whereas the infinitive ends in an /a/ in all verb classes, and this /a/ is maintained in the WL-class in the suffixes for the 1st, 2nd and 3rd pers. sing. both in present and past tense, the corresponding suffixes in the WS-class contain an /i/ (cf. Figure 1). For the Icelandic child the vowel patterning in the present tense may thus function as a cue to class membership of the weak verbs and help distinguish verbs from the small weak class from that of the large weak class. In Norwegian, on the other hand, (at least in the dialect of Norwegian we are investigating), present tense does not differ between the two weak classes, and does not provide the children with such a cue. Furthermore, the Icelandic children have to focus on both the vowel patterns and the consonant patterns to make sense of their language in general - this way they may be more aware of them, and generalise from them more easily. This will be discussed in the following section.

4.2 Role of morphological complexity

Certain cross-linguistic differences between the acquisition of Icelandic and Norwegian past tense morphology appear to be related to the difference in the morphological complexity in the verbal paradigm of the two languages. There are no cross-linguistic differences between correct performances on the WL-class, as both Icelandic and Norwegian subjects are already performing close to ceiling on verbs from this class in the youngest age-group. Overall, however, the Icelandic children are behind the Norwegian ones at age 4 (cf. Table 1), and more so on the S-verbs than on the WS-verbs (cf. Tables 2 and 3). This situation had changed already at age 6. Although the age-range of our subjects does not allow us to verify this as far as the WL-class is concerned, we suggest that the late start of the Icelanders as compared to the Norwegian children is linked to the greater morphological complexity of the Icelandic inflectional system.

Furthermore, we suggest that the greater morphological complexity of Icelandic may subsequently have a delayed facilitatory effect on children's acquisition of morphology, and contribute to the Icelandic children´s advantage over the Norwegian children at age 6. This suggestion is inspired by a hypothesis put forward by Fortescue (1992) who proposed that morphophonemic complexity may actually serve a positive function in the acquisition of morphologically complex languages. When children discover that the one form – one meaning principle doesn't work, they must focus on the problem and look for different realisations of the same morpheme in different contexts. Fortescue originally made this proposal in connection with polysynthetic languages, but the same idea may apply to Icelandic: The complex morphology of this language, with a wide variety of suffixes, vowel changes and other morhophonemic patterns, not only in the verbs, but in the other word classes as well, may compel the child to focus on discovering the patterns.

Our findings suggest that morphological complexity may play different roles at different stages in development. At the outset, the greater morphological complexity of Icelandic made the Icelandic children perform less well than their Norwegian peers. At some point before age 6, however, a change has taken place: the challenge offered by the complex morphological structure of Icelandic has actually stimulated their processing resources and driven them to perform better than the Norwegian children, with their less demanding morphological task.

5. Conclusion

In our opinion, Icelandic and Norwegian offer an important addition to the existing database for the acquisition of past tense, providing a new perspective on the nature of the developmental task for the children, on the role of input factors in acquisition, and consequently, on the validity of acquisition models put forward mainly on the basis of English.

The dual mechanism model, advocated by Pinker & Prince 1988, Marcus & al. 1992, Prasada & Pinker 1993; assumes that there are two separate mechanisms at work in acquisition: a rule-based mechanism which is applied to the weak or regular verbs, and a lexical retrieval mechanism handling the strong or irregular verbs. The single mechanism model, on the other hand, associated with a connectionist framework (Plunkett & Marchman 1991, 1993, 1996) and a cognitive grammar approach (Bybee 1988, 1995, Langacker 1987), assumes that the same mechanism is at work in the acquisition of all verbs. On this view, all verb types are sensitive to input factors like type and token frequency and the phonological properties of verbs.

In both Icelandic and Norwegian, the large weak class is clearly the most productive, and should be the most robust one to form generalisations over. This is also what we find in the 4 year olds. However, over the course of development, our data show that both the weak classes, and even some strong classes, are used as bases for generalisation. Gradually more classes are used productively, and their influence on performance changes over time. Type frequency seems to play a central role here, as well as phonological features. The more verbs the child acquires, the larger the basis for generalisation. We also seem to find evidence for a mass action effect in phonology: when the phonological patterns to generalise over are subtle, there is a need to acquire a large mass of forms before generalisations can be drawn.

Our data seem to be consistent with a single mechanism account of inflectional morphology, since the same factors seem to be contributing to the profile of errors and mastery across all the verb classes in both languages. This uniformity in the influence of input factors across verb type and language suggest a homogeneity in the nature of the processes associated with past tense formation.

REFERENCES

Bokmaalsordboka 1986. Oslo: Universitetsforlaget.

Bjerkan, K.M. & Simonsen, H.G. 1995: Past tense processing in Norwegian: experimental evidence from children and adults. Paper presented at NELAS 4, Jyväskylä, Finland, September 9, 1995.

Bybee, J. L. & Slobin, D.I. 1982: Rules and schemas in the development and use of English past tense. *Language* 58. 265-289.

Bybee, J.L. 1988: Morphology as lexical organisation. Hammond, M. & Noonan, M. (eds.): *Theoretical morphology: Approaches in modern linguistics.* New York: Academic Press. 119-141.

Bybee, J.L. 1995: Regular morphology and the lexicon. *Language and Cognitive Processes* 10 (5). 425-455.

Fortescue, M. 1992: Morphophonemic complexity and typological stability in a polysynthetic language family. *International Journal of American Linguistics* 58: 242-248.

Magnússon, F. & Briem, S. 1991. *Íslensk orðtíðnibók.* Jörgen Pind (red.). Reykjavík: Orðabók Háskólans.

Hagen, J.E. 1994: Svake verb på *-Vde* og *-Vte* i bokmål og deres paradigmetilhørighet. Myking, J., Sandøy, H. & Utne, I. (red.): *Helsing til Lars Vassenden på 70-årsdagen.* Bergen: Nordisk institutt, 57-67.

Langacker, R. 1987: *Foundations of cognitive grammar. Vol.1, Theoretical prerequisites.* Stanford, CA: Stanford University Press.

Marcus, G.F., Pinker, S., Ullman, M., Hollander, M., Rosen, T.J., & Xu, F. 1992: Overregularisation in language acquisition. *Monographs of the society for research in child development,* 57 (4).

Pinker, S., & Prince, A. (1988). On language and connectionism: Analysis of a parallel distributed processing model of language acquisition. *Cognition,* 28, 73-193.

Plunkett, K., & Marchman, V. 1991. U-Shaped learning and frequency effects in a multi-layered perceptron: Implications for child language acquisition. *Cognition,* 38, 43-102.

Plunkett, K. & Marchman V. 1993: From rote learning to system building. Acquiring verb morphology in children and connectionist nets. *Cognition* 48, 21-69.

Plunkett, K., & Marchman, V. 1996. Learning from a connectionist model of the English past tense. *Cognition.*

Prasada, S. & Pinker, S. 1993: Generalisation of regular and irregular morphological patterns. *Language and Cognitive Processes* 8 (1), 1-56.

Ragnarsdóttir, H., Simonsen, H.G., & Plunkett, K. (in preparation): The acquisition of past tense morphology in Icelandic and Norwegian children. An experimental study.

The Linguistic Encoding of Spatial Relations in Scandinavian Child Language Development

HRAFNHILDUR RAGNARSDÓTTIR & SVEN STRÖMQVIST
University College of Education, Reykjavík & University of Gothenburg

1 Introduction

The present study [1] is concerned with cross–linguistic comparisons of the development of aspects of grammar for talking about spatial relations. It explores the linguistic variation among the indigenous languages of the Nordic countries as a "natural linguistic laboratory" (Strömqvist et al. 1995b), focussing on within–language–group comparisons. The data come from longitudinal case studies and from a narrative task with children in age groups from 5 to 15 plus adult controls. The linguistic items analysed are adverbs, particles, prepositions and case marking. Items such as *in*, *on*, *up* and *down* will be referred to as "particles/adverbs", "verb particles/adverbs", or "prepositions" depending on their syntactic and prosodic properties. Illustrations are given in examples (1)–(3).

(1) one–word utterance   *in*   "particle/adverb"
(2) V prt/adv   go *in*   "verb particle/adverb"
(3) prep NP   *in* the house   "preposition"

Particles/adverbs in the sense just defined are used in all languages under study, that is, in Danish, Finnish, Icelandic, and Swedish, although to a varying degree and with partly different syntactic and prosodic characteristics. Prepositions are used in Danish and Swedish, a rich case system in Finnish, and Icelandic uses prepositions together with a few case distinctions.

A cross–linguistic summary overview of the acquisition order of the first few grammatical morphemes encoding spatial relations is given in table 1. The data underlying the descriptive generalizations in table 1 come from longitudinal case studies in the age range 12–42 months, except for the Icelandic data where the earliest age range is represented by "Edda" 8–25 months, and later age ranges by "Ari" and "Birna" from 24 months onwards. The "Oulu sample" of Finnish is composed of 25 case studies of partly overlapping age ranges. Among other things, we find that

---

[1] The present study relates to the project "Language Development — a Scandinavian Perspective", which is supported by NOS–H (Nordiska Samarbetsnämnden för Humanistisk Forskning).

TABLE 1
Acquisition order of the first few grammatical morphemes encoding spatial relations in Swedish, Danish, Finnish and Icelandic

Swedish		Danish		Finnish	Icelandic	
Markus	Harry	Jens	Anne	Oulu sample	Edda	Birna and Ari
in 'IN$_{dir}$'	*in* 'IN$_{dir}$'	*op* 'UP$_{dir}$'	*op* 'UP$_{dir}$'	Illative 'IN$_{dir}$'	*oní* 'DOWN-INTO$_{loc/dir}$'	*á* 'ON'
∨	∨	∨	∨	∨	∨	+ Ndative$_{loc}$
ut, 'OUT$_{dir}$',	*upp* 'UP$_{dir}$',	*ned* 'DOWN$_{dir}$'	*af* 'OFF$_{dir}$'	Adessive 'ON$_{loc}$'	*uppí* 'UP-IN$_{loc/dir}$'	or + Naccusative$_{dir}$
upp 'UP$_{dir}$'	*i* 'IN$_{loc/dir}$'	∨	∨	∨	*uppi* 'UP-IN$_{loc}$'	
∨	∨	*af* 'OFF$_{dir}$',	*ned* 'DOWN$_{dir}$'	Inessive 'IN$_{loc}$',	*í* 'IN$_{loc/dir}$',	*í* 'IN'
i 'IN$_{loc/dir}$',	*på* 'ON$_{loc/dir}$'	*ud* 'OUT$_{dir}$'	∨	Allative 'ON$_{dir}$'	*inn* 'IN$_{dir}$'	+ Ndative$_{loc}$
på 'ON$_{loc/dir}$',	∨	∨	*ud* 'OUT$_{dir}$'	∨	∨	or + Naccusative$_{dir}$
av 'OFF$_{dir}$'	*med* 'WITH$_{com.com}$'	*i* 'IN$_{loc/dir}$',	∨	Elative 'FROM$_{dir}$'	*undir* 'BELOW$_{loc/dir}$'	
	∨	*på* 'ON$_{loc/dir}$'	*på* 'ON$_{loc/dir}$'		*niður* 'DOWN$_{dir}$'	*til* 'TO$_{dir}$'
	ner 'DOWN$_{dir}$'		∨		∨	+ Ngenitive$_{dir}$
			i 'IN$_{dir}$'		*uppá* 'UP-ON$_{loc/dir}$'	
					inní 'IN$_{loc/dir}$'	*inn* 'IN$_{dir}$'
						upp 'UP$_{dir}$'
						niður 'DOWN$_{dir}$'

- the first few morphemes encode similar concepts, notably, IN, ON, UP (Finnish constitutes an exception, see below)
- acquisition order cannot be predicted from semantic complexity:
  - directional concepts are encoded as early as locational
  - compound prt/adv in Icelandic emerge as early as non–compound; note that the morphemes listed for Edda constitute the first few morphemes, whereas for Ari and Birna a great number of morphemes, including several compound ones, are already in place by 24 months of age; the handful of morphemes listed in the table constitute the most frequent ones
- morphemes with both high input frequency and stress emerge earlier than morphemes with high input frequency but no stress; This means that prt/adv emerge earlier than prepositions and case marking, except in Finnish, where prt/adv are infrequent in the input and extremely rare in children's production data (only a dozen of tokens in the whole Oulu sample of over 20 children; in effect, Finnish children — much in contrast to Danish, Icelandic and Swedish children — talk very little about distinctions of vertical space, since concepts like UP and DOWN are not coded by Finnish case morphology (see table 1); In Danish, Icelandic and Swedish, phonological forms which are ambiguous between prt/adv and preposition make their debut as prt/adv, that is, with stress (see Strömqvist et al. 1995a)

In our descriptive overview so far we have made reference to input frequency, prosodic prominence, syntactic and semantic properties. Our developmental data cannot be accounted for with reference to any one of these dimensions alone. There may be a lot to learn, however, from the way the dimensions interact. The empirical challenge, then, is that we do not yet know exactly how they interact, and so we need to explore this interaction carefully, when analysing developmental data from any given language. The rest of this paper is dedicated to a contrastive exploration of this kind between Icelandic and Swedish.

2 A contrastive comparison of the acquisition of prt/adv and PP in Icelandic and Swedish

Some prosodic and syntactic differences between Icelandic and Swedish are illustrated in examples (4)–(7).

(4) Icel **taka** *thað* **ut**   'take it out'
(5) Sw   *ta* **ut** *det*   'take out it'
(6) Icel **taka** *thað utúr* **ofn**-i-num   'take it out-from oven-DAT-DEF:DAT'
(7) Sw   *ta* **ut** *det ur* **ugn**-en   'take out it from oven-DEF'
    where boldface indicates stressed words

TABLE 2
The distribution of prt/adv on one-word vs multi-word utterances
in the Icelandic child Edda from 08;00 to 25;00
and in the Swedish child Markus from 15;19 to 24;09

	Icelandic, Edda, 8–25 months	
Period	1-word utterances with spat prt/adv	multi-word utterances with spat prt/adv
8;00–19;00	0	0
20;03–22;14	19	29
23;27–25;01	1	22
	Swedish, Markus, 15–24 months	
Period	1-word utterances with spat prt/adv	multi-word utterances with spat prt/adv
15;19–20;05	0	0
21;07–22;25	0	18
23;00–24;09	1	92

Icelandic has separate stress on the verb and on the prt/adv. Swedish has phrasal stress on the prt/adv. Icelandic places syntactic material between the verb and the prt/adv. In Swedish there is syntactic contiguity between the verb and the prt/adv. See examples (4) and (5). We hypothesize that the Icelandic pattern is more conducive to analysis on the part of the child (the verb and the prt/adv are analysed as two distinct units), whereas the Swedish pattern is more conducive to synthesis, that is, keeping the verb and the particle together as a unit.

To test these hypotheses, data were derived from two longitudinal case studies, the Icelandic child Edda starting at 08;00 and extending to 25;00, and the Swedish child Markus starting at 15;19 and extending to 33;29. Compare the distribution of prt/adv on one-word vs multi-word utterances in Edda from 08;00 to 25;00 to Markus from 15;19 to 24;09. See table 2.

When Edda starts using prt/adv her usage varies between one-word and multi-word utterances. This is consistent with the analysis hypothesis. In contrast, when Markus starts using prt/adv his usage is constrained to multi-word utterances, where the great majority of collocations are between a verb and the prt/adv. This distribution is consistent with the synthesis hypothesis.

Moreover, Edda and Markus display a very similar spatial verb vocabulary. They both use 26 different verbs and 19 of their respective 26 verbs are the same or closest equivalents between Icelandic and Swedish. Edda and Markus thus constitute a "matched pair" of case studies, not only in terms of age but also in terms of spatial verbs. We are therefore confident in ruling out differences in early verb vocabulary as a source of the variation in prt/adv observed. See table 3.

TABLE 3
Spatial verbs used by Edda 08;00–25;00
and Markus 15;19 to 24;09

Markus (Swedish)	Edda (Icelandic)	Closest equivalent in English
Ta	Taka	take
Ramla	Detta	fall
Komma	Koma	come
Lägga	Lúlla	lie down
Hoppa	Hoppa	jump
Kasta	Kasta	throw
Ligga	Liggja	lie
Öppna	Opna	open
Sätta	Láta	put
Stå	(Vera)	stand (be)
Sitta	Sitja	sit
Dra	Draga	pull
Gå	Labba	walk
Rinna	–	
Röra	–	touch
Snurra	Snúa	turn/revolve
Åka	Fara	go
Plocka	–	pick
Stänga	Loka	close
Tappa	Missa	drop
Dansa	Dansa	dance
Hasa	–	drag oneself along
Jaga	–	hunt
Köra	Keyra	drive
Rulla	–	roll
Slänga	–	
–	Fljúga	fly
–	Hlaupa	run
–	Halda	hold
–	Leiða	hold hands
–	Hjóla	bicycle
–	Klifra	climb
–	Náí	get, fetch
–	Sturta	throw/let fall violently

When a verb phrase is further elaborated with a prepositional phrase in Icelandic, the prt/adv is attracted to the PP and enters into a compound preposition, thus shifting the elaboration of spatial semantics from the verb to the noun. See example (6). In Swedish, by contrast, the prt/adv remains faithful to the verb. See example (7). This difference in distribution of spatial semantics between Icelandic and Swedish can be described as a difference in "packaging" in the sense of Berman and Slobin 1994. That is, the same or very similar information (about the motion event) is encoded (or "packaged") linguistically in different ways.

Now, how does spatial verb argument structure (in a broad sense) in terms of prt/adv and PPs develop in Icelandic and Swedish? Let us turn to a second "matched pair" comparison, this time between Ari 24–26 months and Markus 24–26 months. The case study data from Ari comprise in total 33 data points from 24 to 70 months, and the data from Markus comprise 28 data points from 15 to 33 months, all transcribed in CHAT-format. The age-matched comparison 24–26 months comprise 5 data points from each child, each data point containing various everyday activities in the home.

The five data points from each child were treated as two corpora and the contexts of the top 12 spatial verbs in each corpus were analyzed for occurrences of prt/adv and PP. The "matched pair" character of the comparison is strengthened by the fact that Ari and Markus use a very similar spatial verb vocabulary during the period of comparison: 10 of their respective top 12 verbs are the same or closest equivalents between Icelandic and Swedish.

The findings are summarized in figure (1) (PPs) and (2) (prt/adv). The vertical axis shows the proportion of verb contexts where an argument is articulated. The horizontal axis shows the lexical variation, i.e., how many different prt/adv or prepositions were used with the verb in question.

The distribution of PPs and prt/adv show language specific effects:

- there are more PPs than prt/adv in Icelandic
- there are more prt/adv than PPs in Swedish
- this distributional asymmetry is true of the input to the child as well as of the child's production data

Moreover, Ari uses 12 different prepositions including 4 compound ones, whereas Markus uses only 3 (all non-compound). Again, since Ari and Markus are closely matched for spatial verb vocabulary, we feel confident in ruling out the possibility that the observed difference in argument structure is related to a difference in, say, the inherent semantics of their respective sets of spatial verbs.

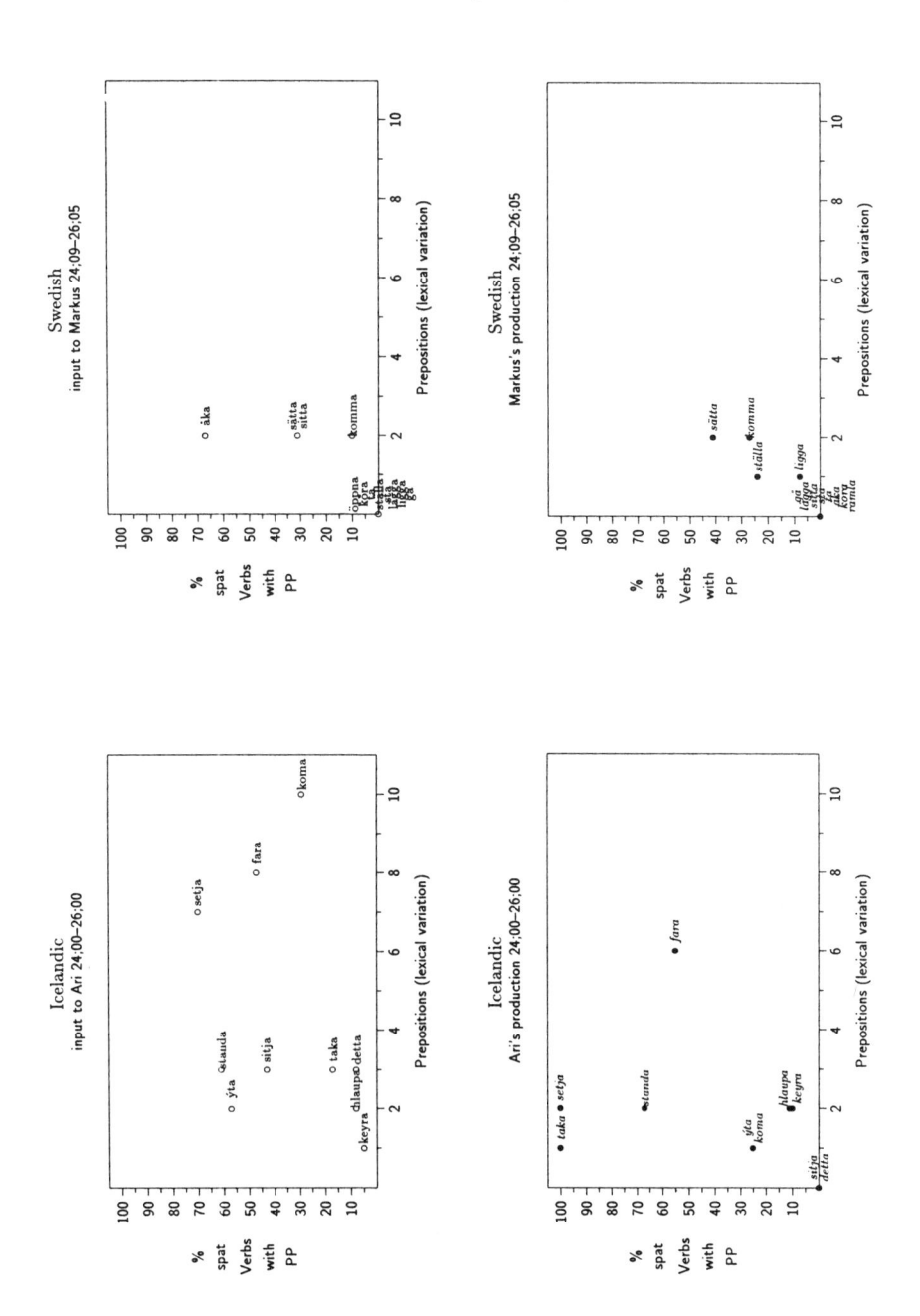

FIGURE 1
The top 12 spatial verbs and the distribution of spatial PPs
in Ari's and Markus's input and production

FIGURE 2
The top 12 spatial verbs and the distribution of spatial prt/adv
in Ari's and Markus's input and production

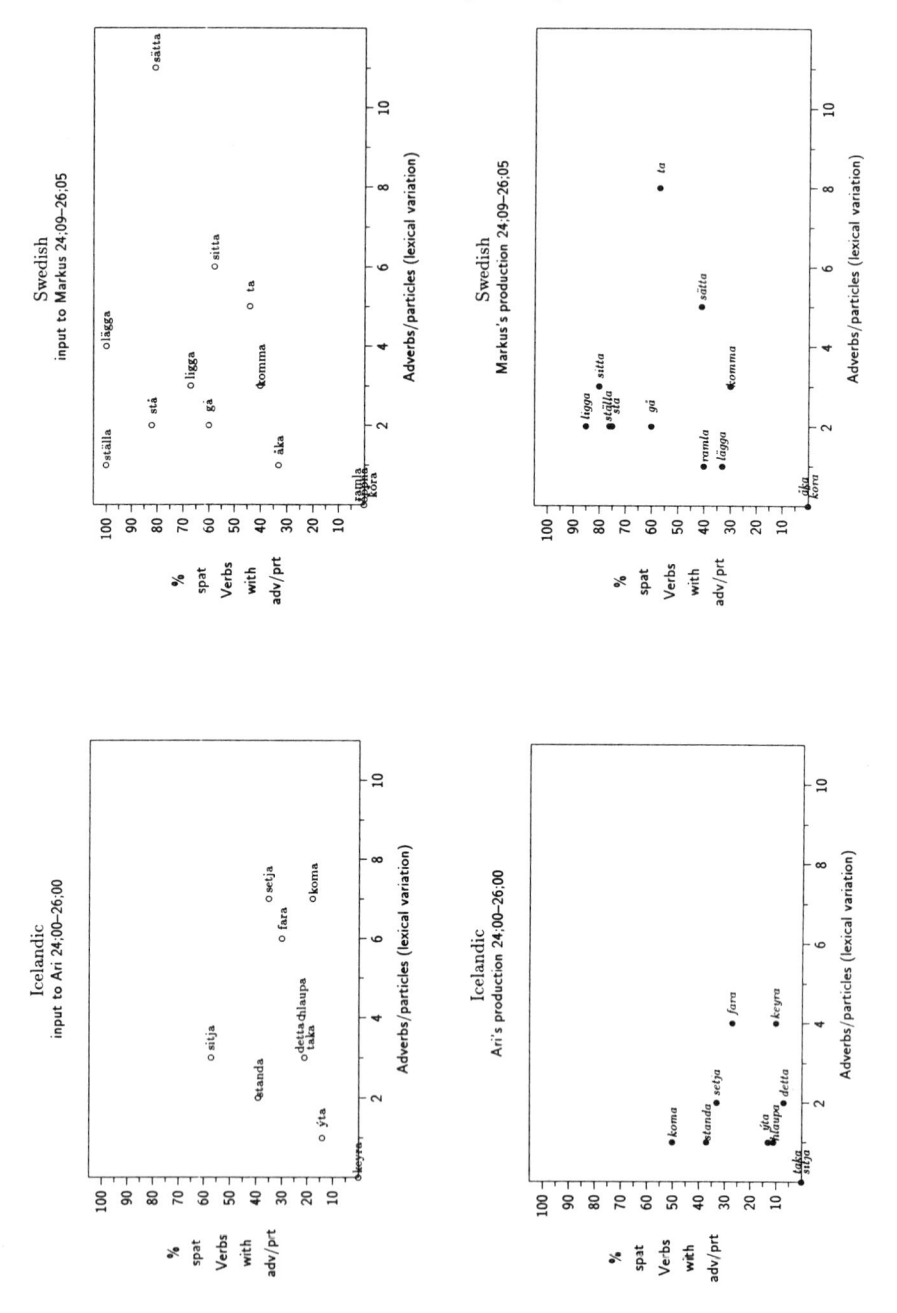

We further suggest that there is a developmental continuity with the previous phase of development (the one–word and two–word stage evidenced in the comparison between Markus and Edda): the Swedish phrasal stress on the particle is a cue to keep the elaboration of spatial semantics with the verb; whereas in Icelandic there are three "attractors" guiding the child to elaborate the spatial semantics further away from the verb, in relation to the noun:

- separate stress on the verb and the prt/adv
- prt/adv enters into compound prep
- prepositions interact with case marking in PP

Let us now consider the data from the narrative task/picture story experiment. In the experiment "Frog, where are you?", a wordless picture story book by Mayer 1969, was used as an elicitation instrument.[2] By this technique, which is closely modelled on the work by Berman and Slobin 1994, narratives were elicited from 41 Swedish and 38 Icelandic subjects in the age groups 5, 9, and 15 years plus an adult control group. There were approximately 10 subjects in each group.

The degree to which the subjects elaborated descriptions of the various events/pictures of the frog story varied a great deal. One event which attracted the interest of all subjects, however, irrespective of age, was "the fall from the cliff".[3] For the purpose of a matched comparison, we here present an analysis of motion verbs and their spatial arguments from precisely that subset of event descriptions that concerns the fall from the cliff. Table 4 summarizes the grammatical constructions used by the Swedish and the Icelandic subjects in descriptions of the motion event "the fall from the cliff". All Icelandic subjects are here treated as one group and all Swedish subjects as one group, irrespective of age differences.

The distribution of prt/adv and PP in the narrative data shows the same tendential asymmetry as in the longitudinal data: V + prt/adv is more frequent in the Swedish than in the Icelandic descriptions, whereas PPs are more frequent in the Icelandic descriptions. Note, further, that the tendential difference between Icelandic and Swedish does not merely represent a difference in "packaging", but a difference in "filtering" in the sense of Berman and Slobin 1994. More precisely, referential information about landmarks (i.e., source, path and goal; see Langacker 1987) are filtered out when the V + prt/adv construction is used (as is typically the case in

---

[2] The booklet depicts the adventures of a little boy and his dog as they go out into the woods to search for a frog which has disappeared from the boy's room. Each subject was first asked to browse through the booklet, so as to get acquainted with the overall content of the story. The subject was then asked to narrate the story, picture by picture, in his own words.

[3] In this event, the boy falls down from off the antlers of a deer down into a pond. The fall is caused by the deer, who, after having carried the boy for some time, stops abruptly at the edge of the cliff.

TABLE 4
Grammatical constructions used by Swedish and Icelandic subjects
in descriptions of a motion event

Language	V only	sentences describing boy's fall from the cliff constructed with			N sentences	N subjects
		V+prt/adv	V+prt/adv +prep+NP(case)	V+prep +NP(case)		
Sw	4%	41%	53%	0%	49	41
Icel	8%	14%	22%	52%	50	38

TABLE 5
The encoding of landmarks in
Swedish and Icelandic descriptions of a motion event

language	sentences describing boy's fall from the cliff constructed with			N sentences
	0 lm	1 lm	2 lm	
Swedish	45%	53%	2%	49
Icelandic	22%	74%	4%	50

Swedish), whereas it filters through when the PP construction is used (as is typically the case in Icelandic): whereas the NP in a PP like *from the cliff* explicitly refers to a landmark (the cliff, SOURCE), the landmarks are implied (and not explicitly referred to) when the VP is elaborated with a prt/adv only, as in, for example, *fell down*. We thus have evidence not only of language specific packaging effects, but also of language specific filtering effects. See table 5 (where landmark is abbreviated "lm").

Now, in the analysis presented in table 5 the age group differences in the data were neutralized. How do age differences interact with the filtering effects observed? Is there a pattern of development beyond the first half of the pre-school age (the early period which we analysed on the basis of longitudinal case studies)?

In table 6 we contrast the youngest and oldest age groups in our Icelandic and Swedish samples. The result is striking: the language specific effect shows a peak in the youngest age group (5-year-olds), and it has levelled out in the oldest age group (adult controls). Example (8) shows a typical description of the fall from the cliff by a Swedish 5-year-old, and example (9) a typical description by an Icelandic 5-year-old.

(8) Swedish *pojken ramla ner*
  'the boy fell down'

(9) Icelandic *og svo datt hundurinn og strákurinn ofaní sjó*
  'and then fell dog and boy [$_{prep}$ above-into] sea:ACC$_{dir}$'

TABLE 6
The encoding of landmarks in Swedish and Icelandic descriptions
of a motion event: youngest and oldest age-groups

language	age-groups	sentences describing boy's fall from the cliff constructed with			N sentences
		0 lm	1 lm	2 lm	
Swedish	5 years	62%	38%	0%	13
	adults	39%	58%	3%	16
Icelandic	5 years	10%	90%	0%	11
	adults	28%	58%	14%	10

3 Discussion

Previous cross-linguistic studies of the encoding of spatial relations in child language development have shown that children are sensitive to details of their linguistic environment from very early on. Given the cross-linguistic diversity of lexicalized and grammaticized distinctions in the conceptual domain of spatial relations, this means that children growing up with different languages can show language specific preferences in their linguistic encoding of spatial relations already towards the end of their second year. (See, e.g., Choi and Bowerman 1991; Sinha et al. 1995; and Slobin 1991.) Our present study adds to this line of evidence. Further, the combination of longitudinal case studies from early phases of language development on the one hand and narrative data from age groups from five to adults on the other provides a window on truly long term development.

From Roman Jakobson's visionary ideas, relating child language acquisition to assumed language universals and particulars (see Jakobson 1941), one would predict that maximal cross-linguistic similarity should be found across early child languages and that samples from more advanced learners should exhibit more particular traits as children come to conquer language particular details only in later phases of acquisition.

Our results from the linguistic domain of spatial relations suggest something different. The encoding of spatial relations in Scandinavian child language development shows language specific effects already in a very early phase of acquisition, resulting in clearly different developmental profiles between matched case studies in within-language-group comparisons. And our truly broad time window on the developmental process in terms of data from infancy to adulthood supports the generalization that these early language specific profiles tend to level out — rather than to become more pronounced — as language users approach adulthood. However, since Jakobson's tenants were based on observations in the domain of phonology, our findings in the semantic domain of spatial relations need not be interpreted as a contradiction to Jakobson's views. Rather, the comparison may help indicate domain specific properties of language development.

We assume, however, the mechanisms behind the particular developmental patterns to be universal. Children are sensitive to details of their particular linguistic environment from very early on, and they look for meaning and strive to express meaning from early on. Those features of the input that are salient from a perceptual and information processing point of view and which meet the child's demand for meaning filter through into the child's process of constructing a language, — irrespective of whether these features are cross-linguistically valid or typical of an individual language. In the latter case, they give rise to a language particular profile of the child's early grammatical development. This distinctive profile later levels out as the learner broadens his linguistic repertoire and can lift the restrictions on his early expressive capacity.

References

Berman, R. A., and D. I. Slobin. 1994. *Relating events in narrative. A Crosslinguistic Developmental Study.* Hillsdale, New Jersey: Lawrence Erlbaum.

Choi, S., and M. Bowerman. 1991. Learning to express motion events in English and Korean: the influence of language–specific lexicalization patterns. *Cognition* 41:83–121.

Jakobson, R. 1941. *Kindersprache, Aphasie und allgemeine Lautgesetze.* Uppsala: Almqvist & Wiksell.

Langacker, R.W. 1987. *Foundations of Cognitive Grammar, Vol 1.* Stanford: Stanford University Press.

Mayer, M. 1969. *Frog, where are you?* New York: Dial Press.

Sinha, C., L. Thorseng, M. Hayashi, and K. Plunkett. 1995. Comparative spatial semantics and language acquisition: evidence from Danish, English and Japanese. *Journal of Semantics.*

Slobin, D. I. 1991. Learning to think for speaking: Native language, cognition, and rhetorical style. *Pragmatics* 1:7–26.

Strömqvist, S., A. Peters, and H. Ragnarsdóttir. 1995a. Particles and prepositions in Scandinavian child language development: effects of prosodic spotlight? in Proceedings of the XIII International Congress of Phonetic Sciences, Royal Institute of Technology, Stockholm, Vol 4, pages 38–45.

Strömqvist, S., H. Ragnarsdóttir, O. Engstrand, Helga Jonsdóttir, E. Lanza, M. Leiwo, Å. Nordqvist, Ann Peters, K. Plunkett, Ulla Richtoff, H. G. Simonsen, J. Toivainen, and K. Toivainen. 1995b. The Inter–Nordic Study of Language Acquisition. *Nordic Journal of Linguistics* 18:3–29.

Using the Semantics Associated with Syntactic Frames for Interpretation without the Aid of Context[1]

NITYA SETHURAMAN, ADELE E. GOLDBERG, & JUDITH C. GOODMAN
University of California, San Diego & University of Missouri, Columbia

1. Introduction

The Syntactic Bootstrapping hypothesis argues that children are able to derive the meanings of new verbs from the syntactic structures in which the verb is heard. In its strongest version, every syntactic frame in which a verb occurs is said to reflect a particular component of the verb's meaning.[2] This view implies that knowledge of verb meaning can be gleaned from the set of syntactic frames alone, without additional context.

A somewhat weaker interpretation of the claim that syntactic frames aid in the acquisition of verb meaning is the idea that the semantics associated with a syntactic frame acts as a sort of "zoom lens",

---

[1]This work was supported by a grant from the John D. and Catherine T. MacArthur foundation to the third author. The authors also wish to thank Jennifer Jahn-Samilo, Aarre Laakso, Tracy Love, William Morris, Jenny Shao, Matthew Walenski, Nils Engle, and Amanda Kohl for their assistance with various aspects of this project.
[2]This is one reading of Landau and Gleitman (1985).

encouraging the learner to take a particular perspective on a given real or imagined situation. That is, the frame encourages the listener to focus on appropriate aspects of the situational context (Fisher et al. 1994; Gleitman 1994). For example, the ditransitive frame (Subj V Obj Obj2) would encourage the listener to construe the situation as one involving transfer since the frame is tightly associated with the notion transfer; likewise, the "caused-motion" frame (Subj V Obj Obl) would encourage the listener to view the situation as involving caused motion (see Goldberg 1995 for motivation for associating semantics directly with these and other sentential frames).

Verb meanings can be determined by choosing the most salient action within the scene picked out by the construction. For example, upon hearing *Chris mooped Pat the ball*, the learner could infer from the ditransitive frame that a scene of transfer was being described. The verb *moop* could then be interpreted to designate the most salient action within that scene, possibly "give", "kick", or "slip", depending on the context. This version of the Syntactic Bootstrapping hypothesis does not rely solely on linguistic frames for learning verb meanings, since extra-linguistic context is required to determine the most salient action (see also Pinker 1989; Pinker 1994).

It is not clear whether the Syntactic Bootstrapping hypothesis is responsible for how children learn their first verbs, as Landau and Gleitman (1985) originally suggested, or if children begin to use it only after they have started to learn some early verbs. This issue raises the question as to whether all frames are known before any verbs. If frames are innately given or learned before any verbs, then one might expect that all syntactic frames should be equally available at the time when verbs are acquired: there would be no gradual learning of frames as verbs are learned. Alternatively, the use of different sorts of frames may emerge over time as children's familiarity with those frames and with the verbs participating in those frames increases.

Pinker (1994) questions whether the strong version of the Syntactic Bootstrapping hypothesis can really work, suggesting a means of testing it:

> There is an extremely simple experiment that would test whether children can learn a verb root's semantic content from multiple frames. . . . For example, children would hear only *She pilked; She pilked me something; She pilked the thing from the other things; She pilked the other things into the thing; She pilked one thing to another*, and so on. If children can acquire a verb's content from multiple frames, they should be able to infer that the verb basically means "create by attaching" (Levin 1985). . . . It would be an interesting finding if children (or adults) could learn significant aspects of a verb's content from syntactic cues, as this experiment would demonstrate (p. 407).

The present experiment aims to put Pinker's challenge to the test. In this study, children between two and four years of age and adults were asked to enact sets of sentences consisting of novel verbs in four different syntactic frames. Such sentences provide listeners with few clues about the novel verbs' meanings besides the information derived from the syntactic frames themselves. We aimed to determine whether children attempt to form a semantic representation of the verb on the basis of the information from the syntactic frames. The actions participants performed for different verbs and different frame types were used to infer their semantic representation of the novel words (our paradigm is based on that of Naigles 1988 and Naigles, Gleitman, and Gleitman 1993; see section 3.1.1 for discussion).

2. Experimental Methodology
2.1 Participants
Forty-four children between 2;4 and 4;1 from the UCSD Developmental Psychology subject pool, and fourteen UCSD psychology undergraduates participated in this study. The subject pool consisted of children whose parents had responded to newspaper advertisements asking families to participate in a variety of developmental studies. Participants were divided into three age groups: 27 two-year-olds (range: 2;4 to 3;0, mean age = 2;8), 17 three-year-olds (range: 3;1 to 4;1, mean age = 3;8), and 14 adults.

2.2 Materials
The test equipment consisted of a plastic boat with a plastic slide attached to the side; a bear, tiger, cow, and pig; and a girl doll and a boy doll. A wall-mounted video camera recorded participants' responses for later coding.

2.3 Stimuli
The stimuli consisted of three pretest sentences, *The plane flies, The pig rides in the truck, The plane pushes the tiger*. The test sentences involved nonsense verbs in four different frames, adapted from Naigles et al. The four frames used in the study were: intransitive (NP V); intransitive with a prepositional phrase (NP V PP); transitive (NP V NP); and transitive with a preposition phrase (NP V NP PP). Each nonsense word was presented four times in succession in each of the four frames; the four frames were presented in varying orders. Following Naigles et al., the youngest group was given 20 sentences, due to their shorter attention span, and the older groups were tested with 40 stimuli[3] (example sentences from both studies are given in Table 1).

Table 1: *Examples of Stimulus Sentences*

Frame	Present Study	Naigles{grammatical/ungrammatical}
NP V	The bear sibs.	The elephant {falls/brings}.
NP V PP	The pig sibs on the boat.	The bird {goes/puts} to/in the ark.
NP V NP	The cow sibs the tiger.	The
NP V NP PP	The tiger sibs the cow to the boat.	The lion {brings/comes} the pig to the ark.

2.4 Procedure
The child and his or her caretaker were taken into the testing area where the session began with a brief period of free-play to familiarize the child with the

---
[3] More subjects were tested in the youngest age group than in the older age group to compensate for the fewer data points.

room and the experimenter. When the child was at ease, he or she was seated at a table and shown the test stimuli, which had been hidden under a cloth. The child was asked to identify each toy and incorrect responses were immediately corrected.

The child was told that the boy and girl dolls had a funny language that they used when speaking with the animals. The experimenter asked the child to help her figure out what the dolls were saying by enacting various sentences with the animals. The child was asked to choose the animals necessary for each sentence, perform the enactment, and replace the animals in the line-up when the action was completed. The sentences were repeated until an action was performed. Positive feedback was given after all enactments. Adults followed the same procedure except that they were not given a free-play period.

2.5 Coding
Following Naigles et al., enactments of intransitive frames (NP V and NP V PP) were counted as frame compliant if the action performed was either "symmetrical" (two entities acting upon each other simultaneously) or "unilateral" (one entity acting independently of another entity). The sentence *The bear sibs to the tiger* would be interpreted intransitively if, for example, the participant enacts a scene in which the bear approaches the tiger but there is no physical contact. Enactments of transitive frames (NP V NP and NP V NP PP) counted as frame compliant if the action was prototypically transitive, where one entity physically acted upon a second entity. The sentence *The bear sibs the tiger* would be interpreted transitively if, for example, the participant enacted a scene in which the bear hit the pig.

Enactments were judged to be either "Frame Compliant" or "Not Frame Compliant".[4] 17.3% of the participants' responses were not included in the analyses, because the wrong animals were chosen or there was no response at all.

3. Results and Discussion
3.1 Frame Compliance and Frame Learning
Table 2 shows the percentage of scored responses that were frame compliant for each frame type and age group.

Table 2: *Frame Compliance by age for each frame type*

Age	NP V	NP V PP	NP V NP	NP V NP PP
Two-year-olds	97%	91%	54%	44%
Three-year-olds	97%	79%	61%	60%
Adults	99%	86%	82%	86%

---

[4] Since Frame Compliance as defined by Naigles et al. tests only whether children paid attention to the transitivity of the syntactic frames, we also coded for "strong frame compliance," namely whether participants enacted the prepositional phrase as well as the frame's transitivity correctly. We found essentially the same trends in the data analyzed that way; space constraints prevent us from giving the details of that analysis here.

We conducted t-tests for each age group and frame type to determine whether the proportion of frame-compliant responses differed significantly from chance (50%). All age groups were found to be influenced by syntactic information in their enactments to some degree: adults made significantly more frame-compliant responses than expected by chance for all four frames. Two- and three-year-olds made a significant percentage of frame-compliant responses for their enactments of the intransitive (NP V and NP V PP) frames. These findings are all significant at the $p < .01$ level. This finding is in accord with many previous studies which indicate that children are sensitive to the semantics associated with syntactic frames in interpreting sentences (Naigles 1990; Naigles et al. 1993; Fisher et al. 1994).

However, the percentage of frame-compliant responses to the transitive (NP V NP and NP V NP PP) frames did not differ significantly from chance for two- and three-year-old children. There is some suggestion that the percentage of frame-compliant responding increases with age. The t-values of the two-year-olds' responses reflect the fact that they are very close to 50% (chance performance) (NP V NP, $t(26) = .57$, $p = .570$; NP V NP PP, $t(26) = .85$, $p = .403$). Three-year-olds are just beginning to show a trend toward more frame-compliant responses (NP V NP, $t(16) = 1.56$, $p = .137$; NP V NP PP, $t(16) = 1.75$, $p = .100$). The difference between children and adults in the percentage of frame-compliant responses to transitive sentences suggests that transitive frames (NP V NP and NP V NP PP) may be gradually learned over time.

A 3 X 2 X 2 repeated measures Anova was conducted on the percentage of frame-compliant responses with age as a between subjects variable and transitivity and the presence or absence of a prepositional phrase as within subjects variables. All three main effects were significant (age: $F(2,55) = 10.83$, $p < .001$; transitivity: $F(1, 55) = 65.67$, $p < .001$; presence of a PP: $F(1,55) = 7.21$, $p < .01$). Scheffe post-hoc tests indicate that two- and three-year olds made fewer frame-compliant responses (71 and 74%, respectively) than adults (88%) ($p < .05$). Intransitive sentences received more frame-compliant responses (92%) than transitive sentences (61%), and frames without a PP received more frame-compliant responses (80%) than frames with a PP (72%). In addition, the interaction between age and transitivity reached significance ($F(2,55) = 10.29$, $p < .001$). Scheffe post-hoc tests reveal that the three age groups performed similarly on intransitive frames. Specifically, adults made significantly more frame-compliant responses to transitive sentences than did two-year-olds ($p < .05$). The percentage of frame-compliant responses made by three-year-olds to transitive frames fell between the other two age groups and did not differ significantly from either. In all, these findings suggest that the ability to use syntactic frames changes with age and is sensitive to factors such as whether or not the frame is transitive and whether or not the frame contains a PP.

The data were further analyzed to determine whether children used their knowledge of the semantics associated with constructions to extract particular meanings for the nonsense verb. Children did not appear to try develop a consistent meaning for the various nonsense verbs across the four presentations. We return to this result in section 3.2.

3.1.1. Comparison with Naigles, Gleitman, and Gleitman (1993)

One of the strongest sources of experimental support for the general idea that children pay attention to the semantics associated with syntactic frames comes from a study reported by Naigles (1988) and Naigles et al. (1993). In this section we provide an explicit comparison of the results from the two experiments.

In Naigles' study, participants were asked to enact grammatical and ungrammatical sentences consisting of known transitive and intransitive verbs in transitive and intransitive syntactic frames (see Table 1 above for example sentences). Of interest were frame-compliant responses to ungrammatical sentences. Specifically, if a listener treated an intransitive motion verb heard in a transitive frame as a transitive verb (e.g., enacting *The zebra falls the lion into the ark* as if the zebra causes the lion to fall), the response was scored as Frame Compliant. Similarly, if a listener treated a transitive motion verb heard in an intransitive frame as an intransitive verb (e.g., enacting *The lion puts in the ark* as if the lion goes in the ark), the response was scored as Frame Compliant. The percentage of frame compliance found by Naigles, et al. is presented in Table 3 below:

Table 3: *Frame compliance for each frame type (Naigles 1988)*

Sentence Type	NP V	NP V PP	NP V NP	NP V NP PP
Two-year-olds	65%	60%	69%	-----[5]
Three-year-olds	40%	64%	70%	79%
Four-year-olds	45%	70%	72%	79%
Adults	34%	30%	50%	76%

Naigles et al. interpreted their results as showing that children are influenced by syntactic cues when interpreting the meaning of a known verb after hearing the verb in just one new syntactic environment. However, since their study used known verbs and frames, they provided participants with information from at least two different sources. The extent to which the participants' semantic representations of the known verbs played a role in their interpretation of the sentences is unclear.

The present study aimed to narrow down which factors were critical to determining the verb meaning in the Naigles et al. study, by performing Pinker's challenge: we substituted nonsense verbs for known verbs in the

---

[5] As in the present study, Naigles et al. found that their two-year-old participants had difficulty with this frame; they did not include items from this frame in their test stimuli.

same syntactic environments used by Naigles et al. This way, verb semantics cannot play a role, because all the verbs are novel.

Both our study and Naigles et al. found that the degree to which participants use the given syntactic information when enacting the sentence depends on the age of the participant and the transitivity of the frame. However, the particular generalizations found in the two studies differ markedly. These points of contrast are discussed in turn.

When participants are given an unknown verb in a syntactic frame, they have only the information from the frame for interpreting the expression. We found that adult participants, who are more familiar with the frames and their meanings, were highly frame compliant on all four frames. As discussed above, adults show significantly more frame-compliant responses than children. We interpret this result as suggesting that proficiency on the frames continues to increase beyond three years of age.

At the same time, Naigles et al. found that when participants are given a *known* verb in a syntactic frame, younger participants are actually more frame compliant than adults. These contrasting findings are actually expected, however. Naigles et al. suggest that when younger participants are given a known verb in a mismatched syntactic frame, they are likely to assume the ungrammaticality of the sentence is due to their own lack of familiarity with all the properties of the given verb. They are willing to accept a new structure as being one that they have not learned yet. Adults, on the other hand, crucially believe they already have all the information about the known verb and therefore are less likely to be influenced by the syntactic frame. Adults are therefore somewhat less frame compliant than younger participants when a known verb is involved.

The transitivity of the stimulus frame influences frame compliance in both studies. When children are given novel verbs in various frames, they tend to be more frame compliant for intransitive frames than transitive frames. Akhtar and Tomasello (in press) provide an explanation of why children do better on intransitive than transitive sentences. They found that in English, children younger than three-and-a-half have difficulty acquiring and using word order in transitive sentences which are "reversible:" either the first or second NP could semantically be interpreted as an agent. Children are found to be equally likely to put the patient in the preverbal slot as they are the agent. It is therefore not surprising that young children would have difficulty enacting the transitive sentences correctly in this study. Intransitive sentences are less complex and encode fewer relationships and are therefore easier. This explanation again relies on the idea that the correlation between syntactic frames and their semantic interpretation is at least in part, learned. As expected, adults did not show a significant difference between intransitive and transitive frames.

Unlike the present study, Naigles et al. found that, given known verbs, children are actually more frame compliant for transitive frames than intransitive frames. They suggest that participants may have interpreted intransitive frames as transitive frames in which the direct object underwent ellipsis. A sentence such as *The zebra brings* may be interpreted as "the zebra is bringing (something)" where the direct object is simply omitted. Participants would be expected to treat such an interpretation as transitive. Transitive sentences such as *The zebra goes the lion* have a direct object and participants trying to account for all the present information would correctly interpret the frame transitively. When unknown verbs are involved as in the present experiment, there is no reason to assume that any argument is omitted. Therefore one would not expect intransitive frames to be at this disadvantage.

3.2 Using the Semantics Associated with Syntactic Frames for Interpretation of Verb Meaning

The extent to which a participant attempted to create a meaning for the nonsense verbs was determined by examining each enactment in turn. We compared how likely a participant was to preserve the same core action for the same novel verb (in a new frame) with how likely (s)he was to simply repeat the same action when a different novel verb was introduced. Recall that each novel verb was repeated in four consecutive frames before a new novel verb was introduced. If the participant attempted to determine a single core meaning for a given nonsense verb, we would expect the same action to be repeated significantly more across repetitions of the same novel verb than when a new nonsense verb was introduced.

Table 4 presents a comparison between the likelihood that participant performed the same action on Trial X + 1 when either the same novel verb or a different novel verb occurred on Trial X. A one-way Anova on the difference score was conducted, and the effect of age was significant ($F_{(2,55)} = 12.22$, $p < .001$). Scheffe post-hoc analyses indicated that the adults were significantly more likely to repeat an action given the same novel verb than a new novel verb than were the children ($p < .05$). The two- and three-year-olds did not differ significantly from one another.

Table 4: *Tendency to preserve the same action for the same nonsense verb compared with the tendency to repeat the same action for different verbs.*

Age	Same Verb, Act Repeated	Different Verb, Act Repeated	Difference
Two	128/392 = .33	34/107 = .32	.01
Three	146/495 = .29	40/160 = .25	.04
Adult	158/422 = .37	7/124 = .06	.31

Our results show that although children paid attention to the frame meaning, they did not appear to try to develop a consistent meaning for the various nonsense verbs across the four presentations. An example is given in Table 5: although the same nonsense verb *ork* is presented four times, the child performed four different actions:

Table 5. *Example of responses by a child aged 4;0 to the same and different nonsense words in various syntactic frames*

Stimulus	Action
The tiger **orks**.	tiger **rolls over** and off table
The bear **orks** the pig on the slide.	bear **pushes** pig down slide
The boy **orks** in the boat.	boy **sits** in boat
The cow **orks** the tiger.	tiger **stands** behind cow
The tiger **blicks** the girl near the slide.	tiger **stands behind** the girl

The fact that children performed different actions for the same verb is not because it is impossible to successfully formulate a root meaning for the verb, since several English verbs appear in all four frames, including *push, roll,* and *slide.* And yet neither two- nor three-year-olds showed any tendency to try to come up with a single root meaning for the nonsense verbs. Adults, on the other hand, are more likely to preserve the same root meaning for each nonsense verb across its four presentations; they also tend to change to a new action for a new nonsense word as can be seen in the example in Table 6 below.

Table 6. *Example of responses by an adult S.W. to the same and different nonsense words in various syntactic frames*

Stimulus	Action
The tiger **orks**.	tiger **turns around**
The bear **orks** the pig on the slide.	bear on pig on slide, **turns around**
The boy **orks** in the boat.	boy **turns around** on slide
The cow **orks** the tiger.	cow put on tiger, **turns around**
The tiger **blicks** the girl near the slide.[6]	girl put on slide, tiger **hits** her

We find that two- and three-year-olds do not appear to use the syntactic information in order to specifically determine the verb's meaning. In particular, our results show that two- and three-year-olds, on average, did not pay attention to whether the same unknown verb was involved in their enactments. That is, we found no tendency for either two- or three-year-olds to repeat the same action over all presentations of the same nonsense verb while changing the action for a new nonsense verb. We suggest that children do not pay attention to the verb because the frame meaning alone does not give children enough information to infer anything about the verb's "root" meaning.

On the other hand, adults do show a tendency to preserve the same action for each instance of one nonsense verb and to change the action when given a new nonsense verb. Although adults are not given any more information than the children are, adults are consciously aware that each sound pattern has a particular meaning and that different sound patterns contrast in meaning. Thus, we suspect that adults tried to consciously problem-solve in a way that naive learners could not, by trying to preserve the same action for the same verb and change it for new verbs. It is interesting to note that even though adults show a tendency to preserve the same action for the same novel verb while changing the action for a new novel verb, this strategy is not applied consistently (.31). We believe that this is because adults as well as children rely in part on real or imagined context to conclusively determine the meaning of an unknown verb.

6. Conclusion

Pinker (1994) suggested a prediction of the strong version of the Syntactic Bootstrapping hypothesis: a child given a novel verb in a number of syntactic frames should be able to deduce the root meaning of the verb. We set out to test this idea by providing children with unknown verbs in four different syntactic frames. While our results show a clear tendency to pay attention to the semantics associated with the syntactic frame for the overall interpretation of the sentence, we do not find that the children show any tendency to try to determine what the root meaning of the nonsense verb might be. Our results suggest that children do not posit verb meanings solely based on such syntactic information. We conclude that in order to attempt to learn verb meanings, more than the linguistic information from syntactic frames is needed: additional semantic information provided by linguistic and extralinguistic contexts is necessary, as well. Furthermore, the ability to use Syntactic Bootstrapping as a strategy for learning verb meanings, at least with more complex sentence types, seems to emerge with development.

At the same time, the "zoom lens" proposal of Gleitman (1994) and Fisher et al. (1994) is entirely consistent with our findings. On this view, the semantics associated with a particular syntactic frame serves to narrow down the perspective taken on a particular situation, while context is used in order to pick out a salient action within that situation to associate with the verb as the verb's core meaning.

References

Akhtar, N. and Tomasello, M. in press. Young Children's Productivity with Word Order and Verb Morphology. *Developmental Psychology.*

Fisher, C., Hall, D.G., Rakowitz, S., and Gleitman, L. 1994. When it is Better to Receive than to Give: Syntactic and Conceptual Constraints on Vocabulary Growth. In L. Gleitman and B. Landau (eds.), *The Acquisition of the Lexicon.* Cambridge, MA: The MIT Press, pp. 333-376.

Gleitman, L. 1994. The Structural Sources of Verb Meanings. In Paul Bloom (ed.), *Language Acquisition: Core Readings.* Cambridge: The MIT Press, pp. 174-221.

Goldberg, A. E. 1995. *Constructions: A Construction Grammar Approach to Argument Structure*. Chicago: University of Chicago Press.

Landau, B. and Gleitman, L. 1985. *Language and Experience: Evidence from the Blind Child*. Cambridge: Harvard University Press.

Levin, B. 1985. Lexical Semantics in Review: An Introduction. In B. Levin (ed.) Lexical Semantics in Review. Lexicon Project Working Papers #1. Cambridge, MA: MIT Center for Cognitive Science. (cited in Pinker 1994).

Naigles, L. 1990. Children Use Syntax to Learn Verb Meanings. *Journal of Child Language*, **17**: 357-374.

Naigles, L. 1988. Syntactic Bootstrapping as a Procedure for Verb Learning. Unpublished Doctoral Dissertation, University of Pennsylvania, Philadelphia.

Naigles, L., Gleitman, H., & Gleitman, L. R. 1993. Children Acquire Word Meaning Components from Syntactic Evidence. In. E. Dromi (ed.), *Language and Cognition: A Developmental Perspective*. Norwood, N. J.: Ablex, pp. 104-140.

Pinker, S. 1989. *Learnability and Cognition: The Acquisition of Argument Structure*. Cambridge, MA: The MIT Press.

Pinker, S. 1994. How Could A Child Use Verb Syntax to Learn Verb Semantics? In L. Gleitman and B. Landau (eds.), *The Acquisition of the Lexicon*. Cambridge, MA: The MIT Press, pp. 377-410.

The Verbalization of Motion Events in Arrernte (Central Australia)[1]

DAVID P. WILKINS
Max Planck Institute for Psycholinguistics

At the time of first colonization, there were approximately 250 distinct and healthy languages indigenous to Australia. Now, only about 20 Australian languages are still being acquired by children as a first language. Arrernte[2], spoken in the deserts of Central Australia, is one of those 20 viable languages, as is its better known neighbor to the northwest, Warlpiri. While the acquisition of Warlpiri has been studied extensively, primarily through the work of Bavin (1993; 1992; 1991; 1990), there has been very little consolidated work on the acquisition of the other healthy Australian languages, and the study to be reported here represents the first investigation of any kind into the acquisition of Arrernte. In particular, this paper will examine the construction of complex motion events in Arrernte narratives from both a developmental and cross-linguistic perspective, and in so doing it attempts to bring together two distinct domains of research — ethnographic and ethnolinguistic research among Aboriginal communities in Central Australia, on the one hand, and crosslinguistic developmental research on the acquisition of narrative rhetorical style, on the other.

1. Background and Hypotheses

The Desert area of Australia, particularly the Central Desert area where the Arrernte and Warlpiri live, has long been recognized as a cultural area within

---

[1] Data collection was supervised and supported by the Yipirinya School, for which I am grateful. Carmel Ryan, in particular, is to be acknowledged for her part in the collection and the analysis of the Arrernte children's data. Margaret Heffernan's help and support in the field was invaluable, as was that of Robert Hoogenraad and Penny Evans. I would also like to thank Shanley Allen, Melissa Bowerman, Eve Danziger, Ken Drozd, Dan Slobin and Barbara Villanova for helpful advice with respect to the research, analysis and/or data presentation.
[2] Until recently, Arrernte was most commonly rendered as Aranda.

which a number of different Aboriginal communities share certain cultural and linguistic traits. For instance, it has been common for primarily English-speaking anthropologists and linguists to give emphasis in their descriptions to the observation that Desert Aborigines appear to have a unique and special concern for orientation in space and for giving detailed attention to motion paths and journeys (e.g. Lewis 1976; Laughren 1978; Glass 1980; Koch 1984; Myers 1986; Munn 1986; Wilkins 1991). The following quotes illustrate this observation:

> Australian Aborigines are well known as being a nomadic people. As such, travel was an intrinsic part of their daily life. ... In the desert, in particular, they travelled long distances. It is not surprising therefore that the languages of the Australian Aborigines should have a variety of lexical, morphological and syntactic devices to deal especially with travel. (Glass 1980:123)

> Warlpiri children of 3, 4 and 5 handle directional terminology (up, down, on, under, hither, thither, here, there, etc.) including the points of the compass and positions and directions relative to the points of the compass with ease and competence. (Laughren 1978)

> Orientation in space is a prime concern for the Pintupi. Even their dreams are cast in the framework of spatial co-ordinates. (Myers 1986)

> The concept of locale and journey provides the framework for men's songs and narratives about ancestral events. (Munn 1986: 132)

The research into this special concern for travel and the linguistic attention given to motion events has tended to be, at best, only implicitly comparative, and has had no developmental examination.

This brings us to the second domain of research, which is explicitly comparative and developmentally oriented, namely the "Frog Story" work of Slobin and his colleagues (Slobin 1996, 1991, Berman and Slobin 1994, Slobin and Bocaz 1988). Three points are suggested by that research which are of particular relevance to this paper:
(i) even 9-year olds have not fully acquired the rhetorical style of their speech community (Berman and Slobin 1994:593,599);
(ii) from early in acquisition, learners stick closely to the set of semantic distinctions provided by their language and tend not to improvise distinctions (Berman and Slobin 1994:641);
(iii) there appears to be a correlation between the semantic type of language and its rhetorical structuring of motion events, in particular it is suggested that Talmy's (1985) distinction between verb-framed and satellite-framed languages correlates with the degree of narrative attention devoted to the dynamics of movement in the description of a *journey*[3] (with satellite-

---

[3] This paper uses Slobin's (1996) notion of *journey*, which refers to a complex path built up from a series of linked paths, or is an extended path with subgoals.

framed languages devoting greater attention to the dynamic structuring of motion events than verb-framed languages (Slobin 1996)).

Against the background of these two research domains, comparative and developmental hypotheses can be formulated and investigated. On the basis of the ethnographic and ethnolinguistic research, one could try to find support for the following comparative hypothesis:

> HYPOTHESIS 1A: The special Arrernte concern for motion and orientation will manifest itself even in elicited narratives and as a consequence of this the structuring of motion events in Arrernte will be both qualitatively and quantitatively different from that of English. For example, Arrernte speakers should deploy spatial language to construct MORE elaborated paths and journeys than English speakers.

However, since Arrernte is a verb-framed language (like Spanish) rather than a satellite-framed language (like English), Slobin's (1996) typological observations suggest a counter-hypothesis:

> HYPOTHESIS 1B: Since Arrernte is typologically a verb-framed language, we would expect it to have a rhetorical style which devotes less narrative attention to the dynamics of movement than English, which is a satellite-framed language. Arrernte speakers should deploy spatial language to construct LESS elaborated paths and journeys than English speakers.

In short, if there are any differences between the narrative treatment of motion events in Arrernte and English, will they be in line with areal cultural predictions or predictions from linguistic typology?

Along with these comparative hypotheses, the paper will also examine the following developmental hypothesis:

> HYPOTHESIS 2: Although children around the age of 9 are not expected to have fully adult-like narrative event structure, Arrernte children's productions will, nonetheless, look more like those of Arrernte adults, than those of English-speaking children.

2. The 'Frog Story' Task and Subjects

To investigate the above hypotheses, elicited narratives were collected following the procedures outlined by Slobin and Berman (1994: 20-28). In this task: (i) subjects are shown a copy of the wordless, picture storybook entitled *Frog where are you?* by Mercer Mayer (1969); (ii) subjects are told in advance that they are going to be asked to tell a story (the story that is shown in the book); (iii) subjects first go through looking at the book, picture-by-picture; (iv) after looking through the book once (to see what the story is about), the subject is then asked to tell the story to the investigator, while again going through picture-by-picture from beginning to end; (v) the investigator works with each subject individually, and makes an audio-recording of the story; and (vi) the investigator keeps track of which picture(s) the narrator is attending to when relating a certain portion of text.

This task was undertaken with 6 children and 6 adults residing in Alice Springs. The 6 Arrernte children were all students in the Central Arrernte primary class of the Yipirinya School (an Aboriginal-controlled bilingual and bicultural school). There were 2 x 7-year-olds; 2 x 8-year-olds; 1 x 9-year-old, and 1 x 10-year-old. While Arrernte is the first language of these children, all are also speakers of some variety of English. The Arrernte children's data was collected in September 1993 by a Central Arrernte person, Carmel Ryan, the children's teacher. She was instructed in the procedure by the author, and she herself identified the best means for conveying the instructions in Arrernte.

The data for the six Arandic adults (aged between 25 and 55) was collected by the author in the period 1992-1995. There are four distinct (mutually intelligible) Arandic varieties represented in the adult group: 3 x Central Arrernte speakers; 1 x Eastern Arrernte speaker; 1 x Western Arrernte speaker and 1 Alyawarr speaker. Like the children, all the adults also speak some variety of English, and most also speak another Central Australian language.

In what follows, the elicited Arrernte narratives will be compared with the American English narratives that were used for analysis in Berman and Slobin (1994) and Slobin (1996). Dan Slobin kindly provided the transcripts of these American English 'frog stories', and the comparison here will involve the 12 x 9-year-olds and the 12 adults.

The investigation will focus on two narratively significant 'journeys' from the frog story: 'the journey from the jar' and 'the journey off the cliff'.

3. Some Facts about Arrernte Grammar

Since this study is concerned with identifying how spatial language is deployed to render complex motion events (journeys) within narratives, there are three aspects of Arrernte grammar that are relevant to the discussion. First, Arrernte has an extensive system of case marking involving fourteen distinct cases which are marked on the final element of the NP (Wilkins 1989). For current purposes, the three most relevant spatial cases are: **-nge** 'ABLATIVE'; **-werne** 'ALLATIVE ; and **-ke** DATIVE. With a motion verb like *tnye-* ' fall', the allative case would only indicate motion towards the goal, without entailing that the goal is reached, while the dative case would indicate motion to the goal, entailing that the goal is reached. Second, in Talmy's (1985) terms, Arrernte is verb-framed (like Spanish) rather than satellite-framed. That is, it is the motion verb that tends to encode path information, rather than a satellite to the motion verb. Thus, for example, it typically uses monomorphemic path incorporating verbs which translate 'enter' and 'exit', rather than complex phrases like 'go in' and 'go out'. English, by contrast, is satellite-framed. Third, a particularly interesting feature of the verb morphology is a distinct slot for an elaborate category of inflections called *the category of associated motion*, which is used to indicate that the verb stem action happens against the background of a motion event with a specific orientation in space. These inflections have meanings like 'do verb stem act while going upwards'; 'do verb stem act while moving past'; 'do verb stem act and then start to go off', etc. (Wilkins 1991, 1989). It must be stressed that such inflections conflate motion and path, can attach to any verb stem (e.g. 'sit', 'eat', 'know', 'sing', 'fall', etc.), and fall outside Talmy's 'verb-framed' vs. 'satellite-framed' typology.

4. The 'Journey from the Jar'

In this section, the motion descriptions which accompany the second picture of the storybook are discussed.[4] The preceding picture had shown a boy's bedroom in which a boy and his dog were looking at a frog in a jar. In the picture we are concerned with, the boy and dog are asleep, and the frog is depicted in the midst of raising himself out of the jar (just one leg is out of the jar). The following picture shows the boy and dog awake looking at the empty jar. In all three pictures the bedroom window is partly opened.

Examples of the motion description are given in (1)-(4)

(1)   ... and the frog is getting out of the jar. [Engl. Child 9D]

(2)   The frog gets out of the bottle and escapes through the open window. [Engl. Adult 20L]

(3)   ..., *kenhe nhenhe frog-frog   nhenge   mameye*
        ..., BUT   here   frog   REMEMB   mother
        ikwere-nhe   mape-werne   alpe-rlenge
        3SG-G   mob-ALLATIVE   go.back-DIFF.S
        '..., while here, that frog is going back to his mother and family'
        [Arrernte Child AR - 8 years old]

(4)   ..., *antyetyerre   re   kenhe   arrate-rle.lhe-me-le*
        ..., frog   3SG:S   BUT   exit-DO&GO-PR-SAME.S
        alwirre-me-le   alhe-rlenge
        run.away-PR-SAME.S   go.away-DIFF.S
        '..., while the frog got out (of the jar) and started going off, fleeing away, leaving (the scene)' [lit. 'go off having fled, having exited and started moving off.'] [Arrernte Adult MM]

As the above examples show, it is possible to identify two distinct path segments in the description of the motion scene, the first segment can be labelled 'FROG LEAVES JAR' and the second can be labelled 'FROG DEPARTS SCENE'. Examples (2) and (4) show an English adult and an Arrernte adult who encode both path segments in their telling (i.e. 'frog

---

[4] For people who don't have access to Mercer Mayer's *Frog where are you?*, the pictures are reproduced in Berman and Slobin (1994: 647-654).

leaves jar and then departs scene'). As a contrast, the English child in (1) only encodes the first path segment 'FROG LEAVES JAR', and the Arrernte child in (3) only encodes the second path segment 'FROG DEPARTS SCENE'.

Considering all the story tellers, it is possible to compare the different age and language groups with respect to how common it is to code one or other or both of these two path segments in describing the motion event associated with the second picture of the storybook. The results of this comparison are given in Figure 1.

	PATH SEGMENT #1 "FROG LEAVES JAR" [e.g. 'exit'; 'get out of'; 'emerge from'; escape from; ...]	PATH SEGMENT #2 "FROG DEPARTS SCENE" [e.g. 'rush away'; 'run away to'; 'get away'; 'escape'; 'leave'; 'return to'; ...]
English Children	92% (11)	33% (4)
Arrernte Children	17% (1)	100% (6)
English Adults	92% (11)	50% (6)
Arrernte Adults	100% (6)	100% (6)

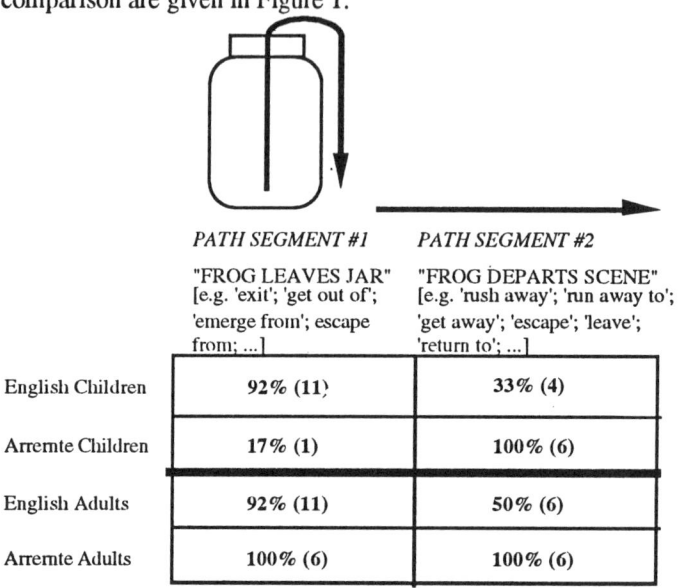

Figure 1. Comparison of segment coding for the 'journey form the jar'

Figure 1 shows that all but one of the English children overtly mention that 'the frog leaves the jar', while only a third of them mention that 'the frog departs the scene'. This is in stark contrast to the Arrernte children, all of whom overtly encode that 'the frog departs the scene', while only one child also encodes that 'the frog leaves the jar'. This suggests that, in Berman and Slobin's terms (1994: 613), the Arrernte children's narratives show a different channeling of attention in comparison to those of the English children.

Looking at the adults, Figure 1 shows that English adults were very similar to the English children — once again, all but one of the twelve encode the first path segment in their telling, and the number of story tellers that encode the second path segment increases from 33% to 50%. The Arrernte adults are the only group who, without exception, overtly encode both path segments in their narrative.

One thing that Figure 1 does not reveal is the fact that Arrernte adults do indeed show a similar channeling of attention to that of Arrernte children. Whenever an English speaker encoded both path segments for this journey, it was always through a sequence of simple conjoined clauses. However, 83% (5/6) of the Arrernte adults encode the description of the second path segment ('frog departs scene') as the head verb (primary clause), upon which the description of the first path segment ('frog leaves jar') is dependent. In other words, the Arrernte children all encode the one segment which the Arrernte adults treat as the head, and they overwhelmingly neglect the segment which Arrernte adults treat as the dependent clause.

As Slobin and Berman (1994: 153) observe, one developmental trend in the English encoding of this motion event is the fact that no English child selects the lexical item 'escape' in their description, whereas 58% of the adults do. It is worth pointing out however, that 25% use 'escape' to describe the first path segment ('escaped from the jar') and 33% use it to describe the second path segment ('escaped through the window'). Similarly, while 66% of the Arrernte adults use the associated motion inflection *-rle.lhe* 'do verb stem act and then start to go off' (e.g. 'exit and start to go off' as in example (4)), none of the Arrernte children use this or any other associated motion inflection.

5. The 'Journey off the Cliff'

In this section, the narrative descriptions given for pictures 15-18 of *Frog where are you?* are considered. These pictures depict a 'journey' which is given close scrutiny in Slobin's (1996) investigation of the rhetorical structuring of motion events in Spanish and English, and which is called by him 'the scene of the fall from the cliff'. Examples (5) and (6), from an English and Arrernte child respectively, give some sense of this journey.

(5) [p15] Then there was a deer living behind the rock and he got caught,

[p16] and then ran and ran and Ralph was right in front of them.

[p17] Then the deer bucked him off

[p18] and he fell into the pond with the rocks. [English Child 9J]

(6) [p15] *Then thing re-nhe ine-ke, alhe-ke*
then thing 3SG-ACC get-PA, go-PA

[p16] *Kele re thing-ke antye-ke anteme kwele*
O.K. 3SG:S thing-D ride-PA now QUOT

itere-werne, re lhe-ke anteme kwele ante
side-ALLATIVE 3SG:S go-PA now QUOT and

kngwelye nhenge kweke too.
dog REMEMB little too

302 / DAVID P. WILKINS

[p17] *Re   tnye-ke   anteme   kwele.   Kngwelye anteme.*
      3SG:S   fall-PA   now   QUOT.   dog   now.
      Re   first,   and then   kngwelye tnye-me   itere-nge.
      3SG:S   first,   and then   dog   fall-PR   side-ABLATIVE
[p18] *Kele kngwelye-Ø   ikwere   kertne,*
      O.K. dog-S   3SG:D   top,
      re-therre   kwatye-ke   tnye-tyalpe-ke.
      3DL:S   water-D   fall-return-PA

[p15] 'Then something got him (i.e. the boy), and went.' [p16] 'So he rode the thing now towards the edge, he went now, and so did the dog.' [p17] 'He fell now, apparently. The dog now. Him first, and then the dog are falling from the edge.' [p18] 'So the dog is on top of him, and the two of them fell back down in the water.'
[Arrernte Child JR - 9 years old]

In such descriptions, the continuous path trajectory of the boy is the focus of interest - from when the boy is picked up by the deer to where the boy lands in the water. In examples such as (5) and (6), it is possible to identify and abstract out the linguistically coded path segments. In (5) the English speaking child builds the journey using four distinct path segments - the deer goes off with the boy ("ran and ran"); the boy moves from the deer ("the deer bucked him off"); the boy moves downwards ("he fell"); and the boy moves to be in water ("fell into the pond"). In (6), the Arrernte child encodes three of the same path segments as the English child, but instead of encoding that 'the boy moves from the deer', she uses another distinct path segment 'the boy moves from the cliff' ("Him first, and the dog are falling from the edge").

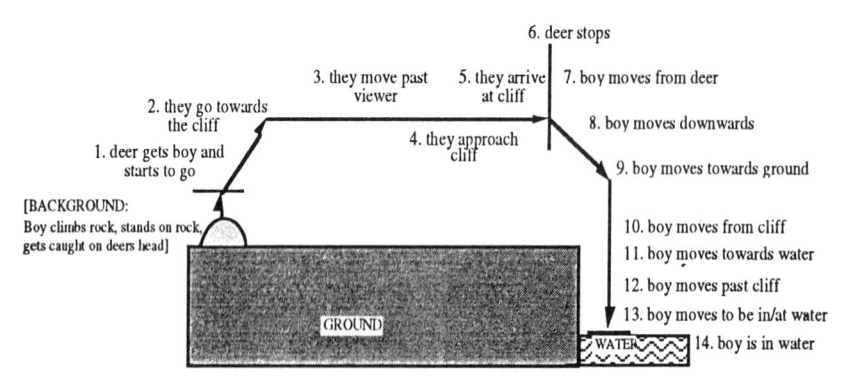

Figure 2. Schematization of the 14 path segments of the 'cliff journey'

Taking all 36 narratives together, it is possible to identify 14 distinct path segments each of which receives overt linguistic encoding in at least one of the narratives. These are presented in Figure 2 (and Table 1). There is no claim here that this is the logical number of segments out of which the path is constructed, only that these segments emerge from the Arrernte and English data examined. In this, the segmental comparison is different from that of Slobin (1996). It is easy to imagine how other languages (or other narrators) could break the path into further segments. Moreover, a similar two-language comparison may identify fewer (or different) segments.

If English speakers and Arrernte speakers are different with respect to the degree of narrative attention they devote to the dynamics of motion events, then this should be reflected in differences in the number of path segments the speakers of each language string together in building their account of the 'journey off the cliff'. Figure 3 shows that Arrernte adults average 7.8 path segments in their description of this journey. This is roughly 3 path segments more than English speaking adults, who show a mean of 4.7 segments. English adults average approximately 1 segment more than English speaking children, who show a mean of 3.8. The Arrernte children's mean of 4.5 segments is down around the English speakers, but is much closer to the English Adult average than it is to the English speaking children's average. Thus, Arrernte adults appear to build much more elaborated 'journeys' than any of the other groups, and Arrernte children are much further from the Adult target than English speaking children are. However, Arrernte children do appear to build slightly more complex journey descriptions than the English Children.

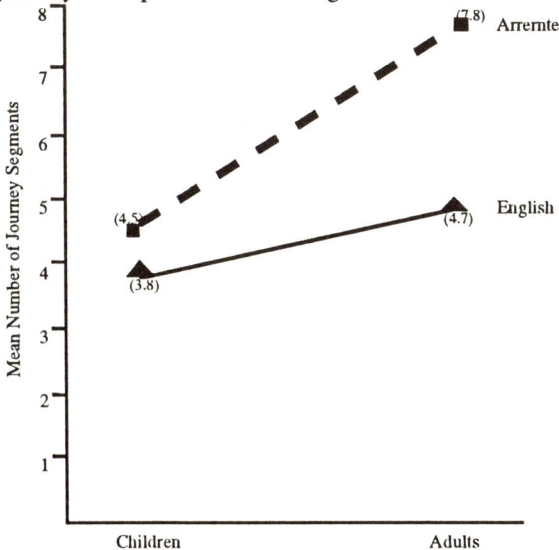

Figure 3. Comparison of mean number of segments in 'journey off the cliff'

These differences may be easier to detect in the data plot shown in Figure 4, which reveals how many segments are encoded by individual narrators. While both of the child groups show a range of 3 to 5 segments, most of the English children build paths of 4 segments, while most of the Arrernte children build paths of 5 segments. English adults show a range of 4 to 6 segments, but half of the adults build paths of 5 segments (much like the Arrernte children). By contrast, the Arrernte adults have a range which begins where the English adult range ends (i.e. 6 segments) and which goes all the way up to 9 distinct path segments. In fact, half the Arrernte adult group encode 9 path segments in their narration of 'the cliff journey'.

Number of path segments narrators use to 'build' the 'cliff-journey'

	3	4	5	6	7	8	9
English Children	.25 (3)	.67 (8)	.08 (1)				
Arrernte Children	.17 (1)	.17 (1)	.66 (4)				
English Adults		.42 (5)	.50 (6)	.08 (1)			
Arrernte Adults				.33 (2)		.17 (1)	.50 (3)

Figure 4. Data plot of how many segments narrators use for 'cliff-journey'

A further question is whether the groups differ in terms of which of the 14 path segments they are most likely to encode in their narratives. Table 1 gives this comparison. Note that, while all 14 path segments are needed to account for the Arrernte data, only 10 segments would have been needed to account for the English data on its own. That is, the number of path segments emerging from the English narratives is a proper subset of the number that emerges from the Arrernte narratives. In fact, there are 3 path segments which are only found in adult Arrernte narratives - 3. 'move past viewer'; 9. 'boy move toward the ground'; and 12. 'boy/dog move past cliff'. Interestingly, each of these three path segments is instantiated through the use of 'associated motion' inflections, and all six speakers encode one or other of these three segments. Further, it should be pointed out that all Arrernte adults mention the path segment 'start to go', while none of the Arrernte children overtly code this, and only 1 English child and 3 English adults include this segment in their telling. Of the 6 Arrernte adults, 5 render this particular segment using the 'associated motion' inflection meaning 'do act and then start to go off' (e.g. *ine-rle.lhe-ke* get-DO&GO-PA 'got and then started to go off').

TABLE 1. Group comparison of journey segments that receive overt coding

	English Children [n=12]	English Adults [n=12]	Arrernte Children [n=6]	Arrernte Adults [n=6]
1. start to go {e.g. deer gets him and starts to go; the deer takes off with him}	8% (1)	25% (3)	—	100% (6)
2. go (towards the cliff) {e.g. the deer carries the boy; the boy rides the deer; the boy sits while going}	67% (8)	67% (8)	100% (6)	100% (6)
3. move past viewer {e.g. he lies while moving past}	—	—	—	33% (2)
4. approach cliff {e.g. they're approaching a cliff}	—	8% (1)	17% (1)	—
5. go be at cliff {e.g. the deer ran to a cliff; the 'demon' arrived at the cliff}	25% (3)	33% (4)	—	17% (1)
6. deer stop (at cliff) {e.g. the deer just stopped; the deer put the brakes on}	8% (1)	25% (3)	17% (1)	33% (2)
7. boy move from deer {e.g. deer leaves boy behind; boy comes off the deer; the deer bucks the boy off}	50% (6)	58% (7)	33% (2)	100% (6)
8. boy move downwards {e.g. the boy falls; the deer drops the boy; thrown downwards}	67% (8)	83% (10)	100% (6)	100% (6)
9. boy move toward the ground {e.g. deer brings him down to ground}	—	—	—	33% (2)
10. boy/dog move from cliff {e.g. the deer has thrown the boy over the cliff; the boy and dog fall off the ledge}	58% (7)	58% (7)	50% (3)	66% (4)
11. boy/dog move waterwards {e.g. the two of them fell down towards the water; they're heading for a pond}	—	8% (1)	17% (1)	66% (4)
12. boy/dog move past cliff {e.g. So the child fell past the (body of) the cliff towards the water}	—	—	—	33% (2)
13. boy/dog move to be.in water {e.g. they both fall into some water; the boy and dog land in the water}	100% (12)	100% (12)	100% (6)	83% (5)
14. boy/dog be.in water				

The fact that all Arrernte adults encode a 'start to go' component seems to correspond to another regularity that is revealed in Table 2. The majority of Arrernte adults, 83%, start their narration of the actual journey (i.e. give their first translocational motion encoding) when their attention is on picture 15 in the storybook. No English speaker, child or adult, starts their motion account when their attention is on this picture, in fact the vast majority give their first motion description when their attention is on picture 16. In picture 15, the deer is standing behind the rock with the boy on his head. The Arrernte adults overwhelmingly choose to see this as the logical prelude to the translocational motion event that will follow and indicate that the deer (and boy) 'start to go' at this stage. Importantly, even though none of the Arrernte children encode a 'start to go' path segment, 50% of them do use their first translocational motion verb in the account of this journey when their attention is on picture 15 (see example (6) above). In short, the Arrernte children once again show a similar channeling of attention to the Arrernte adults. In this case they identify the rhetorically 'correct' place to begin the account of the 'journey' even if they do not use the same linguistic means.

TABLE 2. Where do subjects begin their 'journey'?

	Picture 15	Picture 16	Picture 17
English Children	—	100% (12)	—
Arrernte Children	50% (3)	50% (3)	—
English Adults	—	83% (9)	17% (2)
Arrernte Adults	83% (5)	17% (1)	—

6. Discussion

Regarding the comparative hypotheses outlined in section 1, we do see qualitative and quantitative differences between Arrernte and English speakers with respect to the construction of motion paths. Against the typological prediction (i.e. Hypothesis 1B), speaker's of Arrernte, a verb-framed language, build more complex motion paths than speakers of English, a satellite-framed language. Thus, it is the areal ethnographic observations that informed Hypothesis 1A that here appear to be more predictive of the findings. Of course, the fact that Arrernte adults build more complex motion descriptions is likely to be closely connected to the availability of another 'motion-dedicated' linguistic resource which lies outside the satellite-framed vs. verb-framed typology, namely the associated motion inflections introduced in section 3.

With respect to Hypothesis 2, the developmental hypothesis, we can say that, although Arrernte children may not be closer to Arrernte adults than they are to English speakers in terms of the complexity of the paths they build, they do show some evidence of greater motion event complexity than the English speaking children (see section 5). More significant, however, is the fact that the Arrernte children show unique Adult-like channeling of attention which is very different from their English-speaking counterparts.

Berman and Slobin (1994: 641) correctly observe that each language shapes its own world of expression, and children are sensitive to that, even if they are not masters of it. However, exactly how they become sensitized to the rhetorical predispositions of their speech community remains an open question. For instance, the Arrernte data show that it is not a simple matter of verb-framed vs. satellite-framed typology which predicts whether speakers rhetorically code journeys with more or fewer path segments. In fact, I would predict that speakers of Central Australian desert languages would behave essentially the same way, independent of language type, due to areal cultural factors. Moreover, while Arrernte children do not always use the same spatial language and patterns of event construction as Adults, they still demonstrate certain adult patterns of 'thinking-for-speaking', and it seems reasonable to question whether language is the only contributor to this.[5] Indeed, Berman and Slobin (1994: 594) suggest an interesting possibility when they write:

> ... in the course of developmtent, the child learns to use the expressive options of a particular native language to carry out general discourse functions. Further, those general functions are, to some extent, shaped and channeled by features of individual languages (*and — though not considered here — by cultures as well*). [emphasis mine - DPW]

We are left to ponder, then, what is the relative contribution of linguistic typology vs. culture in sensitizing children to the narrative interests and rhetorical style preferred by the adult members of their speech community. This paper does not pretend to address that question, only raise it.

References

Bavin, Edith. 1993. Language and Culture: Socialisation in a Warlpiri Community. In Michael Walsh and Colin Yallop eds., *Language and Culture in Aboriginal Australia*, 85-96. Canberra: Aboriginal Studies Press.

Bavin, Edith. 1992. The Acquisition of Warlpiri. In Dan Slobin ed., *The Crosslinguistic Study of Language Acquisition Volume 3*, 309-372. Hillsdale, NJ: Erlbaum.

Bavin, Edith. 1991. The Acquisition of Warlpiri Kin Terms. *Pragmatics* 1:319-344.

Bavin, Edith. 1990. Locative Terms and Warlpiri Acquisition. *Journal of Child Language*. 17:43-66

---

[5] In Central Australia, narratives of all sorts tend to be supported and augmented by two other semiotic systems, sand-drawings and absolutely-oriented gestures. Either system, or both together, could draw a child's attention to certain aspects of the rhetorical structuring of narrative and lead them to hypotheses concerning the critical features of adult-like 'thinking-for-narrating'.

Berman, Ruth A. and Slobin, Dan Isaac. 1994. *Relating Events in Narrative: A Crosslinguistic Developmental Study*. Hillsdale, NJ:Erlbaum

Glass, Amee D. 1980. *Cohesion in Ngaanyatjarra Discourse*. Masters thesis, The Australian National University.

Koch, Harold. 1984. The Category of 'Associated Motion' in Kaytej. *Language in Central Australia* 1:23-34.

Laughren, Mary. 1978. Directional Terminology in Warlpiri. *Working Papers in Language and Linguistics*. 8:1-16 (Tasmanian College of Advanced Education, Launceston).

Lewis, David. 1976. Route Finding by Desert Aborigines in Australia. *The Journal of Navigation* 29:21-38.

Mayer, Mercer. 1969. *Frog, where are you?* New York: Dial Press.

Munn, Nancy D. 1986. *Walbiri Iconography: Graphic Representation and Cultural Symbolism in a Central Australian Society*. Chicago: University of Chicago Press.

Myers, Fred. 1986. *Pintupi Country, Pintupi Self*. Canberra:AIAS

Slobin, Dan I. 1991. Learning to Think for Speaking: Native Language, Cognition and Rhetorical Style. *Pragmatics* 1:7-26

Slobin, Dan I. 1996. Two Ways to Travel: Verbs of Motion in English and Spanish. In Masayoshi Shibatani and Sandra A. Thompson eds. *Grammatical Constructions: Their Form and Meaning*, 195-217. Oxford: Clarendon Press

Slobin, Dan I. and Bocaz, Aura. 1988. Learning to Talk about Movement through Time and Space: The Development of Narrative Abilities in Spanish and English. *Lenguas Modernas* 15:2-24.

Talmy, Leonard. 1985. Lexicalization Patterns: Semantic Structure in Lexical Forms. In Timothy Shopen ed., *Language Typology and Syntactic Description III: Grammatical Categories and the Lexicon*, 57-149. Cambridge: CUP.

Wilkins, David P. 1989. *Mparntwe Arrernte (Aranda): Studies in the Structure and Semantics of Grammar*. Doctoral dissertation, Australian National University.

Wilkins, David P. 1991. The Semantics, Pragmatics and Diachronic Development of 'Associated Motion' in Mparntwe Arrernte. *Buffalo Papers in Linguistics*. 207-257